Religious Symbols in F
Unveiling

A Comparative Analysis of Dutch, English and Frencn Justifications for
Limiting the Freedom of Public Officials to Display Religious Symbols

Cover image © Suze M. de Wit

Typesetting: G.J. Wiarda Institute for Legal Research, Utrecht University

SCHOOL OF HUMAN RIGHTS RESEARCH SERIES, Volume 58

A commercial editon of this dissertation will be published by Intersentia under
ISBN 978-1-78068-119-1

The titles published in this series are listed at the end of this volume.

Religious Symbols in Public Functions:
Unveiling State Neutrality
A Comparative Analysis of Dutch, English and French Justifications
for Limiting the Freedom of Public Officials
to Display Religious Symbols

Religieuze symbolen in publieke functies: het ontsluieren van staatsneutraliteit
Een vergelijkende analyse van Nederlandse, Engelse en Franse
rechtvaardigingsgronden voor beperkingen op de vrijheid van publieke
functionarissen om religieuze symbolen te tonen

(*met een samenvatting in het Nederlands*)

Les symboles religieux dans les fonctions publiques: dévoilement de la
neutralité de l'Etat
Une étude comparative des justifications néerlandaises, anglaises et françaises aux
limitations de la liberté des agents publics d'exposer des symboles religieux

(*avec un résumé en français*)

PROEFSCHRIFT

ter verkrijging van de graad van doctor aan de Universiteit Utrecht
op gezag van de rector magnificus, prof.dr. G.J. van der Zwaan,
ingevolge het besluit van het college voor promoties
in het openbaar te verdedigen
op vrijdag 23 november 2012
des middags te 12.45 uur

door

Hana Maria Agnes Elisabeth van Ooijen

geboren op 19 oktober 1980
te Seoul, Zuid-Korea

Promotoren: Prof.mr. M.L.P. Loenen
Prof.mr. B.P. Vermeulen

PREFACE

The book which cannot be improved by (erasing) another word has probably not yet been written. This devilish 'opus magnum thought' lured me to protract this Ph.D. project eternally, but it was offered counterweight by the wisdom that 'the best dissertation is a done dissertation'. The main text being 'done', no word paying due credit to those having helped me in this research could be a word too many. Their large number does not allow me to mention them all by name and makes it likely that my memory will prove deficient, which has nothing to do with the actual value someone has had.

I am greatly indebted to the two people who guided me in carrying out this research: my supervisors Titia Loenen and Ben Vermeulen. I have much appreciated the extent to which they have offered that valuable asset of these days: time. Moreover, their willingness to engage intensively in my research, to help me clarify the strangling lines of thought and yet to give me room to find my own ways to tackle certain problems has been extremely valuable. I am grateful to my reading committee, Wibren van der Burg, Paul Cliteur, Jenny Goldschmidt, Remco Nehmelman and Lucy Vickers, for spending precious summer days reading my manuscript and providing suggestions for improving the final text.

I have been fortunate to carry out the ultimately solitary undertaking of a Ph.D. in a place full of human rights experts: the Netherlands Institute of Human Rights (SIM). Thanks to my colleagues for enriching the daily life of work whether during meetings and presentations or during lunches and dinners. I am thanking the Ph.D. lot for sharing and brightening my lot. In particular, I am grateful to have shared my office – though not at the same time – with the most pleasant roommates who enlivened my working day with discussions, chats and litres of tea: Antoine Buyse, Katharine Fortin and Marthe Lot Vermeulen. Thanks to Hanneke van Denderen, Esther Heldenbergh-Bode and Marcella Kiel for helping out on practical things and more. Thanks to Saskia Bal and Maaike Hogenkamp from our Documentation Centre for being willing to help out with research-related questions or to point out interesting publications. Thanks to Ida Lintel for helping with loose ends. My thanks go out to my colleagues of Comparative Human Rights which I have (co-)lectured with so much pleasure. In particular I would like to mention Marjolein van den Brink to whom I owe additional thanks for her spirited energy in keeping me abreast of interesting publications or activities and in commenting on my work. I am grateful for the insightful and unintentionally (too?) enjoyable meetings I have had with Kim Hermans, Merel Jonker, Reile Meyers, Marloes van Noorloos and Rianka Rijnhout.

I am indebted to many in academia and beyond for their dedicating time and efforts which enriches the solitude of academic research with encouragement, enthusiasm and partnership. In particular I would like to thank the group of experts who have commented on a preliminary draft of my conclusions: Matthijs de Blois, Antoine Buyse, Marjolein van den Brink, Jenny Goldschmidt, Sarah Haverkort-Speekenbrink, Esther Janssen, Wibo van Rossum and Channa Samkalden. I would specifically like to express my gratitude to Janneke Gerards who as a commentator has given me some pivotal suggestions to improve my conclusions.

The academic engagement has also been helpful across boundaries. My gratitude extends to Peter Edge for his generous welcome and help, in organizing a place for me to work, introducing me to other people and in clarifying my research in relation to the English context. In addition, I would like to thank Javad Gohari for kindly and humorously helping me with the more practical side of things and for acquainting me with (the coffee of) one of the finest bookstores in England. I would also like to mention Lucy Vickers for the stimulating discussions and comments on my work.

In France, I have had the privilege to be based at two reputable human rights centres: the PRISME centre in Strasbourg and the CREDOF in Paris. I would like to thank Elisabeth Lambert Abdelgawad for hosting me in the SDRE group of the PRISME centre. In particular, I would like to thank Anne Fornerod for being tirelessly helpful in getting me acquainted with the French situation both substantially and practically, even after my stay and for her indispensable comments on my work. I would also like to thank Françoise Curtit for offering me some valuable leads and helping me out with all kinds of questions. My thanks go out to Victor Canales who gave me advice in finding ways within the Council of Europe. As regards my stay in Paris, I would like to thank Eric Millard for connecting me to the CREDOF. My gratitude extends to Véronique Champeil-Desplats for receiving me, giving helpful comments and organizing a debate on my topic.

I have twice had the honour to participate in the International Summer School on Religion and Public Life which with its mix of reflection, candour and depth offers a unique programme. My gratitude extends especially to Adam Seligman, Rahel Wasserfall and David Montgomery for generously allowing me to take part in this exceptional experience. Thanks for enriching my Dutch bicycle which I hope to ride more often in the future.

One of the things I greatly enjoyed in carrying out research as a 'linguaphile' and as a lawyer is to work with words and with language. Unfortunately, what you love is not necessarily something what you are flawless at, and so I am grateful to all those who have been willing to help me in getting my dissertation not only done, but also in rendering it comprehensible, whether by helping me out with language-related questions or by correcting entire pieces of work. My thanks go to two of our native speakers at SIM, Katharine Fortin and Brianne McGonigle Leyh, for being available for language-related questions. Audrey Déléris and Jayshree Mangubhai have proven that physical distance has not precluded them from delivering outstanding work at a distance. I am grateful to them for enabling me to get it just right. I am obliged to the Wiarda Institute which showed itself to be so professional in being able to work together with the whimsical flows of a Ph.D. project. In particular I would like to mention Klaartje Hoeberechts, Titia Kloos and Peter Morris. Thanks also to Alison Morley for going through my texts with so much scrutiny as well as delicacy; your suggestions have again taught me some more about writing 'true' English. But even in my native language I still have enough to learn. Thanks to José Verouden for offering invaluable suggestions for my Dutch summary. Needless to say that all errors, whether in the English, French or Dutch text are entirely mine.

If my 'seconds' would still have to fulfil the ancient task of physical protection I am not sure whether they would have been very thrilled to fulfil that task but still even then I would at least have felt confident in having these two wonderful and experienced persons by my side. Judith Raven and Marthe Lot Vermeulen, I feel privileged to have already walked so many paths of life together with you and I can only hope to continue to do so after I have followed in both your footsteps. I thank you for bringing warmth, humour and wisdom to my life over tea, coffee or wine. Separating work/private life is less applicable today than it once was and even less so for a PhD research. Accordingly, I am also grateful to all those who played a valuable role in my private life. My gratitude extends to my parents for having equipped me with tools which can serve me throughout my life. I thank my friends, family and in-laws for being involved in my life and for caring. I would like to mention my brother and sisters in particular for being that which seems so self-evident but really is not. I would also like to thank Shiko Boxman and Suze de Wit for making the juggle of various tasks so much easier. Additionally, I would like to thank the latter for sparing me to use more than a thousand words (although twenty-eight words is still a lot). Suze, if only I had the same visual power you possess in that little pencil of yours to draw my gratitude for having you around in my life. Thank you for using that extraordinary gift of yours for the benefit of my book and for adding beauty to my life. Finally, I suspect that my life, whether private or professional, would just not have looked quite the same if I had not shared an important part of it with Caspar. Perhaps surprisingly, but I feel enormously rich and privileged by your persistence in urging me not to settle and to look outside the box, whether it is by you letting me write on a window or by imagining the unimaginable. May such exercises continue to fill our lives and that of Illion.

Amsterdam, 19 September 2012

The information contained in this book reflects, as far as possible, the state of affairs on 1 June 2012.

TABLE OF CONTENTS

CHAPTER 3   THE DUTCH DEBATE

CHAPTER 4   CONCEPTUAL FRAMEWORK

CHAPTER 5   EUROPEAN CONVENTION ON HUMAN RIGHTS

CHAPTER 1
INTRODUCTION

1.1 RELIGIOUS SYMBOLS ... ONCE MORE

In March 2011, a Member of Parliament in the Netherlands[1] caused an uproar which seemed to pass as swiftly as it had emerged. In an interview, she had advocated a ban on municipal employees wearing headscarves or other religious symbols.[2] For a few days, a surge of op-ed articles reacted to this plea after which the discussion died down.[3] To think that it merely concerns a media-induced triviality would be a mistake though. Three reasons make closer scrutiny worthwhile.

First of all, it was not the first time that headscarves or religious symbols in public functions had given rise to debate in the Netherlands. At least ten years ago, there had been a fierce debate on whether religious symbols in the judiciary should be prohibited more expressly.[4] Not many concrete results have been achieved thus far, apart from a clause in the 2010 Coalition Agreement announcing a ban on headscarves in the judiciary and the police.[5] Nonetheless, this provision shows that the issue has remained on the agenda for the past ten years. In other words, the row following the interview should not be seen as an isolated instance but as part of a long-running debate which flares up once in a while.

The persistence of contention is related to the second reason for thorough investigation, which is that the debate is broader than it appears at first glance. The question of religious symbols in public functions can be placed in a context in which religious symbols or even religious issues altogether have become contested more generally. Whether it concerns employees wearing religious symbols or registrars refusing to carry out same-sex marriages for religious reasons, debate on religion-

---

1   Ms. Jeanine Hennis-Plasschaert of the People's Party for Freedom and Democracy (*VVD*).

2   K. Bessems, 'Doe niet zo hysterisch', *De Pers* (Amsterdam, 15 March 2011), pp. 8-9.

3   For example A.H. den Boef, 'Seculiere staat kan echt veel slimmer; Goed dat Hennis wil praten over kerk en staat, maar begin niet met hoofddoekjes', *NRC Handelsblad* (Rotterdam, 22 March 2011). See also C. Brummer, 'Neem VVD'er Hennis toch eens serieus; Overheid moet neutraal zijn', *nrc.next* (Rotterdam, 21 March 2011).

4   This debate had ensued from a law student's claim before the Dutch Equal Treatment Commission. Her application for the position of deputy court clerk had been rejected because she was not willing to take off her headscarf in court, see Chapter 2, Section 2.4.4.

5   Coalitieakkoord 'Vrijheid en Verantwoordelijkheid' <www.rijksoverheid.nl/documenten-en-publicaties/rapporten/2010/09/30/regeerakkoord-vvd-cda.html>. An English translation can be found on <www.government.nl/government/cabinet/coalition-agreement>. All websites in this study have been last accessed on 1 August 2012.

related matters stirs up feelings. In the heat of the debate, a great part of which takes place in newspapers, on television and on the Internet, underlying and larger questions remain unanswered. For instance, one of the notions regularly dragged into the discussions is the separation of church and state. Where does the church stand with regard to religious symbols? What exactly does this constitutional principle require from public officials?[6] These and similar questions on this notion and others merit more attention than they have yet received in public debate.

There is also a third reason which makes closer scrutiny worthwhile. The Dutch MP referred to Turkey and France in suggesting that the Netherlands is making too much of a fuss about religious symbols.[7] While the validity of her suggestion can be questioned, the practice of other countries does indeed show that discussions and developments on religious symbols extend beyond the Netherlands. Furthermore, other countries have adopted a variety of approaches. Some countries have introduced an absolute ban on religious symbols; others have limited such bans to specific institutions; and yet others have not introduced any ban at all. In sum, the issue of religious symbols in public functions is worth examining because it has been on the agenda for a long time, touches on larger questions and crosses national borders.

1.2 THE MAIN RESEARCH QUESTION

Specific as it may seem, the issue of religious symbols in public functions thus harbours some important wider questions. It is precisely this specificity which allows these wider questions to be examined in depth. Public officials' religious freedom[8] presents the tension between the freedom of religion and state neutrality. While both of these concepts have been studied in depth, their effect on public officials' religious freedom has not yet been thoroughly examined. As individuals, public officials in the Netherlands can in principle rely on the freedom of religion. Of course, this protection is not absolute, but it is not entirely clear to which limitations it can be subject.

Moreover, there is a sense that public officials differ from other individuals in a way that might be reflected in how their freedom of religion can be curbed. This is couched in the statement that public officials represent the state and consequently should be neutral, which means that they should refrain from wearing religious

---

6   The term 'public officials' has been chosen as a catch-all for the employees in the three public functions selected for this study, namely the judiciary, the police and public education. Although notice has been taken of the fact that the term is not commonly used and might even conjure up other associations, notably in American English, it is considered to best express two similarities of all three functions: the public character, and the official state representative aspect.

7   She is cited as saying 'Soms denk ik, als ik kijk naar hoe het tot voor kort in Turkije was: wat doen we hier toch moeilijk met z'n allen.', Bessems in De Pers (2011), p. 9.

8   This term is employed in the study as including freedom of religion or belief as well as the right not to be discriminated against on the basis of religion or belief. See also *infra* Section 1.2.1.

symbols. This line of thought seems to inform the spirit of the age which is borne out by the current political tendency. Nevertheless, instead of offering an answer, this line of thought only gives rise to further questions. What does it mean that public officials represent the state? Does a judge represent the state in the same way as a police officer does? And why would neutrality require abstention from wearing religious symbols? While the Dutch MP focused her attention on municipal employees, the broader debate on religious symbols in public functions ensued from instances involving the judiciary and the police. Additionally, debate on religious symbols in public education has taken place across Europe. Accordingly, the present study focuses on these three public functions in answering the following question:

> Does state neutrality in the Netherlands justify and/or necessitate limitations on the freedom of public officials in the judiciary, the police and public education to manifest their religion or belief by displaying symbols?

1.2.1 Two pillars

This study starts off from two concepts informing the issue of religious symbols in public functions: state neutrality and religious freedom. Unsurprisingly, the first concept conjures up the idea that the state should be neutral regarding religion or belief. However, the underlying theory is not as straightforward as the terminology seems to suggest. Of course state neutrality has been well reflected on; however, such reflections have not necessarily led to clarity. Three factors contribute to the complexity of the concept of state neutrality.[9]

Firstly, state neutrality falls short of being a concept of positive law in the Netherlands. This holds true for other states which lack an explicit legal provision while nonetheless assuming state neutrality to apply. What is more, state neutrality is not even a purely legal notion to begin with. This is the second factor which complicates a clear understanding of state neutrality. State neutrality stems rather from philosophy and accordingly it has been analysed to its very core as Chapter 4 shows. Analyses of state neutrality extend to fundamental questions concerning how the state should deal with what is commonly called 'the good life'. In attempting to construe an encompassing view, they pertain to an abstract level. Initial questions are: 'Should the state determine what is good or bad for citizens?' 'How should the state influence choices made by citizens?' They are not the smallest or simplest of questions and it is not surprising that an overwhelming number of theories on state neutrality have been proposed. The resulting analyses are useful in understanding the possible application of state neutrality in policy. At the same time, they precisely demonstrate how complex the implications of state neutrality are, as the concept can

---

9   The concept of state neutrality is discussed in Chapter 4.

3

lead to divergent results. This can be illustrated by applying an often-used theoretical distinction between formal and substantive neutrality to the research matter of this study. Plainly described, the first version of neutrality considers religion or belief as an irrelevant category for state policy. In other words, the state should disregard religion or belief altogether when taking measures. By contrast, when a state acts on the basis of substantive neutrality, it is not precluded from taking into account religion or belief as a relevant category for its policies, in which it strives for even-handedness. Formal neutrality is more likely to cause the state to take its intention for policies as a criterion for neutrality, whereas substantive neutrality also requires the state to look at the actual results of its policies. A formally neutral rule could be the exclusion of all head coverings for public officials. It can be argued that such a rule is at odds with substantive neutrality, because such a rule is likely to affect Muslim women more than others. There is thus no unequivocal meaning of state neutrality leading to one result only. A third factor adding to the complexity of the concept of state neutrality is the connection made with other related concepts such as the separation of church and state or secularism. These notions are casually introduced in discussions on state neutrality; at times, they are even erroneously equated. In sum, three factors make it difficult to grasp the notion of state neutrality. First, state neutrality has not been clearly defined in positive law. The first factor is even more problematic in light of the second factor which concerns the nature of the concept of state neutrality which is philosophical rather than legal. One of the implications of this second factor is that state neutrality has the potential to lead to divergent outcomes. The third factor is that state neutrality is subject to being confused with other ambiguous notions.

The second concept central to the issue of religious symbols in public functions, religious freedom, has given rise to at least as much literature as state neutrality.[10] Its roots go back a long way, but today this concept is likely to be associated with recent human rights law as laid down in a number of international conventions. On the basis of these conventions, individuals are entitled to the right to have and manifest a religion or belief and to the right not to be discriminated against on the basis of religion or belief. The study at hand employs the term religious freedom to cover both rights. Like state neutrality, religious freedom is not a straightforward notion, although religious freedom has been codified. To begin with, while aiming for a universal standard, human rights conventions can do no more than promulgate a minimum standard; the exact implementation may well still vary across member states. Additionally, the object of religious freedom, religions or beliefs, cannot be interpreted unequivocally. To ask what exactly qualifies as a religion or belief generates enormous contention. It should not be too surprising that the term religion or belief has not been defined substantially by law. In part, this lack of definition is

---

10   The concept of religious freedom is also discussed in Chapter 4.

caused by the inability of law to assess theological questions. Courts have sought to remedy this lack by defining formal criteria. Finally, like many other human rights, freedom of religion is not absolute and can be subject to limitations. The grounds for limitations leave room for interpretation.

So here we are presented with two concepts, both of which have a fairly abstract nature. Their meaning cannot be easily captured because they appear to represent ideals. Therefore, they have been described in terms of theoretical classifications or minimum standards. Both notions in themselves have been thoroughly studied, but their interplay and ensuing effect on public officials' scope for religious manifestations have not. The very issue of public officials manifesting their religion or belief by displaying symbols enables such an in-depth examination. Accordingly, the study attempts to further contemplate the meaning of state neutrality and religious freedom beyond the merely abstract level by examining its concrete implications. What consequences do the theoretical classifications of state neutrality have for the specific issue? What guidelines for public officials' religious freedom emanate from the minimum standards posed by human rights law? Furthermore, distinguishing the concepts from as well as connecting them to other concepts such as the separation of church and state is also expected to bring further clarification.

1.2.2 The Dutch debate

The introductory section explained that the issue of religious symbols is an international one, and regular reference has been made to other countries. Be that as it may, the study focuses primarily on the debate in the Netherlands both as a starting point and as the research object. The formulation of the problem is thus informed by how the issue is looked at in the Netherlands. It is the inconclusive status of state neutrality and its relation to public officials' religious freedom which allows for debate. By looking closely at the debate, as it has taken place in the public, political and academic arena, the study identifies specific arguments. The focus on the Dutch debate also implies that the results of the study are primarily aimed at the Netherlands.

Although the initial part and the end part of the study are thus directed towards the Netherlands, the study does not shy away from incorporating an examination of the practice in other countries along the way. This look across borders serves to substantiate the answer to the research question beyond a merely theoretical exploration. In other words, the answer to how state neutrality is to be deployed in the Netherlands can be guided by theoretical analyses, but it can also be inspired by how other states have dealt with it. Such an inspiration is likely to provide a more solid substantiation of the answer. It is said that you should not ask a fish about water. Of course, provided it could communicate, a fish could indicate that it finds water fresh and soothing, but only in itself, not in relation to air. In the same vein, state neutrality as it plays out for public officials in the Netherlands can be assessed in itself, but it is likely to gain more depth when related to how it plays out in other countries. Examining the practice of other countries enables: situations to be looked at in a different way; questions to be asked about what is otherwise taken for granted; and solutions to be envisaged which would otherwise not even be thought of.

As it is, the Netherlands seems to take a middle position regarding the issue of religious symbols in public functions. While inclined to exclude religious symbols in the judiciary for instance, Dutch policy does not seem to consider them problematic in state schools. On the basis of theory alone, both policies seem to fit into the boundaries of state neutrality. As briefly explained in the previous subsection, state neutrality represents an ideal, the implementation of which can lead to divergent outcomes. If a spectrum were to be envisaged, the two extremes of these outcomes could be taken as excluding religious symbols from public functions or including them in public functions. While such extremes are unlikely to be found in their pure form in practice, they are often considered as represented in two countries: France and England respectively. Therefore, these countries are particularly apt to offer a more profound enquiry into the effect of state neutrality on public officials' religious freedom. In sum, while the beginning and end of the study are geared towards the Netherlands, comparison with other countries serves to deepen the evaluation of the Dutch debate.

1.2.3 Three functions

The main research question clearly indicates the three functions central to the study: the judiciary, the police and public education. As indicated, these functions have been at the forefront in the Dutch debate. Another reason for selecting these three functions is that they very neatly illustrate the variety of roles and tasks fulfilled by 'the state'.

To begin with, the public sector in the Netherlands is generally seen as different from the private sector.[11] Three features which are typical of the public sector are relevant for this study. Firstly, unlike the private sector, the public sector does not pursue profit but is considered to look after the 'general interest'. For example, a shoe-selling company can target a very specific audience, say businessmen, and can direct its policy to this purpose. By contrast, the state is seen as serving everybody's interest, and accordingly as being available to all. This ties up with the second feature of the public sector: to serve the general interest, and for this public officials are often endowed with special powers and competences on which they have the monopoly. Despite the enormous amount of money the director of a shoe-selling company might

---

11   See also an Advice of the Council of State (*Raad van State*) which refers to a bill regarding civil servants' status (*Advies over het initiatiefvoorstel Wet normalisering rechtspositie ambtenaren*) discussed in Chapter 2, Section 2.3. This Advice underscores the typical nature of public service, *Kamerstukken II* 2010/11, 32 550, no. 4.

be making, he does not have any more legal competences than other citizens. A police officer, however, has the competence to arrest and detain suspects. Lastly, where the particular image of companies can be cherished and exploited, the image of the state cannot be seen separately from society at large. The shoe-selling company is allowed to choose its logo, business colours and the interior of its shops in such a way as to attract businessmen: briefly, it can shape its entire image around businessmen. But any 'branding' of the state is relevant to the whole Dutch population.[12] In sum, the public sector as a whole has several particular features distinguishing it from the private sector. It should be noticed that this study does not aim at dealing with public officials in terms of employment law. Therefore, the fact that specifically different rules concerning, for instance, hiring and dismissal are in place for the two sectors is acknowledged but not focused on. Instead, the study approaches the public officials in question on a more conceptual level.

Although public functions have particular features in common, these common features at the same time shape each public function in a distinct manner. While each of the functions looks after the general interest, it does so in divergent ways. The judiciary is endowed with the task of preserving justice; the police are entrusted with safeguarding public order and safety; and public education[13] has a pedagogic function in educating individuals. Accordingly, while all are public functions, their competences vary considerably. The exclusivity of their tasks differs too. For instance, contrary to the judicial[14] administration of justice, education can also be taken care of by private parties. As to the previously mentioned third particular feature, the distance which a public official is assumed to have from society also varies. It has sometimes been said that there is a gap between the judiciary and society. Such statements address the idea that the members of the judiciary mostly derive from a particular group of people which does not broadly represent society. An obvious cause for this selective representation lies in the required qualifications. By contrast, state schoolteachers are felt to be closer to society, even if only because many citizens come frequently into contact with them.

A final remark regarding the selection of public officials examined is needed. The number of different types of public officials in the service of a particular public function is rather large. While the image of police officers may conjure up the classic police officer in uniform patrolling the streets, the police officer at the desk working

---

12   The Advice of the Council of State put it in other words by qualifying the relation between the state and citizens as entwined with the democratic constitutional state, pp. 2 and 13.

13   Chapter 2 further elaborates on the Dutch school system. Simply stated, public education in the Dutch context can be distinguished from (independently run) education based on a particular denomination, not necessarily religious. The study uses the term public education as well for the equivalent part of education in England and France. However, it uses 'state schools' instead of 'public schools' to avoid any association with the British public schools.

14   Thus, apart from mechanisms such as mediation.

on reports all day is a police officer as well. In not dealing with the complexities of different types of public officials, this study takes public visibility as a criterion. As the research question emphasizes the visibility of symbols, it only concerns those public functions where there is someone to perceive these symbols. Therefore, the study is in principle limited to those public officials who are considered to perform the core task of the public function at hand and to do so in contact with the public. Only when it is instrumental to illustrate relevant factors might the study pay attention to public officials holding a position in the said functions but who are not in direct contact with the public. On a different note, neutrality in public education in this study concerns primary and secondary education, not vocational and higher education. Accordingly, state school teachers in this study include teachers at primary and secondary state schools.

1.2.4 Symbols manifesting religion or belief

Human rights discourse conceptualizes the freedom of religion by distinguishing between, on the one hand, the freedom to have and to hold a religion or belief and, on the other hand, the freedom to manifest religion or belief. Whereas the former freedom is absolute, the latter can be subject to limitations. The range of possible manifestations is broad albeit not endless, encompassing worship, dietary requirements and teaching. The most obvious reason for focusing the study on symbols manifesting religion or belief is that it is this religious manifestation which has been the cause of discussion in the context of public functions. In addition, some inherent characteristics of dress and symbols make their wearing a controversial issue. First, it might almost be too obvious to state, but dress and symbols are visible items to other people. The whole idea underlying the previously mentioned distinction is that religion is something which can be kept within oneself but which can be expressed on the outside as well. Be that as it may, one manifestation might be more visible than others. When someone does not eat pork for religious reasons, this may not always be apparent to the outside world. Dress and symbols however are visible. Their visibility is compounded by the second reason, namely that dress and symbols are not necessarily bound to a particular context. Praying, for instance, is a religious manifestation which is mainly done in the confines of someone's private sphere or within a religious building. By contrast, dress and symbols may be worn permanently and hence also publicly. The final reason is the ambiguous nature of dress and symbols. Although they could be argued to constitute a passive act, they are nevertheless often understood as actively conveying messages.

Discussions on religious dress and symbols tend to get bogged down in speculations on the religious nature of dress and symbols. The question of religious motivation is difficult to determine for all religious manifestations, and is even more pertinent for dress and symbols because the distinction with non-religious dress and symbols may not always be evident. When someone is praying, few persons would contest the religious nature of this act, whereas a head covering may be worn for many reasons. However, this study does not intend to define what a religious symbol is in essence and what it is not. Therefore, the research question has been formulated in such a way that it emphasizes the public officials' religious motivation in displaying symbols. It thus shifts the question from whether a symbol is religious or not to whether a public official is allowed to display symbols which are assumed to manifest his[15] religion or belief. By using the term 'displaying', the question envisages those symbols which are visible to others. Furthermore, although symbol in the literal sense might be quite restricted, it is meant here in a wide sense to include items such as head coverings, beards and jewellery. Again, the emphasis is on the manifestation of religion or belief; it is less important by which symbol a public official chooses to do so.

The intricate formulation 'manifest their religion or belief by displaying symbols' is deliberately chosen as it avoids the question as to what inherently constitutes a religious symbol. Moreover, this study follows the line chosen by judicial bodies not to define religion or belief materially. So it does not focus on the question whether something is a religious symbol, but instead takes the view that a public official is assumed to manifest his religion or belief by displaying a particular symbol. 'Displaying' conveys the sense that the symbol is perceived by others, and thus only excludes those symbols that are, say, worn beneath clothing.[16] That said, for purposes of easy reading, the study does not avoid using '(wearing/displaying) religious symbols'.

It cannot be overlooked that Islam has primarily drawn attention in the Dutch debate. The items that have caused most contention are probably the Muslim headscarf and face veil.[17] Therefore, it is inevitable that these will be mentioned more often than others. Nonetheless, it should be emphasized that the study is not limited to Muslim symbols, but is directed towards the broader question of public officials manifesting religion or belief irrespective of which religion or belief. In that regard,

---

15 For purposes of easy reading, this study uses 'he', and all derived forms of this pronoun when indicating s/he and all derived forms, except when the context clearly concerns a woman.

16 In part, the term 'displaying' seeks to circumvent objections inherent to the term 'wearing' as eloquently explained by M.D. Evans in his *Manual on the Wearing of Religious Symbols in Public Areas* (Martinus Nijhoff Publishers, The Hague, 2009). He says: 'The focus on the "wearing" of a religious symbol has the capacity to distort our understanding of what a religious symbol actually is …' (p. 70). Furthermore, he illustrates that the term 'wearing' may be evident for some types of religious manifestations such as a headscarf but less so for items, such as a *kirpan* or for a beard where one would generally not use the term 'wearing' (p. 71).

17 These two items out of the diversity of Muslim dress have been most prominently discussed in the European context. This study employs the terms 'headscarf' and 'face veil' as generic terms to encompass a variety of garments. The term 'headscarf' refers to all types of dress which cover the head and leave the face uncovered, also often referred to as *hijab*. The term 'face veil' is meant to indicate all types of garments that cover the face, the most well-known of which are the *niqab* and the *burqa*.

symbols regarded as Muslim are considered in this study as having catalysed the discussion on religious symbols in general.

1.3   PURPOSE OF THE STUDY

1.3.1 Threefold objective

The study has a threefold objective. Firstly, it analyses in depth the Dutch debate on the issue of religious symbols in public functions; this analysis can be thought of as the argumentation level and it aims at going beyond anecdotal media hype and to provide a systemic and comprehensive account. It is clear that multiple and contrasting positions can be taken on the issue of religious symbols in public functions. How is such divergence possible? By mapping out the different arguments, the study dissects the structure of the debate.

Secondly, this study intends to elaborate on existing theory. As explained, the two notions playing a leading part in the study, religious freedom and state neutrality, have been thoroughly studied in themselves but mostly not in relation to the specific problem of public officials manifesting their religion or belief. This study seizes the opportunity to fill that gap. By applying the notions to the main question, it seeks to further conceptualize both notions and their interplay. Accordingly, it can be said that this endeavour pertains to the conceptual level.

Thirdly and finally, the study seeks to evaluate the various approaches taken towards public officials manifesting their religion or belief. It then aims to employ this evaluation to answer the research question. As suggested previously, the current political tendency seems to take its course without taking full advantage of the existing theory and the academic and public debate. It can be said that the result of the first two objectives serves to underpin the third. Having carried out a detailed analysis of the arguments in the debate and a conceptualization of the key notions, the study closes with an answer to the main research question. This answer is relevant to what may be considered as the practical level.

It is submitted that the expected growing participation of religious minority groups in the public functions examined in this study will cause controversy to increase. It should be noted that the whole concept of state neutrality does not allow for the simple qualification of an approach to religious symbols in public functions as right or wrong. The formulation of the research question leaves room for defining a particular bandwidth within which state neutrality justifies and necessitates limitations. Inevitably, the frequency of state neutrality chosen within that bandwidth is likely to impact on the scope for public officials' religious manifestations. In this study, the interpretation of state neutrality and the ensuing policies are instead evaluated in terms of suiting the given context to a greater or a lesser extent. This is further explained when elaborating on the approach of the study. A final matter should be pointed out. It may be assumed that the debate only leaves room for two positions: public officials can either wear religious symbols or they cannot. Although such polarity is understandable given the positions in the public debate, it may overlook the actual range of policy options available to the state. Therefore, the study has used the term 'limitations' in the main research question to leave open the possibility that the answer does not have to be as black and white as suggested in the debate. A clear example of a grey answer would be to incorporate a standard head-covering item in the judicial costume.[18]

1.3.2 Limitations and reservations

As explained, state neutrality is presented as the typical ground to limit public officials' religious freedom. Albeit typical, it is not the only one. The grounds to limit religious manifestations also include public order, safety, health and morals. In the issue of religious symbols in public functions, limitations may also be advocated on the basis of these other grounds. For instance, it may be argued that police officers should not wear religious symbols because they may disturb public order. While it can be argued that safeguarding state neutrality indirectly concerns public order, state neutrality serves as the primary ground for assessing the issue of religious symbols in public functions.

Although the study does not shy away from broader discussions on religious symbols, it limits its findings to the three functions selected for this study, to the Netherlands and to symbols manifesting religion or belief. Where relevant the study explores bypaths. For example, to understand the public debate in France on religious symbols, a brief description of the law on religious symbols at state schools and the related upheavals is indispensable. That said, these explorations are used to the fullest extent to tie in with the issue of religious symbols in public functions.

Obvious as it may be, the underlying academic discipline of this study, namely the legal discipline, needs to be qualified as a limiting factor. Religion-related matters tend to cross disciplines. While they are evidently part of religious studies or theological studies, they are equally part of sociology, psychology or history. It is perfectly possible that the question of public officials manifesting their religion or belief by displaying symbols would be studied from a sociological perspective using empirical methods. As is alleged at times, in studying minority groups, researchers seem to pass by the groups themselves. However, as said before, this study is not about minority groups. While the headscarf undoubtedly recurs regularly in this study, it is not so much the object of this study as it is the catalyst of a larger underlying question: that

---

18 As suggested by amongst others T. Barkhuysen in a public debate, e.g. in a report of Kosmopolis, see: <www.kosmopolis.nl/fileadmin/media-archive/corporate/projecten/Verslag_Geloof_en_Staat.pdf>. See also J. Tigchelaar, 'Het kledingprobleem van Vrouwe Justitia: kan een hoofddoek op een toga?', (2001) 17(4) *Nemesis: tijdschrift over vrouwen en recht*, pp. 138-140.

of religious symbols in public functions. Hence, this study is not about particular individuals or particular groups, but about the three types of public officials and the scope they have to manifest their religion or belief in their functions. Furthermore, it takes a legal perspective, including legal theory.

Finally, there is no intention to carry out a full-blown comparison of the different legal systems included in this study. The inclusion of France and England should rather be seen as providing contexts shifting the perspective on the discussion about religious symbols in public functions. It is not the systems informing the comparison. First and foremost is the particular debate on religious symbols in public functions, the underlying notions in relation to this debate and the arguments substantiating one or the other position in the debate.

1.4 SET-UP OF THE STUDY

1.4.1 'Argumentative' approach

Defining the approach for the study does not end with choosing the discipline. Within the legal discipline a variety of approaches are also available. By centring the research on the debate on religious symbols in public functions as it has taken place in the Netherlands, the study is informed by an approach as expounded by Jan Smits.[19] The following explains how the application of this approach to this study plays out.

Smits qualifies the legal discipline as an argumentative discipline, a 'science of competing arguments'. Contrary to physics for instance, legal science is not about objective laws of nature; it is about laws of men. Therefore, it is at all times subject to debate, it is constantly evolving to suit the society it applies to and it is intertwined with the culture it thrives in. Accordingly, there will be different opinions on what the law should say; normative positions necessarily diverge. Despite constant contention though, rules are made and enforced. This is certainly defensible; in the end, a society has to be regulated. Nevertheless, the rules opted for do not represent the objective truth. Smits argues that the role of legal science lies in carefully scrutinizing the arguments underlying rules. Indeed, this study aims at going beyond the (advocated) rules concerning religious symbols in public functions by focusing on the underlying arguments. This is briefly elaborated.

People already feel strongly about religious symbols and even more so when public officials wear these symbols. Whether discussing it in the newspaper, on the Internet or at a birthday party, people are inclined to articulate their stance in favour of or against it, almost as if they are intuitively driven. Of course, when argued in

---

19 J.M. Smits, *Omstreden rechtswetenschap. Over aard, methode en organisatie van de juridische discipline* (Boom Juridische Uitgevers, The Hague, 2009). See also J.M. Smits, 'Redefining Normative Legal Science: Towards an Argumentative Discipline' in A.P.M. Coomans and F. Grünfeld (eds), *Methods of human rights research* (Intersentia, Antwerp, 2009).

newspaper or academic articles, positions on the issue are more substantiated. These positions can thus range from being entirely in favour or entirely against religious symbols in public functions. As explained, state neutrality is a pivotal notion for understanding the particular position of public officials. Nevertheless, a host of other points further elaborates or complements the interpretation of state neutrality. For example, a police officer's duty to be neutral is underpinned by the statement that he represents the state. Subsequently, however, this statement is taken both ways. Either such representation is taken to preclude any association with religions or beliefs, or it is taken to allow for – though even-handed – inclusion of religions or beliefs. This illustrates first of all that normative positions diverge and secondly that these divergences can be traced back to divergence in the underpinning assumptions. Therefore, to understand the various normative positions properly, it is crucial to reflect really thoroughly on the arguments brought forward.

In the end, this study does aim at a normative evaluation of the current political tendency to exclude religious symbols specifically and of the possible ways to go about religious symbols in public functions in general. But preliminary steps are needed to get there, based on Smit's view of legal science as an argumentative discipline. Accordingly, the study first disentangles the debate in the Netherlands by identifying the arguments brought forward. It explores the underlying theory on state neutrality and religious freedom and examines how the arguments tie into the theory. Taking arguments and theory together, the study builds a conceptual framework that subsequently serves to consider the question within various contexts: the European Convention on Human Rights (ECHR), England and France respectively. By bringing down the issue from abstract concepts to specific arguments, the study aims to achieve a result which can do more justice to the context. This also corresponds with Smits' view on how normative positions can be evaluated in the end. Taking the underpinning arguments as the point of departure, he proposes that a normative evaluation can be substantiated by finding the arguments which best suit the context and the prevailing 'doctrinal system'.

1.4.2 Sources and methods

The central role of the Dutch debate may be clear by now. But where is this debate to be found? As described at the outset of this chapter, part of it has taken place in public through news media. News reports and op-eds provide interesting sources to construe the public debate on religious symbols in public functions. Nonetheless, being primarily a legal study, this research focuses on the debate as it has taken place in legal academic circles. Accordingly, academic literature and case law are the primary sources for this study. It supplements the description by using other sources, such as the news media. It does so for the Dutch debate, as well as for the French and English ones. Because it concerns a debate, it describes this debate by identifying the lines of argument advanced to bolster one or the other position. In other words, it disentangles the mishmash of numerous points into identifiable lines of logic. In sum, Chapters 2 and 3 are mainly descriptive in character, outlining the background and contents of the debate.

Subsequently, the study turns to a thorough analysis of the theory underlying the key concepts. To do so, it makes use of academic literature, both legal and politico-philosophical. It uses existing theories to describe these notions and analyses these theories to come to its own reconceptualization. This might be labelled as systemizing the knowledge on state neutrality and religious freedom to fit into the mould of religious symbols in public functions. Such systemization is applied in Chapter 4. After having dissected the debate, explored the underlying theory in depth and constructed a conceptual framework, the study moves on to place the issue at hand against the background of various legal systems. Accordingly, Chapters 5, 6 and 7 contain a comparative description.

Chapter 5 begins by describing and analysing the ECHR case law. By doing so, this study seeks to find the human rights standards defining the minimum standards which any limitation would have to meet. The study uses the ECHR because of its pivotal importance for human rights norms in European states. Admittedly, the analysis cannot lead to the promulgation of any general doctrinal or conceptual explanations of how religious freedom plays out in relation to state neutrality. The task of the ECHR supervising bodies is limited to assessing a particular measure and its compatibility with the Convention. Therefore, ECHR judgments are primarily context-driven. Be that as it may, guidelines can be derived from the ECHR case law, and in any event measures constituting a violation indicate at least some boundaries which cannot be crossed.

The next two chapters, Chapters 6 and 7, move from the regional human rights system to the French and the English systems. The role of these country studies is not to indicate guidelines that can be applied directly to the Dutch legal order. Instead, their position on opposite ends of the spectrum 'excluding or including religious symbols' is used to provide information on how these countries have dealt with this issue, to the most divergent extent possible. This also implies that the study is focused on the main thrust of their approach, in the knowledge that like many things in reality their approach is not free from nuances and contradictions. Stating the obvious, *the* French system or *the* English system does not exist. Both have their own history and complexities. Viewed in themselves, each system has an inner consistency. As a consequence, they are not suitable as a template for the Dutch context. Practices of other countries do not offer ready-to-transplant solutions. After all, these practices are intrinsically entwined with the particular characteristics of the specific context. Therefore, copying any practice without at least modifying it in accordance with the local context would be like transplanting an organ without preparing a body for it. The likely result of such an act would be rejection. The practices of other countries can instead be used to critically question our own practices and to enlarge our frame of reference. In accordance with Smits' approach, the information of the other legal orders is considered as providing empirical material as to how they have dealt with religious symbols. The chapters first describe and then analyse the results on the basis of the conceptual model. This enables a comparison with the Dutch debate and an evaluation.

A specific method is case studies. As explained, the study is limited to three particular public functions: the judiciary, the police and public education. The particular features of the public functions are taken account of to illustrate how they may be relevant for the differences between them. Additionally, part of the research has been conducted in England and France. During these visits, interviews have been conducted, mainly with scholars and incidentally with members of the public functions examined in this study, human rights institutions and government officials. These interviews mostly serve illustrative purposes to see whether the information from the books corresponds with reality.

1.4.3 Outline

Presentation of the problem	Chapter 1: Introduction Chapter 2: The Dutch context Chapter 3: The Dutch debate
Conceptual framework	Chapter 4: Conceptual framework
Human rights standards	Chapter 5: The ECHR
Comparison	Chapter 6: France Chapter 7: England
Conclusion	Chapter 8: Conclusion

The study is divided into five parts. The first part is mainly descriptive and expounds the problem. Chapter 2 describes the Dutch context and examines how the question of religious symbols in public functions has emerged. Chapter 3 looks more in detail at how the debate has been conducted and which lines of argument can be identified. The questions investigated in Chapters 2 and 3 are as follows:

1. What is the current scope for public officials in the judiciary, the police and public education in the Netherlands to manifest their religion or belief by displaying symbols?
2. How has the scope for public officials in the judiciary, the police and public education in the Netherlands to manifest their religion or belief by displaying symbols come to be contested?
3. How is state neutrality in the Dutch debate argued to impact on the scope for public officials in the judiciary, the police and public education in the Netherlands to manifest their religion or belief by displaying symbols?

Subsequently, Chapter 4 explores the underlying theory on the basis of which it proposes a conceptual framework to capture the Dutch debate and to lead the subsequent examination.

4. How can theory offer a conceptual framework to assess the arguments underlying limitations on the freedom of public officials to manifest their religion or belief by displaying symbols?

Chapter 5 aims at determining the minimum human rights standards. In so doing, it refers mainly to the ECHR, as this is the most important human rights convention for the state involved in this study and as it lays down binding norms.

5. How is state neutrality considered in the ECHR framework to justify limitations on public officials in the judiciary, the police and public education to manifest their religion by displaying symbols?

The study then moves on to an assessment of the issue against the background of the two legal systems representing the extreme ends of the spectrum in dealing with religious symbols. Chapters 6 and 7 first describe the context of France and England respectively and subsequently analyse how the problem has been dealt with in these contexts.

6. How is state neutrality considered in the French context to justify and/or necessitate limitations on public officials in the judiciary, the police and public education to manifest their religion by displaying symbols?
7. How is state neutrality considered in the English context to justify and/or necessitate limitations on public officials in the judiciary, the police and public education to manifest their religion by displaying symbols?

Chapter 8 uses the results of the examination of the ECHR and the two legal systems together for evaluating whether state neutrality in the Netherlands can be said to justify and/or necessitate limitations on the freedom of public officials to manifest religion or belief by displaying symbols.

1.5   CONCLUSION

The seemingly short-lived attention directed at municipal employees displaying religious symbols may suggest that the issue of religious symbols in public functions only has incidental relevance. Such an understanding would erroneously downplay the issue, though. While the newspapers only report on incidents for a short while, there has already been a long-running and international debate on religious symbols in public functions. A closer look reveals furthermore that this issue has broader implications than may be suggested on the face of it. Therefore, the present study aims at examining in depth the issue of public officials displaying religious symbols, on a conceptual level as well as on an argumentative level. It is hoped that doing this leads to a clearer basis for a more thorough evaluation of whether state neutrality justifies and/or necessitates limitations on public officials' freedom to display religious symbols.

CHAPTER 2
THE DUTCH CONTEXT

2.1 INTRODUCTION

Brief as it was, the uproar referred to in the introductory chapter was telling. On the one hand, the situation was clear in the sense that municipal employees or public officials were as yet not precluded from displaying religious symbols. On the other hand, it was unclear enough to be contested. The present chapter sets the stage for analysing the contents of the debate more thoroughly by describing some of the background. More specifically, it looks at the scope for public officials to manifest their religion or belief by displaying symbols. Additionally, it pays particular attention to how the debate emerged and also to how such a debate impacted on public officials' freedom to display religious symbols. Accordingly, the two questions central to the present chapter are formulated as follows:

> 1. What is the current scope for public officials in the judiciary, the police and public education in the Netherlands to manifest their religion or belief by displaying symbols?
> 2. How has the scope for public officials in the judiciary, the police and public education in the Netherlands to manifest their religion or belief by displaying symbols come to be contested?

In describing the backdrop to the debate, the chapter sets out by addressing three issues relevant to the study within the context of the Netherlands: religious freedom; the position of religion in the public sphere; and state neutrality.[1] Subsequently, it elaborates on public officials' freedom to display religious symbols, specifically in regard to the three particular groups in this study. In tracing the origins of the debate,

---

1   The three issues have been derived from three principles which have been proposed by Van Bijsterveld as traditionally describing the relation between state and religion: freedom of religion or belief; state neutrality; and church–state separation, see S. van Bijsterveld, 'Scheiding van kerk en staat: een klassieke norm in een moderne tijd' in W.B.H.J. van de Donk and others (eds), *Geloven in het publieke domein. Verkenningen van een dubbele transformatie. WRR Verkenningen, nr. 13* (Amsterdam University Press, Amsterdam 2006), p. 228. See also S.C. van Bijsterveld, *Godsdienstvrijheid in Europees perspectief* (W.E.J. Tjeenk Willink, Deventer 1998), p. 21. Van der Burg has a broader take on the principles which are central to discussions on the multicultural society and adds the principles of equal treatment and of freedom of expression, see W. van der Burg, *Het ideaal van de neutrale staat. Inclusieve, exclusieve en compenserende visies op godsdienst en cultuur* (Boom Juridische uitgevers, The Hague 2009), p. 7.

the second part of the chapter pays attention to the developments on a legislative, political and (quasi) judicial level.

2.2 RELIGION IN THE NETHERLANDS

It was thought, not too long ago, that religion-related matters would give little reason for further examination. In a secularized world, these matters were expected to disappear from the public agenda.[2] Reality has convincingly disproved this expectation to the extent that the term 'desecularization'[3] has been coined. The challenge for today's scholar working in so contentious an area is not so much finding enough issues but rather confining his work to a limited number of issues. The three issues selected for the present section can be considered as crucial ones for beginning to understand the role of religion in the Dutch context. In discussing these issues quickly to give an overall impression of this context, this section is far from exhaustive. Rather than providing a comprehensive account of these issues,[4] it attunes these issues as much as possible to the topic of the study.

2.2.1 Religious freedom

The Netherlands has long since been known for its tolerance in a range of fields, whether it is with regard to its liberal drugs policy or for its approach towards abortion and euthanasia. A similar tolerance has been associated with the Dutch approach towards religion. This probably goes back to the Republic of the United Provinces when the Netherlands provided sanctuary to religious minorities persecuted elsewhere.[5] At that time the now well-known Dutch consent-based approach was

---

2   Wim van de Donk and Rob Plum have succinctly reminded scholars of the 'secularization thesis'. Since the beginning of sociology in the 19th century, this thesis has been one of the central tenets of (religious) sociology and it has become part and parcel of Western common sense, see W. van de Donk and R. Plum, 'Begripsverkenning' in Van de Donk and others (eds) (2006), pp. 27-28.
3   P.L. Berger (ed), *The Desecularization of the World. Resurgent Religion and World Politics* (Ethics and Public Policy Center/William B. Eerdmans, Washington D.C./Grand Rapids 1999), p. 2 ff. Cliteur notices a 'nearly universal consensus' among scholars that the secularization thesis has failed, P. Cliteur, *The secular outlook: in defense of moral and political secularism* (Wiley-Blackwell, Oxford 2010), p. 1.
4   Studies that have dealt more extensively with these issues are for example S.C. Van Bijsterveld, *Overheid en godsdienst. Herijking van een onderlinge relatie.* (Wolf Legal Publishers, Nijmegen 2008), F.T. Oldenhuis, *Schurende relaties tussen recht en religie* (Van Gorcum, Assen 2007) and H. Post, *Godsdienstvrijheid aan banden* (Wolf Legal Publishers, Nijmegen 2011).
5   See e.g. the detailed description by H. Knippenberg, 'The changing relationship between state and church/religion in the Netherlands' (2006) 67(4) *International Journal on Geography*, p. 319; B.P. Vermeulen, 'On Freedom, Equality and Citizenship: Changing Fundamentals of Dutch Minority Policy and Law (Immigration, Integration, Education and Religion)' in M. Foblets and others (eds), *Cultural diversity and the law. State responses from around the world* (Bruylant [etc.], Brussels 2010), p. 7.

already in place: despite the Reformed Church being the formally established church, other denominations were permitted a certain number of freedoms.[6] Religious freedom was the first human rights guarantee to be explicitly articulated.[7] Today, its codification has materialized on an international, regional and a national level. In the Dutch Constitution (*Grondwet*, hereinafter: Constitution) it can be found in Article 6:

> 1. Everyone shall have the right to profess freely his religion or belief, either individually or in community with others, without prejudice to his responsibility under the law.[8]

The constitutional provision has played a limited role in case law, partly because it includes a limitation clause giving the legislature much leeway to impose restrictions.[9] Questions touching on the foundations of religious freedom, such as the definition or scope of religion or belief, are discussed with reference to human rights treaties.[10] As mentioned in the introductory chapter, Article 9 of the European Convention on Human Rights (ECHR) is notably of importance for the study and will be further elaborated on in Chapters 4 and 5.

As with law in general, legal guarantees of religious freedom do not function in a vacuum. Once a legal provision has been adopted, society does not stop evolving. Such an evolution might shed new light on a legal provision, raising new questions, requiring a renewed interpretation or even bringing its very legitimacy into question. This is no different with the legal guarantees of religious freedom. The adoption of Article 9 ECHR – as well as of Article 6 of the Constitution – goes back a long way; the more recent one, Article 9 ECHR, entered into force in 1953. In the many years since, Dutch society has gone through a number of changes possibly impacting

---

6   They did not enjoy full freedom of religion and discrimination certainly took place. However, within the context at that time, the possibility for them to congregate in secret, for instance, was relatively speaking already quite some freedom, see Knippenberg (2006), and Vermeulen in Foblets and others (eds) (2010)

7   S.C. van Bijsterveld, 'Freedom of religion in the Netherlands' (1995) 29(2) *Brigham Young University Law Review*, p. 555.

8   Grondwet voor het Koninkrijk der Nederlanden van 24 augustus 1815 (Grondwet). A formal translation of the Dutch Constitution can be retrieved from the website of the Dutch Government <www.government.nl>. A detailed description of the legislative history of this provision can be found in B.C. Labuschagne, *Godsdienstvrijheid en niet-gevestigde religies. Een grondrechtelijk-rechtsfilosofische studie naar de betekenis en grenzen van religieuze tolerantie* (PhD Rijksuniversiteit Groningen, Wolters-Noordhoff, Groningen 1994), p. 27 ff. and S.C. den Dekker-van Bijsterveld, *De verhouding tussen kerk en staat in het licht van de grondrechten* (PhD Katholieke Universiteit Brabant, W.E.J. Tjeenk Willink, Zwolle, 1988), p. 48 ff.

9   Vermeulen in Foblets and others (eds) (2010), p. 14.

10   Ibid.

on the application of the provisions on religious freedom.[11] Two of them are worth mentioning here.

To begin with, religion as a relevant sociological factor has changed in two seemingly paradoxical ways. Firstly and regularly referred to, Dutch society has rapidly secularized since the 1960s.[12] It should be emphasized, however, that such secularization mostly extended to church attendance. In other words, it might be more exact to say that Dutch society has religiously de-institutionalized.[13] This proposition is corroborated by the second development, namely of religion seemingly having a revival.[14] A significant number of people still consider themselves as religious, religion has attracted the interest of scholars and nowadays it often proves to be a publicly debated topic. This was thought to be inconceivable in the 1990s, which saw wide support for the thesis that the world would increasingly secularize to the point where religion would completely lose relevance.[15]

An additional change of a demographic nature relates to the character of the Dutch religious landscape. Whereas the Netherlands can traditionally be considered a Christian society, today it is host to a wide variety of religions. The previously mentioned de-institutionalization coupled with individuality can partly account for this variety. No longer do individuals merely profess religions attached to churches, but they also seek their own religious orientation, possibly ending up with more esoteric practices not clearly connected with institutions.[16] Additionally, decolonization and immigration have introduced religions and beliefs different from the traditional Christian ones in the Netherlands. For instance, the number of Muslims in the Netherlands has increased exponentially since the 1960s, ensuing

---

11 See also Van Bijsterveld in Van der Donk and others (eds) (2006), p. 228.

12 S.V. Monsma and J.C. Soper, *The Challenge of Pluralism: Church and State in Five Democracies* (Religious Forces in the Modern Political World, Rowman & Littlefield Publishers, Inc., Lanham (New York, Boulder, Oxford) 1997), p. 53.

13 M. Buwalda, 'De terugkeer van religie in het publieke domein' in Wetenschappelijk Onderzoeks- en Documentatiecentrum (WODC) (ed), *Religie en Grondrechten* (Justitiële Verkenningen, Wetenschappelijk Onderzoeks- en Documentatiecentrum, The Hague 2007), pp. 10-11, Van Bijsterveld (1998), pp. 7-8, E. Sengers, 'Kwantitatief onderzoek naar religie in Nederland' in M. ter Borg and E. Borgman (eds), *Handboek religie in Nederland: perspectief, overzicht, debat* (Meinema, Zoetermeer 2008), p. 68 ff.

14 It is also succinctly described as the return or comeback of religion. At the same time, it is a matter of debate as to whether it can truly be considered a comeback; Alan Wolfe for instance rather speaks of a transformation of religion, see Van de Donk and Plum in Van de Donk and others (eds) (2006), pp. 13, 32-33.

15 See e.g. M.P.C. Scheepmaker, 'Voorwoord', in WODC (ed) (2007), p 5. See also Van de Donk and Plum in Van de Donk and others (eds) (2006), p. 13 and Berger (1999).

16 T. Bernts, G. de Jong and H. Yar, 'Een religieuze atlas van Nederland' in Van de Donk and others (eds) (2006), p. 89. See also J. Kennedy and M. Valenta, 'Religious Pluralism and the Dutch State: Reflections on the Future of Article 23' in Van de Donk and others (eds) (2006), p. 341.

from decolonization and labour migration.[17] The majority are from Morocco and Turkey.[18]

In sum, some notable contextual changes have impacted on how religious freedom is perceived. It can be imagined that such changes might have equal importance for the other notions as well. The next section discusses the position of religion in the public sphere and the changes which it has undergone both on a legal and a conceptual level.

2.2.2 The position of religion in the public sphere

The previous section has pointed to the predominantly Christian heritage in the Netherlands. This heritage can be related not only to the composition of the population but also to the Calvinist Church as the privileged church even in the nineteenth century.[19] At that time, no equal and full religious freedom was formally available to other religions. Adherents of other religions were granted some liberty to exercise their faith, but they depended on the goodwill of local authorities.[20] In 1795, the Batavian Revolution brought the privileged position of the Calvinist Church to an end, after which church and state became more separated, although this separation fell short of being complete.[21] Over the years, the separation gradually progressed until in 1983 the final remaining provision concerning the (financial) relationship between church and state was removed from the Constitution.[22] Since then, the Netherlands has commonly been considered as having a system of church–state separation.[23]

It should be noted, though, that the degree of the separation is moderate in leaving some privileges for the church untouched, including the special legal position of a church community.[24] Moreover, the church–state separation does not mean that state and religion are so strictly separated that the state can be qualified as secular. In fact, it should not be understood otherwise than indicating that church and state do not have any mutual institutional authority.[25] The narrow meaning of the church–state separation also implies its limited ability to provide clarity on questions concerning

---

17 Bernts, De Jong and Yar in Van de Donk and others (eds) (2006), p. 113.
18 Ibid, p. 114.
19 Monsma and Soper (1997), p. 55, Knippenberg (2006), p. 318.
20 Knippenberg (2006), p. 319.
21 For example, ministers of the Calvinist Church who already received state salaries and pensions retained that right, ibid, p. 320.
22 Ibid, p. 323, See also S.C. den Dekker-van Bijsterveld and others, *Kerk en staat. Hun onderlinge verhouding binnen de Nederlandse samenleving* (Annalen van het Thijmgenootschap, Ambo, Baarn 1987), p. 34. For a brief overview of the stages marking the progressive separation of church and state see B. Koolen, 'Intermezzo: stappen in de tijd' in Van de Donk and others (eds) 2006), p. 261 ff.
23 Monsma and Soper (1997), p. 71.
24 Den Dekker-Van Bijsterveld and others (1987), p. 36.
25 Ibid.

the relation between religion and state; such questions are determined by the interplay between several notions of which church–state separation is one.[26]

The moderate degree of the church–state separation is underscored by how religion is dealt with in policies. In accordance with the constitutional provision on religious freedom, legal protection extends to religion as it does to (non-religious) belief. Something obviously illustrating the equal footing on which religion and belief are treated is the equal state funding of both public and denominational education. Another example is that the state cannot withhold subsidy for welfare institutions with a religious basis by reason of this basis alone.[27] Besides the remaining presence of religion in policy considerations, religious remnants can be traced throughout the public sphere. For instance, the preamble of Acts includes the standard formula 'by the grace of God'. In the same vein, the Queen refers to 'God's blessing' in her yearly Speech from the Throne.

The above goes to show that the Netherlands has traditionally coped with a diversity of religions, the management of which it has approached quite pragmatically. Equality for all religions and beliefs has been formalized and the traditionally dominant church has become increasingly separated from the state. However, this separation has by no means resulted in the exclusion of religion from the public sphere. This resonates with the predominantly pluralistic view taken on religion-related issues. Furthermore, it has not been wholly rejected that the Dutch state can have an active role in religion-related affairs. The pluralistic view has been favourable to the emergence of so-called pillarization.[28] This socio-political and organizational system enabled multiple denominations to coexist in separate spheres within the public domain.[29] More specifically, it meant that Roman Catholic, Protestant and Socialist groups were able to live separately from each other in the public domain[30] by having television channels, newspapers, schools, hospitals and other facilities tailored to their own (religious or philosophical) orientation.[31] It proved to be a suitable accommodation

---

26 Van Bijsterveld in Van der Donk and others (eds) (2006), p. 248.
27 A memo was written by the Vereniging van Nederlandse Gemeenten (VNG) and the Ministry of Interior, 'Tweeluik religie en publiek domein' (2009), p. 14, to be found on <www.vng.nl> search term 'Tweeluik'. As a rule, it is not the religious basis of an organization which determines whether subsidy can be provided, but the extent to which the objectives for which the subsidy is given can actually be attained.
28 See Monsma and Soper (1997), p. 61, B.P. Vermeulen. 'Religieus pluralisme als uitdaging aan de 'neutrale' rechter', Themanummer 'Ieder z'n recht, magistraat in een pluriforme samenleving' (2005) *Trema*, p. 244.
29 Knippenberg (2006), p. 322.
30 See for a detailed description of the pillarization in the Netherlands, e.g. A. Lijphart, *Verzuiling, pacificatie en kentering in de Nederlandse politiek* (J.H. de Bussy, Amsterdam 1984). He points out that the pillars each 'lived in their own world, isolated from the other pillars.' Furthermore, he emphasizes that this isolation was primarily characterized by social criteria, not by geographic ones, p. 29.
31 He points out that the pillarization was manifested in the system of political parties but also in the system of interest groups like trade unions, in media and in education, ibid, pp. 47, 51.

until the 1960s[32] when it disintegrated because of socio-cultural changes, which were so profound that they have been labelled a cultural revolution.[33] It was reported that trends of secularization and individualization coupled with an influx of immigrants bringing new religions changed Dutch society.

The advent of these religions and beliefs challenged the position of religion in the public sphere as well. On the one hand, they benefited from the pillar structure in, for example, being able to establish denominational schools. On the other hand, they could not be fully positioned within the pillar structure,[34] which was anyhow disintegrating. As a consequence, the demands of religious minorities could not be met sufficiently within the given structure. With the generally shifting relations between religion and state, these demands put the existing structures under pressure.[35] At this point, it also became clear that the undeniably Christian heritage had left its mark on the Dutch state, which possibly posed larger obstacles for minority religions.[36] The main research problem in this study exemplifies the tension of Christian assumptions underlying religious freedom in the Netherlands; in principle, religious symbols do not have such an essential importance for Christians as they may have for adherents of minority religions. The next section discusses more in depth the attitude of the state towards religion by examining state neutrality.

2.2.3 State neutrality

In leaving the arduous task of conceptually studying state neutrality to Chapter 4, the present chapter confines itself to briefly going over its status in the Dutch context. It must first be noted that state neutrality has not been explicitly laid down in Dutch law. What is more, it has generally remained underexposed and undeveloped in Dutch constitutional law.[37] What comes closest to a legal articulation of state neutrality is deducing the idea of state neutrality from a combination of legal provisions. It has been proposed that Articles 1, 3, 6 and 23(3) of the Constitution imply state

---

32   Lijphart indicates 1967 as the end of the 'era of pillars'; in that year the general elections marked a new era. At the same time, he emphasizes that both the emergence and the decline of the pillars have been a gradual process, ibid, p. 27.

33   Knippenberg (2006), p. 322. See also M. van Noorloos, *Hate Speech Revisited* (PhD Universiteit Utrecht, Intersentia, Antwerp, 2011), p. 207.

34   Scheffer points out that the position of Muslims in relation to the pillars differs in a few respects from the position of the groups formerly placed within the pillars. In referring to Lijphart, he underscores that albeit separated, the pillars were united by one roof. Furthermore, the group of Muslims is ethnically diverse and socio-economically homogeneous, P. Scheffer, *Het land van aankomst* (De Bezige Bij, Amsterdam 2007), pp. 171-173.

35   See for the context for the discussion on the topical developments of the relationship between state and religion Van Bijsterveld (2008), p. 1.

36   Den Dekker-Van Bijsterveld and others (1987), p. 38.

37   Van der Burg (2009), p. 9.

neutrality.[38] These provisions read in conjunction express two essential elements of state neutrality. First of all, the state should treat individuals equally, which is formulated in Article 1 as follows:

> All persons in the Netherlands shall be treated equally in equal circumstances. Discrimination on the grounds of religion, belief, political opinion, race or sex or on any other grounds whatsoever shall not be permitted.

State neutrality in the context of this study specifically concerns the grounds of religion or belief, which have been expressly mentioned in this provision. The principle of equal treatment is of significant importance. This is even more so since the adoption of three EU Directives on Equal Treatment,[39] seeking to harmonize legal regulations on equal treatment throughout the European Union. Dutch law has progressively elaborated equal treatment legislation in detail in the Equal Treatment Act (*Algemene Wet Gelijke Behandeling*).[40] This Act has established a quasi-judicial body, the Equal Treatment Commission (*Commissie Gelijke Behandeling*, hereinafter: the Commission),[41] which has developed an extensive body of opinions. In 2012, the Commission was incorporated into the new National Human Rights Institute.[42] Because this institutional change does not affect the opinions of the Commission discussed in this study, it is left outside the scope of this study. The work of the Commission has considerably influenced the approach to questions concerning differential treatment on the basis of religion or belief.

Equal treatment regarding appointment in public service has been specifically addressed in Article 3:

---

38 Vermeulen in Foblets and others (eds) (2010), p. 18.
39 Council Directive 2000/78/EC of 27 November 2000 establishing a general framework for equal treatment in employment and occupation 2000 2000/78/EC, Council Directive 2000/43/EC of 29 June 2000 implementing the principle of equal treatment between persons irrespective of racial or ethnic origin 2000 2000/43/EC, Council Directive 2006/54/EC of 5 July 2006 on the implementation of the principle of equal opportunities and equal treatment of men and women in matters of employment and occupation 2000 2000/54/EC. The first one is the most relevant one for this study. As the name of the Directive indicates, the scope of application of the Directive is restricted to the employment sphere.
40 Wet van 2 maart 1994, houdende algemene regels ter bescherming tegen discriminatie op grond van godsdienst, levensovertuiging, politieke gezindheid, ras, geslacht, nationaliteit, hetero- of homoseksuele gerichtheid of burgerlijke staat (Algemene Wet Gelijke Behandeling).
41 Ibid, Section 11. According to Section 12, the Commission may conduct an investigation to determine whether discrimination in terms of the Act has taken or is taking place. Section 13 stipulates that the Commission may make recommendations, meaning that these are not legally binding.
42 Wet van 24 november 2011, houdende de oprichting van het College voor de rechten van de mens (Wet College voor de rechten van de mens), Staatsblad 2011, 573 see also <www.naareenmensenrechteninstituut.nl>.

All Dutch nationals shall be equally eligible for appointment to public service.[43]

The provision originally intended to qualify access for non-nationals to the public service, although it does not absolutely exclude non-nationals from the public service.[44] This provision thus guarantees that the state should not favour or disfavour Dutch nationals on the basis of *inter alia* religion or belief in appointing them for public service.

The second essential element of state neutrality is that the state should remain aloof from religious questions. As explained in the previous section on religious freedom, the state is required to refrain from interfering with individuals' right to believe, and to justify any limitations it imposes on individuals' right to manifest their religion or belief. Article 6 of the Constitution guarantees this in part while Article 9 ECHR provides an important basis for protecting this right. Specifically with regard to education, Article 23(3) of the Constitution formulated neutrality of education provided by the state as follows:

3. Education provided by public authorities shall be regulated by Act of Parliament, paying due respect to everyone's religion or belief.

In sum, state neutrality can be derived from several principles in the Constitution. However, its definitive meaning has not been clarified in Dutch law.[45] Furthermore, what is important yet complicated, for understanding the role of state neutrality in context is its normative connotation. As a concept, it is not merely instrumental in describing reality, it also points to an ideal that is yet to be realized.[46] Combined with what was said previously, state neutrality can be qualified as an intermediary ideal, which derives its force from the other key principles just as it confers force and meaning on these principles.[47] At this point, the description already begins to address state neutrality as a conceptual idea and will therefore be continued in Chapter 4.

The return of religion-related issues on the agenda has similarly increased the interest in state neutrality. As a consequence, the question as to what state neutrality means and signifies has become more pertinent, even more so because of the previously described societal changes. It may well be that these changes bear on the interpretation of state neutrality, and on the other principles. The fluidity of state neutrality presents a challenge to understanding how it applies to public officials' religious freedom. The notion is essential in understanding the possibly different

---

43   Original text: 'Alle Nederlanders zijn op gelijke voet in openbare dienst benoembaar.'
44   See N. Beenen, *Citizenship, Nationality and Access to Public Service Employment. The Impact of European Community Law*, (PhD Universiteit Utrecht, Europa Law Publishing, Groningen 2001), pp. 172 and 176.
45   See also Van Bijsterveld (2008), p. 21.
46   Ibid, pp. 21-22. See also Van Bijsterveld in Van der Donk and others (eds) (2006), p. 230.
47   Van der Burg (2009), pp. 9-10.

scope of human rights available to public officials. Human rights traditionally protect an individual against the state, whereas the public official in a way represents the state.[48] The next section starts by describing public officials' entitlement to individual freedoms in general and to religious freedom in particular. This is discussed firstly for the group of public officials as a whole and subsequently for the three groups in this study: the judiciary, the police and state school teachers.

2.3 PUBLIC OFFICIALS' FREEDOM TO DISPLAY RELIGIOUS SYMBOLS

As the introductory chapter made clear, the distinction between the public sector and the private sector basically implies that public officials have a different status from that of employees of private enterprises. Consequently, in several respects different rules may apply to public officials, for instance when it comes to their appointment and dismissal. This is not entirely free from controversy. In 2011, a bill was proposed to abolish public officials' special status.[49] This bill is probably motivated primarily by a wish to equalize the rules on dismissal in the public sector with those in the private sector and it is not expected to take effect before 2015. Therefore, it does not in itself set aside the assumption that public officials may be subject to special rules concerning the freedom to manifest religion or belief.

One source for general rules concerning public officials is the Central and Local Government Personnel Act (*Ambtenarenwet*, hereinafter: CLGP Act).[50] It defines a public official as 'someone who has been appointed to work in public service'.[51] 'Public service' comprises 'all services and utilities which are run by the State and

---

48 The specific question of public officials manifesting their religion or belief has made Cliteur distinguish three different relations in which human rights can be relied on to a greater or lesser extent. Firstly, in the relation between a citizen in the public domain and the state, human rights apply fully. Secondly, when a special regime applies between a citizen and the church for instance, human rights apply to a limited extent. And thirdly, in employment relations where the function at hand is to the fore, human rights apply to a limited extent as well. In his view, public servants should submit to these limitations, see P.B. Cliteur, 'Hoofddoekje past niet bij neutrale rechter', *NRC Handelsblad* (30 June 2001). Brekelmans and Vermeulen also question whether fundamental rights apply to internal relations of state organizations, F.H.J.G. Brekelmans and B.P. Vermeulen, 'Enkele beschouwingen over de relevantie van religie, politieke overtuiging en overheidsneutraliteit voor de rechtspositie van de leraar' in R. de Lange and L.J.J. Rogier (eds), *Onderwijs en onderwijsrecht in een pluriforme samenleving: opstellen aangeboden aan prof. mr. dr. D. Mentink* (Boom Juridische Uitgevers, The Hague 2008), p. 27.

49 Voorstel van wet van de leden Koşer Kaya en Van Hijum tot wijziging van de Ambtenarenwet en enige andere wetten in verband met het in overeenstemming brengen van de rechtspositie van ambtenaren met die van werknemers met een arbeidsovereenkomst naar burgerlijk recht (Wet normalisering rechtspositie ambtenaren) *Kamerstukken II*, 2010/11, 32 550, no. 5.

50 Wet van 12 december 1929, houdende regelen betreffende den rechtstoestand van ambtenaren (Ambtenarenwet).

51 Ambtenarenwet, Article 1(1).

public bodies'.[52] It was previously mentioned that the Constitution also includes the term 'public service' for which it guarantees all Dutch nationals the right of equal eligibility.[53] Public officials do not have a uniform employee status but it is not uncommon to regard them as a group. In any case, as explained in Chapter 1, this study does not examine public officials' employment status and neither has it selected the research domain on the basis of this criterion, but rather it looks at public officials on a more conceptual level.

Over the years, it has become accepted that public officials can rely on the protection of human rights.[54] Ongoing discussions on this issue take into consideration the special nature of the relationship that public officials have with the state compared with other individuals.[55] Therefore, there is a special dimension to the interest of a public official's proper functioning. This came to the fore for instance in the 1972 Explanatory Memorandum which mentioned loyalty as the basis for limitations on a public official's freedom of expression.[56] Today, a similar idea is expressed in the CLGP Act which imposes a duty on public officials to 'diligently perform their office'.[57] Earlier discussions on special limitations on public officials' individual rights demonstrate that some rights are more likely to be subject to limitations than others. Discussions have also considered the question whether a distinction between the effect of individual rights within and outside office may be useful. Specifically, there were discussions in 2004 on public officials' scope of freedom of expression. The approach of the Government made it clear that this freedom was not absolute and

---

52 Ibid, Article 1(2). At the time of the introduction of Article 3 into the Constitution, the notion of public service was not defined and thus left room for applying the notion in varying circumstances. In the discussions, the Government emphasized that the formal definition of public service pointed to bodies governed by public law, see Beenen (2001), p. 174.

53 Article 3 of the Dutch Constitution.

54 This has not always been the case. Since the end of the nineteenth century the views have changed, see E. Verhulp, *Vrijheid van meningsuiting van werknemers en ambtenaren* (PhD Universiteit van Amsterdam, Sdu, The Hague 1996), p. 198. See also Wijziging van de Ambtenarenwet 1929 ter zake van de uitoefening van grondrechten, Memorie van Toelichting, *Kamerstukken II*, 1985/86, 19 495, no. 3, p. 2. C.R. Niessen. 'Ambtenaar en grondrechten, ofwel: leve het poldermodel.' (1999) 24(7) *NJCM-Bulletin: Nederlands tijdschrift voor de mensenrechten*, p. 955. Brekelmans and Vermeulen in De Lange and Rogier (eds) (2008), p. 26. This has been confirmed in a Government Memo, see Ministerie van Binnenlandse Zaken, Nota 'Grondrechten in een pluriforme samenleving', *Kamerstukken II* 2003/04, 29 614, no. 2, p. 15. Nevertheless, it should be remembered that human rights may be limited. Special limitations may apply for public officials. For instance, the right to freedom of expression particularly provides for limitations aimed at safeguarding the impartiality and authority of the judiciary, see Article 10(2) ECHR.

55 It is this special relation which can justify special limitations on public officials' individual rights, see Verhulp (1996), pp. 199, 201, 203.

56 Ibid, p. 201.

57 Ambtenarenwet, Article 15ter.

that limitations could be imposed depending on factors such as the extent to which a public official is associated with a particular policy on which he expresses his view.[58]

The accepted approach to the question of public officials and their individual rights is that any limitation on the exercise of these rights should be based on the limitation clauses in the Constitution or treaties.[59] This means that the assessment of the legitimacy of limitations depends on the limitation clauses of the constitutional or treaty provision in question.

In 1988, special provisions relating to the limitation of public officials' individual rights were adopted. In particular, Article 125a of the CLGP Act lays down a clear justification for limitation. It stipulates that public officials should 'refrain from disclosing thoughts or feelings ... if because of the exercise of these rights the proper fulfilment of his function or the proper functioning of his service would not be reasonably guaranteed'.[60] While this provision indicates the possible criteria for limiting an individual right, it cannot be taken to cover religious manifestations.[61] Presumably, at the time when this provision was adopted, questions concerning religious symbols were not anticipated.

The specific discussion on religious symbols emerged at the turn of this century, prompted by the individual cases further discussed in the next section. In 2004, the Dutch House of Representatives (hereinafter: the Dutch House) held a debate on the question whether public officials could be prohibited from displaying religious symbols.[62] During the debate, Member of Parliament Eerdmans submitted a motion, which requested the Government to adopt a legal ban on public officials wearing religious symbols.[63] A large majority dismissed this motion.[64] Six weeks later, the Government published a Memorandum on fundamental rights in a plural society

---

58 E.g. the Periodic Report submitted by the Netherlands to the Human Rights Committee, the Netherlands, 'Fourth Periodic Report submitted to the Human Rights Committee' (30 July) 9 May 2007 CCPR/C/NET/4.

59 Wijziging van de Ambtenarenwet (1985/86), Memorie van Toelichting.

60 Original text: 'De ambtenaar dient zich te onthouden van het openbaren van gedachten of gevoelens of van de uitoefening van het recht tot vereniging, tot vergadering en tot betoging, indien door de uitoefening van deze rechten de goede vervulling van zijn functie of de goede functionering van de openbare dienst, voor zover deze in verband staat met zijn functievervulling, niet in redelijkheid zou zijn verzekerd.'

61 See the criteria as formulated in Verhulp (1996), p. 208. See also Wijziging van de Ambtenarenwet (1985/86) Memorie van Toelichting.

62 *Handelingen II* 2003/04, no. 45, p. 3880 ff.

63 Ibid. The initial text proposed a legal prohibition on the 'manifestation of a religious conviction by provocative garb and/or jewellery by public officials ...' Later on, the author modified the text into 'a general prohibition on the manifestation of a religious conviction by ostentatious garb and or jewellery by public officials' (Original text: *een algemeen verbod op het uitdragen van een religieuze overtuiging door middel van overheersende kleding- stukken en/of sieraden door ambtenaren*), *Kamerstukken II* 2003/04, 29 200, no. 48.

64 129 votes against to 7 votes in favour. 31 maart 2004, *Handelingen II*, no. 61, p. 3966.

(*Nota Grondrechten in een pluriforme samenleving*, hereinafter: Memorandum).[65] It stated that in principle displaying religious symbols does not in itself hinder public officials from properly fulfilling their functions.[66]

Nevertheless, it anticipated two situations where religious symbols might be problematic. The first situation is when such symbols would impede or completely prevent a public official's proper functioning; it mainly seemed to point to practical interference, such as that possibly posed by a face-covering garment. The second situation involved functions the authority of which benefits in particular from an impersonal or uniformed appearance.[67] Typical examples of such functions are the judiciary and the police. Subsequent sections of this study further discuss more recent government plans to introduce legal limitations for these two groups. These plans were incorporated in the Government Agreement of 2010, which expresses the intention to limit the wearing of headscarves in the judiciary and the police.[68]

The discussion goes to show that a general ban on the display of religious symbols by all public officials has not enjoyed wide support. Instead, plans for limitations have focused on specific groups of public officials. Accordingly, such limitations could well diverge depending on the type of public official.[69] The next sections discuss, in connection with the public functions particularly examined in this study, which limitations on the freedom to display religious symbols, if any, are in place.

2.3.1 Judges' freedom to display religious symbols

Randomly ask someone to describe a judge and he probably mentions a robe as one of the first things. Generally, the robe is seen as an essential element to the image of a judge. Anglo-Saxon films and television programmes broadcast in the Netherlands may even add a wig to this image. In other words, a judge is associated with a clear and traditional appearance. In reality, the judiciary and its image are more diverse. To begin with, the judicial organization encompasses a range of judicial officers not all of whom can be called a judge *senso strictu*. The types of judicial officers can be found in the Judicial Organization Act (*Wet op de Rechterlijke Organisatie*, hereinafter:

---

65   Nota 'Grondrechten in een pluriforme samenleving' (2004).
66   Ibid, p. 16, which has been reiterated in the municipal memorandum 'Tweeluik' (2009), p. 10.
67   Nota 'Grondrechten in een pluriforme samenleving' (2004), p. 16. 'Tweeluik' (2009), p. 10.
68   Coalitieakkoord 'Vrijheid en Verantwoordelijkheid' on <www.rijksoverheid.nl/documenten-en-publicaties/rapporten/2010/09/30/regeerakkoord-vvd-cda.html>. An English translation can be found on <www.government.nl/government/cabinet/coalition-agreement>. It includes: 'In voorschriften wordt opgenomen dat de politie en leden van de rechterlijke macht geen hoofddoek dragen.' Strikingly, this article uses the specific term of headscarves (and thereby clearly alludes to the Muslim headscarf) instead of a neutral term.
69   Article 125 creates the possibility of further rules on the position of public officials, including their appointment and other rights and duties.

JO Act).[70] The JO Act lays down rules on the administration of justice and public prosecution. The first provision defines several categories of judicial officers, one of which comprises those who are charged with the administration of justice.[71] In its turn, this category explicitly breaks down into several types of judges, including but not limited to the President of the Supreme Court (*Hoge Raad*) vice-presidents, justices and judges.[72] Apart from the distinction between different types of judges, the distinction between different types of proceedings must be kept in mind. A judge administering justice in constitutional law cases does not deal with the same issues as a family law judge. Furthermore, some types of judges are so *sui generis* that they in principle fall outside the scope of the study. The Council of State (*Raad van State*) for example is not part of the judiciary and arbitration judges are not part of the judiciary either.

Within the judiciary, state neutrality finds expression through the paramount principle of judicial independence and impartiality.[73] This principle has been acknowledged as indispensable for a democratic state that endorses the rule of law. It has been encapsulated in the right to a fair trial, as testified by human rights law. For example, Article 6 ECHR reads:

> ... everyone is entitled to a fair and public hearing within a reasonable time by an independent and impartial tribunal established by law. ...[74]

In other words, the principle of judicial independence and impartiality is not an ideal, an unwritten rule or a good custom, it is a legal duty aimed at preserving rights and freedoms of others. When taking office, judges implicitly subscribe to the duty by

---

70 Wet van den 18den April 1827, op de zamenstelling der Regterlijke magt en het beleid der Justitie (*Wet op de rechterlijke organisatie*).

71 Original text: 'rechterlijke ambtenaren met rechtspraak belast: de rechterlijke ambtenaren, genoemd in onderdeel b, onder 1° en 2°'.

72 Original text: '1°. de president van de Hoge Raad; 2°. de coördinerend vice-presidenten van, de vice-presidenten van, de raadsheren in, de raadsheren in buitengewone dienst bij, de raadsheren-plaatsvervangers in, de rechters in en de rechters-plaatsvervangers in de gerechten'. Nonetheless, where appropriate, other members of the judiciary are included in the study, if it has any bearing on the category focused on.

73 More specifically, it concerns subjective impartiality which refers to the personal impartiality of a judge. It is presumed as long as the contrary has not been proved. Objective impartiality refers to the way in which a tribunal is organized, see P. van Dijk and others (eds), *Theory and practice of the European Convention on Human Rights* (4th edn Intersentia, Antwerp [etc.] 2006), p. 616.

74 As is evident from this phrase, judicial impartiality goes hand in hand with judicial independence. As judicial impartiality mostly reflects the idea of state neutrality, this study focuses on this prong of judicial fairness. To guarantee judicial independence, the judiciary was separated from the Ministry of Justice. On 1 January 2002, the Council for the judiciary was established as a link between the courts and the Ministry of Justice.

declaring *inter alia*[75] that they will comply with the Constitution and all other laws.[76] Interestingly, in the Netherlands, a judge can choose between a religious oath and a secular pledge. The former concludes with an explicit reference to God.

The question relevant to this study is how the duty of judicial impartiality relates to the dress of the judiciary: does this duty also imply limitations on judicial dress? Specific dress rules for the judiciary have been laid down in the Regulation on judicial costume of 1997 (*Kostuum- en Titulatuur besluit rechterlijke organisatie*, hereinafter: the Regulation).[77] Article 2(1) of the Regulation stipulates that judges are obliged to be dressed in the costume prescribed for their function when they are undertaking their judicial task; the costume prescribed is a robe with bands and a cap.[78] No mention is made of the possibility of displaying religious symbols. This could be taken to indicate that the current law leaves no room for displaying such symbols, but the reverse could just as well be argued.[79]

Another relevant question for determining the scope for religious symbols is whether adherence to the dress code is mandatory for upholding the principles of judicial independence and impartiality. Neither the Regulation itself nor the explanatory memorandum makes any explicit note of the link of the Regulation with these principles. On the basis of practice, it can be stated that wearing the judicial robe is not a condition *sine qua non* of judicial impartiality. Some types of judges, such as those in the field of family law, do not wear their robe in court at all times.[80] At any

---

75 Wet van 29 november 1996 tot vaststelling van de gewijzigde Wet rechtspositie rechterlijke ambtenaren (Wrra) (aanvulling met onder meer de onderwerpen omvang van de taak, arbeidstijd, vakantie en verlof) Tweede Kamer der Staten-Generaal, *Stb.* 2003, 381 Article 5g, para. 1. Een rechterlijk ambtenaar legt bij een benoeming in een ambt voorafgaand aan de datum van indiensttreding de eed of belofte af volgens het formulier zoals dat is vastgesteld in de eerste bijlage bij de wet.

76 Original text: 'Ik zweer/beloof dat ik trouw zal zijn aan de Koning, en dat ik de Grondwet en alle overige wetten zal onderhouden en nakomen.', (Wrra) Bijlage I.

77 Besluit van 22 december 1997 betreffende de titulatuur en het kostuum der rechterlijke ambtenaren alsmede het kostuum van de advocaten en van de procureurs (Reglement II) (Kostuum- en titulatuurbesluit rechterlijke organisatie). These rules could be made pursuant to the Act stipulating that rules can be made on costume by a general decree of government.

78 Original text Article 2: 'De in artikel 1 genoemde rechterlijke ambtenaren, en degenen die door het bestuur zijn aangewezen of benoemd voor het verrichten van griffierswerkzaamheden en de waarnemend griffiers bij de Hoge Raad zijn gekleed in het voor hun ambt of functie voorgeschreven kostuum, bestaande uit een toga en een bef en, met inachtneming van de volgende artikelen, een baret, wanneer zij binnen een gebouw, dat als gerechtsgebouw dienst doet, in de uitoefening van hun ambt of functie aanwezig zijn op een terechtzitting of wanneer zij in een gebouw als vorenbedoeld anders dan ter terechtzitting een ambtsverrichting vervullen, waarbij het dragen van het kostuum gepast is.'

79 The lack of the inclusion of religious garments and symbols can also be interpreted as not prohibiting them, cf. T. Wolff, *Multiculturalisme & Neutraliteit* (PhD Universiteit van Amsterdam, Vossiuspers, Amsterdam 2005), p. 195.

80 Cf. *Oordeel 2001-53* (CGB, 22 June 2001), para. 4.11. A reason for doing so is to reduce the 'distance' between the judge and the court user. This also applies to judges in administrative procedures, such

rate, it is certain that the current lack of a clear rule has left room for argument. For at least ten years since contention emerged, the governmental approach has striven for an explicit prohibition on religious symbols within the judiciary. Thus far, such a prohibition has not passed the stage of a Ministerial announcement that legislation is to be adopted.[81]

2.3.2 Police officers' freedom to display religious symbols

No less than a judge does a police officer evoke a clear image. Instead of a robe, though, a police officer is likely to be visualized as someone with a uniform and the necessary equipment. This image is linked with his authoritative role. After all, the police are one of the parties exclusively authorized by the law to exercise force. This responsibility can be found in the 1993 Police Act (*Politiewet*) which endows the police with the task of ensuring that the legal order is enforced and that those in need are aided.[82] Like the judiciary, the police are not a monolithic organization with a single type of police officer. The Police Act distinguishes several categories of police officers. In addition to those assigned to police tasks, police officers may be assigned to technical, administrative or other tasks in the police service. Furthermore, individuals may also work with the police on a voluntary basis.

On taking office, police officers take an oath or pledge, just like judges. By doing so, they express their adherence to the professionalism of the police and their loyalty to the state. Moreover, loyalty to the law should also be declared. Police officers can also choose between a religious oath and a secular pledge.

Pursuant to Article 49 of the Police Act, the Minister of the Interior can make rules concerning dress. Similar to the Regulation for the judiciary, the regulation on police uniforms[83] does not provide for religious symbols, thus similarly raising the question whether the omission should be interpreted as either prohibiting religious symbols or leaving leeway for them. Practice seems to indicate that administrative police personnel are allowed to display religious dress.[84] Besides, it is not unambiguously

---

as with the Council of State.

81 Although this has been implemented in practice as meaning that religious symbols are not allowed.

82 Original text: 'De politie heeft tot taak in ondergeschiktheid aan het bevoegde gezag en in overeenstemming met de geldende rechtsregels te zorgen voor de daadwerkelijke handhaving van de rechtsorde en het verlenen van hulp aan hen die deze behoeven.'

83 Regeling van de Minister van Binnenlandse Zaken, nr. EA94/U907, houdende regels voor de kleding van de politie 1994 *Stcrt.* 1994, 64 (Regeling Kleding Politie), which specifies in detail which garments are part of the uniform.

84 Commissie Gelijke Behandeling, 'Advies Commissie Gelijke Behandeling inzake uiterlijke verschijningsvormen politie. Pluriform uniform?' (CGB Advice) (2007) 2007/8. See also S. Saharso and O. Verhaar, 'Headscarves in the Policeforce and the Court: Does Context Matter?' (2006) 41(1) *Acta politica: tijdschrift voor politicologie.*

clear whether the uniform is only prescribed for one of the categories of police officers and how the uniform relates to the scope for religious symbols.

2.3.3 State schoolteachers' freedom to display religious symbols

Schools can be established either by the state or by private parties, i.e. individual or private organizations.[85] The state provides funds for both types of education.[86] Non-state schools may have a denominational or a non-denominational basis. That is to say, they can be based on a particular religion or belief. Furthermore, they are not required to respect everyone's religion or belief. This allows them leeway for example to select teachers and pupils on the basis of religion or belief.[87] By contrast, state schools have no such leeway but have to be open and accessible to everyone,[88] regardless of religion or belief. In other words, they must pay due respect to everyone's religion or belief[89] and furthermore be neutral as to religion or belief.[90]

Because state schools are established by the state, it is no surprise that state school teachers are public officials. In appointing teachers, state schools are precluded from applying ideological or philosophical criteria. In his turn, the teacher, in his teaching, should respect everyone's religion or belief. While denominationally neutral, public education has come to apply this neutrality in an increasingly inclusive way.[91] It has not completely excluded religious education. The upshot is that, in terms of denominational or not, the distinction between public education and non-state education has faded somewhat.[92] That said, state neutrality in public education remains constitutionally enshrined in Article 23 of the Constitution requiring public education to observe respect for each person's religion or belief.[93] Furthermore, the neutral character of public education has been specified in the Primary Education Act (*Wet op het primair onderwijs*) and the Secondary Education Act (*Wet op het voortgezet onderwijs*). These Acts explicitly guarantee equal access to public education. Furthermore, they determine that public education contributes to the

---

85   E.g. the governmental website: <www.government.nl/issues/education>. See also Brekelmans and Vermeulen in De Lange and Rogier (eds) (2008), p. 19.

86   See for the historical background of the Dutch school system and the influence of the pillarization system Vermeulen in Foblets and others (eds) (2010), pp. 6-7.

87   Brekelmans and Vermeulen in De Lange and Rogier (eds) (2008), p. 19.

88   K.A.M. Henrard, 'De neutraliteit van openbaar onderwijs en de staatsplicht de filosofische en religieuze overtuigingen van ouders te respecteren: een zoektocht naar de gepaste grenzen in concreto' in De Lange and Rogier (eds) (2008), p. 59.

89   Cf. the Dutch Constitution (*Grondwet*), Article 23.

90   Brekelmans and Vermeulen in De Lange and Rogier (2008), p. 18.

91   Henrard in De Lange and Rogier (eds) (2008), p. 59.

92   See P.J.J. Zoontjens, 'Bijzonder en openbaar onderwijs' in T. Bertens (ed), *Recht en religie* (Ars Aequi, Nijmegen, 2003), Section 6.

93   Original text of Article 23(3): '3. Het openbaar onderwijs wordt , met eerbiediging van ieders godsdienst of levensovertuiging, bij de wet geregeld.'

development of pupils in taking account of the diversity of values, be they religious, philosophical or social, in Dutch society.[94]

Ensuing from this provision, teachers may have an important role in conveying the character of public education. The importance of their appearance, more specifically of their dress, has not been made explicit. A lack of clarity, similar to that in the judiciary and the police, exists as to the possibility of dress limitations. Unlike judges and police officers though, state school teachers are not bound by any legal rules on dress requirements. Moreover, they do not wear a prescribed uniform. Rules were only made when contention arose, which is further described in Section 2.4.6 below. In response to the growing need for clarity, the Government issued a Guideline in 2003.[95] This Guideline confirmed that schools are in principle free to adopt dress regulations. However, it equally underscored the duty of schools to observe fundamental principles, such as the principle of non-discrimination and the freedom of expression, when adopting such regulations. A school should also make sure to publish the regulations in the necessary public documents, such as the school prospectus. The Guideline was quite outspoken regarding religious dress, in pointing out that a ban on religious dress violates equal treatment law, save for objective justification.

2.4 THE INITIAL INDICATIONS OF A CHALLENGE

The previous sections of this chapter have mainly given a descriptive account of the context. In so doing, they have paid attention to the background of religious freedom in the Netherlands and to public officials' freedom to manifest their religion or belief by displaying symbols. The latter part revealed the lack of clarity of the law concerning this freedom. For a long time, this lack of clarity was irrelevant, given the context in the Netherlands. The changes in that context have caused the lack of clarity to raise a challenge to the standing law. The present section aims at tracing the roots of this contention. It commences by describing how debate on religion in the Netherlands emerged generally and continues by discussing specific debates on the three types of public functions.

2.4.1 Increasing debate on religion

The first section of this chapter has described how two major societal changes have affected the interpretation of the principles relevant to religious freedom in the

---

94 Wet van 2 juli 1981, houdende Wet op het basisonderwijs (Wet op het Primair Onderwijs) 1981 *Stb.* 1981, 468, 14428, Article 46 and the Wet van 14 februari 1963, tot regeling van het voortgezet onderwijs 1963 *Stb.* 1963, KST 5350, no. 40, Article 42 respectively.

95 Following an Advice of the Equal Treatment Commission, the then Minister of Education, Culture and Science issued a Guideline on 11 November 2003, see 'Leidraad kleding op scholen'.

Netherlands. One change of the past decades concerned the role of religion in society: it has become less prominent by deinstitutionalization and at the same time more prominent by revival. The other change was demographic in nature and has resulted in a religious landscape different from the one of approximately fifty years ago. Both changes have flavoured the debate in their own way.

The changed role of religion can be pointed to as directly underlying the room for argument. At the time when the role and nature of religion were relatively homogeneous, they were little questioned. Having assumed a greater variety now, they have become subject to closer and more critical scrutiny. Stated simply, the mere existence and presence of religion is not accepted as self-evidently as it used to be.[96] This may be seen for instance in the popularity of religious critiques, which have been articulated for example in the form of well-selling books.[97] Calls to push back religion to the private sphere found some support. In the Netherlands, this has culminated in a relatively serious plea by politicians and also by scholars in favour of abolishing the legal guarantee of religious freedom.[98] A major argument put forward in favour of such a change was that religion should not enjoy a more privileged position than other ideas or opinions. This was coupled with the statement that the protection of religious freedom could be sufficiently effectuated by other human rights guarantees, such as the freedom of expression. Thus far, this plea has not been put into effect, but it does show the extent to which the debate stretches to question the very basis of religious freedom.

The change of the religious landscape can be related to the wider debate on multicultural societies. As mentioned, the steady immigration which has taken place since the 1960s has introduced a wide variety of cultures, religions and ethnicities into Dutch society. The Netherlands has gone through a development comparable to other Western European societies. The multicultural mosaic has raised questions about how to reconcile the different cultures that make up society. In dealing with such questions, some publications[99] have spurred a lively public debate on immigration and integration in Dutch society. The debate was fuelled by the events on 11 September 2001, which served as a catalyst in branding Islam as problematic. In the aftermath, immigrants' religion has become a source of suspicion.[100] This was illustrated in

---

96   Cf. Post referring to Borgman who has pointed out that Dutch people seem to have forgotten how to cope with religious and philosophical differences. Accordingly, people do not realize anymore that basic needs and values are actually coloured by philosophical beliefs, see Post (2011), p. 237.

97   E.g. R. Dawkins, *The God delusion* (Houghton Mifflin Company, Boston 2006).

98   E.g. H.M.A.E. van Ooijen and others (eds), *Godsdienstvrijheid: afschaffen of beschermen?* (Stichting NJCM-Boekerij, Leiden 2008).

99   E.g. P. Fortuyn, *Tegen de islamisering van onze cultuur* (A.W. Bruna Uitgevers, Utrecht 1997); P. Scheffer, 'Het multiculturele drama' in *NRC Handelsblad* (29 January 2000).

100 See e.g. Vermeulen in Foblets and others (eds) (2010), p. 100. Scheffer points out that it is unique, both in the history of Islam and in the history of Europe that Muslims are a minority in a secular environment, Scheffer (2007), p. 356.

public debate where the tone concerning immigrants' religion and related issues has harshened.[101] Furthermore, the increasingly suspicious stance towards notably Islam was borne out by political events which were not necessarily related but seemed part of a general tendency.[102] As a consequence, the image of the Netherlands as a tolerant and peaceful sanctuary for all kinds of religions has been slowly but surely eroded.[103]

While it is true that Islam attracted special attention in the debates, it also shed a new light on other religions.[104] More than ever, the realization dawned that many customs had originated from Christian soil. Islam not only raised suspicion towards itself, it also reinvigorated more scrutiny towards these customs. Obviously, this scrutiny was also part of the previously mentioned trend of a growing general suspicion towards religion. Anyhow, not only did relatively new religion-related phenomena create debate, but formerly unquestioned practices were brought back into debate as well. The examples in the next section illustrate this.

2.4.2 The particularity of the central issue

The scope of disputes involving religious issues in the Netherlands is so wide that it may help to distinguish two of them in the context of this study. First of all, various cases of conscientious objection have been central to public debate. Such cases involved both majority, i.e. Christian, and minority religions. The concept of conscientious objection has hereby been stretched considerably. The more 'traditional' cases of conscientious

---

101 Cf. the contributions of Pim Fortuyn, mentioned *supra* in note 96. At the time, he was considered to be unusually outspoken about immigrants and Islam, although other politicians like Frits Bolkestein had also been so. Some welcomed Fortuyn's style as straightforward and free from politically correct terms. His style seemed to have paved the way for a harsher tone in public debate. See also 'Grondrechten in een pluriforme samenleving' (2004), p. 1.

102 As the leader of the party 'Lijst Pim Fortuyn' (LPF), Fortuyn took part in the general elections in 2002 and was heading for great electoral success. He was assassinated nine days before the election. The LPF won twenty-six seats. Someone who did not shy away from bold statements on Islam and Muslims either was the publicist Theo van Gogh. In 2004, he was assassinated by a fundamentalist Muslim. In 2010, the party of Geert Wilders, the Freedom Party, won twenty-four seats in the general elections. Wilders also has fierce criticism of Islam. See for a description of the assassination on Van Gogh and its context e.g. I. Buruma, *Murder in Amsterdam: The Death of Theo van Gogh and the Limits of Tolerance* (Penguin Books, New York 2006).

103 E.g. R. Cohen, 'Dutch virtue of tolerance under strain', *New York Times* (7 November 2005) <www.nytimes.com/2005/10/16/world/europe/16iht-islam1.html>. See also R. Hardy, 'Europe's young angry Muslims', *BBC* (14 March 2006) <news.bbc.co.uk/2/hi/europe/4802388.stm> and A. Daruvalla, 'The Netherlands: Limits of Tolerance', *Time* (27 September 2001) <www.time.com/time/world/article/0,8599,176640,00.html>.

104 Van Bijsterveld (2008), p. 1. An example of an issue which received renewed attention was the extent to which non-state schools can treat individuals differently on the basis of their religious ethos, see e.g. R. Nehmelman, 'Hoe een enkel feit tot een nieuwe schoolstrijd leidt? Over het spanningsveld tussen de bijzondere school en de homoseksuele docent' in H. Broeksteeg and A. Terlouw (eds), *Overheid, recht en religie* (Kluwer, Deventer 2011).

objection involve individuals refusing to serve in the army or to pay taxes. Jehovah's Witnesses had already added the refusal of blood transfusions or of other medical treatment. Around 2008, novel types of conscientious objection emerged, at least two of which were subject to heated debate.[105] One had been lingering since 2001 when it became possible for same-sex couples to marry. Not all registrars were willing to officiate at such marriages and relied on conscientious objection. The 2007 Coalition Agreement caused upheaval by creating leeway for municipalities to accommodate registrars' conscientious objection.[106] Both within and outside Parliament, a debate took place on the room to be left for such conscientious objection.[107] The other novel type of conscientious objection had been widely covered in the media in 2004, when an imam refused to shake hands with the then Minister of Integration; his refusal was based on the fact that she was female. These instances raise fascinating questions concerning the extent to which individuals can be exempted from (legal) duties, whether their conscientious objection amounts to discrimination and so on. They show how observation of religious duties can interfere with other interests such as other individuals' rights and freedoms.[108] Additionally, they illustrate that newer as well as traditional religions can give rise to controversy. Sitting on the boundary between the *forum internum* and the *forum externum* of religious freedom, conscientious objection is almost something of a separate category of religious manifestations. As indicated in the introduction, this type falls outside the parameters of the study.

The second type of dispute relates to those cases which can be considered as typical examples of the *forum externum*. This type covers a wide variety of manifestations, ranging from ritual slaughter to religious oaths. In this category of dispute, religious symbols and Muslim symbols in particular have drawn significant attention. Much

---

105 These are prominent forms of conscientious objection, although other forms of conscientious objection have emerged too, such as *halal* mortgages to accommodate objection to interest, objection to handling alcoholic beverages, objection to handling pork etc. Another objection which has received media coverage concerned a Muslim barrister (to be) who refused to rise when the judges entered. This issue culminated in disciplinary proceedings which did not result in a disciplinary penalty though, see *Beslissing in de zaak onder nummer van: 5499* (Hof van Discipline, 11 December 2009).

106 As long as municipalities would guarantee the right for same-sex couples to marry, registrars could refuse to officiate at such marriages by having a colleague officiate. The original text: '... zorgvuldige omgang met gewetensbezwaarde ambtenaren van de burgerlijke stand [brengt] met zich dat in onderling overleg in plaats van de gewetensbezwaarde een andere ambtenaar van de burgerlijke stand een huwelijk tussen personen van hetzelfde geslacht voltrekt, mits in elke gemeente de voltrekking van een dergelijk huwelijk mogelijk blijft. Mochten er in de gemeentelijke praktijk problemen ontstaan, dan zullen initiatieven worden genomen om de rechtszekerheid van gewetensbezwaarde ambtenaren veilig te stellen.'

107 For an overview of the debate see e.g. J.P. Loof (ed), *Juridische ruimte voor gewetensbezwaren?* (Stichting NJCM-Boekerij, Leiden 2007).

108 To a certain extent, it has been accepted that fundamental rights have relevance for private law, see e.g. R. Nehmelman, 'Private vrijheid! Over de werking van grondrechten in het privaatrecht' (2011) (1) *Letsel & Schade*, p. 18.

controversy arose regarding the Muslim face veil, like the *burka* and the *niqab*.[109] These garments were put on the political agenda by a motion in 2005. This motion proposed to ban the wearing of the *burka* in public and it was accepted by a majority of the Dutch House.[110] In spite of this majority vote, it still took a long sequence of reports and bills before a ban on face veils began to near the stage of becoming law.[111] Most importantly, there was debate on whether a ban was necessary and justified in the first place. Multiple reasons, related to the religious as well as the face-covering aspect of the face veil, were advanced to this end. Additionally, the exact form of a ban was subject to dispute. It was discussed whether a ban should take a neutral form in addressing all face coverings or whether it should target specific face coverings such as the *burka* and the *niqab*. Another question concerned the scope of a ban: should it be a general ban applicable to the entire public space or should it only apply to particular situations such as education or public transport? In the end, the Government submitted a neutrally worded bill[112] applicable to the entire public space, which was still critically reviewed by the Council of State.[113] The Netherlands was not exceptional in aiming at a ban on face veils. At the time other European states had already adopted such a ban[114] or were in the process of adopting one.[115] The long run-up demonstrates that questions of the legal and practical feasibility of a ban impede a straightforward adoption of such a ban. In the end, a great part of the discussions on the face veil have focused rather on the face-covering character than on the religious character of face veils. Therefore, face veils are not further considered as apposite

---

109 The public debate was ignited when a Member of Parliament, Geert Wilders, submitted a resolution to introduce a general ban on the burqa and niqab, see for a description of the developments 'Overwegingen bij een boerka verbod. Zienswijze van de deskundigen inzake een verbod op gezichtsbedekkende kleding' (The Hague 2006), Annex to *Kamerstukken II* 2010/11, 29754 no. 91.
110 Motie Wilders, *Kamerstukken II* 2005-2006, 29 745, no. 41.
111 See for a description of the backdrop to the legislative developments e.g. A. Overbeeke and H.M.A.E. van Ooijen, 'Les politiques relatives à la burqa aux Pays-Bas: une tradition pluraliste démasquée?' (provisional title) in D. Koussens and O. Roy (eds), *Quand la burqa passe à l'Ouest, enjeux éthiques, politiques et juridiques* (Sciences des religions, Presses universitaires de Rennes, 2013 (forthcoming)); H.M.A.E. van Ooijen, 'Boerka of bivakmuts: verbod in de openbare ruimte? Het wetsvoorstel Kamp nader onder de loep genomen' (2008) 33(2) *NJCM-Bulletin: Nederlands tijdschrift voor de mensenrechten*, pp. 160-176.
112 Voorstel van wet houdende de instelling van een algemeen verbod op het dragen van gelaatsbedekkende kleding *Kamerstukken II*, 2011/12, 33 165, no. 2.
113 Raad van State, 'Advies ten aanzien van het Voorstel van wet houdende de instelling van een algemeen verbod op het dragen van gelaatsbedekkende kleding, met memorie van toelichting', *Kamerstukken II*, 2011/12, 33 165, no. 4, Section 2. It remains to be seen how the European Court of Human Rights would assess a general ban on face veils in public. The judgment in the case *Ahmet Arslan and Others v. Turkey* seems to indicate that such a ban would not lightly pass the test of the Court (Appl. no. 41135/98 ECtHR, 23 February 2010).
114 In July 2011, a face veil ban entered into force in Belgium (Instelling van een algemeen verbod op het dragen van gelaatsbedekkende kleding). In April of the same year, a French ban on face veils had already entered into force, see Chapter 6.
115 E.g. Koussens and Roy (eds) (2013 forthcoming).

to the central question of the study, because the main research question turns on the (allegedly) religious character of symbols. The *hijab*, or Muslim headscarf, figures in all cases pointed out in this study as marking the emergence of the separate debates. Apparently, it remains capable of generating discussion in particular contexts although it seems to have been accepted long since in Dutch society.

The prominence of Muslim symbols in Dutch debate demonstrates how the distinction between Christianity and minority religions is all the more pertinent in discussions on religious symbols. These discussions show the different weight which different religions appear to attribute to the importance of dress and symbols. In principle, manifestation by display of symbols seems to have less importance for Christianity than it has for Islam and other religions.[116] In the same vein, Muslim individuals seem to have asserted their right to display religious symbols more positively than others. Conversely, limitations on religious symbols are likely to have affected Muslims more than others. Obviously, specific instances can be pointed out as exceptions to this rule. For instance, a tram driver was precluded from displaying a cross by clothing regulations. In complaining to have been discriminated against, he went to court. One of his arguments was that Muslim colleagues were allowed to wear a headscarf. This argument was to no avail, because the court ruled that the limitation on the display of a cross was nonetheless justified.[117]

Another point which defines the issue central to the study concerns the reason examined for limitations. Where religious symbols are concerned, a host of reasons have been put forward in support of limitations which resound beyond the domestic context. A reason regularly advanced is that a ban on religious symbols guarantees safety, for instance in sports. It was only after a long-running discussion that the International Federation of Association Football decided to run a test allowing female soccer players to wear a headscarf during soccer games.[118] Another ground for prohibiting religious symbols might be health, which can sometimes be closely related to the argument of safety. A situation where this ground for limitations is conceivable is the food processing industry. In addition, there may also be less direct and less legal grounds for prohibiting or allowing for religious symbols. For example, a state may pursue the emancipation of women or minorities in the labour market. For this reason, the state may either prohibit or permit religious symbols. Depending on the reason put forward in a particular case, the debates on prohibiting or allowing for religious symbols can vary considerably. As was emphasized before, in the discussions relating to public officials, the argument of state neutrality has specific pertinence as a ground for imposing limitations. This is an important if not essential

---

116 The same holds true for other religions such as Hinduism. However, as described, Islam has been most prominent in the public debates.

117 *Trambestuurder t. GVB* (Rechtbank Amsterdam, 14 December 2009) LJN: BK6378, to be found on <zoeken.rechtspraak.nl>.

118 See e.g. M. Collett, 'Prince Ali stunned by FIFA experts' hijab knock back', *Guardian* (25 May 2012).

feature which distinguishes the particular debate concerning public officials from a debate concerning other individuals.

While at times the issue of public officials and religious symbols was addressed as being uniform, separate instances can be pointed out for each of the public functions examined in this study as having ignited the various debates. In describing the debates, the subsequent sections start out with cases, which are exemplary for the debate concerning each public function. For all three types of public functions, there have been cases before the previously mentioned (Equal Treatment) Commission, which have animated the debate significantly. The complainants in these cases do not correspond exactly to the categories of public officials in this study. Be that as it may, their function is relevant to or sufficiently akin to the functions examined in this study. At any rate, the issues addressed in these cases are relevant. What is more, precisely the difference of function brings relevant aspects to the fore. Before discussion of the emerging debates in relation to the public functions and the particular Commission cases, a preliminary note concerning the legal framework of the Commission should be made.

2.4.3 The decision scheme of the Equal Treatment Commission

It was mentioned previously that the Commission had been established within the framework of the (Equal Treatment) Act.[119] The Act also serves as the legal framework for the work of the Commission. It prohibits discrimination in different situations, notably those relating to employment and services.[120] The issue of dress codes for public officials at any rate falls within the ambit of the Act. Discrimination can either be direct or indirect. Direct discrimination can be established when differential treatment takes place explicitly on grounds of e.g. religion or belief. An example would be a rule prohibiting headscarves worn for religious reasons. Direct discrimination is prohibited except for legally defined exceptions. By contrast, seemingly neutral rules which nonetheless affect particular religious groups more than others may constitute indirect discrimination. For instance, a rule prohibiting head covering on grounds of safety may affect Muslim women wearing headscarves more than others. A rule resulting in indirect discrimination may be authorized when it is objectively justified. In this case, it needs to pursue a legitimate aim and use means which are appropriate and necessary.[121]

The next sections briefly describe, by highlighting Commission opinions, how the debate came about. In so doing, they do not examine the opinions in depth yet;

---

119 Algemene Wet Gelijke Behandeling, Section 11.
120 Ibid, Sections 5-7.
121 Ibid, Section 2(1).

such in-depth analysis with particular attention to the arguments is left to be discussed in Chapter 3.

2.4.4 The deputy court clerk

The previous description of the current law made it clear that it did not mention anything about judicial officers' freedom to display religious symbols. This omission might be interpreted either way: display of religious symbols is prohibited or authorized. Until 2001, there had been no public outcry over the legislative silence on religious symbols in public functions.[122] In that year, a law student, having applied for the position of a deputy court clerk, brought a complaint of direct discrimination on grounds of religion or belief before the Commission.[123] She had not been considered for the position, because she had declared that she would not take off her headscarf during court sessions, should she obtain the position. The respondent, the court, considered this garment to be at odds with the previously mentioned Regulation on court dress, which in its view aimed at safeguarding judicial independence and impartiality. The Commission first established that, in referring to the Regulation, the decision not to employ the student did not constitute direct discrimination but indirect discrimination. It accepted the legitimacy of the aim pursued by the court, namely safeguarding judicial independence and impartiality. However, it considered that the means chosen to pursue this aim, i.e. by applying the dress regulation so strictly as to exclude applicants with a headscarf from the position of deputy court clerk, was not objectively justified. In making this finding, it referred to several societal tendencies including the aspiration for a transparent judiciary.

The above opinion concerned the position of a deputy court clerk and it left obscure what the view of the Commission was regarding other members of the judiciary, such as judges.[124] Thus, there was room for speculating on what the Commission might say about them. This vagueness resounded in public debate which extended to the judiciary as a whole.[125] The opinion of the Commission primarily concerned a court clerk's right to wear a headscarf and could thus not resolve uncertainty surrounding judges' rights to wear headscarves. This uncertainty caused Members of Parliament to submit questions to the Minister of Justice. They inquired whether he would

---

122 While this silence might be taken as accepting an implicit ban on religious symbols, it should be noted that, at that time, some courts, such as the Amsterdam District Court, already allowed individual court clerks to wear a headscarf for instance.

123 *Oordeel 2001-53,* (CGB, 22 June 2001), paras. 3.8-3.9.

124 Although the Commission noted that the court clerk's function is different from the judge's function and implied that it might have opined otherwise had it concerned a judge, it limited its opinion to the case in hand. It refrained from expressly stating that it did not consider its opinion to be applicable to judges as well.

125 E.g. C.W. Maris-Van Sandelingenambacht, 'Hoofddoek of blinddoek?' in N.F. van Manen (ed), (Ars Aequi Libri, Nijmegen 2002), p. 181 ff.

be prepared to consider amending the policy so as to meet the principle of equal treatment. He declared that he was not in favour of mitigating the requirements for fulfilling judicial functions. He emphasized that a judge should not actively manifest his personal convictions. A court clerk in that regard should be equated with a judge for now, as those attending or appearing in court might not be able to distinguish between the two.[126] Moreover, he announced that a bill for a general law prohibiting religious symbols for judicial officers would be submitted. His position was endorsed by the Council for the Judiciary (*Raad voor de Rechtspraak*) which agreed that religious symbols should not be allowed in the courts.[127]

The then Government confirmed its approach in the previously mentioned Memorandum (on fundamental rights in a plural society). It expressly left room for the option to restrict public officials' individual religious freedom by stating that there might be situations in which displaying religious symbols inhibit a proper functioning of public officials.[128] This position was far from broadly shared by the political parties, as can be seen from a parliamentary debate;[129] in other words, there was no consensus on the possibility of banning judicial officers from displaying religious symbols. The debates were not merely held in terms of positive law terms but also rather concentrated on the underlying legal arguments. In other words, instead of settling the issue with a reference to the law as it stood, the debates elaborately examined the underlying issues of this law. The same holds true for the academic debates. The emphasis has thus been on the material question whether judicial officers, administering justice or not, can display religious symbols. This question extends beyond the mere question of compatibility of religious symbols with the judicial robe.

---

126 However, the Minister of Justice did note the plans for making a more prominent distinction between the judge and court clerk and stated a willingness to possibly examine the situation again at that time, see Annex to *Handelingen II* 2001/02, no. 1652, p. 3445.

127 O. Verhaar and S. Saharso, 'The Weight of Context: Headscarves in Holland' (2004) 7(2) *Ethical Theory and Moral Practice*, p. 188.

128 Original text: 'Hoewel het dragen van kledingstukken en/of sieraden die mogelijk uitdrukking geven aan een religieuze overtuiging in beginsel aan het goed ambtenaarschap niet in de weg staan, zijn er omstandigheden waaronder dit toch het geval kan zijn... Aldus kunnen er in verband met de aard van de functie redenen zijn met betrekking tot veiligheid, functionaliteit of onpersoonlijke gezagsuitoefening die kunnen leiden tot de dringende noodzaak voor het stellen van kledingvoorschriften.', Nota 'Grondrechten in een pluriforme samenleving' (2004), p. 16.

129 Debat over religieuze uitingen ambtenaren, *Handelingen II* 29 200-VII, no. 24, pp. 3880-3896. The debate was initiated at the request of Joost Eerdmans of the List Pim Fortuyn (Lijst Pim Fortuyn) who firmly defended a neutral state which would not allow public officials to manifest their religion or belief. At that time, there was no majority for a ban on public officials displaying religious symbols.

2.4.5 The non-uniformed police officers

In 2000, the Council of Chief Commissioners of Police (*Raad van Hoofdcommissarissen*, hereinafter: the Council) initiated a plan for enabling police officers to wear religious headgear.[130] This plan particularly aimed at the uniformed police, as in practice administrative police personnel were already allowed to wear such clothing.[131] However, when meeting with fierce criticism, which was mainly based on the prevalent importance of the neutrality principle, it was never carried out. The criticism proved effective, as the new uniform, presented a year afterwards, did not provide for religious headgear.[132] What is more, instead of incorporating religious symbols into the uniform, the development took an opposite turn in explicitly excluding religious symbols from the police uniform.

In 2004, the Council adopted the National Clothing Regulation (*Kledingreglement*). Prior to this regulation, a special committee, the Dutch Police Advisory Committee on Clothing (*Adviescommissie Kleding Nederlandse politie*), had given some advice stressing the importance of the police being 'lifestyle neutral'. One of its points of departure was that police officers wearing civilian clothing and having contact with the public should wear neutral clothing and accessories. The National Clothing Regulation was tailored to that advice and thus did not provide for the possibility of wearing religious headgear.[133] It can be observed that this tendency has been extrapolated on a political level. At the same time, it has not remained free from dispute. Several individuals have brought complaints before the Commission, two of which are discussed below. The complaints are relatively complex due to disagreement between the parties on the facts, the ongoing developments concerning dress regulations for the police and the distinction between uniformed and non-uniformed service within the police.

The first of these complaints was dealt with by the Commission in March 2006.[134] The complainant, a former senior police officer, decided to start wearing a headscarf when she had already been working with the uniformed police in Rotterdam for twelve years. This decision did not immediately lead to dismissal, but her employer did inform her that she could no longer retain her position in the uniformed police which she agreed with. An alternative position in the non-uniformed police would be looked for. What followed was a complex sequence of events in which the

---

130 They did so mainly because of two interrelated reasons: in response to a lack of personnel and the felt need to mirror society in its ethnic diversity. See also S. Saharso and O. Verhaar (2006), p. 78.
131 Ibid.
132 As the article mentions, the reasons for withdrawing the plan were unclear, see ibid. Or, as reported in the press, the plan had been silently shelved, e.g. 'Alternatief politiepet van de baan; Plan voor keppeltjes, hoofddoeken en tulbanden blijkt stille dood gestorven' *NRC Handelsblad* (8 May 2003).
133 Adviescommissie Kleding Nederlandse Politie aan de Raad van Hoofdcommissarissen, Notitie Landelijk Kledingreglement, 16 januari 2004, also referred to in 'Pluriform uniform?' (2007), p. 6.
134 *Oordeel 2006-30* (CGB, 2 March 2006).

complainant was prohibited several times from wearing her headscarf. In the end, the employer informed her that no suitable alternative position could be found and terminated her employment. The complainant emphasized the duty of the employer to find an alternative position and qualified its insufficient endeavours to do so as direct discrimination. In addressing the complaint, the Commission set out the various duties incumbent on the employer, and in the end concluded that the employer had committed direct discrimination on grounds of sex and religion by not including in its search positions in the non-uniformed police where contact with the public is involved.

In the same month, the Council sent a letter to the Minister asking for the dress regulation to be revised so as to impose a uniform policy on the whole police force.[135] A year after, on 24 May 2007, the Minister asked the Commission for advice. Her request specifically concerned the principle of 'lifestyle neutrality' as a leading principle for police officers' dress and appearance and asked how this principle related to the non-discrimination principle.[136] The Council had asked for the principle of lifestyle neutrality to be included in the dress regulation and to apply this principle to all police officers who had dealings with the public. The Commission acknowledged that the police fulfil a special task in society; therefore typical police tasks differentiate police officers from other public servants. It established that the requirement of lifestyle neutrality results in indirect discrimination, because some police officers adhering to religions with more outward manifestations will be more affected.[137] Subsequently, it examined whether such discrimination can be objectively justified. It concluded that the aim of a neutral and representative appearance, in order to promote public trust in the police and public acceptance of police authority, is legitimate. It also considered that dress regulations based on the criterion of lifestyle neutrality can be appropriate. However, it left open whether such a regulation is necessary and imposed the burden on the Minister to adduce arguments in order to justify 'such a strict regulation'. The Commission stressed that while the special position of the police enlarged the Minister's margin of appreciation, the infringement of the proposed regulation revision on constitutionally protected interests substantially decreased this margin.[138] It recalled that the criteria of representativeness and neutrality can be fleshed out in different ways. In so doing, it referred to foreign police forces with uniforms especially designed to enable police officers to wear religious clothing.

In response, the Dutch House adopted a resolution pronouncing that it was *absolutely undesirable* that a police officer in the Netherlands should wear a headscarf

---

135 The Chief of the National Police of the National Council sent a letter to the Minister of the Interior on 28 March 2006 regarding the appearance of the Dutch police (*Uiterlijke verschijningsvormen Nederlandse Politie*).

136 'Pluriform uniform?' (2007), p. 6.

137 Ibid, p. 16.

138 Ibid, p. 17.

(emphasis added).[139] Moreover, Parliamentary Members submitted questions to the Minister in order to see whether she agreed with the advice of the Commission.[140] One of the questions for example was whether she rejected the advice.[141] The Minister announced that she would consult the parties involved and take a position on the issue by February 2008 at the latest. She mentioned that she would take the resolution adopted by the Dutch House into consideration. However, she also pointed to the importance of the human rights framework.

While the Minister's position was still pending, the second complaint was examined by the Commission on 23 October 2008. This time, it concerned a dispute between the Amsterdam regional police force and a non-uniformed extraordinary police investigator, who had been working with the police for ten years. Contrary to the police officer in the previous case, she had already been wearing a headscarf since 2003 without any problems. It was not her change in dress which caused problems, but a change in policy within the police in 2007. This change affected her duties in two ways: firstly, her duties were extended to tasks in the cells and secondly, for both the tasks in the cells and her already existing desk duties she was obliged to wear a uniform. The main reason for this policy change was the possibility of investigators coming into contact with the public.[142]

The Commission established that the new uniform policy constituted indirect discrimination. The police force had declared that its new policy aimed at the police being identifiable and neutral. The Commission deemed these aims to be legitimate and the means of the uniform policy appropriate. However, in assessing the necessity of the dress code, it distinguished between the duties in the cells and desk duties. In relation to the former duties, it noted that the applicant was not formally obliged to be in contact with third persons. Basically, such contact would consist of chance encounters in the hallway, for which she could identify herself with a badge. Therefore, the Commission considered the uniform precept to be unnecessary and hence not objectively justified. However, in relation to desk duties, the Commission considered that the police force had the discretion to attribute significant weight to the interests of the police to be identifiable and neutral. Therefore, the distinction made by the uniform precept for desk duties was objectively justified. The Commission refrained from responding to the alternative request of the applicant to the Commission to rule

---

139 Original text: '… spreekt uit, dat het absoluut onwenselijk is dat in Nederland een politieagente met een hoofddoek loopt'.
140 Parliamentary Questions Vragen van de leden Brinkman, Fritsma en Wilders (allen PVV) aan de ministers van Binnenlandse Zaken en Koninkrijksrelaties en voor Wonen, Wijken en Integratie over het advies van de commissie gelijke behandeling over het dragen van hoofddoekjes door politieagenten, Annex to *Handelingen II* 2007/08), no. 941, p. 2007 ff.
141 Ibid, Question 2.
142 For the facts, see *Oordeel 2008-123* (CGB, 23 October 2008).

on the ban on wearing a headscarf with the police uniform as such. In so doing, it referred to the intention of the Minister to take a position on the issue.[143]

On 14 November 2008, the Minister published this position by way of a letter to the Dutch House.[144] In this letter, she concluded that 'expressions which can undermine the desirable neutrality of the police, such as expressions of belief, religion, and expressions which undermine the authority of the police as well as expressions which entail a certain safety risk' should not be allowed. She applied this conclusion to police officers wearing a uniform and police officers charged with 'public functions', in other words police officers who have contact with the public, while not wearing a uniform.

2.4.6 The state school intern

Unlike judges and police officers, state school teachers are not subject to a duty to wear a uniform. Therefore, the question of religious symbols did not concern their compatibility with a uniform. But the notion of neutrality did play an important role in the debates. This was the case in the context of state schools which are bound to a duty of neutrality in line with their constitutional duty of even-handed respect for all religions and beliefs. But equally, the notion has cropped up in relation to a non-state denominational school, which appeared to be founded on neutrality. Disputes in the school context appeared quite early on before the Commission; even by 9 February 1999 the Commission had given an opinion on a student's complaint.[145] She had been requested to take off her headscarf during an internship at a primary state school, which was part of her training as a school teacher. She had refused to meet this request and had not returned to the school. Before the Commission, the student complained that she had been discriminated against on grounds of religion.

The point of contention between her and the school pertained to what the public character of the school specifically required of its teachers. While they both agreed on the need for teachers to have an open attitude, they disagreed on whether such an open attitude precluded the wearing of religious symbols.[146] The Commission observed

---

143 With regard to this opinion of the Commission, Uzman has addressed the question as to how the opinions of the Commission relate to issues that the legislature has not yet definitively dealt with, see J. Uzman, 'Procola-spook of broedende kip? Noot bij oordeel 2008-123' in J.H. Gerards and P.J.J. Zoontjens (eds), *Gelijke behandeling: oordelen en commentaar 2008* (Wolf Legal Publishers, Nijmegen 2008), p. 332 ff.

144 Brief van de Minister van Binnenlandse Zaken en Koninkrijksrelaties *Kamerstukken II* 2008/09, 29 628, no. 109.

145 *Oordeel 1999-18* (CGB, 9 February 1999). This case concerned a state school, but there have been more disputes concerning religious clothing at schools, two of which have resulted in a complaint before the Commission.

146 The school stated that the public character of the school implied an open attitude of all teaching personnel. Such an attitude entailed great reticence of behaviour, including the way of dressing. It

that it had been neither stated nor proved that the applicant did not have this open attitude. In the opinion of the Commission, the school simply assumed that wearing a headscarf showed a certain, unwanted religious view. Therefore, the Commission concluded that the request of the school constituted direct discrimination.[147]

The decision of the Commission did not stop further bans on religious symbols in schools. In response, the Commission gave an Advice on Dress Regulations in schools in 2003.[148] It allowed schools to adopt dress policies, as long as they were aware that some of these requirements might affect persons of a particular religion. At the same time, it explicitly stated that state schools cannot require their teachers and pupils not to wear a headscarf. Although a teacher can be required to propagate neutrality in exercising her duties, such neutrality does not in itself impede the wearing of a headscarf. The Advice emphasized that the legal criteria objectively justifying indirect discrimination are very strict.

Neither the Advice nor the previously mentioned ministerial Guideline succeeded in settling the disputes revolving around the concept of educational neutrality and its compatibility with religious symbols. Disputes kept being brought before the Commission. On 11 February 2005, a complaint of a student who was on a teacher training course was dealt with by the Commission.[149] The student alleged that she did not qualify for a teaching practice post since she wore a headscarf. It must be mentioned that this case did not concern a state school, but a private denominational school, explicitly founded on the principle of neutrality - it had enshrined it in its statutes. This basis was at the centre of the argument of the school, explaining that religion was excluded. However, when scrutinizing these statutes, the Commission concluded that this foundation had not been articulated sufficiently. Therefore, the school could not qualify as a denominational school and consequently it could not rely on the exception to the rule that schools cannot discriminate directly. This case makes it clear that it may be possible for denominational schools to interpret neutrality very strictly, as long as it has been clearly laid down in its statutes.

---

then considered this reticence to be even more applicable to a way of dressing which identified the wearer with 'a grouping, which does not only observe very strict views for itself, but also displays little tolerance towards dissenters within the same religion'. It considered it self-evident that a woman wearing a headscarf, even within the privacy of a classroom, adhered to very strict views; therefore, 'she could implicitly come across as threatening for the women and girls within the same religion adhering to less strict ideas'. The school continued that the wearing of the headscarf was considered as a symbol of oppression of women in Turkey; retaining this symbol was therefore not desirable in a state school, para. 3.4 ff.

147 *Oordeel 1999-18*, para. 5.
148 E.g. Advice of the Commissie Gelijke Behandeling concerning clothing at schools (*Advies Commissie Gelijke Behandeling inzake Gezichtssluiers en hoofddoeken op scholen*) (16 April 2003) 2003/01.
149 *Oordeel 2005-19* (CGB, 11 February 2005).

In 2006, the Commission confirmed this approach in a case in which another student on a teacher training course complained that she had been discriminated against because of her headscarf.[150] The competent authority for primary schools in Utrecht arranged with the teacher training authority that it would look for a different teaching practice post from the initial one.

2.5 CONCLUSION

The purpose of the present chapter was to describe the background to the Dutch debate. In so doing, the chapter has focused on two aspects: firstly, the situation concerning public officials' freedom to display religious symbols as it existed before the debate emerged, and secondly, how this situation subsequently became contested. In examining these two aspects, the chapter has included the national legislation, (quasi) judicial case law and academic literature.

It appeared that there is room for interpretation concerning religious freedom, the position of religion in the public sphere and state neutrality. Moreover, these notions continuously evolve in tune with the changes in the social context in which they are applied. Indeed, the traditional pragmatic approach which the Netherlands has taken in coping with religious diversity has come to face challenges due to societal changes. On the one hand, the changing role of religion diminished as well as increased the relevance of religion in society. On the other hand, demographic changes ensuing from immigration brought with them a variety of religions. These 'new' religions encompassed different religious manifestations and placed religious freedom in a different light. As to public officials' religious freedom, it has nowadays become accepted that public officials enjoy individual rights, although views on their freedom have varied over the years. At the same time, it goes without saying that public officials are not like other employees. Their exercise of state authority is considered to entail some special responsibility. That said, no explicit rules were in place regarding dress codes and the room they left for religious symbols. This omission enabled disputes to arise.

For the judiciary and public education, individual challenging of bans on religious symbols was crucial for igniting a wider debate on the question of public officials wearing religious symbols. By contrast, the police itself met with opposition when it attempted to adopt rules incorporating religious symbols into police uniform. This opposition was corroborated by the intervention of politics and individual complaints.[151] What is striking is that the main individual disputes only came before

---

150 *Oordeel 2006-70* (CGB 14 April 2006).

151 Cf. the voting record of the general assembly of the Dutch Association of Lawyers (*Nederlandse Juristen-Vereniging, NJV*) on the question whether it should be possible to combine the police uniform with items like headscarves, kippahs or turbans. The majority of the assembly supported a negative answer to this question, Handelingen NJV, 'Multiculturaliteit en Recht' (Dordrecht,

the Commission and were not taken to court. In other words, there is little or no 'real' case law on this issue.

In sum, the emergence of the debate is the result of interplay between an increasingly wider debate on the role of religion in the Netherlands and argument on specific questions relating to the public services examined in this study. The description of the debate demonstrates clearly how these two issues have reinforced each other, and how all the disputes originated in the same period of time. The reaction to the conflict for each of the public services in terms of rulemaking did not proceed at an identical pace. At the time when plans to adopt bans on religious symbols within the judiciary and the police are pending, no such plans have been initiated for public education except in relation to face veils.[152] Irrespective of the legislative and political developments, a real understanding of the underlying issues necessitates looking at the merits of the debate. Accordingly, the next chapter turns to the points of contention central to the debate.

---

13 June 2008, vol. 138 (2)), p. 88.

152 More generally, the judiciary and the police tend to be put on a par in being considered to be carrying out functions directly falling to the state, more so than public education. This is also reflected in the Advice of the Council of State on the bill on normalizing the legal position of public officials; it advises creating an exemption not only for the judiciary but for all public officials authorized to used force, hence including the police, see Raad van State (2011), para. 3d.

CHAPTER 3
THE DUTCH DEBATE

3.1 INTRODUCTION

In the previous chapter, this study took a bird's-eye view of the debate on religious symbols in public functions by describing the context. The present chapter zooms in on the contents of the debate. In so doing, this chapter starts off by identifying the separate arguments put forward in support of both affirming and refuting a leading question in this study: does state neutrality justify and/or necessitate limitations on the freedom of public officials to manifest their religion or belief by displaying symbols? Focusing on these arguments may be of explanatory value for the differences of opinion. This approach is in tune with the argumentative approach, which underscores the importance of fundamentally contemplating the arguments figuring in a debate, subsequent to identifying the arguments. The emphasis on the substance of the arguments diminishes the relevance of the authority of the source; in other words, the views of the legislature and judges serve as a source of arguments rather than as a source of rules. Apart from legislation and case law, policy documents and scholarly literature are resorted to for finding arguments. In the process of identifying the arguments, the study aims at making the connection with state neutrality. Accordingly, the question central to the present chapter is:

> How is state neutrality in the Dutch debate argued to impact on the scope for public officials in the judiciary, the police and public education in the Netherlands to manifest their religion or belief by displaying symbols?

Despite some overlap, the (origins of the) debates for each public function differ. Therefore, a separate examination of the different debates is warranted. The study first turns to individual complaints before the Equal Treatment Commission (the Commission), dealing with the main issue. As previously noted, the Commission does not issue legally binding judgments, but it has produced an authoritative body of jurisprudence in the field of equal treatment law. Therefore, its opinions shed a useful light on how the different points of view are put forward. The description also takes into account how the arguments have resounded on other levels and whether additional arguments have been put forward.

In sum, the chapter has a two-step approach. In line with the approach of the study, it first identifies and describes arguments as they were put forward in the cases before the Commission and as they resounded in the ensuing debate. Subsequently, it takes the description further in reflecting on the arguments and making the connection with the main research question. Using the cases before the Commission as a starting point for the description implies three things.

Firstly, because the cases concern public functions, state neutrality is implicitly present in the cases. That is not to say that all arguments have equal pertinence to state neutrality. For the sake of clarity though, the analysis first considers which main points were dealt with in the cases. In presenting the points put forward, the discussion specifically examines their relation to state neutrality. In the end, after having presented the bulk of arguments, it highlights those arguments with a clear link to state neutrality. Secondly, as a result of the inherently polarized nature of (quasi) judicial disputes, the description presents a relatively bipolar point of view. The examination endeavours to abstract from the particular claims to identify the points of contention between the parties and the premises underlying these points of contention. Thirdly, it should be noted that the legal framework of the complaints entails that the obvious recurring question is whether differential treatment has taken place and when that is the case whether that differential treatment can be qualified as direct or indirect discrimination. This is not so much an argument but rather the central point of contention. Be that as it may, the way in which the point of differential treatment is put across is mixed up with how state neutrality plays out in these particular cases. Therefore, the point of differential treatment is presented first in all three separate debates.

3.2 THE DEBATE ON THE JUDICIARY

As described in the previous chapter, the law student who brought a complaint before the Commission had applied for the position of deputy court clerk. Her case prompted a broader debate on the judiciary, which really boiled down to the question of judges and religious symbols. Even though it concerned a deputy court clerk and not a judge, the point of judicial impartiality was addressed. At the same time, it was precisely the difference between a deputy court clerk and a judge that was invoked to support the complainant's argument. These two points are discussed after the point of differential treatment. In addition, two other points raised concern the role of the Regulation on judicial dress (hereinafter: the Regulation) and the separation of church and state. The remainder of this section discusses how these points were put forward, what relation they have to state neutrality and possibly whether they resounded in other sources.

3.2.1 Direct or indirect discrimination

Before the Commission, the complainant argued that the decision of the respondent not to employ her because judges and court clerks should not manifest their religion or belief by wearing particular dress constituted direct discrimination. In response, the respondent put forward that any sign, which is recognizable to litigants as a *visible sign of personal views* (emphasis added), is incompatible with the Regulation. In its view, the ban on signs expressing personal views included but was not limited to religious dress and symbols, thus falling short of being discriminatory. The Commission took a slightly different angle in interpreting the Regulation. It first noticed that the respondent had referred to the Regulation, which indeed contained no reference to religion or belief. The Commission established that the Regulation prohibited *any type of head covering* (emphasis added), irrespective of the religious character of such head covering. The Commission recognized that Muslim women might be particularly affected and, as a result, it found indirect discrimination. The remainder of the opinion assessed whether the indirect discrimination could be objectively justified. The assessment centred on the point of judicial impartiality, on which Section 2.2 will elaborate.

It is evident from the previous chapter that the Minister of Justice did not consider the Regulation to constitute direct discrimination. Furthermore, to his mind judicial impartiality justified limitations on judicial officials' freedom to manifest religion or belief. In the academic world, there were some scholars making a fervent call to consider the Regulation as direct discrimination.[1] These scholars emphasized that the reason of the respondent not to employ the complainant as a deputy court clerk was her refusal to take off the headscarf. This reasoning, according to these scholars, refers directly to religion or belief. Other scholars agreed with the finding of indirect discrimination. However, some of them agreed with the Commission in not finding the indirect discrimination objectively justified, whereas others considered such indirect discrimination to be objectively justified.[2] The interpretation of judicial impartiality is of importance concerning which position is favoured.

3.2.2 Judicial impartiality and independence

In accordance with the equal treatment legislation, an objective justification of a measure constituting indirect discrimination first requires the measure to pursue a legitimate aim. Fulfilment of the additional requirements, appropriateness and necessity of the practice, depends on this aim. The respondent argued that safeguarding

---

1   E.g. J. Tigchelaar, 'Het kledingprobleem van Vrouwe Justitia: kan een hoofddoek op een toga?' (2001) 17(4) *Nemesis: tijdschrift over vrouwen en recht*, p. 138. Also Nieuwenhuis points out that the reference by the court to 'any sign of personal views' and, in particular, religious symbols may easily qualify as direct discrimination, see A.J. Nieuwenhuis. 'Tussen *laïcité* en AWGB: Hoofddoek en openbaar onderwijs in Frankrijk, Duitsland, Nederland en onder het EVRM' (2004) 18 *Nederlands Juristenblad*, p. 945.

2   E.g. two articles in the (2001) 26(7) *NJCM-Bulletin: Nederlands tijdschrift voor de mensenrechten*: T. Loenen, 'Hoofddoeken voor de klas en in de rechtbank: op weg naar een multicultureel publiek domein?', p. 38 and M. Kuijer, 'Vrouwe Justitia: blinddoek of hoofddoek? (Annotatie bij Commissie Gelijke Behandeling 22 juni 2001, oordeel 2001-53)', p. 898.

judicial independence and impartiality[3] was the primary interest served by limitations on religious dress and symbols within the judiciary.[4] The Commission identified three questions, which it needed to answer in the case in hand. Firstly, did the Regulation aim at safeguarding judicial impartiality? Secondly, was this aim free from any discriminatory intent? Thirdly, was compliance with the Regulation necessary and did it meet the standards of proportionality and subsidiarity?[5]

The first two questions have not been the focus of dissent.[6] What is more, the importance of the principle of judicial impartiality itself simply stood uncontested.[7] The last question, though, did give rise to contention, in the case itself as well as in the ensuing political and scholarly discussions. And it is this question which is most relevant to the main research question in this study. In the case before the Commission, the complainant questioned the necessity of the Regulation by arguing that judicial impartiality does not depend on appearance. She articulated the core of her argument by stating: 'there is no reason to assume that a judge in a robe *with* a headscarf judges less neutrally and impartially than a judge in a robe *without* a headscarf' (emphasis added).[8] To bolster her point she referred to the theory that a composition of the judiciary which is representative of the composition of the population in society is beneficial to public trust in the judiciary. Such a composition would allow litigants, coming from a variety of backgrounds, to identify with the judiciary. By contrast,

---

3 The terms 'judicial neutrality', 'independence' and 'impartiality' figure interchangeably in the debate. While the differences between these terms are marginal, 'judicial impartiality' is preferred over the other terms. Judicial officers' personal preferences, such as religious ones, mainly affect judicial impartiality; this section thus uses this term.

4 In addition to the previous footnote, it can be noted that this section specifically focuses on judicial impartiality since it pertains to the substantive value of state neutrality, whereas judicial independence rather points to organizational independence.

5 Cf. *Oordeel 2001-53* (CGB, 22 June 2001).

6 While the complainant did not state anything explicit about the aim of the Regulation, she did not contest it either.

7 As Cliteur states, we have always been impressed by the tremendous power which we have conferred on the judiciary. Whereas they once decided on matters of life and death, they still decide on hugely significant interests of those being judged, see P.B. Cliteur, 'Hoofddoekje past niet bij neutrale rechter', *NRC Handelsblad* (30 June 2001). He emphasizes that it has been we who endowed the judiciary with this power and that in doing so we have made this conditional on requirements of the principle of legality and of judicial independence. Maris also refers to the early theory of John Locke on the social contract to explain the importance of the judiciary being impartial and of church and state being principally separated, see C.W. Maris van Sandelingenambacht, 'Hoofddoek of blinddoek?' in N.F. van Manen (ed), (Ars Aequi Libri, Nijmegen 2002), p. 185. See also B. van Mourik, 'Het islamitisch hoofddoekje en het Franse *laïcité* (2004) 29(3) NJCM-Bulletin: Nederlands tijdschrift voor de mensenrechten, p. 312.

8 Original text: 'Er is geen reden om aan te nemen dat een rechter in toga met een hoofddoek minder neutraal en onpartijdig oordeelt dan een rechter in toga zonder hoofddoek', see *Oordeel 2001-53*. See also F. Bruinsma, 'Symbolische kleding (Mening over de stelling 'In een multiculturele samenleving is een rechter in toga met een hoofddoek een aanwinst')' (2001) 21 *Nederlands Juristenblad*, p. 993.

exclusion of symbols like the headscarf would entail exclusion of an entire group of newcomers.

Despite the uncontested importance of judicial impartiality, the respondent still went to great lengths to emphasize it, in referring to the constitutionally founded position of the judiciary in the Dutch constitutional system and to Article 6 ECHR. In the opinion of the respondent, the dress limitations in the Regulation endorsed the requirements of judicial impartiality.[9] The respondent emphasized that it was exactly these limitations which furthered litigants' trust in the judiciary. Moreover, the respondent referred to ECHR case law in stating that the mere appearance of partiality suffices for violation of Article 6 ECHR. It concluded this line of reasoning by underscoring that a litigant should not feel favoured or disfavoured by the judge's or court clerk's dress.

The Commission found in favour of the complainant by considering that the Regulation was not necessary; it was not proportional and subsidiary to meet the aim of judicial impartiality. In so doing, it observed that this aim had not been made explicit since 1960. Moreover, several facts and trends, of which the Commission mentioned three, have diminished the need for strictly applying the Regulation. Firstly, it pointed to the fact that some types of judges do not wear their robe in session. Secondly, it mentioned that the state had been striving for a judiciary which represented the composition of the population in society as much as possible. Thirdly, the Commission stated that the judiciary was on its way to being transformed into a modern, transparent organization. It viewed these facts and trends as demonstrating that the need for dress rules should be put into perspective; this diminished the need for strict application of these rules. Finally, it was relevant that this case concerned a court clerk whose specific role could have a bearing on the reasoning. Section 2.4 elaborates on this.

Just as the argument of judicial impartiality had been at the centre of the deputy court clerk case, so it received a good deal of attention in the ensuing debates. These debates focused on the question as to how a judge's appearance in particular and the judiciary's appearance in general relate to judicial impartiality. This is a pivotal question for this study, which focuses on religious manifestation by symbols. Moreover, it directly involves state neutrality, because judicial impartiality derives from state neutrality. Specifically, the judge's appearance raises the question of the significance of the robe for judicial impartiality.

The complainant downplayed the significance of the robe for judicial impartiality. According to her, the judgment is a much better indicator of impartiality, which met with the agreement of some scholars.[10] In support of this, some have pointed out that

---

9   The term 'judicial independence' is used by the court.
10   In other words, judges still need to prove themselves, regardless of their robes, e.g. Bruinsma (2001), p. 993.

mechanisms to remedy a judge's partiality are available, like judicial challenge.[11] In other words, such mechanisms diminish the need for the robe as a token of judicial impartiality. The robe[12] is actually no more than the outer appearance, or rather a *symbol* for the underlying ideal of judicial impartiality.[13] The relation between this symbol and its underlying ideal has been called conventional,[14] which suggests that other symbols are just as conceivable.

On the other hand, the importance which the respondent attributed to the robe has been equally met with approval by scholars.[15] This view qualified the robe as symbolizing the judicial task. Contrary to downplaying this symbol, it considered such symbolization as essential for safeguarding the underlying ideal.[16] Its advocates pointed to the depersonalization effectuated by the robe.[17] One author phrased it rather poetically by labelling the judiciary as 'a profession without a soul or engagement'.[18] Dress or symbols *par excellence* can serve to underline this impartiality.[19] The Dutch Government has acknowledged the particular importance of dress for specific public functions, such as the judiciary, in conveying neutrality.[20]

The debate has elaborated further on the relation between the robe and judicial impartiality in touching on two underlying points: first of all, the drawing of a parallel

---

11 Ibid.

12 E.g. Tigchelaar (2001), p. 139. She questions whether a judicial costume is necessary for attaining judicial impartiality.

13 E.g. W. van der Burg, C.J.M. Schuyt and J.H. Nieuwenhuis, *Multiculturaliteit en recht* (Verslag van de op 13 juni 2008 te Dordrecht gehouden algemene vergadering van de Nederlandse Juristen-Vereniging, vol. 138, Kluwer, Deventer 2008). See also S. Harchaoui, 'Gevraagd: Analytisch vermogen (Mening over de stelling 'In een multiculturele samenleving is een rechter in toga met een hoofddoek een aanwinst')' (2001) 21 *Nederlands Juristenblad*, p. 994; Bruinsma (2001), p. 993; and Loenen (2001), p. 865.

14 Tigchelaar (2001), p. 139.

15 E.g. Cliteur in *NRC Handelsblad* (2001), P.B. Cliteur, 'Opzij en Zwolse rechter hebben gelijk; Hoofddoek past niet bij ambt zonder ziel of engagement' *Trouw* (18 April 2001), A. Ellian and P. Zoontjens, 'Bij een blinddoek past geen hoofddoek' *De Volkskrant* (9 May 2001). In the case before the Equal Treatment Commission, the court also stated that the requirements in the Regulation on clothing aim to substantiate requirements of judicial impartiality, paras 3.13 and 3.14.

16 C.A.J.M. Kortmann, 'Tekenen' ((Mening over de stelling 'In een multiculturele samenleving is een rechter in toga met een hoofddoek een aanwinst')' (2001) 21 *Nederlands Juristenblad*, p. 995. This view builds on a distinction between public and private, see also Maris van Sandelingenambacht in Van Manen (2002), p. 190.

17 Kortmann (2001); A.F.M. Brenninkmeijer, 'Verwarring', (Mening over de stelling 'In een multiculturele samenleving is een rechter in toga met een hoofddoek een aanwinst')' (2001) 21 *Nederlands Juristenblad*, p. 995.

18 Cliteur in *Trouw* (2001).

19 This view is supported by the interpretation of judicial impartiality as proposed by Kuijer (2001), p. 897.

20 Ministerie van Binnenlandse Zaken, Nota 'Grondrechten in een pluriforme samenleving', *Kamerstukken II* 2003/04, 29 614, no. 2, referred to in the 2006 case, para. 3.3.

between religious expressions and other expressions and secondly, the relation of religious expression and inner motivation.

With respect to the first point, some scholars pointed out that the idea of a judge with a headscarf being partial was based on no more than prejudice.[21] To bolster this point they drew a parallel with other personal features and stated that a judge's appearance can never be entirely neutral. Any feature of a judge's looks, the allegedly immutable ones, be it skin colour or gender, as well as the mutable ones, such as specific earrings or hair style can provoke prejudice in the litigant.[22] The drawing of this parallel reveals the complicated nature of religious expressions. On the one hand, it can be argued that a religious expression, such as a headscarf, can be taken off, in contrast with skin colour.[23] On the other hand, this might be more difficult with a beard which is worn for religious reasons. Furthermore, it is debatable whether taking off a headscarf equals taking off earrings which are worn for decorative purposes. This relates to the second point: the relation between religious expressions and inner motivation.

Some scholars pointed out that the wearing of religious dress raises a warranted concern about the judge's impartiality. They not only emphasized the visible aspect of the headscarf and the possible impression of partiality but they also suggested that the refusal to take off religious dress or symbols implied a refusal to allow the rule of law to prevail over personal convictions.[24] In other words, they made the point that a judge declared his being impartial by taking off religious dress or symbols. This point can be put into perspective by the statement that taking off religious dress or symbols does not equal omitting the underlying religion or belief. What is more, this statement has been taken further in making the point that a judge will always retain personal views. As a result, it would be more transparent to allow these views to be expressed.[25]

On the level of the judiciary as a whole, the debate related judicial impartiality to public trust in the judiciary. It discerned two elements of this relation: the first was the question of equal access for those pursuing a career in the judiciary and the

---

21   W. van der Burg, *Het ideaal van de neutrale staat. Inclusieve, exclusieve en compenserende visies op godsdienst en cultuur* (Boom Juridische uitgevers, The Hague 2009), p. 58. T. Wolff, *Multiculturalisme & Neutraliteit* (PhD Universiteit van Amsterdam, Vossiuspers, Amsterdam 2005), p. 196.

22   Wolff (2005), p. 197. T. Loenen, *Geloof in het geding: Juridische grenzen van religieus pluralisme in het perspectief van de mensenrechten* (Sdu Uitgevers, The Hague 2006), p. 85.

23   C.J.M. Schuyt, 'Publiekrecht in een multiculturele samenleving' in Van der Burg, Schuyt and Nieuwenhuis (eds) (2008), p. 114.

24   Cliteur in *Trouw* (2001). Maris van Sandelingenambacht in Van Manen (2002), p. 188. This resonates with the assumption that wearing a religious garment or symbol is a matter of personal choice, see Ellian and Zoontjens in *De Volkskrant* (2001).

25   According to Loenen, at least the litigant then knows with whom he has to deal, see Loenen (2006), p. 85.

second was the degree to which the judiciary was seen to represent the population and accordingly to be impartial. More specifically, these elements were relevant to the candidate judge and the litigant or even the wider public respectively.

With respect to the first element, the complainant's point that dress limitations might effectively result in the exclusion of particular groups from the judiciary resonated with some scholars who even spoke of 'categorical exclusion' of groups.[26] They coupled this with the concern that such exclusion might impede the emancipation and integration of such groups.[27] Other scholars have argued in response that individuals have the choice to comply with the dress policy or not; according to this view, individuals would choose whether to be excluded or not. What is more, taking off religious dress or symbols may actually be conducive to emancipation and integration. One may ask again whether religious dress and symbols are based on a voluntary choice in the same way as decorative jewellery is.

As to the second element, the complainant made the point that a judiciary consisting of all kinds of groups would convey to litigants that it is inclusive of all kinds of groups in society.[28] This point has resonated with some scholars who agree that such a message indicates that the judiciary is representative of society, which allegedly furthers public trust in the judiciary.[29] Conversely, other scholars have contended that the more diverse a society is, the more the judiciary is required to have a neutral, or actually blank image. This view finds such an image best both for fostering public trust and for preventing the judiciary from becoming too politicized.[30]

3.2.3 Role of the Regulation

Because the Regulation has laid down the rules concerning judicial dress, its status has been the subject of attention in the debates. In the deputy court clerk case before

---

26 Categorical exclusion is also an element to include in the balancing test, see van der Burg (2009), p. 58. The Equal Treatment Commission pointed out that a prohibition on a headscarf will exclude a considerable number of Muslim women and will thus have consequences for the diversity strived for by the police, *Oordeel 2008-123* (CGB, 23 October 2008), para. 5. See also S. Saharso and O. Verhaar, 'Headscarves in the Policeforce and the Court: Does Context Matter?' (2006) 41(1) *Acta politica: tijdschrift voor politicologie*, pp. 80-81. They point out that 'police officers wearing headscarves would lead to a greater public trust in the impartiality of the police, and thus promote the police's legitimacy and improve its performances.' See also Loenen (2006), p. 83. As noted by the National Centre of Expertise for Diversity (*Landelijk ExpertiseCentrum Diversiteit*), when certain groups do not see the police as 'their' police, this results in a direct loss of legitimacy, see the report 'Politie voor ééenieder. Een eigentijdse visie op diversiteit' (Politieacademie, Apeldoorn, 2009) to be found on e.g. <zoek.officielebekendmakingen.nl/>, p. 9.
27 Ibid.
28 Ibid.
29 Loenen (2001), p. 866. Loenen (2006), p. 85. W. de Been, 'Hoofddoek past in rechtszaal', *De Volkskrant* (16 May 2001).
30 Maris van Sandelingenambacht in Van Manen (2002), p. 186.

the Commission, this attention focused on the relation of the Regulation to the Equal Treatment Act. At the material time, an exception concerning the applicability of the Act was made for Acts of Parliament[31] which had been passed prior to entry into force of the Act.[32] The difference of opinion between the parties before the Commission concerned the nature of the Regulation as well as the moment of its entry into force. These issues mattered for determining the extent to which the Regulation would fall within the ambit of the Equal Treatment Act; the Commission ruled that the Equal Treatment Act was fully applicable to the Regulation. Furthermore, it pointed to recent societal changes having reduced the need to interpret the Regulation very strictly.[33] In the scholarly discussions, the exact procedural status of the Regulation itself drew little if any attention.

This issue is not very interesting for the academic debate on the judiciary and religious symbols, at least not in the way it was put across before the Commission. However, the underlying substantive point of the ambiguity surrounding state neutrality and the rules which are associated with it is of interest. The omission of explicit rules on religious dress and symbols within the judiciary raised the question whether such silence should be interpreted as prohibiting or authorizing such dress and symbols.[34] Even so, it could be questioned whether the dress code has kept pace with time. As described, religious diversity in Dutch society has increased and introduced dress and symbols which were not foreseen at the time of drafting the Regulation. Apart from the rules in the Regulation itself, its underlying rationale has been said to refer to state neutrality. This point recurs in the discussion of judicial impartiality and independence.

3.2.4 Court clerk in relation to the judge

The case before the Commission concerned a deputy court clerk, but the debate automatically raised the question of the relation of that official to a judge. The complainant separated the two by emphasizing the supportive nature of a court clerk's function; a court clerk does not administer the law and cannot be challenged. Therefore, she considered her line of reasoning with regard to judicial impartiality and independence to hold even more true for a court clerk. By contrast, the respondent stressed that the close connection between a court clerk's function and a judge's function made its considerations with regard to a judge hold equally true for a court clerk. It considered a court clerk's presence and appearance to be one of the factors

31 It concerns '*wetgeving in formele zin*', which refers to the adoption of laws by the government and Parliament, as prescribed in Article 81 of the Dutch Constitution.
32 This provision was deleted from the Act in 2002.
33 *Oordeel 2001-53* para. 4.11.
34 Kuijer has pointed out that the challenge to the Regulation is part of stimulating a normal evolution of law, Kuijer (2001), p. 897.

determining the image of the court. The respondent used precisely the fact that a court clerk cannot be challenged as a reason to avoid any appearance of partiality.

In agreement with the complainant, the Commission emphasized the supportive character of a court clerk's function. Together with the other considerations mentioned, the Commission considered the exclusion of applicants with a headscarf for the deputy court clerk's position a far-reaching measure. It noted that the dress rules in the Regulation did not in themselves preclude the wearing of a headscarf in combination with the robe. Therefore, the Commission found the dress requirement disproportional. This was even more the case for deputy court clerks. It considered that other means could be employed to demonstrate a clear distinction between a judge and a deputy court clerk.

The public debate did not emphasize the distinction between a court clerk's position and a judge's, but rather extended the question of religious dress and symbols to the judiciary as a whole.[35] The Minister of Justice concurred with the respondent in the deputy court clerk case in taking the litigant's perception as paramount; he observed that it is difficult for the litigant to distinguish between court clerks and judges.

While the point as such has little relevance for the main research question, it does raise the point as to who can be considered as bearers of state authority and accordingly as subject to the duty of state neutrality. Moreover, it is of interest for the question as to what should serve as the yardstick to measure judicial impartiality. Is it indeed the litigant's perspective, and if so, does this render the perspective subjective? Or is it possible to make the perspective objective by moving away from the litigant's perspective to that of the average reasonable observer?

3.2.5 Separation of church and state

The respondent in the deputy court clerk case casually dragged in a major concept at the end of its pleading; it noted that the wearing of a religious symbol during the exercise of a judicial function 'touches on the separation of church and state'.[36] In the debate, the opponents of religious dress and symbols in public functions have also included the separation of church and state as an argument against the wearing of such

---

35 E.g. Parliamentary Questions 'Vragen van het lid Halsema (GroenLinks) aan de minister van Justitie over het dragen van hoofddoeken door ambtenaren' Annex to *Handelingen II* 2001/02, no. 1652.

36 E.g. E. Jurgens, 'Het recht op onpartijdige ambtenaren', *Trouw* (12 July 2001). Vermeulen relates the separation of church and state to the requirement of philosophical neutrality and acknowledges that these principles are not unequivocal, see B.P. Vermeulen, 'Religieus pluralisme als uitdaging aan de "neutrale" rechter' (2005) *Trema* (Theme: 'Ieder z'n recht, magistraat in een pluriforme samenleving'). In the case before the Equal Treatment Commission, the court also stated that the wearing of a religious symbol in the exercise of a judicial function touches on the separation of church and state, para. 3.18.

items [37] In so doing, they have coupled the notion to secularism and state neutrality by arguing that the separation of church and state entails secularity in public functions such as the judiciary.[38]

3.3 THE DEBATE ON THE POLICE

The debate on the police focused on police officers wearing a uniform or being in contact with the public. Nonetheless, as is already clear from the previous chapter, the cases before the Commission did not concern police officers who could be plainly identified as uniformed police. The discussion of the arguments again starts with the question of direct or indirect discrimination. Additionally, the type of neutrality relevant to the police is lifestyle neutrality. Other arguments concerned factors which were specific for the functioning of the police: the previously mentioned distinction between the uniformed and the non-uniformed service and contact with the public. Finally, the argument concerning the separation of church and state has also emerged in the context of the police.

3.3.1 Direct or indirect discrimination

The previous chapter described how two complaints involving police officers had come before the Commission. The first one, in 2006,[39] demonstrated that banning religious dress and symbols was not limited to the uniformed service alone. Although the complainant had agreed not to wear the headscarf in uniformed service, the respondent regarded contact with the public as an additional ground for excluding the headscarf, even in non-uniformed service. Before the Commission, the complainant alleged that the respondent's failure to offer an alternative, non-uniformed position constituted direct discrimination. The respondent argued that the ban on the headscarf also applied to non-uniformed positions where contact with the public was involved. Moreover, its reasoning did not maintain a clear distinction between uniformed and non-uniformed service: it rather dealt with the exclusion of particular garb and symbols by referring to the general lifestyle neutrality required of the police. Its line of argument furthermore focused on the procedural developments in the dispute with the complainant and suggested that she herself had contributed to the difficulty of finding an alternative position. The Commission underscored the fact that the respondent had used contact with the public as a criterion to bar the complainant from wearing a headscarf. Accordingly, it considered that the respondent had based this ban on the possibility of the public seeing the complainant's religion from the

---

37   E.g. Ellian and Zoontjens, in *De Volkskrant* (2001).
38   Jurgens in *Trouw* (2001). Ellian and Zoontjens in *De Volkskrant* (2001).
39   *Oordeel 2006-30* (CGB, 2 March 2006).

wearing of the headscarf. The Commission found this consideration to constitute direct discrimination.

In the second complaint, in 2008,[40] the complainant did not contest the incompatibility of religious symbols with the uniform, but the transformation of formerly non-uniformed tasks into uniformed tasks. The respondent indicated that contact with the public was the very reason for this transformation. It further explained that the uniform made individuals identifiable as police officers to third parties.[41] Moreover, it argued that the uniform and the exclusion of personal symbols would guarantee neutrality. Contrary to its previous decision, the Commission did not consider the transformation of certain tasks into uniformed tasks, which implied exclusion of religious symbols, to constitute direct discrimination. It established indirect discrimination because the transformation of non-uniformed tasks into uniformed tasks did adversely affect individuals wearing a headscarf for religious reasons. The Commission continued by assessing whether the transformation of the tasks was necessary to ensure the neutrality and the recognisability of the police. The reasoning of the Commission identified two factors which were relevant to such necessity. The first one was the degree of contact which a police officer actually has with the public and the second one was the availability of alternative ways to be identified as a police officer. Depending on these factors, the imposition of a uniform duty and the ensuing exclusion of religious symbols could be objectively justified.

While the divergence of the two decisions in finding direct or indirect discrimination is confusing, it has not been central to debate elsewhere. The point which has drawn attention, mostly on a political level, is the question of lifestyle neutrality.

3.3.2 Lifestyle neutrality and uniformity

The police have explicitly coined the term lifestyle neutrality.[42] This term envisaged a wider scope than religious neutrality. What is more, it has been suggested that other expressions, such as tattoos and hairstyles, have ignited the debate even more than religious symbols.[43] The first complaint before the Commission made it clear that it is not quite obvious exactly to which tasks lifestyle neutrality applied. Be that as it may, lifestyle neutrality has been referred to as the basis of dress codes within the

---

40 *Oordeel 2008-123*, (23 October 2008).

41 Ibid, para. 3.13.

42 E.g. Adviescommissie Kleding Nederlandse Politie aan de Raad van Hoofdcommissarissen, Notitie Landelijk Kledingreglement, 16 januari 2004.

43 Cf. *Appellant t. de Korpsbeheerder van de politieregio Rotterdam-Rijnmond* (Centrale Raad van Beroep, 24 December 2009) LJN: BK8782 to be found on <zoeken.rechtspraak.nl>. This case concerned a police officer wearing a mohican haircut. While this case postdated the origins of the debate on police dress, it demonstrates that disputes concerning such manifestations have led to actual court cases.

police. Moreover, it has been considered necessary in an ever-diversifying society. The respondent in the first case before the Commission corroborated its point by referring to the previously mentioned governmental memo, which acknowledged the relevance of an impersonal or uniformed exercise of police tasks.[44] The respondent in the second case specifically spoke of police tasks involving contact with the public in referring to lifestyle neutrality. Moreover, it pointed out that neutrality did not only apply to religious manifestations, but to other 'personal' manifestations as well, like certain hairstyles and jewellery.[45]

The argument of lifestyle neutrality clearly resounded in the approach proposed by the Minister of the Interior referred to in the previous chapter. In explaining this approach, she coupled neutrality with two other notions: authority and safety. In this way, she built her line of reasoning which concluded with the necessity of excluding religious dress and symbols. In her explanation, the three notions complemented each other.

For instance, with regard to authority she pointed to the special position of the police within society; in order to enforce the law, the police may use special competences. What is more, the police are endowed with the exclusive authority to exert force.[46] As a result, the role of the police is a special one not only within society but also in relation to the state.[47] The Minister of the Interior emphasized that an appearance which conveys authority is of the utmost importance for a proper fulfilment of police tasks. Accordingly, any expression undermining this authority should be excluded.

In the same vein, she argued that neutrality upheld the uniformity and professionalism of the police. She considered that conveying impartiality and objectivity constituted a condition for the legitimacy of the police in exercising its special task. Again, any expression which might undermine the impartial appearance of the police should be avoided. Another interest of neutrality lies in police officers being identifiable as such, an issue which came to the fore in the second complaint before the Commission.[48]

Finally, the Minister of the Interior related the argument of safety primarily to the possible harm arising from accessories such as large earrings and necklaces. In this form, this argument is irrelevant to the study. Nonetheless, another interpretation of this argument tying it more closely into neutrality may be of more relevance.

---

44 *Oordeel 2006-30,* para. 3.3.
45 *Oordeel 2008-123,* para. 3.3.
46 Cf. Commissie Gelijke Behandeling, 'Advies Commissie Gelijke Behandeling inzake uiterlijke verschijningsvormen politie. Pluriform uniform?' (CGB Advice) (2007) 2007/8, p. 13. The litigant in *Oordeel 2008-123* also emphasized the role of the police as a law enforcer and as a monopolist in the use of force to support the argument for the relevance of a neutral appearance, para. 3.16.
47 CGB Advice, p. 13. See also Nota 'Grondrechten in een pluriforme samenleving', p. 16, which mentions that the state manifests itself by way of the police.
48 *Oordeel 2008-123*, para. 3.3. See also Saharso and Verhaar (2006), p. 80.

The argument of safety can also be connected with the neutrality of the police. This interpretation would consider the risk of a non-neutral appearance of the police as provoking aggression or other reactions, thereby putting the police's safety at risk.[49]

Generally, the debate on the police has been less elaborate than the one on the judiciary, perhaps precisely because all arguments had already been put forward in the latter debate. In any event, the underlying points of contention are similar to those discussed in the context of the judiciary and will therefore be elaborated on in the section which reflects on the arguments.

3.3.3 Uniformed and non-uniformed service

The distinction between uniformed and non-uniformed service has differentiated the discussion concerning the police more than the one concerning the judiciary. At first sight, the distinction seemed to suggest a clear-cut policy: religious symbols were prohibited in uniformed service and allowed in non-uniformed service. In the first case before the Commission, the complainant had agreed with the respondent that the headscarf was incompatible with the uniform. It was this very distinction which had prompted the National Council in 2000 to propose the incorporation of religious symbols into the police uniform. As mentioned in the previous chapter, in Section 2.4.5, this proposal focused specifically on the uniformed service, as non-uniformed police officers already enjoyed more freedom to wear religious dress and symbols. The previous chapter also described the failure of this plan and the reversal of the approach in the following years. Instead of aiming at incorporation of religious symbols in the uniform, the policy became to exclude such symbols. Part of this development was the departure from the uniformed versus non-uniformed distinction; the two cases before the Commission underscore this distinction.

The cases showed that the police based exclusion of the headscarf on contact with the public, even where non-uniformed tasks were concerned. Nevertheless, the incompatibility of the headscarf with the uniform has also been contested, for instance by the complainant in the second case.[50] However, the National Clothing Regulation of 2004 which recommended lifestyle neutrality had also abandoned the distinction between uniformed and non-uniformed service: the criterion whether police officers had contact with the public proved to be more important. Subsequent documents concerning religious symbols and the police followed the same line.

---

49   Cf. reaction of Schuyt in the discussion during the yearly general assembly of the Dutch Association of Lawyers (*Nederlandse Juristen-Vereniging, NJV*) about the topic multiculturalism and law, see Handelingen NJV, 'Multiculturaliteit en Recht' (Dordrecht, 13 June 2008, vol. 138 (2)), p. 84.

50   Cf. the opinion of Vermeulen in the yearly *NJV*-meeting. He emphasized that uniformed public officials hold functions in which the state manifests its authority, see ibid, p. 77.

3.3.4 Contact with the public

The cases before the Commission made it clear that the criterion of contact with the public cut across the distinction between uniformed and non-uniformed service. Both uniformed and non-uniformed police officers had tasks involving contact with the public. The first case before the Commission demonstrated that it was not clear initially whether the headscarf could be prohibited in connection with tasks performed in contact with the public. The second case confirmed that there was a lack of clarity. Instead of implementing a policy which prohibited the headscarf from being worn by police officers undertaking public tasks, the employer had transformed formerly non-uniformed tasks into uniformed tasks. Its reasoning showed that the reason for doing so was that these tasks involved contact with the public. In other words, each employer attempted to avoid promulgating an outright ban on the headscarf in public tasks, but nonetheless made it clear indirectly that it considered the wearing of the headscarf by officers undertaking public tasks to be unacceptable.

An opposite assessment of whether public contact is a legitimate reason for prohibiting the headscarf is precisely the reason for the divergence of both Commission decisions. In the first case, the Commission decided that the consideration of public contact as a ground for excluding the headscarf or symbols was direct discrimination. Precisely because citizens' perceptions served as the benchmark on the basis of which the headscarf was excluded, this exclusion was considered to be discriminatory. In the second case, the Commission also took into consideration that citizens could take notice of the headscarf. However, in that case the Commission considered that this perception justified the (indirectly discriminatory) policy of excluding the headscarf. The second approach now seems to have taken root in the Netherlands, a fact which is confirmed by subsequent policy. The Minister of the Interior declared her plans for a regulation laying down lifestyle neutrality which would be applicable both to the uniformed service and to non-uniformed police officers undertaking tasks which brought them into contact with the public.

3.3.5 Separation of church and state

In the debate on the police, the separation of church and state has also been referred to, though not very prominently. One scholar argued that in public office, such as the police, there should be no place for ideologies wishing to abolish the separation of church and state.[51] This principled point of view does not differentiate between different types of police officers nor does this point of view seem to be supported in policy. The Minister of the Interior has noted that the separation of church and state in itself does not entail the complete exclusion of religious manifestation by police

---

51   Referred to by Saharso and Verhaar (2006), p. 79.

officers – or other public servants.[52] In reference to the Memorandum on fundamental rights in a plural society, the Minister has stressed the institutional nature of the separation of church and state. Furthermore, she pointed to its important relationship with the freedom of religion.

3.4 THE DEBATE ON PUBLIC EDUCATION

The previous chapter described how the question of religious symbols at state schools has developed. Whereas political plans point in the direction of introducing legal prohibitions on religious symbols within the judiciary and the police, no such plans have been made for state schools (yet). Be that as it may, state education has not been free from debate on religious symbols. Accordingly, complaints have been brought before the Commission, policy documents have been drafted and articles have been written. As hinted at before, the complaint discussed in this study follows the line of the complaints discussed in the context of the judiciary and the police in that it is in fact atypical of the debate. While the debate has focused on teachers, the complainant in this case was not actually a teacher but an intern. Nonetheless, the issues raised were relevant to a teacher's position as well. The discussion of the arguments again starts with the point of direct or indirect discrimination. It then pays attention to the other points raised, of which neutrality has yet again been the focus of the debate. The remaining points concerned a teacher's special role, in particular in relation to their pupils, the rights and freedoms of these pupils as well as of their parents, and finally the separation of church and state.

3.4.1 Direct or indirect discrimination

Strictly speaking, it is questionable in the 1999 case whether differential treatment had really taken place. It did not concern an explicit decision of dismissal or rejection, but an oral notification by the respondent that the wearing of the headscarf in class was undesirable. Nonetheless, this procedural point was brushed aside by the Commission, which dealt with the oral notification as constituting differential treatment.[53]

The complainant put forward a case that direct discrimination had taken place because the school had treated her differently from others on the basis of her religion by considering her headscarf to be problematic. She pointed to the public character of the school, which precluded the school from applying admission requirements which

---

52 Response to Parliamentary Questions 'Antwoorden op vragen PVV over het dragen van hoofddoekjes door politieagenten' *Handelingen II* 2007/08), no. 941.
53 Which was probably also informed by the respondent's indication that it would appreciate a decision on the merits, see *Oordeel 1999-18* (CGB, 9 February 1999), para. 3.5.

denominational schools can do.[54] To her mind, 'no requirements regarding practising or not practising a religion' could be imposed. The respondent did not frame its argument in terms of direct or indirect discrimination, but it clearly implied that its differential treatment was objectively justified. It simply put forward denominational neutrality of state education as a ground for such justification. The Commission acknowledged that requiring teaching personnel to have an open attitude is not at odds with the Equal Treatment Act. However, it emphasized that the complainant's headscarf did not preclude her from having such an open attitude. The assumption of the school that the headscarf showed a religious conviction which was unacceptable to the school's open attitude therefore constituted direct discrimination.

3.4.2 Denominational neutrality

The previous section made clear that the dispute between both parties turned on the interpretation of denominational neutrality. The complainant interpreted the denominational character of the school as precluding the imposition of any requirements concerning practising or not practising religion. By contrast, the respondent used the very same denominational neutrality to justify its policy of excluding symbols such as the headscarf. It noted that the exclusion applied to teachers alone and not to pupils. To its mind, the exclusion underscored teachers' open attitudes, in showing restraint on their side, which was expressed in the way they dressed.

The school used what may be called a material assessment of the headscarf and of Islam in substantiating its argument. It considered its reasoning to apply even more in the case of dress connected to a religion which professed strict ideas and was not very tolerant of dissenters within the religion. In the view of the school, a teacher choosing to wear a headscarf, even within the private surroundings of a classroom, 'evidently demonstrates very strict ideas'.[55] Moreover, this may 'come across as intimidating towards female coreligionists who have often only acquired the right for themselves to a more liberal way of life with a good deal of trouble'.[56]

Just as with the debate on the judiciary and the police, the debate on state school education does not question the importance of denominational neutrality. Instead, it focuses on how such neutrality is expressed and how the appearance of teachers should be seen in this regard. The question raised is what a teacher's appearance says about

---

54 Ibid, para. 3.2.
55 Original text, ibid, para. 3.4: 'Het lijkt evident dat een Islamitische vrouw die zelfs in de beslotenheid van het eigen klaslokaal meent de hoofddoek te moeten dragen, ook in vergelijking met de grote meerderheid van haar geloofsgenoten, getuigt van zeer stringente opvattingen …'.
56 Original text, ibid, para. 3.4: '… en daarmee impliciet bedreigend kan overkomen op de vrouwen en meisjes van dezelfde godsdienst, die zich veelal met grote moeite het recht op een vrijere leefwijze hebben verworven.'

her neutrality or her open attitude. The decision of the Commission demonstrated that it considered the assumption of the school that the headscarf was incompatible with a teacher's open attitude as no more than that: an unfounded assumption. It emphasized that a teacher wearing a headscarf might still very well have the open attitude required.[57] The subsequent policy documents have followed this line which has been equally subscribed to in academic literature.[58]

3.4.3 Teachers and their exemplary role

The respondent placed much weight in its pleadings on the role of teaching personnel in relation to pupils. It mentioned the exemplary role of teaching personnel and placed this role against the background of discussions on the headscarf within the school environment. It implied that the headscarf had been the cause of tension within the school. In its decision, the Commission did not take this point into consideration. Policy documents have acknowledged that teaching personnel fulfil an exemplary role, but such documents have not specified this role with regard to wearing religious symbols. In other words, the policy documents have not generally determined that such symbols are incompatible with the exemplary role of teaching personnel.

3.4.4 Parents' and pupils' rights

Just as the duty of judicial impartiality is mirrored by the right to a fair trial, including an impartial judiciary, the duty of denominational neutrality is mirrored by parents' and pupils' rights to education. The freedom of education includes the right to be educated in conformity with the parents' religion or belief. In any event, teaching at state schools should respect all religions and beliefs. The respondent seemed to hint at having the protection of other pupils' rights in mind in arguing against the headscarf, in implying that previously the headscarf had resulted in the pestering of pupils, and thus indirectly resulting in disrespect for their religion or belief. In disregarding this part of the respondent's argument, the decision of the Commission can be interpreted as not accepting that rights and freedoms of others can act in this way to limit a teacher's freedom to wear religious symbols.

The subsequent Advice of the Commission also did not seem to consider the rights and freedoms of others to constitute an argument for limiting the scope for religious symbols at state schools.

---

57 Original text, ibid, para. 4.5: 'Echter het feit dat verzoekster een bepaalde godsdienst belijdt en deze door het dragen van een hoofddoek uit, sluit niet uit dat zij deze open instelling heeft …'.

58 Loenen (2001), Saharso and Verhaar (2006) p. 8.

3.4.5 Separation of church and state

The issue of the separation of church and state did not come to the fore in the Commission case. Nonetheless, it has indirect relevance to the question of religious symbols in state education. The principle of denominational neutrality emanates from the separation of church and state.[59] Apparently, this does not preclude denominational neutrality from being compatible with religious symbols. Generally, the discussion involving separation of church and state in the Netherlands focuses more on the state subsidizing non-state denominational education,[60] than on the compatibility of denominational neutrality with religious symbols.

3.5 THE RELEVANT POINTS OF CONTENTION

The exploration thus far was the first stage in disentangling the debate. It has used the Commission cases as a primary source to pave the way across the wilderness of arguments. As had been anticipated, it turned out that not all arguments have a similar weight for state neutrality. Additionally, the debates appeared to be both specific as to the function in question and generic in showing threads common to all functions. When the relevant points of contention running through the debates are singled out, they can be systemized as proposed in the present section. The discussion focuses on common factors between the three public functions, but it does not overlook the fact that their effect can play out differently according to the particular features of each public function. The present chapter briefly illustrates the variable effects while leaving in-depth discussion to be dealt with in the next chapter. Before the systemization is presented, a caveat is in order.

The systemization opted for cannot escape a degree of arbitrariness. In the end, alternative systemizations are usually conceivable. Systemization is often shaped by a particular way of looking at things, which is unlikely to be free from judgment. Furthermore, it should not be forgotten that distinction may serve clarity but does not necessarily neatly separate the things distinguished; in other words, albeit distinguished, these things may still be entwined with one another.

With this in mind, a threefold grouping of the points of contention comes to the fore. The first set of points of contention is grouped under the relation between the state and the public official. The second one concerns the relation of the public official

---

59   Commissie Gelijke Behandeling, Advice concerning equal treatment at schools 'Naar een discriminatievrije school', (2008) 2008/3, to be found on <www.cgb.nl>, p. 25.

60   E.g. G. Snik and J. de Jong. 'Moet een liberale overheid bijzondere scholen bekostigen?' (2001) 21(3) *Pedagogiek, wetenschappelijk forum voor opvoeding, onderwijs en vorming*. See also B.P. Vermeulen, 'On Freedom, Equality and Citizenship: Changing Fundamentals of Dutch Minority Policy and Law (Immigration, Integration, Education and Religion)' in M. Foblets and others (eds), *Cultural diversity and the law. State responses from around the world* (Bruylant [etc.], Brussels 2010), p. 125.

to those with whom he has dealings, which varies according to the public official's function. The remaining issues are taken together in a third line of arguments dealing with what may be denoted as the institutional aspects of the state. The following sections further explain the points of contention.

3.5.1 Relation between the state and the public official

The public official is the one who has lodged a complaint against his employer, the state, before the Commission. Accordingly, the complaints centre precisely on the relation between the two parties. It was explained that the primary question in a case before the Commission is whether the complainant has been subject to differential treatment by the respondent. Accordingly, the first point of contention concerns the extent to which limitations on religious symbols have implications for the equal treatment of a public official. Such implications can play out when a person aspires to take on a public function as well as when a person has already undertaken such a function. It can be derived from the debates that the difference between the parties in the debate lies in the interpretation of equality. Those favouring limitations state that such limitations would apply equally to everyone and would thus forego any arbitrariness. Those against limitations, however, point out that these limitations affect some people more negatively than others. For instance, a rule excluding symbols expressing personal views would generally affect Muslim women more than Christian women because the former consider it their religious duty to wear such a symbol whereas the latter do not.

The Commission's opinions and the ensuing debates showed the relevance of the particular formulation of a measure limiting the display of religious symbols. The precise impact of a measure depends in part on that formulation. For example, some measures had explicitly prohibited headscarves, whereas other measures placed the focus on excluding all symbols expressing personal views.

The choice of one or the other interpretation of equality may also depend on the character of the particular public function. More specifically, although both have the status of a public official, a judge and a state schoolteacher have different positions vis-à-vis their 'employer', the state. Moreover, the policies to employ them differ. Whereas judges are recruited by way of a strict selection procedure, teachers follow an arguably more conventional path to obtain a position. Accordingly, it can be imagined that the imposition of limitations on the display of religious symbols is rated differently as to its proportionality.

The question as to which policy would best safeguard equality could be considered to be a generic question, which is relevant to any employment relation. A second point which typifies the relation between a public official and the state concerns the question whether a public official can be considered to personify the state. As briefly touched on in the introductory chapter, the public sector is distinguished from the private sector in, for instance, looking after the general interest. In contrast to private companies, state institutions are in principle available to all citizens. In the same vein, the representatives of these institutions are at the service of all citizens. The importance of a public function is for some public officials underscored by the endowment of special competences. More than for employees in the private sector, the question is raised as to what extent a public official's capacity is divided and should be seen as divided from his private capacity. This is an incredibly complex question, not least because the very contrast between official and private capacity can be contested in the first place. No less complex is the endeavour to subsequently decide what should be considered as inherent to the private or to the official capacity. Proponents of limitations on religious symbols seem to suggest that it goes without saying that religion is part of a person's private identity. This standpoint though is informed by a very particular view of the place of religion in society, which in itself is not free from debate. That aside, it is debatable whether requiring a public official to take off a religious symbol would effectively result in making him less religious in the official sphere.

3.5.2 Rights and freedoms of others

The debates demonstrated that the point of state neutrality automatically involved the perspectives of those with whom public officials have dealings. It seemed to be that the neutrality of a symbol is something which is mostly established by virtue of other people's perception. Accordingly, an important point of contention proved to be the extent to which others who see a public official displaying a religious symbol may infer bias on the part of that public official. Although inevitable, it is this indirect connection of a symbol with neutrality which complicates the matter by introducing a subjective and varying element: the perception of others. That said, the point of contention is surrounded by three difficulties.

To begin with, it remains up for debate what weight such perception should have; in other words, should the perception of others even be taken into account as a benchmark? The other, more delicate, questions emanate from the controversy of relating bias to a religious symbol. Can a religious person – insofar as 'religiousness' religiosity can be established in the first place – be rightly qualified as more susceptible to bias than a non-religious person? Thirdly, how is 'being religious' different from other personal traits such as 'being male' or 'being Dutch'? The last two characteristics may similarly be argued to at least influence someone's judgment. The much-heard rebuttal for this point is that, unlike religion, gender and nationality or ethnicity are immutable. This rebuttal is flawed in oversimplifying the mutability of all these characteristics and, in any case, the question remains how this difference is relevant to the effect which all personal characteristics may have.

These three difficulties account for the intricacy of answering the question to what extent measures limiting the display of religious symbols could enhance neutrality. Such measures may indeed prevent others from perceiving a public official to display religious symbols. It remains to be seen though whether they would actually increase the public official's neutrality. In the debates, a link with the divide between a public official's private and official capacity has been alluded to. The line of argument assumes that in taking on his official capacity, insofar as it can be put on like a coat, an individual should refrain from displaying religious symbols. Such refraining would also effectively result in more neutrality because the public official consciously steps into his official function. A possible objection to this line of argument could be that leaving off religious symbols might also give the public official the feeling of having a licence to judge free from his religious beliefs.

While applicable to all functions, this point of contention could be imagined to play out variably, because judges and police offices wear uniforms, whereas state schoolteachers do not. Additionally, the relation between the public official and the person he has dealings with differs. More specifically, a litigant coming before a judge may have other grounds for being suspicious about the judge's appearance than a citizen on the street seeing a police officer on patrol. Furthermore, the difference would be even more acute if the litigant were to be standing trial for defamation of Islam, and the judge in question were to be wearing a headscarf.

Another point of contention having to do with the perspective of others takes a slightly different angle on the issue. Instead of connecting religious symbols to bias, this point connects religious symbols to their possibly undue influence on those perceiving them. In other words, it raises the question whether a public official who displays a religious symbol runs the risk of improperly proselytizing others. This point remained relatively underexposed in the Dutch debates although it did come to the fore in the context of public education. Be that as it may, in representing an essential take on the rights and freedoms of other, it is worth being discussed separately. The difference between the public functions regarding this point can be expected to lie, for a large part, in the person with whom a public official has dealings. Thus, a schoolchild may run a different risk of being influenced from an adult appearing in court.

3.5.3 State and society

This section deals with the remaining two points of contention, which may be said to concern the more abstract level of the state. It was implied, for instance in the deputy court clerk case, that the appearance of public officials bears on the image of the public service in question. The interest of safeguarding public trust in a public service was pointed to. It can be asked in what way the appearance of the public service can contribute to safeguarding such trust. Two options seemed to emerge from the debates: a public service whose officials can be taken to mirror the composition of the population[61] and a public service whose officials observe a particular distance from the population in being detached from it.

This point is exemplary for the complexities inherent in the term 'state neutrality'. It has become clear by now that neutrality does not represent a rule but a fuzzy concept the interpretation of which can be variable, or even widely divergent. With regard to the relation between state and public official, this can lead to different policies. In the context of this point, it can lead to different images. In a way, such different images may be seen as metaphorical for the different versions of neutrality, which were previously touched on and will be elaborated in the next chapter. These versions grapple with the question as to how neutrality is best expressed. In essence, 'state neutrality' alludes to a lack of bias and to equality. But how is this shown? On the abstract level of the state, this question invokes another which is how the state should be related to society. In the deputy court clerk case, the complainant portrayed a neutral state as mirroring the diversity in society. Another position would be to promote a state which keeps its distance from the diversity in society by not showing anything of it. In a way, this point can be seen as analogous, albeit on a macro level, to the previously mentioned point of how a public official should convey a lack of bias to a citizen. It may again be asked, who gets to determine what is neutral? Should the citizen's perception serve as a yardstick?

The other point of contention figured in all three debates, albeit not so prominently. It concerns the separation of church and state. According to those who referred to this institutional principle, it basically implies that public institutions have a secular character. The difficulty in determining the impact of this point mostly lies in its interpretation and relevance in the Dutch context. It was suggested that the separation of church and state is mostly institutional in nature and does not necessarily entail secularism. If so, then this point would have no direct impact on the freedom of public officials to manifest religion or belief.

Similar to the other points, these points may elucidate the differences between the public functions in the study. The need for the corpus of teachers to represent society may entail different interests from the need for the judiciary to do the same. In other words, the different features of the task involved, of the citizens and of the relation between the public official and the user may be of relevance.

3.5.4 Overview

The previous subsections have proposed and explained the points of contention which are considered as central to the debate in the Netherlands. The following table

---

61 Cf. B. Sloot. 'Moeten rechters lijken op de Nederlandse bevolking? Over de wenselijkheid van descriptieve representatie door de rechterlijke macht' (2004) 2 *Trema*.

summarizes these points of contention, as schematic overviews can add to mere text in providing clarity.

Table 3.1: Points of contention

Point of contention	Explanation
(1) Equal treatment of the public official	The state should ensure equal access to those pursuing a position in public service and moreover it should treat public officials equally. The question is how such equality is best safeguarded, by an invariable policy or by a differentiating policy?
(2) Personification of the state	Does a public official personify the state? On the one hand, a public official still has a personal capacity endowing him with individual rights. On the other hand, being a public official he possesses an official capacity and incurs an obligation of state neutrality vis-à-vis others. Therefore, the question can be asked, to what extent does his professional obligation encroach on his individual rights?
(3) Public officials' bias	The question can be asked whether public officials manifesting their religion or belief by displaying symbols convey bias. An ensuing question is whether they violate another person's right to equal treatment. This violation is mainly created by the impression which public officials give of being biased towards another person with whom they have dealings. This might justify limiting public officials' freedom to manifest their religion or belief.
(4) Risk of proselytism	This point also relates to the effect of the appearance of public officials on the rights of others. In contrast to the previous point, though, this one extends this effect further in considering the possibility of their appearance exerting an improper influence on others. This argument thus addresses the risk of imposing a religion or belief on others.
(5) Image of the state	In serving citizens of the state, public officials need to convey that the state is available for all. The question is how they can best do so, for instance by embodying some blank entity or by emphasizing their individuality and link to society?
(6) Separation of church and state	It has been suggested that the separation of church and state directly requires that public officials refrain from manifesting their religion or belief by wearing symbols. The argument presupposes public officials as personifying the state.

Basically, the systemization distinguishes three groups, each comprising two points of contention. The first group concerns the relation between the state and the public official. (1) It firstly deals with how the state should ensure that a dress policy is in conformity with equal treatment of public officials. (2) Secondly, it asks whether a public official's capacity stands apart from his private capacity, or in other words, to what extent a public official can be taken to personify the state. The second group can be related to the rights and freedoms of others. The points of contention are related to the extent to which a public official displaying a religious symbol jeopardizes these rights and freedoms, more specifically (3) the right to equal treatment and (4) the right to freedom of religion or belief. Finally, two points of contention relate to the state in the abstract. (5) One of them concerns the question in what manner a state can materially convey neutrality. (6) The other asks how a state can institutionally convey neutrality, in other words to what extent the separation of church and state impacts on public officials' freedom to manifest religion or belief.

3.6 Conclusion

Where the previous chapter hovered over the debate in sketching its context, the present chapter has zoomed in on the contents of the debate. Instead of describing the debate in chronological order, this examination focused on identifying the underlying points of contention. In so doing, the examination looked at the points primarily put forward in cases before the Commission and it emphasized the points which are relevant for this study. Furthermore, the examination looked at how these points resonated on other levels. It turned out that while dealing with the specific functions at hand, the debates turned on common threads. Common as they are though, the threads may still play out differently for each of the public functions. In total, the chapter has identified six points of contention. In addition to identifying the points of contention, the chapter proposed a systemization of them. The previous subsection listed these points of contention in Table 3.1.

The stage for further analysis has now been set. The previous chapters have endeavoured to include sufficient information on the context and contents of the Dutch debate so as to allow for a comparison. Before the debate is evaluated against the background of different normative contexts though, the next chapter focuses on clarifying the concepts which are so important, yet so elusive: state neutrality and religious freedom. It aims at going beyond merely describing these concepts in relating them to the central issue in the study.

CHAPTER 4
CONCEPTUAL FRAMEWORK

4.1 INTRODUCTION

The lines of argument, rather like knotty threads, were disentangled in the previous chapter. The present chapter turns to the underlying key concepts. As pointed out previously, the question of public officials manifesting their religion or belief sits right on the intersection of religious freedom and state neutrality. The relation between the two concepts though is not linear but multi-layered. This aspect already came to the fore in the previous chapter where it was shown that, while being interrelated, the points of contention at issue are not on the same level. Where one set of points of contention mostly looked at the relation between the state and the public official, the other one was based on the interaction between the public official and the individual he is dealing with. Although disentangling the points of contention helped to distinguish the separate lines of reasoning, thinking about the interplay between religious freedom and state neutrality ends up in a mind-boggling labyrinth of thought.

The initial consideration is still fairly simple. As an individual, a public official can rely on religious freedom. His right to manifest religion or belief though is not unlimited; it can be subject to limitations. This is no different for other individuals. The particularity may lie in the ground for limitation. Because he is a public official, he may be bound to a duty of state neutrality, which could provide a typical reason to limit the religious freedom of public officials. Seen in this regard, state neutrality is inherent to a public function imposing limitations on public officials' religious freedom. So far, all is clear. It becomes more complicated when you start thinking more deeply. To begin with, you might wonder who it is that state neutrality seeks to protect. In the initial line of thinking it seems obvious that it is the citizen with whom the public official has dealings. By virtue of representing the state, public officials have a special position and often special means or powers at their disposal. It is evident that they should not deploy or abuse this position to harm citizens' rights. As to religious freedom, it is obvious that state neutrality precludes public officials from converting citizens, for example. It is less obvious though whether their special position precludes them from manifesting religion or belief altogether. Is it conceivable that they can carry out religious practices without harming the rights and freedoms of others, or does their special position imply such harm per se? Or would such practices even be incompatible with state neutrality altogether, irrespective of whether they harm the rights and freedoms of others? The practice of displaying symbols takes the complication even further. Apart from the question as to what extent this practice would be harmful to others, the question arises as to what extent erasing such symbols would effectively guarantee the rights and freedoms of others. The removal of symbols does not remove the underlying religion or belief. And aside from this, is it only citizens who are protected by state neutrality? Could it also be that state neutrality aims at protecting the public official from the state? In the same way that public officials, as representatives of the state, should not violate state neutrality towards citizens, so should the state, as an employer, refrain from violating state neutrality in its dealings with public officials? Again it is debatable what this implies for the display of symbols. Precluding public officials from wearing religious symbols interferes with their right to manifest religion or belief. But perhaps this is the only way to guarantee that the state refrains from interfering with the public official's religion or belief. After all, the state would not, in the absence of a displayed symbol, be capable of knowing the public official's religion or belief. Anyhow, this brief exercise shows how intricate the dynamics of state neutrality and religious freedom are.

This chapter seeks to deal with these dynamics. Generally, it aims to unravel state neutrality and its relation with religious freedom. In doing so, this chapter builds a conceptual framework for two purposes. On the one hand, it helps to get a grasp on the many arguments in the Dutch debate. On the other hand, it offers a tool of analysis for the remainder of the study. The question on which this chapter is based is:

> How can theory offer a conceptual framework to assess the arguments underlying limitations on the freedom of public officials to manifest their religion or belief by displaying symbols?

It has been shown that the issue of public officials displaying religious symbols raises a host of interrelated, overlapping or contradictory questions. Furthermore, its real understanding must begin at an abstract level. At face value, the issue seems concrete enough. You could capture this problem in terms of conflicting rights and duties on the level of positive law. Nevertheless, both state neutrality and religious freedom actually represent abstract ideals. They harbour important assumptions about man, the world and their relation to each other. Without pretending to apply a fully-fledged fundamental analysis, the following sections undertake a brief exploration of the fundaments of state neutrality and its relation with religious freedom. Because this elaboration is mainly on a conceptual level, it draws from academic literature. For state neutrality the sources are not exclusively legal but also politico-philosophical. For religious freedom, the books consulted are mainly legal.

4.2 EXPLORING STATE NEUTRALITY

4.2.1 Definition

It was explained in the previous chapter that Dutch law does not explicitly define state neutrality in law. There are a few constitutional provisions the contents of which form the building blocks of state neutrality. Any definition of state neutrality would thus have to be found indirectly. If such a definition were only to be explicitly lacking from the Dutch legal order,[1] then it might not be so complicated to find. Unfortunately, however, there is no generally agreed consensus about the definition of state neutrality on a definitional level or a conceptual level either.[2] Three reasons may contribute to this lack of consensus. First of all, in being a constitutional concept, state neutrality is closely entwined with the particular social and political context of states.[3] Moreover, it interacts with other constitutional concepts such as the separation of church and state and secularism.[4] Obviously, another constitutional concept, namely religious freedom, cannot be overlooked here. A second reason for the lack of consensus is that state neutrality is not exclusively a legal concept. On the contrary, it can rather be considered as a concept on the brink of various disciplines and accordingly, it has been dealt with in political science, law and philosophy. As Babylonian hurdles can sometimes inhibit different disciplines from finding a common language, it is not impossible to imagine the difficulty in finding a common definition of one term. The final reason relates to the very roots of state neutrality. The dominant interpretation of state neutrality, as it is endorsed in most Western European countries, can in and of itself be considered politically coloured, more specifically as being based on a liberal tradition of thinking.[5]

---

1   As Chapter 2 explained, state neutrality can be implicitly derived from a number of Dutch constitutional provisions. It will appear in Chapter 7 that English law also implies state neutrality. By contrast, France has enshrined in its Constitution that the French Republic is *laïc*, from which a duty of state neutrality for public service ensues; Chapter 6 further elaborates on this.

2   E.g. R.J. Ahdar and I. Leigh, *Religious freedom in the liberal state* (Oxford University Press, Oxford [etc.] 2005), p. 87; W. Sadurski, 'Neutrality of law towards religion' (1990) 12 *Sydney Law Review*, p. 421.

3   They offer room for contextual variation, see W. van der Burg, *Het ideaal van de neutrale staat. Inclusieve, exclusieve en compenserende visies op godsdienst en cultuur* (Boom Juridische uitgevers, Den Haag 2009), p. 15.

4   Ibid, p. 17.

5   It is a distinctive or even defining feature of liberalism, Ahdar and Leigh (2005), p. 42; J.T.S. Madeley, 'European Liberal Democracy and the Principle of State Religious Neutrality' in J.T.S. Madeley and Z. Enyedi (eds), *Special Issue on Church and State in Contemporary Europe. The Chimera of Neutrality* (West European Politics, vol. 26, no. 1; Frank Cass & Co., London 2003), p. 5. The importance of state neutrality thus also lies in the fact that liberalism is the principal philosophical foundation for law in modern liberal (political) democracy (and individual liberty), Ahdar and Leigh (2005), p. 38. Liberalism itself originates in efforts to disentangle religion and politics, see W.A. Galston, *Liberal purposes: goods, virtues, and diversity in the liberal state* (Cambridge University Press, Cambridge; New York etc. 1991), p. 13.

The complexity of state neutrality has not in the least discouraged scholars, mainly within the politico-philosophical discipline, from writing extensively on state neutrality. On the contrary, it has proved to inspire them to produce an enormous amount of contemplation, analyses and opinions on state neutrality. Therefore, it is not so much that no definition of state neutrality has been offered but rather that numerous different definitions have been formulated, some being broader than others.[6] Instead of trying to find the one true definition, this study opts for a comprehensive description as a starting point to identify a few essential elements. In a philosophical publication, Steven Wall suggests that 'understood very generally, the principle of state neutrality holds that the state should not favor (or disfavor) any permissible non-neutral conception of the good and nor should it give greater (or lesser) assistance to those who pursue it'.[7] Although the philosophical roots of this definition give an abstract flavour to the formulation, it captures the essential gist derived from many descriptions. Furthermore, it serves well to illustrate the link with religious freedom.

In serving as an inspiration, the description can be specified in one respect to suit the context of the present study. The elusive concept 'conception of the good'[8] can be understood in a particular sense. It has been clearly distinguished to encompass conceptions of goods, conceptions of a good society and conceptions of a good life,[9] the last of which is relevant to this study. By limiting the understanding of state neutrality to this category, the study resists the call to drop the concept of state neutrality altogether. Scholars advocating this call stress that a state can never be entirely neutral.[10] Indeed, it is accepted that the state cannot be neutral regarding conceptions of a good society.[11] The society simply has to be run and this inevitably

---

6   See e.g. S.V. Monsma and J.C. Soper, *The Challenge of Pluralism: Church and State in Five Democracies* (Rowman & Littlefield Publishers, Inc., Lanham (New York, Boulder, Oxford 1997), p. 6; W. van de Donk and R. Plum, 'Begripsverkenning' in W.B.H.J. Van de Donk and others (eds), *Geloven in het publieke domein. Verkenningen van een dubbele transformatie. WRR Verkenningen, nr. 13* (Amsterdam University Press, Amsterdam 2006), p. 45.

7   As formulated by S. Wall 'Neutrality and Responsibility' (2001) 98(8) *Journal of Philosophy*, p. 390. He also specifically explains why he restricts his definition to permissible conceptions of the good; this is supported by the account of T. Wolff, *Multiculturalisme & Neutraliteit* (PhD Universiteit van Amsterdam, Vossiuspers, Amsterdam 2005), p. 123.

8   As this study does not focus on the complicated concept of 'the good life' but rather on the role of the state in this regard, it limits itself with this succinct phrase in G. Graham, *Living the Good Life: an Introduction to Moral Philosophy* (Paragon House, New York 1990), p. 2. Ronald Dworkin relates the good life to 'what gives value to life', referred to *Shingara Mann Singh v. France* (ECtHR, Appl. no. 24479/07, 13 November 2008) in G. Sher, *Beyond Neutrality. Perfectionism and Politics* (Cambridge University Press, Cambridge 1997), p. 20. For further reading on the good life, see e.g. J.J. Kupperman, *Six myths about the good life: thinking about what has value* (Hackett, Indianapolis 2006).

9   Van der Burg (2009), p. 28.

10 Madeley in Madeley and Enyedi (eds) (2003), p. 8. D. Laycock, 'Formal, Substantive and Disaggregated Neutrality toward Religion' (1990) 39 *DePaul Law Review*, p. 993.

11 Wolff (2005), p. 118. Galston (1991), p. 79: 'No form of political life can be justified without some view of what is good for individuals.'

requires choices to be made as to taxes, state budget, legislation and as to all those other infinite policy decisions. The real discussion on neutrality is in regard to conceptions of the *good life*. How should citizens live their lives? What moral choices can they make in shaping their lives? Evidently, religions and beliefs at least inspire such conceptions. Considering the focus of this study on symbols of religion or belief, 'conceptions of the good' can be understood as 'religion or belief'.

This qualification makes the term 'non-neutral' irrelevant, as religions or beliefs are by definition not neutral. Furthermore, Wall has briefly explained that the addition 'permissible' covers those conceptions which are not at odds with other fundamental principles of 'political morality'. To illustrate, he refers to a conception favouring the dominance of some over others, which might be impermissible as it conflicts with the principle of equality. This raises an interesting point, because it is precisely those conceptions which are held in the name of religion or belief that carry the potential to be at odds with fundamental principles of 'political morality'. It would go too far here to address conflicts revolving around religious matters or the relation between religion and tolerance, but it is quite clear that the compatibility of religion or belief with other normative systems is capable of being argued about. More specifically, the previous chapter indicated that the ambiguous relation between manifesting religion or belief and the right to equal treatment is one of the underlying aspects of the debate on state neutrality. A complicating factor is the restraint to be observed in matters of religion or belief. How can it then be ascertained whether or not conceptions in religion or belief are in keeping with other principles? For now, it suffices to establish that 'permissible' is a component of the description of state neutrality. How it plays out for the particular issue in hand is addressed later on.

The heart of the description breaks down into favouring (or disfavouring) a religion or belief on the one hand and giving greater (or lesser) assistance to those pursuing a religion or belief on the other hand. The formulation implies that the addressees of state neutrality are religions or beliefs as well as individuals, or communities for that matter. Moreover, the duties emanating from state neutrality seem to differ.

In particular, the element of neither favouring nor disfavouring strongly conveys a sense of impartiality.[12] While it can be argued that the two concepts do not correspond entirely, they tend to be put on a par in legal discourse. Neutrality seems to be most appropriate to use in relation to an abstract entity such as the state, whereas impartiality is somehow more likely to be used in relation to individuals. That said, this finding is actually not very helpful, as it constitutes a circular reasoning. State neutrality means that the state should be neutral. A way out of this conundrum is by further elaborating 'favouring or disfavouring'. The term encompasses varying degrees. In the most passive sense, the state should not articulate any preference

---

12   Ahdar and Leigh (2005), p. 42.

whatsoever for a religion or belief.[13] *A fortiori*, the state is precluded from promoting or prescribing any religion or belief.[14] It should be noted that preference, promotion or prescription should not be given to a particular religion or belief over another religion or belief or over a secular system as a whole.[15]

A general and more legal translation of 'giving greater or lesser assistance' is that the state should not differentiate in its treatment towards those having or pursuing a religion or belief.[16] This obligation also functions at various levels. The most passive level prohibits the state from evaluating individuals' religion or belief. Moreover, it should not treat them more or less favourably on the basis of their religion or belief, and finally, it should certainly not impose any religion or belief upon them or otherwise use coercion.[17] As will become clear, these concrete duties towards individuals and communities resonate with the neutrality duties of the state concerning religion or belief in general.

In sum, although the one true definition of state neutrality does not exist, some essential elements can be derived from the many available definitions. It becomes clear that state neutrality exists on two levels, a more abstract one towards religion or belief in general, and a more concrete one towards individuals or communities. Additionally, on both levels, the obligation of state neutrality encompasses various degrees of duties, impacting on its passive as well as on its active agency.

4.2.2 Rationale

It was previously pointed out that the type of neutrality endorsed in Western European countries is mainly based on liberal thought. Admittedly, liberal thought can be divided into several currents of thought. Nevertheless, it can generally be said to subscribe to a set of values, five[18] of which can be pointed out here as informing state neutrality:[19] freedom, individuality, rationality, equality, and diversity. These

---

13 Or, in other words, the state should not evaluate the merits of a religion or belief, or it should not make a public ranking, see W. Kymlicka, *Contemporary political philosophy: an introduction* (2nd edn Oxford University Press, Oxford [etc.] 2002), p. 218. Rawls, referred to by Sher (1997), p. 20.

14 Which has led Kymlicka to suggest that antiperfectionism would be a better term, Kymlicka (2002), p. 218; see also Wolff (2005), p. 120. Joseph Raz, referred to by Sher (1997), p. 21. Another way of phrasing it is that the state is precluded from actively inculcating any moral outlook, see Alisdair MacIntyre, referred to by Sher, p. 21.

15 Monsma and Soper (1997), p. 6.

16 Madeley in Madeley and Enyedi (eds) (2003), pp. 4-5; Kymlicka (2002), p. 217.

17 Ahdar and Leigh (2005), p. 45.

18 Obviously, there is room for debate on these values. But in any event, this study submits that state neutrality cannot be reduced to one fundamental value, but instead has been informed by various values, see also Van der Burg (2009), who does not believe that state neutrality can be reduced to one value, p. 19.

19 This aspect, by virtue of its liberal origin, has given rise to even more controversy than the question as to what state neutrality is. As elegantly stated by Sadurski: 'The controversy on state neutrality

five values are interrelated, mutually reinforcing[20] and they converge in the following quintessential rationale of state neutrality: the state should guarantee an arena in which individuals are free to pursue their religion or belief.[21]

The previous section illustrated that the state should refrain from interfering with those holding or pursuing a religion or belief. Such constraint on the state is the obverse of the freedom for the individual to which liberals attach paramount importance. This view places the individual at the forefront.[22] Moreover, the moral primacy of the individual is considered superior to any claim of social collectivity.[23] A degree of autonomy for the individual is therefore indispensable. As an implication, the state is absolutely inhibited from breaching this autonomy, irrespective of its motivation. Put differently, even if the state were to have knowledge about the right religion or belief, it would breach individual freedom were it to impose this knowledge on individuals.[24] Even apart from being fundamentally undesirable, coercion can also be argued to be an inadequate means to internalize knowledge of the right religion or belief.[25]

The above is based on a firm belief in the rationality of individuals. Liberalism assumes that the world has a rational structure to be uncovered through human reason and inquiry.[26] It is these capacities which enable the human individual to carry out his pursuit of religion or belief. The only way to strengthen this pursuit is by debate and argument with others.[27] In no case is force the appropriate means to make individuals adhere to a particular religion or belief. Nonetheless, it is simultaneously acknowledged that there is in fact no rational basis for choosing among religions or beliefs.[28] That accepted, state neutrality is considered the only non-arbitrary response

---

does not so much arise from its semantics as from the reasons for adopting the conception of neutrality', Sadurski (1990), p. 422.

20 Although they can have different normative weight, see ibid, p. 422.

21 MacIntyre, referred to by Sher (1997), p. 21. Ahdar and Leigh (2005), p. 42; Madeley in Madeley and Enyedi (2003), pp. 4-5.

22 As it underpins political democracy, see Ahdar and Leigh (2005), p. 38. Another term used in this context is 'self-determination': liberals consider that state neutrality is required to respect self-determination, see Kymlicka (2002), p. 217. This has also been labelled self-discovery of a personal conception of the good, see Ahdar and Leigh (2005), p. 42. Rawls considered individual choice needed to find out what is valuable in life. What is more, he regards it as a violation of people's essential interests when the state attempts to enforce a particular view of the good life on people. See Rawls, referred to by Kymlicka (2002), p. 217.

23 John Gray, referred to by Ahdar and Leigh (2005), p. 39.

24 No judge on earth can be entrusted with such a task. This was the epistemological neutrality argument for religious tolerance, referred to by Galston (1991), p. 259.

25 Cf. Locke, who explains that inward faith cannot be established by coercion when defending the conscience-based neutrality, referred to by Galston (1991), p. 259. Galston himself considers that freely chosen error is preferable to the coerced pursuit of the good.

26 See Robert Sharpe, referred to by Ahdar and Leigh (2005), p. 40.

27 A. Heywood (2007), Politics (3rd edn, Palgrave Macmillan, Basingstoke 2007), p. 46.

28 Galston, referred to by Ahdar and Leigh (2005), p. 42. And Locke, referred to by Galston, p. 259.

to this state of affairs,[29] because assertions about religion or belief are personal and incorrigible.[30] The desired reluctance of the state to be involved in religious matters has been equally endorsed in religious doctrine. Christian theorists and authorities soon developed the idea that secular authorities have limited powers in matters of religion.[31] This insight brought them early on to envisage an image of two distinct kingdoms, the heavenly and the earthly one. This dichotomy also implied a duality in authority, the spiritual authority and the secular authority. As a consequence, the state has no competence to deal with religious matters.[32] This view still resonates in the assumption in some judicial systems that the state should keep away from substantial judgments on theological postulates.[33] Additionally, this view can be considered to underlie models of separation between church and state.

The last two mentioned of the five liberal values are equality and diversity. Perhaps paradoxically, the previously mentioned individual moral primacy also implies equality of each individual. Because the liberal image of human beings envisages every individual as born with the same moral worth, it is based on foundational equality.[34] This implies the obligation of the state to treat all equally.[35] The equal moral worth of all individuals coupled with the right to freely hold or search for a religion or belief is likely to result in a society thriving on a diversity of religions or beliefs.[36] Liberalism indeed values such diversity, as best fostering

---

29 Galston, referred to by Ahdar and Leigh (2005), p. 42, see John Gray, referred to by Ahdar and Leigh (2005), p. 39.

30 Social institutions and political arrangements cannot be infallible in determining the good life; liberalism has therefore also been qualified as 'meliorist', see Ahdar and Leigh (2005), p. 39.

31 Ahdar and Leigh (2005), p. 34 and R. Robertson, 'Church-State Relations in Comparative Perspective' in T. Robbins and R. Robertson (eds), *Church-State Relations: Tensions and Transitions* (Transaction Books, New Brunswick, New Jersey, [etc.] 1987), p. 154. John Locke brought forward several reasons for the limited power of governments, including the impossibility of rationally adjudicating religious claims and the limitation of government power to protect non-moral goods: goods of the body and external possessions, see Galston (1991), p. 259.

32 S. Ferrari, 'Islam and the Western European Model of Church and State Relations' in W.A.R. Shadid and P.S. van Koningsveld (eds), *Religious Freedom and the Neutrality of the State: the Position of Islam in the European Union* (Peeters, Leuven 2002), p. 9.

33 As also endorsed by the ECtHR, see e.g. M.D. Evans, *Manual on the Wearing of Religious Symbols in Public Areas* (Council of Europe Manuals: Human Rights in Culturally Diverse Societies, Nijhoff, Leiden 2009), p. 44. This point was eloquently touched on by the European Court of Human Rights in the *Kosteski* case, when it said: '[While] the notion of the State sitting in judgment on the state of a citizen's inner and personal beliefs is abhorrent and may smack unhappily of past infamous persecutions ...', see: *Kosteski v. "The Former Yugoslav Republic of Macedonia"* (Appl. no. 55170/00 ECtHR, 13 April 2006), para. 39.

34 Heywood (2007), p. 46. John Gray, referred to by Ahdar and Leigh (2005), p. 39.

35 See Ahdar and Leigh, p. 42.

36 It is relevant here to realize that liberalism is in effect the ideology of the industrialized West, see Heywood (2007), p. 45. Of course, not all societies in the world can be considered to constitute diverse communities, but the whole context and constellation of liberalism is such that a certain level of diversity can be presupposed. The complexity of this is left aside here, as it is not relevant to put emphasis on it.

moral progress[37] as well as a good in itself.[38] Considering the costs of restraining such a basic fact of modern social life[39] further corroborates this, as eloquently articulated by John Locke: 'in circumstances of deep diversity, the consequences of trying to impose uniformity are worse than accepting the existence of controversial opinions'.[40] Therefore, a state endorsing principles without any particular assumption of the good is best for safeguarding diversity.[41] Liberalism has therefore also been regarded as '… an account of the manner in which diverse moral communities can coexist within a single legal community'.[42] This view stresses the importance for these communities to have a common ground, which can be constituted by agreed legal principles. As to religion, the above can be translated as a religiously plural society being[43] best arranged by principles that are not religious themselves. Non-religious legal principles form the neutral communication material through which religious communities can sustain their mutual relationships.

In sum, state neutrality is not a value emerging from and existing in a vacuum. It helps to remain aware of its roots in liberal thinking to understand its purport properly. The understanding of state neutrality in most Western European countries hinges on particular assumptions of man and his pursuit of religion or belief. Furthermore, state neutrality may not be so much an end in itself as rather a means to safeguard other fundamental values. This is an indication of the possible entanglement with human rights, which in their turn can also be regarded as stemming from liberal ideology.

4.2.3 Implementation

The previous sections have made an initial attempt to explore state neutrality conceptually. They have not revealed much on the practical implementation of state neutrality. Then again, it must be cautioned that explorations *in abstracto* are limited in their potential to provide real clarity on this point. It should not be lost from sight that state neutrality is above all a conceptual construct. Moreover, it has a strongly normative connotation; rather than embodying concrete rules for the state,

---

37 A free market of competing ideologies gives a better prospect for moral progress, see Heywood (2007), p. 42.

38 Ahdar and Leigh (2005), p. 42.

39 'Diversity is a basic fact of modern social life and the practical efforts to constrain it would be high.' This argument of Locke, which he labels 'prudential neutrality', is one of five employed by him to endorse religious tolerance, referred to by Galston (1991), p. 259.

40 Referred to by ibid, p. 259.

41 'Society, being composed of a plurality of persons …, is best arranged by principles that do not themselves presuppose any particular conception of the good', cf. Michael Sandel, referred to by Sher (1997), p. 21.

42 Galston (1991), p. 45.

43 Another way of phrasing it is to point out the importance of safeguarding peace in a pluralistic society, see Van der Burg (2009), p. 19.

it represents an ideal.[44] As with ideals, the more concrete the implementation of an ideal, the more variation comes in. As a result, there are various views on how state neutrality should be implemented. Before these views are discussed, a preliminary remark is necessary concerning what it is that has to be neutral.

Most generally and not of great explanatory value, state neutrality is considered to apply to *action* of the government.[45] This covers a wide array, ranging from policy[46] to law[47] and political decisions.[48] Additionally, state neutrality requires more of the state than refraining from interference.[49] The state assumes the responsibility of providing a framework for individuals to pursue a religion or belief.[50] Different modalities of this responsibility can be distinguished. A rather minimalist modality would require the neutral state to confine itself to regulating the conditions for citizens to live with each other, on the basis of equal freedom and opportunities, without articulating on the way in which citizens shape their lives. More responsibility is incurred by the state in the view that it should protect the individuals' capacity to judge for themselves the worth of different religions or beliefs.[51]

So the actual implementation of state neutrality encompasses different modalities. The analytical classifications developed in literature leave this fact intact but they do help to understand the implementation of state neutrality further. The first and widely discussed classification articulates the two ways in which state neutrality can serve as a standard for state action. It distinguishes between neutrality of justification and state neutrality of effect. Whereas the former can be understood as having a procedural take on neutrality, the latter regards neutrality substantively. A parallel can be drawn with another distinction between formal and substantive neutrality respectively.[52]

---

44 Van der Burg qualifies it as an 'intermediary ideal', meaning it derives its force from other ideals, see Van der Burg (2009), p. 17.

45 See Joseph Raz, referred to by Sher (1997), p. 21.

46 Wolff (2005), p. 3.

47 Alisdair MacIntyre, referred to by Sher (1997), p. 21.

48 Dworkin, referred to by ibid, p. 20.

49 Alisdair MacIntyre, referred to by ibid, p. 21.

50 Wolff (2005), p. 11.

51 See Kymlicka (2002), p. 217. Cf. E.M.H. Hirsch Ballin, 'Staat en kerk, kerk en staat' in S.C. den Dekker-van Bijsterveld and others (eds), *Kerk en staat. Hun onderlinge verhouding binnen de Nederlandse samenleving* (Ambo, Baarn 1987), p. 15. This implies that the state permanently guarantees the conditions for personal and social formation, with respect to coherent religious and philosophical values as well.

52 Although being presented separately from neutrality of justification and neutrality of effect, their gist is very similar. It can be argued that formal and substantive neutrality have a slightly broader scope in the sense that they say more about the substantive interpretation of neutrality, but their nature as a procedural criterion prevails.

Neutrality of justification or formal neutrality[53] applies to the intention of government action.[54] It inhibits the state from taking action justified by reasons explicitly related to religion or belief.[55] A more poetic formulation qualifies formal neutrality as 'religion-blindness': the state should engage with individuals without seeing their religion or belief.[56] In particular, a policy justifying the exclusion of headscarves with the intention of minimizing the visible presence of Islam would not meet the criterion of neutrality of justification. By contrast, such a policy would be neutral if it were to aim at excluding head covering to contribute to public order.

Neutrality of effect is a standard applicable to the consequences of the actions of the state. Substantive neutrality adds the element that with regard to religion the state seeks even-handedness.[57] As already suggested by the term, it precludes the state from taking action which, intended or not, positively or negatively, affects the flourishing of any religion or belief.[58] As can be derived from literature, the ultimate underlying aim is 'the ideal that persons should neither enjoy certain advantages or benefits, nor suffer certain disadvantages or handicaps because of their faith – or lack of faith'.[59] In other words, if a policy excluding head covering would affect Muslim women more than other (non-) religious women, it cannot be neutral; even if the justification is the safeguard of safety.

On the one hand, neutrality of effect has been argued to impose an unreasonable burden on the state. Neutrality of justification would provide a more realistic standard.[60] On the other hand, formal neutrality has been critically reviewed. Whilst having an appealingly elegant simplicity,[61] formal neutrality has also been found to

---

53 The former term figures more broadly in relation to conceptions of the good, whereas the latter term is used specifically in regard to religion or belief.

54 A further distinction of state neutrality in the context of liberalism has been made by William Galston, see Galston (1991), p. 100. In addition, Kymlicka (2002), p. 218; Wolff (2005), p. 138; Ahdar and Leigh (2005), p. 45: in this book, the terms 'neutrality of aim' and 'neutrality of effect' are used. Cf. Ahdar and Leigh, p. 87.

55 Wolff (2005), p. 138. In the same vein, formal neutrality is that the state should not use any classification in terms of religion or belief as a standard for its action, '... government cannot utilize religion as a standard for action or inaction because these clauses ... prohibit classification in terms of religion either to confer a benefit or to impose a burden', see Philip Kurland, cited in Laycock (1990), p. 999.

56 Ahdar and Leigh (2005), p. 88.

57 Ibid, p. 89. See also Monsma and Soper (1997), p. 6.

58 Wolff (2005), p. 138.

59 S.V. Monsma, 'Substantive Neutrality as a Basis for Free Exercise-No Establishment Common Ground' (2000) 42(1) *Journal of Church & State*, p. 26.

60 Kymlicka (2002), p. 218; Wolff (2005), p. 138. It is striking that both concede that, initially, one would be inclined to consider state neutrality as neutrality of effect. Full neutrality of effect is practically unimaginable, see Ahdar and Leigh (2005), p. 45. It would require a state to allow all religions or beliefs to prosper, whereas liberals precisely accept that the freedom to choose any religion or belief entails varying disadvantages. Kymlicka (2002), pp. 21 and 218.

61 Ahdar and Leigh (2005), p. 88.

have 'deeply troubling aspects'.[62] Most of all, it lacks the ability to protect minority religions and in any event it carries the risk of affecting religious freedom to a great extent. Nonetheless, substantive neutrality is not without problems either: in being more difficult to apply; it requires more judgment, and it requires a baseline for properly determining whether a religion or belief can be said to be either favoured or disfavoured.[63]

A complicating factor in subjecting the issue in this study to these standards is that religious symbols can be qualified variously depending on the perspective taken. The decision of a state to implement a dress code for its police force would most probably qualify as an action which can be measured against the criterion of either neutrality of justification or neutrality of effect. The action is then regarded as taking place between the state and its public officials. By contrast, the question whether a police officer wearing religious dress or symbols constitutes state action towards others is less simple to answer. It is relevant though in order to enable assessment by the criterion of either neutrality of justification or neutrality of effect.[64]

Just as neutrality of justification and neutrality of effect classify different ways of application, an additional classification offers two different substantive interpretations of state neutrality: inclusive and exclusive neutrality. Again, alternative labels have been offered, which boil down to the same meaning: open and closed neutrality,[65] positive and negative neutrality. These interpretations imply value judgments about the contents of state neutrality. Inclusive neutrality allows religion or belief the broadest scope possible, under the condition of even-handedness.[66] So in reality, individuals and communities would then have the right to enjoy their religious freedom in public, and the state would also enjoy more scope to involve religion or belief in its actions. By contrast, as the term suggests, exclusive neutrality seeks to exclude religion or belief as much as possible from the public domain.[67] It is often associated with the French *laïcité* which completely relegates religion to the private sphere.[68] A state

---

62 Monsma (2000), p. 24. See also Laycock (1990), p. 1000. Most of the time, formal and substantive neutrality diverge.

63 Laycock (1990), p. 1005.

64 But the question cannot be separated from the distinction between neutrality of justification or neutrality of effect, p. 38.

65 H. Werdmölder, 'Headscarves at Public Schools. The Issue of Open Neutrality Reconsidered.' in M.L.P. Loenen and J.E. Goldschmidt (eds), *Religious Pluralism and Human Rights in Europe: Where to Draw the Line?* (Intersentia, Antwerpen-Oxford 2007), p. 155.

66 Van de Donk and Plum in Van de Donk and others (eds) (2006), p. 45. W. van der Burg, C.J.M. Schuyt and J.H. Nieuwenhuis, *Multiculturaliteit en recht* (Verslag van de op 13 juni 2008 te Dordrecht gehouden algemene vergadering van de Nederlandse Juristen-Vereniging, vol. 138; Kluwer, Deventer 2008), p. 46.

67 Van de Donk and Plum in Van de Donk and others (eds) (2006), p. 45. See also Van der Burg, Schuyt and Nieuwenhuis (2008), p. 46.

68 Van der Burg, p. 40. He also points to the Rawlsian version which is more applicable to public reason and is therefore left out of the discussion here.

adhering to a formal neutrality approach is more likely to create exclusive neutrality, whereas a state adhering to a substantive neutrality approach is more likely to create inclusive neutrality. This is not an absolute rule, and situations could be envisaged where this hypothesis is refuted. A third though less-established interpretation is compensatory neutrality. This kind of neutrality allows or even requires the state to compensate for structural or historical inequalities which make it more difficult for minorities to profess their religion on an equal footing.[69]

In conclusion, state neutrality does not pose an unambiguous standard for state action. It depends on how state neutrality operates as a standard to evaluate state action as to whether such action is deemed neutral or not. Furthermore, various standards are likely to be congruent with a particular interpretation of state neutrality.

Before moving to religious freedom, the subsequent sections briefly deal with the question how state neutrality links to two other concepts often referred to: secularism and the separation of church and state. In the debates, these two concepts have sometimes been suggested to be or to imply the same as state neutrality. The following discussion examines whether this is indeed the case.

4.2.4 Secularism

In discussions on state neutrality, secularism is often mentioned too. Sometimes, secularism is simply equated with state neutrality; at other times it is presupposed to have a relation with state neutrality. Secularism resembles state neutrality in at least one respect: it has equally been the subject of countless reflections. This is clear from the many existing definitions and the great deal of discussion on these definitions.[70] It is not surprising that, like state neutrality, secularism is not uniformly defined. Another similarity is that secularism is also closely entwined with the social and political context of a state. Accordingly, just like state neutrality, secularism is not so much a legal concept as a political or social one.

One definition of secularism strikingly resembles that of state neutrality: secularism denotes the idea that the state or political authority should not be in the business of imposing or advancing or privileging any particular religion or religious belief or religion in general.[71] Another definition alludes to the idea of a separation between religion and the state whereby religion belongs to the private realm of citizens: 'At the heart of secularism lies a distinction between the public realm of citizens

---

69   Van der Burg, p. 39. Van de Donk and Plum in Van de Donk and others (eds) (2006), p. 45.
70   As can be derived from C. Taylor, 'Foreword: What is secularism?' in G.B. Levey and T. Modood (eds), *Secularism, Religion and Multicultural Citizenship* (Cambridge University Press, Cambridge 2009), p. xi.
71   G.B. Levey, 'Secularism and religion in a multicultural age' in Levey and Modood (eds) (2009), p. 4.

and policies, and the private realm of belief and worship'.[72] Yet another considers secularism in its simplest and most widely circulated form as calling for a *de facto* if not *de jure* separation between religion and politics.[73] The last two definitions neatly illustrate that despite similarities, secularism is not on a par with state neutrality.

State neutrality has the potential of being integrated into the legal order of state as a constitutional principle, either written or unwritten. By contrast, secularism represents a more comprehensive view advocating that religion should not intrude into worldly affairs, usually reflected in a desire to separate church from state.[74] The two concepts can be said to differ significantly in nature. State neutrality is a principle especially devised as a safeguard for religious freedom, whereas secularism provides a system for the state to give a place to religion. Policies emanating from secularism can be qualified as being in keeping with an exclusive interpretation of state neutrality.

Another brief point worth mentioning is the need to distinguish secularism from secularization: both can lead to a secular society but they encompass two different things. Whereas secularization refers to the social process by which a society becomes increasingly irreligious,[75] secularism is a political choice by the state that defines the place of religion in society.[76] Secularization can lead to a decline in church attendance, in the number of individuals describing themselves as religious, and in a decline of visibility of religion in the public realm. When a state adheres to secularism, it intentionally chooses to keep religion out of its affairs.[77] While the two can certainly go together and reinforce each other,[78] they do not necessarily do so.[79]

---

72 T. Modood, 'Muslims, religious equality and secularism' in Levey and Modood (eds) (2009), p. 177.
73 S. Sayyid, 'Contemporary politics of secularism' in Levey and Modood (eds) (2009), p. 187.
74 J. Rivers, *The Law of Organized Religion. Between Establishment and Secularism* (Oxford University Press, Oxford 2010), p. 328.
75 O. Roy and G. Holoch, *Secularism confronts Islam* (Columbia University Press, New York, N.Y. 2007), pp. 7, 13.
76 Partly derived from Roy (2007), p. 8, who deals with *laïcité*. See also P. Cliteur, *The secular outlook: in defense of moral and political secularism* (Wiley-Blackwell, Oxford 2010), p. 3.
77 E.g. A.H. den Boef, *Nederland seculier! Tegen religieuze privileges in wetten, regels, praktijken, gewoonten en attitudes* (Van Gennep, Amsterdam 2003): 'Secular is a state in which religion merely belongs to the private realm'.
78 Roy (2007), p. viii.
79 For instance, the UK is probably not labelled secular in the ideological sense that it adheres to secularism; on the contrary, the Anglican Church is the established church, the Queen is the head of that church and some bishops hold a seat in the House of Lords. At the same time, however, research demonstrates that the levels of religious belief and activity in the UK are amongst the lowest in the world. This probably means that the UK can be said to be secular in the sociological sense that society is highly secularized. Perhaps this also explains the contrast between the definite statement of Roy that Great Britain is also a secular democracy, whereas Trigg definitely does not consider the UK to be secular. See Roy (2007), p. 13 and R. Trigg, *Religion in public life: must faith be privatized?* (Oxford University Press, Oxford 2007), pp. 24 and 64.

Just like neutrality, secularism is associated with the separation of church and state.[80] The next section discusses this concept.

4.2.5 Separation of church and state

For an understanding as to how the concept of separation of church and state relates to the other two concepts, namely neutrality of the state and secularism, a good starting point is again its definition. With this concept, a semantic interpretation is already significant: separation between church and state means disengaging the institutions of the church and of the state respectively. More specifically: the state should not interfere with the internal relations of the church,[81] nor should the church interfere with state affairs.[82] An illustration of this is that churches have the freedom to assign their own officials but they have no influence in the assignment of state officials. While this is the general description of the separation between church and state, its precise implementation depends on the national context.

For instance, two of the three countries concerned in this research pursue a policy of separation between church and state. In France, this separation is part of the broader political principle[83] *laïcité*, which seeks a radical exclusion of religion from the public domain. This principle results in a strict separation between church and state in France. Nevertheless, some features of the church–state relation in France seem inconsistent with this system. For instance, the French state subsidizes church buildings.[84] The Netherlands is characterized as having a milder implementation of the church–state separation.[85] The Dutch interpretation of this separation does not preclude the state from, for instance, subsidizing schools with a religious basis, which would be inconceivable in other separation systems. Accordingly, other authors have

---

80 See e.g. Ahdar and Leigh (2005), p. 72.
81 It has been observed that the clearest expression of state incompetence in religious affairs is the recognition of the independence and autonomy of religious groups, see Ferrari in Shadid and Van Koningsveld (eds) (2002), p. 9.
82 Cf. for instance the definition of Sophie van Bijsterveld in Den Dekker-Van Bijsterveld and others (1987), p. 11. She explicitly qualifies this definition with regard to the Dutch context, but the description is such that is also applicable to other states.
83 Although in France, secularism can be understood on various levels, namely as an effect of law, as a philosophy and as a political principle, see Roy, p. 17 ff.
84 The possibly underlying justification in French discourse is the benefit for the freedom of religion, which precludes such subsidy from harming the church–state separation, see Ferrari in Shadid and Van Koningsveld (2002), p. 13. That said, the historical dimension cannot be overlooked: after all, it was the state itself which confiscated the church property and thus became accountable for maintaining it.
85 The Dutch themselves characterize the system of the Netherlands as such, see Monsma and Soper (1997), p. 71.

not so much classified the Netherlands as having a separation system, but have rather qualified it as subscribing to a pluralist model.[86]

Apart from the different forms which separation between church and state can take, separation between church and state must be distinguished from a separation between religion and state. Some theoretical descriptions of one or other of the two kinds of separation lightly put them on a par. Such a conflation may obfuscate a clear understanding of the two, because they do differ in some respects. In general, they are not synonyms and they cannot be used interchangeably. More specifically, the separation between church and state is an institutional principle, whereas the separation between religion and state is an ideological principle.[87] The former principle primarily precludes both the state and the church from mutually interfering with each others' internal organization or internal affairs.[88] The latter principle envisages the removal of all religious influences from the public sphere and public institutions[89] by separating ideas, beliefs and other ideological influences by religious institutions from the state.[90] The extent to which the state does this can vary and pertain to divergent areas. The state can be totally indifferent towards religion, or it can practise a sympathizing tolerance towards religion.[91]

---

86   Ibid, p. 51.

87   Temperman defines it as 'the legal-political endeavour which aims at internalizing and consistently preserving a regime in which the state apparatus and religious institutions function independently from each other', J. Temperman, *State-Religion Relationships and Human Rights Law: Towards a Right to Religiously Neutral Governance* (Martinus Nijhoff Publishers, Leiden/Boston 2010), p. 121.

88   S. van Bijsterveld, 'Scheiding van kerk en staat: een klassieke norm in een moderne tijd' in Van de Donk and others (eds) (2006), p. 249. Ahdar and Leigh (2005), p. 72.

89   Ahdar and Leigh, p. 74.

90   Ibid, p. 72. This interpretation has received a great deal of criticism because it renders the idea of separation as artificial. See also H.M. Vroom, '"Church"-state relations in the public square: French laicism and Canadian multiculturalism' in Van de Donk and others (eds) (2006), p. 293: 'On the institutional level, the separation between church and state may be easy enough to realize, but on an ideological level it is more difficult, because traces of worldviews enter the public and political domains.'

91   See also: Ahdar and Leigh (2005), p. 74: either the state refrains from adopting and imposing any established belief or the state actively pursues a policy of established unbelief. Ferrari in Shadid and Van Koningsveld (eds) (2002), p. 20. The latter form can also be found in literature as friendly separation as opposed to hostile separation. Anyhow, the precise composition of the spectrum and the terms used differ from author to author. The purport however is roughly the same. The scholars consider the indifference variant to be applicable to the United States of America. The policy of the former Soviet Union practised towards religion, i.e. actively imposing atheism, is regarded as hostile separation, whereas friendly separation engenders a more pluralistic approach. Another nuance can be found in the motivational forces for a separation. During the Reformation, two movements were striving for separation out of opposite motives. One movement sought to safeguard the church from the state, the other to safeguard the state from the church. Interestingly, these two opposite movements are reflected in the separation systems that were implemented in the United States of America and France respectively.

In light of the previous section, the question arises as to how the separation between church and state or between religion and state relates to secularism. Pursuing either of these separations is basically an implementation of the secular ideal. When the state actively pursues a separation between church and state, it can be said to adhere to secularism. When a state actively separates religion and state it does so even more. The pursuit of separating religion and state may result in a secularized society. This is not necessarily the case when pursuing a separation between church and state. Conversely, other church–state systems can go just as well with either secularism or secularization. The example of the British being amongst the most secular people while living in a state with an established church illustrates this.

As with secularism, an evaluation of a system of separation between church and state in the light of state neutrality depends on the standard of state neutrality. An institutional separation between church and state alone can still be in accordance with both standards of state neutrality. However, making a distinction between realms and putting religion in one of those realms is a very formal way of determining the room for religion in public. Therefore, a separation between religion and state is more likely to resonate with a state policy which pursues neutrality of justification. It can thus be imagined that a separation between state and religion can have a bearing on the freedom of religion. The exact scope of this bearing depends on the extent to which and the manner in which religion and state are separated.

The whole spectrum and approach of church–state systems can also be said to have been built on Judaeo-Christian heritage; because the church is central to this heritage, all church–state models are built on this conception of a religious community. It may even be put forward that these models take a Christian view as the point of departure.[92] Moreover, the secular ideal coupled with the separation between church and state can be traced back to the originally Christian image of the heavenly and earthly realm.

The separation between church and state is an institutional construction to pursue secularism. That is not to say that a state with a separation between church and state is necessarily secular: this separation does not automatically entail a separation between religion and society, or between religion and politics, for that matter. The separation which the Netherlands applies to church and state does not extend to religion and politics; religious parties hold seats in Parliament. Theoretically, a separation between church and state does not guarantee that the state observes neutrality. Conversely, a state which has no separation between church and state can still be neutral: although the UK has a state church, the state subscribes to observing the freedom of religion and neutrality towards religions. Such a state can also still have secular features.

So in addition to the identified core elements of state neutrality and the roots of state neutrality, the classifications of state neutrality make clear that the abstract ideal

---

92   This is conceded expressly by Ahdar and Leigh (2005), p. 67.

has been analysed in order to clarify how it could be applied and which meaning or interpretation it could have. Moreover, despite undeniable links with related concepts such as secularism and separation of church and state, neutrality can in no way be equated with these concepts. The next section further explores the relation of state neutrality with other concepts by looking at religious freedom.

4.3 EXPLORING RELIGIOUS FREEDOM

It has become clear by now that state neutrality is aimed at protecting just that: religious freedom. Like state neutrality, religious freedom can be seen as embodying an ideal although it has been more crystallized into a constitutional human rights concept. The relation between state neutrality and religious freedom is not one-dimensional. With regard to the issue of public officials wearing religious symbols, the effect of state neutrality on religious freedom seems to be primarily limiting. But it turns out that state neutrality is also aimed at protecting religious freedom. The following sections briefly explore the concept of religious freedom in light of state neutrality.

4.3.1 Definition

When dealing with religious freedom on a conceptual level, it is difficult if not impossible to do justice to its significance.[93] Its roots go far back to at least the beginning of the modern state system.[94] During the past few decades though, it has been mainly shaped within human rights discourse.[95] As such, it has been enshrined in a number of international human rights conventions. These conventions have largely given effect to religious freedom in a similar way. The provision of the ECHR, which has been directly inspired by the Universal Declaration of Human Rights (UDHR)[96] and is relied on in this study, is exemplary for how religious freedom is articulated as a human rights provision. For completeness and clarity it is cited in full:

---

93 See for some monographs dealing in depth with religious freedom C. Evans, *Freedom of religion under the European Convention on Human Rights* (Oxford ECHR Series, Oxford University Press, Oxford 2001); M.D. Evans, *Religious liberty and international law in Europe* (Cambridge University Press, Cambridge 1997); B.G. Tahzib, *Freedom of religion or belief. Ensuring Effective International Legal Protection* (PhD Universiteit Utrecht, Martinus Nijhoff Publishers, Leiden 1995); P.M. Taylor, *Freedom of Religion. UN and European Human Rights Law and Practice* (Cambridge University Press, New York 2005).

94 M.D. Evans 'Historical Analysis of Freedom of Religion or Belief as a Technique for Resolving Religious Conflict' in T. Lindholm, W. Cole Durham Jr. and B.G. Tahzib-Lie (eds), *Facilitating Freedom of Religion or Belief: a Deskbook* (Nijhoff, Leiden 2004), p. 1.

95 See also ibid, p. 27.

96 Taylor (2005), p. 26. See for an elaborate description of the legislative history of Article 9 ECHR, M.D. Evans (1997), p. 262 ff.

1. Everyone has the right to freedom of thought, conscience and religion; this right includes freedom to change his religion or belief and freedom, either alone or in community with others and in public or private, to manifest his religion or belief, in worship, teaching, practice and observance.

2. Freedom to manifest one's religion or beliefs shall be subject only to such limitations as are prescribed by law and are necessary in a democratic society in the interests of public safety, for the protection of public order, health or morals, or for the protection of the rights and freedoms of others.

This provision is a good example of how human rights provisions conceptualize the freedom of religion. The format followed is familiar to ECHR provisions and to other human rights provisions for that matter. That is to say that it envisages a right, in the first paragraph, and requirements for imposing limitations on that right, in the second paragraph. This structure seems clear enough, as does the seemingly simple terminology.[97] Be that as it may, the structure of Article 9, and of similar provisions in other human rights treaties, exemplifies how complex the underlying conceptualization of the freedom of religion is.

In part, it is the construction of the freedom of religion around two dimensions with a different scope, which causes this complexity. This distinction goes back to the deliberations for the UDHR.[98] The first dimension of the freedom of religion is the freedom to have thought, conscience and religion, which includes the freedom to change religion or belief. This dimension is commonly referred to as the *forum internum* of the freedom of religion. This term denotes that it relates exclusively to an individual's inner realm. The choice of words makes clear that the protection not only includes religion but also extends beyond it. Against the background of the previous information on state neutrality, this individual freedom forms the obverse of the obligation of the state to refrain from impeding an individual's quest for a good life. Such a quest requires the individual to be able to think freely.

The second dimension explicitly limits the freedom to manifest a religion or belief. In other words, it does not protect the manifestation of thought or conscience absolutely.[99] This manifestation can take place individually or together with others.[100] Additionally, the provision identifies four forms which this manifestation can take. In line with its external character, the right to manifest religion or belief is referred to as the *forum externum* of the freedom of religion. Although the distinction between both

---

97　M.D. Evans (1997), p. 284.
98　M.D. Evans (1997), p. 190; C. Evans (2001), pp. 35 and 40.
99　M.D. Evans (1997), p. 284 ff.
100　The Commission has also decided at an early stage that it is entirely up to the individual whether to manifest his religion of belief individually or collectively. It pronounced that these alternatives are not 'mutually exclusive' and that it is not up to the authorities which alternative an individual prefers, see *X. v. United Kingdom* (Appl. no. 8160/78 ECnHR, 12 March 1981), para. 8.

forums is longstanding, it may be good to note that it has been and still is discussed. Because this discussion has less relevance to the study at hand, only two points are mentioned here. Firstly, it may be asked whether a distinction can actually be applied. Especially in cases of conscientious objection, it cannot always be reasonably established whether the religious act or omission in question is part of the *forum internum* or *forum externum*.[101] Consequently, when a state imposes limitations, these limitations may also qualify as violations of the *forum internum*. Secondly, on a more fundamental level, it has been argued that the dichotomy itself emanates from a limited conception, i.e. a Christian conception, of religion or belief.[102] As a consequence, the dichotomy does not take into account the variable significance which religious manifestations may have for religions or beliefs. It can be recalled that the dichotomous perception of the freedom of religion or belief has been inspired by the Christian dichotomy between the relation between man and society on the one hand and the relation between man and God on the other.[103] Moreover, the implementation of the freedom of religion as laid down in Article 9 ECHR has been said to be guided by a Christian paradigm, due to the Judaeo-Christian heritage in Europe. The link between the *forum internum* and the *forum externum* may be different for other religions. For this study, suffice it to say that religious dress or symbols have been considered as falling within the ambit of the *forum externum*. That having been said however, one of the very issues up for discussion concerning religious dress is the variable link with the *forum internum*.

A more general challenge lies in the definition of the object of religious freedom. Human rights provisions and supervising bodies of the convention concerned have most of the time shied away from materially defining religion or belief. Generally, they leave room for a wide array of convictions.[104] In the same vein, the range of manifestations protected is broad, although they can be limited. The drafting processes for the UDHR and ECHR witnessed controversy on the limitation clause. For the ECHR, the ultimate decision determined that a specific limitation clause would apply

---

101 Cf. Tahzib, who has specified the type of violations which are conceivable both of the *forum internum* and the *forum externum*, see Tahzib (1995), pp. 26-27.
102 C. Evans (2001), p. 205. More generally, the outlook of the European Court of Human Rights itself has been criticized as being too much informed by secular or liberal assumptions, e.g. Z.R. Calo, 'Pluralism, secularism and the European Court of Human Rights' (2011) 26 *Journal of Law and Religion*. See also critiques on particular cases, *infra* the discussion in Chapter 5, e.g. specifically n. 80 and 97.
103 M.D. Evans (1997), p. 190.
104 Cf. UN Human Rights Committee, 'General Comment no. 22: The Right to Freedom of Thought, Conscience and Religion (1993) (48th session) CCPR/C/21/Rev.1/Add.4, to be found through <www.ohchr.org>. This Comment succinctly establishes that theistic, non-theistic and even atheistic convictions qualify as beliefs.

to the freedom of religion.[105] The reasons for this decision can unfortunately not be inferred from the record of the deliberations.[106]

In addition to the guarantee of the freedom of religion or belief, the right to equal treatment protects individuals from being treated differentially on grounds of religion or belief. This is expressed first of all by the accessory provision Article 14 ECHR, which explicitly includes religion as a ground:

> The enjoyment of the rights and freedoms set forth in this Convention shall be secured without discrimination on any ground such as sex, race, colour, language, religion, political or other opinion, national or social origin, association with a national minority, property, birth or other status.

This right can only be relied on in conjunction with another right in the Convention, in this case Article 9 ECHR. A general, independently effective, prohibition of discrimination has also been laid down in the first provision of Protocol 12:

> 1. The enjoyment of any right set forth by law shall be secured without discrimination on any ground such as sex, race, colour, language, religion, political or other opinion, nationalorsocialorigin,associationwithanationalminority,property,birthorotherstatus.
> 2. No one shall be discriminated against by any public authority on any ground such as those mentioned in paragraph 1.

However, this provision has not been prominent in case law on religious freedom. In general, the non-discrimination principle has been addressed mainly as an accessory principle within the context of the ECHR. The importance of non-discrimination as regards religious freedom has increased on a domestic level, presumably in part as a consequence of the anti-discrimination EU Directives.

4.3.2 Rationale

Like state neutrality, human rights discourse can be considered as deriving from liberal ideology. Many values could be identified as fundamentally justifying the protection of religious freedom.[107] But in accordance with the previously mentioned liberal values underpinning state neutrality, the following liberal values underpinning human rights in general and religious freedom in particular can be proposed: freedom,

---

105 C. Evans (2001), p. 41.
106 Ibid, p. 45.
107 E.g. conflict resolution and social inclusion, social cohesion, autonomy and dignity, see L. Vickers, *Religious freedom, religious discrimination and the workplace* (Hart, Oxford [etc.] 2008), pp. 33-40. See for an elaboration on the link between justifying human rights and justifying religious freedom T. Lindholm, 'Philosophical and Religious Justifications of Freedom of Religion or Belief' in Lindholm, Cole Durham Jr. and Tahzib-Lie (eds) (2004), p. 48 ff.

individuality, rationality, equality, and diversity. What these values offer to a certain extent are reasons which do not rely on the acceptance of particular religious views and thus can be accepted by all people.[108]

The first basic value of freedom speaks for itself in relation to human rights. The human rights vernacular in principle puts individual rights and fundamental freedoms on a par, which the ECHR itself testifies to. More specifically, as previously explained, Article 9 is based on the very premise that an individual should be absolutely free as to thought, conscience or religion. In line with the idea enshrined in state neutrality that an individual should be free to pursue his own worldview, religious freedom guarantees that an individual is free to have, choose and therefore also change religion or belief. Consequently, this part is absolutely inviolable from interference by the state. The individuality speaks from the fact that primarily individuals are endowed with the right to religious freedom despite the fact that religious communities also incur rights under Article 9 ECHR and that individuals remain free to manifest their religion or belief in community with others. At its core, human rights discourse is premised on a firm belief in man's rational capacity. So is the guarantee of religious freedom. In principle, the individual motivation to pursue religion or belief can be rational as well as irrational, but the mere legalization of religious freedom can be taken to testify to the importance of human reason.

Individuals can rely on human rights by virtue of their being human. Therefore, equality is an impetus for acknowledging the importance of individual religious freedom. In the same way that everyone is entitled to have freedom of thought, conscience or religion, regardless of background, he should not be treated unequally for so having. At the same time, exactly because everyone is entitled to have and manifest his own religion or belief, albeit the latter right is not unfettered, religious freedom values religious diversity. While some people might prefer one true religion to be recognized, religious diversity is a fact of life.[109] The European Court of Human Rights has endorsed the value of religious diversity by coupling the duty of state neutrality to pluralism and broad-mindedness.[110] In a situation where it is common for a dominant religion to exclude others, the acknowledgement of the equality of minority religions underscores their equal right of assertion to be there. That sounds rather similar to the statement of the Court concerning the duty of the state to ensure the coexistence of various religious communities.[111]

---

108 See also Vickers (2008), p. 32.
109 C. Evans (2001), p. 23.
110 Cf. *Leyla Şahin v. Turkey* (Appl. no. 44774/98 ECtHR, 10 November 2005).
111 *Metropolitan Church of Bessarabia and others v. Moldova* (Appl.no. 45701/99 ECtHR, 13 December 2001), para. 115 ff.

4.3.3 Implementation

The right to freedom of thought, conscience and religion is conferred on 'everyone'.[112] Generally, it does not only fall to individuals but also to communities, such as churches. Additionally, as already mentioned, a variety of convictions can be protected under the human rights guarantee of freedom of religion.

The right conferred on everyone may raise the question as to which scope of obligations on the state it entails. It has long since been recognized that it is insufficient for the state to refrain from interfering with the freedom of religion or belief. A truly and effective enjoyment of this right may require a more active stance on the part of the state. This echoes the previously noted modalities of state neutrality, the rationale of which is mostly to ensure an arena enabling individuals to pursue their religion or belief. Indeed, a state's obligation of neutrality so far as religious life within a state is concerned, seems to have moved on from simply not taking sides to a more active role in ensuring neutrality.[113]

In the same way that state neutrality leaves room for varying implementation, so can the freedom of religion be subject to limitations to a varying degree. Limitations need to meet specific requirements such as pursuing a legitimate aim. Safeguarding neutrality of the state could qualify as such an aim. The intricate relation between state neutrality and religious freedom lies in the fact that the former can thus be a ground for limitation as well as safeguard of the latter. Perhaps it could be stated that religious freedom is the human rights translation of the ideal of state neutrality.

4.4   BUILDING A MODEL

The previous elaboration was necessary to get a good feel for state neutrality and religious freedom. The issue of public officials manifesting their religion or belief by displaying symbols sits right on the interface of both concepts. Therefore, what is even more interesting for the present study is how the key concepts interact with each other. To this end, the following sections examine where the two concepts meet and, where relevant, where they are different. From this integration, the sections aim at building a model to capture the concepts.

---

112 While this formulation seems to envisage primarily individuals as subjects of Article 9 ECHR, the development in the ECHR case law shows that the scope has been extended to legal persons akin to a church. See the development in the case law of the Commission, discussed by M.D. Evans, *Manual on the Wearing of Religious Symbols in Public Areas* (Council of Europe Manuals: Human Rights in Culturally Diverse Societies, Nijhoff, Leiden 2009), pp. 286-287.

113 Ibid, pp. 44-45.

4.4.1 Basic concepts

The analysis of state neutrality as well as that of religious freedom started out with a brief description of the disciplinary roots of the concept at issue. This is where the most striking difference between the two can be found. As already touched on, state neutrality has been elaborated on in numerous, mostly politico-philosophical, theories and has mainly remained in this sphere. Accordingly, it has not been codified in law as a rule; rather, it can often be derived from multiple legal provisions taken together. In contrast, for the past few decades, religious freedom has been integrated into human rights law as one of the fundamental guarantees. With its ancient roots and pertinent role in history, it is regularly considered to be one of the oldest and most controversial of all human rights.[114] Having been shaped mostly in the language of human rights, it is a part of human rights conventions and of most, if not all, European constitutions. Accordingly, it endows individuals with rights which they can invoke against the state.

This is where the similarities come in because, on a substantial level, the similarities stand out more than differences. As to their gist, state neutrality and religious freedom converge in the following aspects. To begin with, both concepts contrast 'the state' with 'the individual'. They are both premised on the assumption that the state is the more powerful actor, which therefore needs to be constrained in order to protect the individual. It might be said that state neutrality has been constructed rather from the perspective of the state whereas human rights operate from the individual's perspective. For the issue in this study, it seems as if the point where the state and the individual come together, i.e. in the person of the public official, has not been elaborated on in either of the underlying theoretical backgrounds. What happens if an individual is the state? The omission of expressly identifying the public official as a separate actor may partly be the reason for the obscurity in the discussion. Therefore, this study proposes to refine the dichotomy between the state and the individual in expressly identifying the public official.

The left-hand figure in Diagram 4.1 shows the binary relation between the state and the individual as it is usually portrayed. The right-hand figure indicates how the public official can be integrated. The individual is shown here as 'citizen' to denote the contrast between 'normal' individuals and individuals with a public function more clearly. The public official could also have been placed right in between the state and the individual. However, what would have gone missing then is the relation between the state and the citizen. It would have implied that all contact from the state with the citizens runs through the public official. And while all actions, policies and decisions, also from the state, can in the end be related to individual, human action, complete dismissal of the state as an abstract entity would miss an important

---

114 Evans in Lindholm, Cole Durham Jr. and Tahzib-Lie (eds) (2004), p. 1.

point. For citizens do have a certain conception of 'the state' or of state organs, such as 'the judiciary', 'the police' or 'state education'. In the context of this study, the issue of religious symbols in public functions has also been discussed in terms of what religious symbols convey about the state in general. Therefore, retaining a relation between 'the state' and 'the citizen' is vital for contemplating the issue of religious symbols in public functions to the fullest extent possible. Obviously, any schematic representation of reality seeks to simplify this reality. Such simplification has the potential to quickly clarify complicated matters, although the downside is that simplification does not do justice to the complexities of this reality. Therefore, this diagram is just one option to capture reality. That said, it clearly shows the actors and relations at stake in the issue of religious symbols in public functions.

Diagram 4.1: Actors

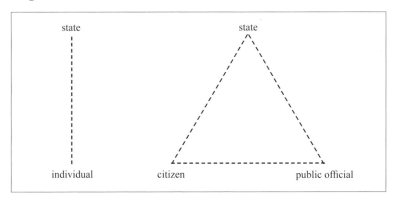

In a way, the public official can be seen as standing between the state and the citizen. A public official represents the state towards the citizen; he is the medium through which the state becomes tangible for the citizen. For example, a police officer keeping surveillance on the street is a very real human being whom citizens can perceive. At the same time, it is clear to citizens that this police officer is doing his service in the name of the state; he wears a uniform and is endowed with competences which normal citizens do not have. In this representation, the actors in questions are individuals who can enter into contact with each other. That is not to say that the state as an abstract entity loses every connection with citizens. Although the police obtains reality for the citizen in the person of the police officer, it is also known to the citizen as an organization *in abstracto*. It is not unusual to speak of 'the police' as an existing organization, a vital part of 'the state'. Finally, in standing between the citizen and the state, the public official maintains a relation with the state as an organization. Being a public official, he is in the service of the state.

The second and most essential point where state neutrality and religious freedom meet and moreover reinforce each other is regarding the contents of the duties emanating from state neutrality. Both theories on state neutrality and human rights indicated that the general obligation of state neutrality could be further broken down to encompass various modalities of duties. Stated briefly, the state should walk a fine line between action and restraint. It is not sufficient, and is arguably impossible, for the state to refrain entirely from interfering with matters of religion or belief. At the same time, when dealing with such matters, it should take care not to violate its duty of neutrality or its obligations to respect citizens' religious freedom. Human rights discourse has qualified these two seemingly opposite categories as positive and negative obligations; rather than being opposite, both categories serve to enhance each other. For example, in order to effectively guarantee citizens the right to pursue a religion or belief, the state should guarantee religious communities the right to build their houses of worship. By refraining from interfering with what religious communities teach in these houses, the state equally guarantees religious freedom. Another thing shown was that state neutrality concerned religions or beliefs *in abstracto* as well as the dealings of the state with the citizen *in concreto*. For example, the state is precluded from proclaiming that Christianity is a superior religion, whether it is by way of public undirected statements or in its direct contact with citizens. While the human rights guarantee of religious freedom does not make that distinction so explicitly, it does imply it. The duty of the state to guarantee individuals' religious freedom is realized in part by its not favouring or disfavouring religions or beliefs. In human rights discourse, this duty can be read into the state having to refrain from stepping into substantial assessment of religions or beliefs. In other words, although the state is to protect religious freedom, it only has limited leeway to establish whether something is truly a religion or belief, or even more so whether a particular practice constitutes a manifestation of religion or belief. It is important to note that the duty of state neutrality extends to religions and beliefs versus secular systems.[115] Within the human rights discourse, this is given effect by the inclusion of secularism into beliefs. While recognizing that other distinctions are possible too, the study distinguishes three core duties emanating from state neutrality on the basis of the examination of state neutrality and religious freedom. This enables a further specification of the formerly identified general definition: 'the principle of state neutrality holds that the state should not favour or disfavour any religion or belief and nor should it give greater or lesser assistance to those who pursue it'. The following list sets out the core duties:

1. the state should not evaluate, favour or disfavour religions or beliefs (in general or in its interaction with individuals and communities);
2. the state should not impose religion or belief (in general or in its interaction with individuals and communities);

---

115 Monsma and Soper (1997), p. 6.

3. the state should not favour or disfavour individuals or communities on the basis of religion or belief (in general or in its interaction with individuals and communities).

Combining these duties with the formerly adjusted representation of the actors in play demonstrates the multi-layered effect of state neutrality. If the obligation of state neutrality could first be represented as being owed by the state to the individual, it now creates triple duties playing out in a tripartite manner. Including this in the diagrams of the actors results in the following images.

Diagram 4.2: Actors and state neutrality

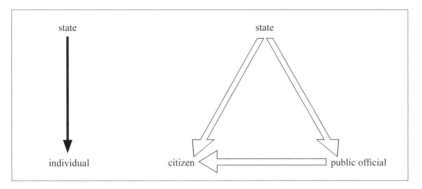

These figures show that the initial change of the binary relation between state and individual into a tripartite relation including the public official equally implies a tripartite effect of state neutrality. The effect of state neutrality between 'the state' and 'the citizen' remains, but it is complemented with the effect of state neutrality between the human being embodying the state, the public official, and the citizen. Moreover, whilst a public function does endow a public official with special competences, it does not per se deprive him of his individual being. Accordingly, in the same way that the state should observe state neutrality towards the citizen, so should it towards the public official. Additionally, the image intends to express that state neutrality towards citizens also operates through the public official. The public official can function as an intermediary between the state in the abstract and citizens: the public official can be seen as embodying the state in exercising state power. The other change concerns the contents of the obligation of state neutrality. These have not so much altered; rather, they have been specified. So, where the closed arrow in the left-hand figure represents a general though rather straightforward obligation of state neutrality, the open arrows in the right-hand figure represent the three core duties encapsulated in state neutrality.

4.4.2 Dynamics

It was said that a vital rationale of state neutrality is to guarantee an arena where individuals can freely pursue their freedom of religion or belief. It seems like stating the obvious to say that religious freedom aims at guaranteeing the same. More generally, it was shown that state neutrality and religious freedom share similar underpinning values. Accordingly, their mutual relation can be qualified as being each other's obverse. State neutrality imposes duties on the state in order to safeguard individuals' rights. As already explained, human rights have been framed so that individuals are entitled to rights towards the state. Or put another way, individuals' human rights should be protected against interference by the state. Whilst it is implied that the duties of state neutrality seek to serve individual rights, it might be helpful to visualize these rights in a diagram.

Diagram 4.3: Actors, state neutrality and individual rights

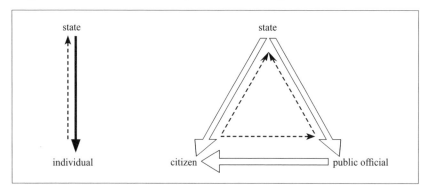

Again, the tripartite relation demonstrates that the dynamics of state neutrality and religious freedom play out on various levels. In the left-hand simple representation it could be said that the state should observe an obligation of state neutrality towards the citizen, who in his turn can invoke religious freedom against the state. Only religious freedom is mentioned here, as this right is primarily entwined with state neutrality. This right comprises multiple aspects as expressed by the freedom of religion or belief and as encompassed in theories of state neutrality. More specifically, an individual has the right to have and to hold freedom of thought, conscience and religion. The duty of the state not to give a particular religion a privileged position or not to impose a religion or belief on individuals may be seen as the obverse of this aspect of religious freedom. Additionally, an individual has the right to manifest religion or belief. This is partly guaranteed by the duty of the state not to treat individuals differentially on the basis of their religion or belief. The right-hand diagram equally includes the relation between the state and the citizen and their mutual dynamics as to rights and duties is no different, if only somewhat more specified. But it shows more clearly that the citizen can also invoke his religious freedom against the public official by virtue of the latter representing the state. At the same time, the public official himself can invoke individual rights against the state. So he is entitled to religious freedom and merits protection from interference by the state. It goes without saying though that the relation which the public official has with the state is different from that of the citizen with the state. In sum, the triangular model also underlines the indivisibility of the manifold effect of state neutrality: a dress policy imposed by the state on the public official impacts on how state neutrality plays out in the relation between the public official and the citizen. Furthermore, the triangle shows that neutrality of the state is conveyed by the symbolic state as well as through the public official's person.

4.4.3 Implications

An important similarity of state neutrality and religious freedom, relevant for their implementation, is their nature as an ideal. In their abstractness, ideals are mostly not fully realized. They represent something to strive for, but leave room as to how this should be done. Their meaning as such can be discussed, and even more can their implementation; they leave room for contextual variation.116 Such variation comes in different forms for both ideals. As may be clear by now, state neutrality does not provide an unambiguous standard for states to rely on. Instead, depending on how it is applied, state neutrality can even result in completely divergent if not opposite policies. It makes a difference whether a state puts the grounds of its policy to the test of neutrality or the effects of its policy. Consequently, state neutrality has been qualified as encompassing different standards. Religious freedom, especially the freedom to manifest religion or belief, comprises an ambit, which can be limited in variable degrees. Their implementation may well be compatible, but the 'how' exactly is not straightforward. In other words, there is an area where both state neutrality and religious freedom can be lived up to. They both imply a certain bandwidth allowing for different policies. The question is what room this bandwidth leaves for prohibiting or allowing public officials to manifest their religion or belief by wearing symbols. Speaking in terms of the diagrams, the question is how a balance can be struck according to the dynamics as portrayed in Diagram 4.3.

The diagrams clarify that the difficulty in striking this balance is partly caused by the multi-level effectuation of state neutrality and the interconnectedness of relations between the actors involved. Stated more specifically, measures aimed at public officials' freedom to display religious symbols obviously impact on the relation between the state and the public official. Accordingly, these measures should meet neutrality requirements effective from the state towards the public official. At

116 Van der Burg (2009), p. 8.

the same time, though, such measures have an influence on the other relations as well. To illustrate this statement, imagine that the state adopts a policy of allowing public officials to display religious symbols. Such a policy would undoubtedly raise questions of the neutrality of both public officials and the state towards citizens. The distinction between neutrality of justification and neutrality of effect does not render unequivocal answers in the issue of public officials displaying religious symbols. Therefore, it may be more instructive to take the points of contention previously identified as paramount for assessing the effect of state neutrality.

4.5 APPLYING THE MODEL TO THE POINTS OF CONTENTION

As previously stated in Section 4.4.1, the model has the benefit of offering a simple visualisation of a complex reality. It is helpful in providing insight into how state neutrality and religious freedom play out regarding the issue of religious symbols in public functions. Additionally, it can clarify the points of contention identified in the previous chapter. It was explained that in approaching state neutrality and how it affects the freedom of public officials to manifest religion or belief, the debate turns on these points of contention. In other words, the points of contention can be considered as each concretising an aspect of the impact of state neutrality. In so doing, they represent the several core duties to a greater or lesser extent. The model cannot only be used to conceptualise state neutrality but also to further systemize the points of contention. More importantly, this exercise subsequently serves to equip the model for evaluating the points of contention.

The initial systemization of the points of contention in the previous chapter has already alluded to a division according to the relations between the different actors. The conceptual model developed in the current chapter elaborates on this division. It brings out the correspondence of the points of contention with the relational dynamics between the three actors. To begin with, the points concerning equal treatment of the public official and personification of the state can be linked to the dynamics between the state and the public official. Both arguments in fact boil down to the question as to how the policy regarding religious symbols affects treatment of public officials by the state. Secondly, the points as to the public official's bias and the risk of proselytism are both relevant to the question whether public officials wearing religious symbols jeopardize the equal treatment and the freedom of religion of citizens. In other words, they correspond with the relation between the public official and the citizen. Finally, the points on the image of the state and the separation of church and state concern the question whether public officials wearing religious symbols compromise the neutral image of the state for citizens. These arguments have to do with the relation between the state and citizens. The following sections further elaborate on this grouping of the points of contention. In so doing, they pay attention to how state neutrality plays out in these different relations.

4.5.1 Neutrality of the state towards the public official

The two points linked to the state–public official relation provide two perspectives; basically, they turn on the same thing, but from different angles. The first one, the equal treatment point, focuses on how state neutrality determines the dress policy of the state which in its turn affects the public official's rights, both when that official takes on his function and when he is in the service of the state. Not only is his right to equal treatment involved, but also his right to freedom of religion or belief. In this perspective, neutrality acts as an obligation of the state towards the public official. In other words, it is a force restraining the state in the interest of the public official. A complicating aspect is that neutrality plays out on two levels: whereas the state may use neutrality as a ground for a policy, that policy itself should be neutral. For example, the Dutch policy in the police is safeguarding lifestyle neutrality, but the policy itself also has to meet the requirements of state neutrality. It should be emphasized that substantiating a policy with reference to state neutrality does not automatically make the policy neutral.

With the theory on state neutrality in mind, the contrasting positions in the debate turn out to be informed by neutrality of justification and neutrality of effect respectively, which run parallel with different conceptions of equality. Those in favour of precluding public officials from wearing religious symbols argue that such a policy provides an equal threshold for all and moreover constitutes equal treatment during the public official's service. This position reflects a formal conception of equality and it corresponds to neutrality of justification. With respect to its dress policy for public officials, the state turns a blind eye to religion or belief and accordingly does not take it into account at all when promulgating dress rules. In this view, such disregard does not violate the public official's freedom of religion. It is not religion or belief on the basis of which the state imposes limitations, but rather on the basis of professional duties. Moreover, were an interference established, it would be considered justified by the requirements of those professional duties. By contrast, the position that does not consider exclusion of religious symbols necessary for state neutrality is based on a substantive conception of equality. Additionally, it is not the reasons which are the yardstick for determining neutrality but the actual effects. On a side note, in this case the addressees of such effects are not citizens in general but public officials. If the policy were thus to affect certain groups more than others, then the policy would take that into account in pursuing equality. Rather than excluding religious symbols, this conception of equality, substantive equality, would favour including them, on the basis of even-handedness. This view thus does not consider that the obligation of state neutrality automatically implies that the public official's religious freedom is limited.

The second perspective, the personification point, revolves around how the obligation of state neutrality has the potential to shape the division between the public official's private and official capacity. The room for religious symbols depends on how strictly this division is envisaged. The one position emphasizes that individuals incur a special responsibility by taking on a public function. As it were, they come to personify the state and as such they come to bear the duties incumbent on the state, including those connected with state neutrality. In this perspective, state neutrality does not act so much as an obligation of the state towards the public official, but rather as a duty incurred by the public official who takes on his function. State neutrality is then considered to be a force imposing limitations on the public official's individual freedom to manifest religion or belief. Or put differently, state neutrality is seen as restraining the public official in the display of religious symbols. Whereas he is fully entitled to his individual freedoms in his private capacity, he may be expected to forgo them (partly) in his official capacity.

4.5.2 Neutrality of the public official towards the citizen

As elaborated on in the previous part of this chapter, individual rights are the obverse of the obligation of state neutrality. This is especially clear in the context of the judiciary, where indirect reference is made to the right to a fair trial. Basically, it is said by one side in the debate that a judge cannot wear a religious symbol, because it would convey bias; such bias is central to the third point of contention. Bias would violate a judge's duty of judicial impartiality, and consequently the citizen's right to an impartial and independent judge. More generally, the bias conveyed by the symbol jeopardizes the citizen's right to equal treatment. A symbol in itself cannot lead to unequal treatment, which is indeed stressed by the other side in the debate. However, the citizen may well perceive himself to have been unequally treated. Another angle focuses on the public official's attitude which has been argued to effectively become more neutral by the act of taking off a religious symbol. The symbol also figures in this view by posing a threat to the citizen's freedom of religion or belief. By displaying his adherence to a religion or belief, a public official might unduly influence, or even proselytize, the citizen (fourth point of contention). By playing down the relevance of the symbol, the other side in the debate does not consider a symbol to have such an effect.

These points of contention thus play out between the individual public official and the individual citizen. This relation is concerned with the balance struck between the rights, which the citizen can invoke against the public official as a state representative, and the duties that the public official should observe towards the citizen. In other words, state neutrality is then a duty which the public official observes towards the citizen. The public official's rights connected to religious freedom remain effective too. In principle though, these are invoked against the state, as shown in the previous section. In this relation, state neutrality does not directly concern a policy of the state impacting on citizens. Rather it is the public official's conduct that has to meet the duties of state neutrality. More specifically, it is by (not) manifesting religion or belief by (not) displaying symbols that he complies with state neutrality. In other words, strictly speaking, it is this conduct and not the underlying policy which has to meet the standard of neutrality. It cannot be determined outright which standard of neutrality informs one or the other position. This has to do with the following.

The crux of the point of contention lies in the effect of the symbol. More specifically, it turns on whether a symbol can rightfully be interpreted as encroaching on citizens' rights in the context of the display of a religious symbol. This is not simple to determine. If a public official were to use his competences to pressure a citizen to convert to a religion or belief, it is clear that he is imposing a religion or belief on that citizen and therefore acting in contravention of his duties of state neutrality. If he were to proclaim towards the citizen the superiority of a religion, he would equally be violating his duties, albeit arguably less so. And finally, if a public official, for example a police officer, were more likely to arrest a citizen who is Muslim, that public official would be committing a violation of his duty of state neutrality. But if a public official 'merely' manifests his religion or belief by displaying a symbol, he might be said to passively convey that he is religious but no more than that.

Nonetheless, it came to the fore in the debate that it is unclear whether the display of a symbol constitutes an act of proselytism. Passive it may be, but a symbol may nevertheless be identified as a marker of a particular religion, which may be significant considering the possibly unequal relation between the public official and the citizen. Moreover, a religious symbol may convey that the public official is biased towards a citizen. So although it is not so much that differential treatment can be directly established, it may nonetheless be inferred from the fact that the public official manifests his religion or belief by a symbol. This goes beyond what may be considered a mere prejudice on the part of the citizen. It can also be argued that by the very act of displaying his religion or belief, the public official becomes per se less neutral. From this perspective, the act of displaying a religious symbol is a conscious act of religious practice impacting on his professional attitude.

4.5.3 Neutrality of the state towards the citizen

The two points of the image of the state (fifth point of contention) and separation of church and state (sixth point of contention) can be related clearly to the theories on state neutrality, which deal with how 'the state' should be neutral towards individuals. The image point considers the room for religious symbols in public functions to put across a particular image. In other words, it reasons that the external appearance of public officials impacts on this image. It is premised on the assumption of state neutrality requiring that the state should be equally available for all citizens, in terms of representation as well as of access. Accordingly, on the one hand, the state should convey that it is at the disposal of its citizens, and that it will serve citizens irrespective of their religion or belief. Additionally, it should present itself as equally accessible for all citizens, should they wish to become a part of a particular public sector. This borders on the point of equal access for public officials.

The two positions advanced in the debate concerning this point of contention reflect an authority-based approach and a representation-based approach respectively. The authority-based approach portrays the state as an entity, which can best remain impersonal for retaining its distanced authority. In this view, any evidence of adherence could be interpreted as alliance and should thus be avoided for risk of partiality. This position was corroborated at times by reference to the separation of church and state which was interpreted to mean that the state was precluded from conveying anything religious. The representation-based approach takes representation as the basis for the state operating for all. By mirroring society and its composition, the state could put across that it is in touch with all kinds of different layers, boxes and segments of society.

These points of contention may be considered to be the most abstract ones as they pertain to the state in the abstract and the citizen in the abstract. As touched on previously, all state action may in the end be related to individual action. It is possible though to speak of the state *in abstracto* when referring to it as an organizational body. In the context of the study, the state has an important role as an actor bearing state neutrality. More specifically, the study deals with a particular function in the abstract, for instance 'the judiciary'. It has to do with how citizens view public functions.

The relation of the different points of contention to the different relations adds the points of contention to the diagram in the following way.

Diagram 4.4: Points of contention

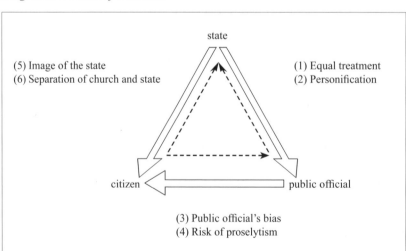

state

(5) Image of the state
(6) Separation of church and state

(1) Equal treatment
(2) Personification

citizen   public official

(3) Public official's bias
(4) Risk of proselytism

4.5.4 Factors to evaluate the points of contention

The third and most concrete asset of the model is that it proffers factors which are possibly helpful for further contemplating and evaluating the points of contention. In corresponding with the relational dynamics between the different actors, the different points of contention imply that the features of the actors and of their respective relations bear on how they can be evaluated separately. Approaching the relational dynamics with common sense brings out factors that are relevant for (evaluating) the points of contention and for bringing to light the differences between the three public functions.

It can well be imagined that in having a different position a judge's bias plays out differently from a state schoolteacher's bias. Whereas the former is bound to observe judicial impartiality and should pronounce a judgment, the latter is not held to such a legal obligation and has a task with a fundamentally different nature. On the basis of the model, three elements can be referred to as organizing the many factors: the actors, their relation and the circumstances.

Looking at what actors are in play in order to evaluate the points of contention implies having regard for what they are and who they are. In other words, it is relevant for instance what kind of competences, duties and rights an actor possesses. For instance, a judge is endowed with the exclusive task of administering justice. A judicial uniform symbolizes the formality or obviously the uniformity of his task. To give another example, litigants can rely on a right to fair trial, which can be seen as the obverse of the judge's duty of impartiality. Moreover, they have the possibility of challenging a judge when they suspect him to be biased. Individuals dealing with police officers do not have the same possibility. This difference may be of relevance when regarding the point of a public official's bias. Additionally, an actor's particular characteristics, such as age or reputation, may influence how a point of contention is decided on.

The second group of factors concerns the relation between the actors. The model has been construed in such as way as to emphasize neutrality as a concept assuming meaning by virtue of the dynamics between the actors. The difficulty in singling out the relevant facets of the relations determining these dynamics is the difference between the types of relations. In being based on employment, the relation between the state and the public official is fundamentally different from the one between the public official and the citizen. There are many facets of a relation which determine the interplay between actors. For example, actors may have a specific balance of power or purpose defining the basis on which they meet. Additionally, the frequency and length of time with which actors come into contact may be of relevance. The contact between the public official and the citizen most clearly illustrates how specific factors determine the relation.

113

The power balance may refer to matters like the tools available to the citizen for acting on violation of neutrality (such as the mechanism of challenging a judge). Otherwise, it may address the extent to which a citizen's reaction to a public official's (presumed) neutrality impacts on the latter's functioning. The possible impact of a public official's appearance on the citizen's willingness to subject himself to the public official's authority may be of relevance for setting rules on this appearance. For example, when a litigant before a judge refuses to be cooperative, this may be less of a problem than a suspect refusing to be cooperative towards a police officer because he suspects the officer to be biased. The presumed asymmetrical relation between a state schoolteacher and a pupil is another example of a particular power balance.

The other facets help to typify the contact between the actors. It matters how frequently actors come into contact, for how long, with what purpose and how direct their contact is. For example, in principle, a judge and a litigant meet briefly, incidentally and for the purpose of administering justice. Moreover, a lawyer may assist the litigant thus serving as some sort of intermediary. By contrast, a teacher and a pupil meet on a long-term basis, frequently and for a pedagogic purpose. They have direct contact. Whereas both a judge and a teacher may be said to operate within confined spaces – a court or a school – a police officer has a wider working area. He may well come into contact with an array of individuals. What is more, in light of the issue of religious symbols, the perception of citizens with whom a police officer is not necessarily in personal contact may be relevant as well.

Finally, all kinds of contextual factors can be thought of as having a bearing on how neutrality plays out in general and on how the points of contention can be contemplated and evaluated in particular. For example, at first sight, the point of contention that a religious symbol may jeopardize a judge's impartiality appears to speak for itself. The business-like nature of proceedings though diminishes such self-evidence. There are many proceedings conceivable where the judge's (assumed) religion is probably quite irrelevant; take for instance administrative proceedings on building permits. Then again, what if the building permit concerns a mosque? Would it then matter if the judge would appear to be a Muslim? And what happens when a female judge sits on a bench dealing with a domestic violence case? Addressing these questions may offer a more solid basis for assessing the impact of religious symbols on neutrality than relying on a general hunch. Features of the system may also be considered. For example, the school system offers an alternative to public education; parents have the freedom to establish a school in conformity with their religion or belief. By contrast, the judicial system is indivisible in that a litigant in court is bound to one court system.

4.6 CONCLUSION

The elusiveness of both state neutrality and religious freedom accounts for an important part of the contention in the debate. The conceptual analysis in the present chapter demonstrated that in being ideals, they leave room for interpretation. In examining their interplay, this study aimed at identifying the core meaning of state neutrality for its impact on the issue of religious symbols in public functions. Subsequently, it proposed a model portraying the dynamics of state neutrality and religious freedom. This model made clear that three actors are involved; in addition to the state in the abstract and the citizen, it expressly included the public official. In so doing, the model also served to demonstrate the indivisibility of the relations between the different actors and the way in which state neutrality is effectuated. More specifically, the way in which the state observes neutrality towards the public official inevitably affects the way in which the public official observes neutrality towards the citizen. Additionally, the triangular model demonstrated the different levels on which the points of contention can be placed. Doing so also indicated the importance of specific factors for assessing the necessity and justifications of limitations on the freedom to display religious symbols. Such factors revolve around the different actors and their relations, and in addition they relate to contextual elements.

This model will serve as a reference framework to analyse the main issue of religious symbols in public functions against the background of three different normative contexts. The subsequent chapters examine the issue within the context of the European Convention on Human Rights, France and England consecutively. The analysis of the issue within the first normative context aims at finding the minimum human rights standards which any limitation on the display of religious symbols in public functions would have to live up to; it has specific regard for how state neutrality has been employed as a ground of justification for limitations. The chapters on France and England serve to find out how these states have dealt with state neutrality in relation to the issue of religious symbols. The organisation of all three chapters consists of a descriptive part and an analytical part. Accordingly, after having described the elements of the contexts in relation to the main issue, the chapters consider the issue in depth through the lens of the framework developed in the present chapter.

CHAPTER 5
EUROPEAN CONVENTION ON HUMAN RIGHTS

5.1   INTRODUCTION

While the European Convention on Human Rights (hereinafter: ECHR or Convention) can rely on a relatively long legacy, the developments of the Convention continue to be scrutinized, and not without criticism. Be that as it may, the significance of the Convention and the corpus of case law connected to it can hardly be overestimated. Moreover, its effect on the legal order of High Contracting States cannot be ignored. It is therefore imperative to take account of the Convention in any study of a human rights issue in the context of a High Contracting State. While judgments primarily address the state involved in a case, they are conducive to guiding the implementation of the Convention. That is to say that the Court pronounces judgment on interferences with ECHR provisions and, in doing so, effectively establishes the minimum standards that High Contracting States should observe. The present chapter studies the ECHR case law on Article 9[1] in relation to the issue of religious symbols in public functions. In so doing, it attempts to examine to what extent the points of contention in Dutch debate have figured in case law.

In several respects, the present chapter includes a broader scope of cases than might be expected on the basis of the research problem as it has been defined. To begin with, while focusing on cases dealt with under Article 9, it does not exclude cases under other provisions if they are relevant to the main issue. Accordingly, although cases concerning the display of symbols are at the centre, cases involving other types of expressions are also examined. Furthermore, it is not a particular timeframe that directs the selection of the cases, but the pertinence to the main issue. As a consequence, the cases included cover a wide time span, i.e. from 1976 to 2012. Thus they include cases before the European Court of Human Rights (hereinafter: ECtHR or Court) as well as before the European Commission of Human Rights (hereinafter: ECnHR or Commission).[2] Finally, the selection has not been restricted to cases with a public official as the applicant, but it has also included cases concerning other

---

1   Subsequent references to provisions, supervisory bodies and case law in the present chapter concern the ECHR system, unless otherwise stated.
2   This chapter uses the term 'supervisory bodies' when denoting both of them. From 1998 onwards, reform of the ECHR system abolished the Commission whose tasks came to be carried out by the Court alone, see Protocol 11.

individuals, provided the cases were relevant. The question that the present chapter seeks to answer is as follows:

How is state neutrality considered in the ECHR framework to justify limitations on public officials in the judiciary, the police and public education to manifest their religion or belief by displaying symbols?

The chapter takes a two-step approach. It first describes the relevant cases and subsequently proceeds to assess the points of contention against the background of these cases. Three preliminary remarks need to be made. Firstly, the examination in specifically the second part may be somewhat unusual in being held against the conceptual model developed in Chapter 4. This exercise is not carried out with the expectation that the case law and conceptual model nicely map onto each other, just as the selection of cases is not made with the expectation that they will nicely map onto the scope of the study. As a result, the ECHR discourse does not naturally resonate with the concepts developed in the previous chapters. The second remark is that the analysis of the case law is in tune with the general approach of the study. Accordingly, the decisions and judgments are primarily analysed as sources of arguments. In other words, this chapter expressly does not intend to provide a general appraisal of the ECHR case law. Therefore, it includes scholarly critique of ECHR case law only to a limited extent. The third remark is also concerned with the way that the case law is employed. The very nature of the case law impedes any analysis undertaken to generate doctrinal truths. The contemplation of the arguments against the background of the Convention is also essentially different from the one undertaken within the French and the English context respectively. Additionally, it is noted that the case law is primarily context-driven. This fact is used to the benefit of applying the conceptual model.

Before the cases are delved into, an exploration of the framework is helpful. After all, any exegesis of findings gains clarity if the text responsible for the findings is known. It would be a step too far, though, to give an extensive account of the Convention here, even more so because such an account has already been the subject of many an apt monograph.[3] Furthermore, it is not essential for a sufficient understanding of Article 9. Therefore, the next section deals only briefly with some preliminary issues concerning the application of Article 9.

---

3   E.g. C. Evans, *Freedom of religion under the European Convention on Human Rights* (Oxford ECHR Series, Oxford University Press, Oxford 2001); M.D. Evans, *Religious liberty and international law in Europe* (Cambridge University Press, Cambridge 1997); P.M. Taylor, *Freedom of Religion. UN and European Human Rights Law and Practice* (Cambridge University Press, New York 2005). R. Uitz, *Freedom of religion: in European constitutional and international case law* (Council of Europe Publishing, Strasbourg 2007).

5.2   THE APPLICATION OF ARTICLE 9

Chapter 4 referred to Article 9 as being exemplary for how provisions on religious freedom are construed in human rights treaties. To reiterate the original text:

> 1. Everyone has the right to freedom of thought, conscience and religion; this right includes freedom to change his religion or belief and freedom, either alone or in community with others and in public or private, to manifest his religion or belief, in worship, teaching, practice and observance. 2. Freedom to manifest one's religion or beliefs shall be subject only to such limitations as are prescribed by law and are necessary in a democratic society in the interests of public safety, for the protection of public order, health or morals, or for the protection of the rights and freedoms of others.

Before the Court addresses the merits of a case, it needs to deal with the admissibility of the claim. While many admissibility decisions do not provide substantive insight into the application of Article 9,[4] some do. This is especially the case with manifestly ill-founded claims, some of which have therefore been included in the present discussion of case law.

Additionally, it is important to briefly note which steps the supervisory bodies take when coming to a judgment on the merits. Judgments on the merits are construed along relatively determinate lines.[5] After presentation of the facts, relevant domestic law and the arguments of both parties are included. Then the supervisory bodies usually arrive at considering and applying the law of the Convention. They often recite general principles on the application of Article 9, examining whether a *prima facie* interference with Article 9 can be established. For this purpose, they briefly look at whether a religion or belief is in play and whether the manifestation in question is indeed a religious manifestation in the sense of Article 9. In a case where such interference can be found, the supervisory bodies examine whether this interference can be justified. Such justification applies when the interference is prescribed by law, pursues a legitimate aim and is necessary in a democratic society. The following sections briefly discuss these steps for considering whether a violation of Article 9 can be established.

---

4   Claims can be declared inadmissible for quite technical reasons, e.g. for not being submitted within six months after the final national decision, or for lack of evidence, see P. van Dijk and others (eds), *Theory and practice of the European Convention on Human Rights* (4th edn Intersentia, Antwerp [etc.] 2006), p. 162 ff. and C. Evans (2001), p. 10.

5   See also Viljanen, who identifies a typical index of judgments of the Court, J. Viljanen, *The European Court of Human Rights as a developer of the general doctrines of human rights law: a study of the limitation clauses of the European Convention on Human Rights* (PhD Tampere University, Tampere University Press, Tampere 2003), p. 47.

5.2.1 Everyone

According to the text of Article 9, the right to freedom of thought, conscience and religion is conferred on 'everyone'.[6] Additionally, the provision implies that the right to manifest religion can also be enjoyed by communities. It has gradually been accepted in case law that churches and other organizations[7] indeed incur rights under Article 9 and as such also have standing.

A specific question in the context of this study is whether 'everyone' includes public officials or whether particular restrictions are inherent to their special position. In EU law, such a special position for public officials has been translated into restricting access to public functions to EU nationals only.[8] Article 9 has not explicitly reserved a special position for public officials. On the contrary, without a doubt, public officials are protected under this provision,[9] which has been confirmed on numerous occasions.[10]

At the same time, two determinations in case law put this general rule into perspective. Firstly, it can be derived from case law that an individual's access to a position in public service may be subject to conditions which impact on his rights under the Convention, as long as these conditions comply with the justification criteria. Thus, it seems that the mere fact that an individual experiences access to a public function to be limited as a consequence of e.g. dress requirements cannot be at the basis of a complaint under the Convention.[11] Secondly, public functions have at times been qualified as entailing a particular legal regime, which implies inherent restrictions on the right under Article 9;[12] Section 5.5.2 of this Chapter further elaborates on.

---

6   While this formulation seems to envisage primarily individuals as subjects of Article 9 ECHR, the development in the case law shows that the scope has been extended to legal persons akin to a church, see the development in the case law of the Commission, discussed by M.D. Evans, pp. 286-287.

7   Van Dijk and others (eds) (2006), p. 765. See for example *Savez Crkava "Riječ Života" and Others v. Croatia* (Appl. no. 7798/08 ECtHR, 9 December 2010).

8   See N. Beenen, *Citizenship, Nationality and Access to Public Service Employment. The Impact of European Community Law* (PhD Universiteit Utrecht 2001, Europa Law Publishing, Groningen).

9   Similarly with respect to Article 10 ECHR, under which cases possibly relevant for this study have been brought.

10 E.g. *Konttinen v. Finland* (Appl. no. 24949/94 ECnHR, 3 December 1996), *Tepeli and others v. Turkey* (Appl. no. 31876/96 ECtHR, 11 September 2001), *Ahmed and others v. United Kingdom* (Appl. nos. 65/1997/849/1056 ECtHR, 2 September 1998), *Vogt v. Germany* (Appl. no. 7/1994/454/535 ECtHR, 2 September 1995).

11 *X. v. United Kingdom* (Appl. no. 8160/78 ECnHR, 12 March 1981). *De Meester v. Belgium* (Appl. no. 8493/79 ECnHR, 8 October 1981). *Vogt v. Germany* (ECtHR 1995).

12 Scholars have identified this as the doctrine of inherent limitations which applies to certain Convention rights exercised by persons of a special legal status or regime, such as civil servants, see Van Dijk and others (eds) (2006), p. 345.

5.2.2 Religion or belief

In accordance with the general approach to religion and belief explained in the previous chapter, Article 9 leaves room for a wide range of personal convictions. Indeed, case law has endorsed a broad interpretation.[13] Convictions falling within the ambit of Article 9 have included mainstream religions, such as Christianity, Islam, and Hinduism. Additionally, minority religions and beliefs like the Church of Scientology and the Moon Sect have been dealt with under Article 9. Secular beliefs such as secularism, atheism and pacifism have been equally included.

Although the supervisory bodies have addressed a wide variety of convictions under Article 9, they have identified some criteria to prevent a completely undefined scope of Article 9.[14] In particular, individualized religions and beliefs or religious practices which were found to lack a certain consistency were considered to fall outside the substantive scope of Article 9.[15] In the seminal case *Campbell and Cosans v. United Kingdom*,[16] the Court set out some formal criteria to distinguish religions or beliefs from opinions and ideas, the last two being protected under Article 10. It considered 'conviction' as included in Article 2 of Protocol 1 to be 'more akin' to 'belief' in Article 9, both denoting 'views that attain a certain level of cogency, seriousness, cohesion and importance'.[17]

In spite of these criteria, the supervisory bodies have not definitively settled what constitutes a religion or belief.[18] In subsequent cases, the supervisory bodies have seemed to rather circumvent the definitional question by dealing with cases on other grounds or by moving directly to the second paragraph of Article 9.[19] Notwithstanding the challenge of this definitional question, the supervisory bodies have in principle refrained from formulating general material criteria for a religion or belief.[20] Cases involving religious manifestations, in particular symbols, illustrate that the supervisory bodies have to walk a fine line in assessing religious manifestations.[21]

---

13 C. Evans describes the approach by the Court and Commission as being generous, see C. Evans (2001), pp. 54-55.

14 E.g. ibid, p. 53 ff.

15 Ibid, p. 57 ff.

16 *Campbell and Cosans v. United Kingdom* (Appl. nos. 7511/76; 7743/76 ECnHR, 25 February 1982).

17 Ibid, para. 36. This case elaborated on an approach that had been initiated earlier, namely in the case of *X. v. Germany* (Appl. no. 8471/79 ECnHR, 10 March 1981), see C. Evans (2001), p. 54.

18 As Carolyn Evans says, they are rather ill-equipped to determine whether something constitutes a religion or belief, see C. Evans (2001), p. 55.

19 C. Evans (2001), p. 56.

20 In general, the Court is precluded from entering into theological assessments, see e.g. F. Cortese, 'The *Lautsi* Case: A Comment from Italy' (2011) 6(3) *Religion and Human Rights*, p. 227.

21 Cf. *Dahlab v. Switzerland (ECtHR 2001)* (Appl. no. 42393/98 ECtHR, 15 February 2001); *Lautsi and others v. Italy* (Appl. no. 30814/06 ECtHR [Grand Chamber], 18 March 2011).

5.2.3 Manifestation of religion or belief

Article 9 includes four categories of manifestations: worship, teaching, practice and observance. The supervisory bodies have determined that these categories make up an exhaustive list.[22] Accordingly, instead of adding categories to the list, they have been rather inclined to interpret the given categories broadly. When dealing with an Article 9 case for the first time, the Court had already given a broad interpretation of 'teaching'. In addressing the complaint of a Jehovah's Witness for being arrested for proselytism, the Court ruled that improper proselytism which goes together with, for instance, offering material or social advantages, falls outside the protection of Article 9.[23] By contrast, bearing witness to one's faith and attempting to convince others of this faith may be qualified as teaching under Article 9.

Otherwise, the category of 'practice' has the potential for covering a wide range of religious manifestations.[24] In 1978, the Commission defined a formal criterion to clarify the limits of 'practice' in *Arrowsmith v. United Kingdom*.[25] In order for a practice to be protected under Article 9, it had to 'actually express' the belief concerned. Such 'actual expression' assumed a stronger link with the underlying religion or belief than being motivated or influenced by a religion or belief. While the exact interpretation of this criterion can still be debated, this distinction has gained force by frequent reiteration in subsequent cases.[26] In any event, religious dress and religious symbols have generally been accepted as a religious manifestation under Article 9.

5.2.4 Limitation clause

As previously explained, in contrast to the right to have or change a religion or belief, the right to manifest a religion or belief can be legitimately subject to limitations. The limitation clause in Article 9(2) is one of the least permissive clauses in the Convention.[27] More specifically, this clause obviously comprises a smaller list of interests that can constitute a legitimate aim than Articles 8(2), 10(2) or 11(2).[28] Nonetheless, in order to justify a particular interference, Contracting Parties need to meet identical requirements: the interference needs to be prescribed by law, pursue a legitimate aim and be necessary in a democratic society. These requirements are

---

22   Cf. *Arrowsmith v. United Kingdom* (Appl. no. 7050/75 ECnHR, 16 May 1977), C. Evans (2001), p. 106.
23   *Kokkinakis v. Greece* (Appl. no. 14307/88 ECtHR, 25 May 1993), para. 48.
24   See e.g. A. Krishnaswami, 'Study of Discrimination in the Matter of Religious Rights and Practices' United Nations (New York 14 October 1959) UN Doc. E/CN.4/Sub.2/200/Rev.1 79.
25   *Arrowsmith v. United Kingdom* (ECnHR 1977).
26   C. Evans (2001), p. 116.
27   Ibid, p. 45.
28   Van Dijk and others (2006), p. 768.

elaborated on the basis of several criteria which in some cases are tested more extensively than in others? For instance, the legal basis for an interference is established with the help of three criteria: foreseeability, accessibility and preciseness of the law.[29] The legitimate aim requirement has assumed less emphasis, because the pursuit of a legitimate aim has very rarely given reason for finding a violation.[30] By contrast, the requirement for an interference to be necessary in a democratic society has proved to be of great significance in establishing a violation.[31] In testing this requirement, the supervisory bodies examine the existence of a pressing social need for interference, the proportionality of interference to the aim pursued and the relevancy and sufficiency of the reasons given by the state authorities.[32] In applying these criteria, the supervisory bodies have underscored time and again that a certain 'margin of appreciation' falls to the state. This concept has gained such an importance for the assessment of limitations that it has come to be one of the authoritative doctrines for the application of the 'necessary in a democratic society' test.[33] That said, it has also generated a great deal of controversy, the difficulty of which is reinforced by the fact that it has emerged from the case law developed by the supervisory bodies.[34]

5.2.5 Margin of appreciation

The doctrine of the margin of appreciation has been defined as the line at which international supervision should give way to a State Party's discretion in enacting or enforcing its laws.[35] Stated simply, in enjoying a margin of appreciation, Contracting Parties retain certain discretion to take decisions and implement measures in the observance of their obligations under the Convention. The supervisory bodies have expressed this by stating that they are not to take the place of the national authorities. This underlying principle does not mean that certain areas protected by the Convention are left outside the supervision of the Court;[36] the margin of appreciation goes hand in hand with European supervision.[37]

---

29 *Sunday Times v. United Kingdom* (Appl. no. 6538/74 ECtHR, 26 April 1979), para. 49 ff., referred to by e.g. Viljanen (2003), p. 185 ff.
30 Van Dijk and others (2006), p. 340.
31 Ibid, pp. 340 and 768.
32 Viljanen (2003), p. 235.
33 H.C. Yourow, *The margin of appreciation doctrine in the dynamics of European human rights jurisprudence* (PhD University of Michigan Law School, Kluwer, The Hague, 1996). Although the book was written some years ago, it remains relevant in having addressed the issue so thoroughly. This section only aims to highlight some relevant points with regard to Article 9 ECHR, Van Dijk and others (2006), p. 340.
34 G. Letsas, 'Two Concepts of the Margin of Appreciation' (2006) 26(4) *Oxford Journal of Legal Studies*, p. 705.
35 Yourow (1996), p. 13.
36 Viljanen (2003), p. 248
37 Henrard states that 'it is obvious that the more extensive the margin of appreciation the Court leaves

Contracting Parties have been granted, relatively speaking, much discretion in Article 9 matters,[38] by the frequently made statement that in 'questions concerning the relationship between religion and state' the 'role of the national decision-making body must be given special importance'.[39] This is in accordance with the subsidiary[40] role of the supervisory bodies, which is confined to reviewing the conformity of the measure in question with the requirements of the Convention.[41] As a corollary, national authorities are considered to be in a better position than the supervisory bodies to assess the necessity of interferences with individuals' rights.[42] The reason for this is that 'opinion in a democratic society may reasonably differ widely'. This consideration reflects national state practice as an important factor,[43] which the supervisory bodies take into account in determining the width of the margin of appreciation. Generally, when state practice across Contracting Parties varies widely, the supervisory bodies are more inclined to grant states a wider margin of appreciation, due to the apparent lack of consensus. The discussion of cases in this chapter will demonstrate that the Court has applied a wide margin of appreciation

---

to states, the more insignificant its own supervision is. Hence, it comes as no surprise that once the Court grants a wide margin of appreciation to a state, it will seldom conclude to a violation of the Convention', K. Henrard, 'Shifting Visions about Indoctrination and the Margin of Appreciation Left to States', Special Issue: The Lautsi Case' 6(3) *Religion and Human Rights* (2011), p. 246.

38 In general, it can be established that a wide margin of appreciation is applicable to Article 9 cases. This has been pointed before now out in the literature. See Yourow (1996), p. 186; he identified a schema in which several groups of rights go with a varying margin of appreciation. In this model, personal freedoms have a rather wide margin of appreciation in comparison with rights to a fair trial, see. See also C. Evans (2001), p. 143.

39 E.g. *Leyla Şahin v. Turkey* (Appl. no. 44774/98 ECtHR [Grand Chamber], 10 November 2005), para. 109.

40 See *Leyla Şahin v. Turkey* (Appl. no. 44774/98 ECtHR [Chamber] 29 June 2004), para. 100. Of course, the supervisory bodies have had to walk a fine line. Indeed, it can be observed, especially as regards cases concerning potentially sensitive subjects that the supervisory bodies cannot ignore reality on the ground. In the *Lautsi* case for example, several commentators considered it prudent for the Court to have regard for the political component of the case, e.g. W. de Been, '*Lautsi*: A Case of "Metaphysical Madness"?' and J.-M. Piret 'A Wise Return to Judicial Restraint' (2011) Special Issue: The Lautsi Case' 6(3) *Religion and Human Rights* (2011), p. 233 and pp. 277-278 respectively; D. McGoldrick, 'Religion in the European Public Square and in European Public Life– Crucifixes in the Classroom?' (2011) 11(3) *Human Rights Law Review*, p. 499.

41 As pointed out in e.g. the *Belgian Linguistics v. Belgium* case, Appl. nos. 1474/62, 1677/62, 1691/62, 1769/63, 1994/63, 2126/64 ECtHR 23 July 1968), referred to by Viljanen (2003), p. 248. See also Yourow (1996), p. 6: '… the Convention organs may most accurately be viewed not as a supranational court of appeal, but in their more limited supervisory role, slowly legitimizing European human rights consensus among the States Parties'.

42 As pointed out in the *Handyside* case, referred to by Viljanen (2003), p. 248 and C. Evans (2001), p. 142.

43 Other factors include the right at stake – as stated, Article 9 generally entails a wider margin of appreciation – and the extent to which a measure interferes with the core of an applicant's private life, see C. Evans (2001), p. 143.

in cases concerning religious symbols.[44] Additionally, it can be observed that the doctrine has been at the forefront in some of the judgements of the Court.

In having briefly clarified the general application of Article 9, the present chapter continues by addressing the case law in depth. For the selection and explanation of the cases, the leading question is how the supervisory bodies have assessed the compatibility with the Convention of limitations on public officials' freedom to manifest their religion or belief by wearing symbols. In so doing, this examination has special regard for state neutrality as a justification. Accordingly, the next section commences with discussing cases where explicit reference to neutrality has been made.

5.3   STATE NEUTRALITY

Chapter 4 discussed the concept of state neutrality against the background of politico-philosophical terminology. The discussion made clear that this concept is fraught with complexities, ranging from the difficulty of defining it to the problems in implementing it. Additionally, it was shown that a conceptual connection could be made with religious freedom; in several ways, the two concepts turned out to resonate with each other. In focusing more on the positive law within the ECHR framework, the present chapter examines the role of neutrality in that framework. Accordingly, the current section analyses to what extent the concept of neutrality has explicitly figured in case law. To the extent possible, the cases are presented according to the public functions central to the study. As will be seen, there are cases handed down by the supervisory bodies relating to the judiciary and education. By contrast, the lack of any cases on the police cannot be overlooked. No cases have been found which involved police officers or comparable officials which were relevant to the main research question of the present study.

Before addressing the specific contexts in which neutrality was found to play a role, the section begins by examining whether neutrality has any relevance on a general level of the Convention.

5.3.1 General principle

State neutrality has not been explicitly mentioned in the text of the Convention. That has not prevented the supervisory bodies from regularly mentioning this concept in Article 9 cases, to the extent that neutrality seems to have become part of the general

---

44   Doing so has not remained without criticism. Some scholars suggested that the Court has at times resorted to the margin of appreciation as a way to circumvent thorny questions, e.g. De Been who calls the margin of appreciation 'the "get-out-of-a-difficult-situation-free" card', De Been (2011), p. 231.

principles.[45] That said, the supervisory bodies have not put forward an unambiguous understanding of neutrality. It has figured in cases involving a variety of states, which had dealt divergently with the role of religion in the public sphere.

Throughout their case law, the supervisory bodies have gradually shaped the general duty of the state to be neutral and impartial into more positive obligations on the part of the state.[46] In earlier case law, they articulated this general duty of the state mostly in relation to the communal aspect of Article 9 as not taking sides in disputes between religious communities.[47] In other words, the supervisory bodies employed the concept of neutrality to prevent the state either from endorsing one religious community at the expense of another or from requiring official recognition of a religious organization in order to make its activities lawful. Another requirement of neutrality concerned the restraint to be observed by the state in not determining the legitimacy of religious beliefs or of the ways in which they are expressed.[48] In other cases, the supervisory bodies have extended the duty of neutrality to encompass positive obligations for the state. An example of this is the terminology qualifying the state as 'the neutral and impartial organiser of the exercise of various religions, faiths and beliefs'.[49] In understanding neutrality in a more active manner, the supervisory bodies coupled neutrality with high-minded values like pluralism, tolerance and broadmindedness. In order to safeguard these values, the state was to take an active stance in ensuring mutual tolerance between groups. Moreover, neutrality was tied into the overarching need to protect the rights and freedoms of others.[50]

Apart from enshrining neutrality in its general principles, the supervisory bodies have made explicit reference to neutrality in specific contexts. Focusing on the main research problem, the analysis discusses cases in a political, judicial and educational context. As previously stated, the cases do not exclusively and exactly map onto the categories of public officials central to this study. In containing relevant indications

---

45   Cf. M.D. Evans, *Manual on the Wearing of Religious Symbols in Public Areas* (Council of Europe Manuals: Human Rights in Culturally Diverse Societies, Nijhoff, Leiden 2009), p. 43 ff. On many occasions, state neutrality figures in the section on general principles in Article 9 cases, in earlier as well as more recent cases, see e.g. *Metropolitan Church of Bessarabia and others v. Moldova*, (Appl. no. 45701/99 ECtHR, 13 December 2001); *Lautsi and others* (ECtHR [Grand Chamber] 2011).

46   Or as formulated by Malcolm Evans: 'There has been a subtle, but significant, shift in the perception of the role of the state in relation to the freedom of religion or belief', M.D. Evans (2009), p. 43.

47   E.g. *Metropolitan Church of Bessarabia and others v. Moldova* (ECtHR 2001).

48   *Manoussakis and others v. Greece* (Appl. no. 18748/91 ECtHR, 29 August 1996); also referred to in M.D. Evans (2009), p. 44.

49   Or as it was stated in the *Refah Partisi v. Turkey* case (Appl. nos. 41340/98, 41342/98, 41343/98 and 41344/98 ECtHR, 13 February 2003): 'In order to perform its role as the neutral and impartial organiser of the exercise of religious beliefs, the State may decide to impose on its serving or future civil servants, who will be required to wield a portion of its sovereign power, the duty to refrain from taking part in the Islamic fundamentalist movement, whose goal and plan of action is to bring about the pre-eminence of religious rules', para. 94. See also M.D. Evans (2009), p. 45.

50   M.D. Evans (2009), p. 50.

though, they have been included and, where possible, analogous reasoning is applied. The subjects figuring in the cases in the political context are civil servants. The cases in the judicial context concern judges. Finally, the cases in the educational context comprise several strands. In tune with the specific-to-general order of the entire chapter, the section begins the discussion of these strands with the one most pertinent to the study, namely with the neutrality of the educational staff. Subsequently, this chapter also deals with students' neutrality and neutrality of the educational environment.

The next section concerns an application lodged by British civil servants concerning the compatibility of political activities with their duty to be politically neutral. It must be noted that the rationale of political neutrality is different from that of religious neutrality. In the same vein, political activities are not the same as religious symbols. Nevertheless, in fundamentally concerning the tension between a professional duty and the exercise of individual freedoms, the case has been included to see whether parallels can be drawn.

5.3.2 Civil servants' neutrality

Some states have imposed restrictions on the freedom of public officials to carry out political activities.[51] In 1998, the Court dealt with such restrictions in *Ahmed and others v. United Kingdom*.[52] Mr. Ahmed and three others were civil servants who had been permanently employed in different capacities by various local authorities. Their complaint was that domestic law violated their right to freedom of expression.

All four of the applicants were politically active in the sense that three of them held positions within a political party while one of them had stood as a candidate for election. Pursuant to regulations that had been adopted in 1990 on the compatibility of carrying out political activity with holding a post as a public official, they were all compelled to withdraw or resign from their political positions. The 1990 regulations were the upshot of a report drawn up by the Widdicombe Committee (the Committee),

---

51 In Germany 'Berufsverbote' were applicable during the 1970s on the basis of which persons were excluded from public service because of their political activities, see e.g. T.L. Bellekom. '"Verfassungsfeinde" en openbare dienst' (PhD Rijksuniversiteit Leiden 1987, Stichting NJCM-Boekerij, Leiden). In the UK, civil servants are divided into three categories which allow various levels of political activity. S. Fredman, 'The legal context: public or private?' in S. Corby and G. White (eds), *Employee relations in the public services: themes and issues* (Routledge, London [etc.] 1999), p. 61.

52 *Ahmed and others v. United Kingdom* (ECtHR, 1998). This case demonstrates pertinent differences of the British approach towards civil servants and their freedom to engage in political activities in comparison with the approach towards the public officials in this study and their freedom to display religious symbols. Specifically, in contrast with the Dutch rules, the British rules concerning political activities in the civil service have been formulated strictly and in the abstract, see also C.R. Niessen, 'Ambtenaar en grondrechten, ofwel: leve het poldermodel.' (1999) 24(7) *NJCM-Bulletin: Nederlands tijdschrift voor de mensenrechten*, pp. 956-957.

which had been specially set up in response to the increasing politicisation of local government and attendant problems in respect of the relationship between named elected members and local officers. The Committee had been vested with the task of inquiring into the respective roles of elected members and officers of local government authorities and of making any necessary recommendations for strengthening the democratic process.

At the centre of its conclusions was 'the established wide agreement that the public service tradition of a permanent corps of politically impartial officers should be retained'. In line with this conclusion, the Committee recommended that:

> the legislation should be amended so that persons who are councillors or who are standing for election as councillors, or who have been councillors within the last year, may not be employed by another authority at the rank of principal officer or above;

Furthermore, steps were recommended to include a prohibition on political activity in the terms and conditions of principal officers or above. These recommendations resulted in the making of the previously mentioned regulations, which laid down rules concerning restrictions on political activity carried out by specific categories of local government officials. Each local authority was obliged to draw up a list of politically restricted posts. The applicants' posts were all included in such a list. They contended that the introduction and application of these regulations constituted an unjustified interference with their right to freedom of expression.

After establishing that the interference had been prescribed by law,[53] the Court continued by assessing whether such interference had pursued a legitimate aim. The Government advanced the claim that 'the Regulations were essential to the proper functioning of the democratic system of local government in the United Kingdom', because they 'were intended to strengthen the tradition of political neutrality on the part of specific categories of local government officers by prohibiting ... forms of political activity which could compromise the duty of loyalty and impartiality ...'.[54] The Court accepted this approach in recognizing the importance of political neutrality for the 'bond of trust between elected members and a permanent corps of local government officers who both advise them on policy and assume responsibility for the implementation of the policies adopted'.[55] In evaluating whether the interference

---

53 The Court took into account that conduct which may call into question an officer's impartiality in the eyes of third parties, cannot be defined with absolute precision. Furthermore, an officer could seek advice beforehand either from the employer or from the union or some other source. Finally, even if an officer was to be disciplined for having breached the Regulations, he could appeal to an industrial tribunal whose decisions over time would undoubtedly help to promote a harmonized approach to the interpretation of the Regulations, see *Ahmed and others v. United Kingdom* (ECtHR, 1998), paras. 46-48.
54 Ibid, para. 50.
55 It places the importance of political neutrality against the broader interest of effective political

was necessary in a democratic society, the Court reiterated three general principles elaborating on the nature of the 'necessary in a democratic society' test. In so doing, the Court emphasized that it was not taking the place of the 'competent national authorities'. Instead, the Court qualified its task as looking 'at the interference complained of in the light of the case as a whole' and determining 'whether it is "proportionate" to the legitimate aim pursued and whether the reasons adduced by the national authorities to justify it are "relevant and sufficient"'.[56]

Apart from the compatibility of the regulations with the recommendations of the Committee, it was mostly the proportionality of the regulations that was at the centre of the dispute. The applicants and the Government disagreed on the relative weight of three factors in particular: the number of political officers subject to restrictions, the range of activities that were limited, and the possibility of exemptions. For instance, the applicants were of the opinion that the categories of posts were 'too broadly conceived and absorbed large numbers of local government employees'.[57] By contrast, the Government stated that the categories of officers 'were clearly defined in accordance with the duties which they performed'.[58]

Whereas the Commission had agreed with the applicants in finding the restrictions 'far-reaching, inflexible and disproportionate',[59] the Court came to an opposite conclusion. The Court started by establishing that the Committee had identified a pressing social need and that the regulations were a valid response to that need.[60] Subsequently, it described the categories of officers subject to limitations as 'carefully defined' in 'as focused a manner as possible'.[61] Additionally, the Court considered the exemption procedure to allow optimum opportunity for an officer to seek exemption from the restrictions. As to the range of activities restricted, the Court noted that not all comment on political matters was meant to be silenced, but merely 'comment of a partisan nature which judged reasonably can be considered as espousing or opposing a party political view'.[62] In the view of the Court, the applicants were still free 'to join a political party or to engage in activities within that party other than the limited

---

democracy, which is not to be interpreted narrowly, see ibid, para. 52. Furthermore, it refers to the 'right of the public' to 'expect that the members whom they voted into office will discharge their mandate in accordance with the commitments they made during an electoral campaign and that the pursuit of that mandate will not founder on the political opposition of their members' own advisers', whereas they also have a right in their dealings with local government to be advised by neutral officers, ibid, para. 53.

56 Ibid, para. 55.
57 Ibid, para. 57.
58 Ibid, para. 59.
59 Ibid, para. 60.
60 At this point, the Court refers to the varying state practices on the organisation of local democracy and the arrangements for local authorities. It uses this point to underscore that the adoption of the Regulations was within the respondent State's margin of appreciation, see ibid, para. 62.
61 Ibid, para. 63.
62 Ibid.

restrictions'.[63] Furthermore, the Court took into account that a distinction applied between 'the duties and responsibilities, which the applicants owed to their local authorities and the pursuit by them of their own personal activities'.[64] In sum, the Court concluded that the restrictions could not be said to amount to a disproportionate interference with the applicants' rights under Article 10, which accordingly had not been violated.[65]

5.3.3 Judicial impartiality

Just as public officials in general are entitled to protection of their personal freedoms, so too are judicial officials.[66] Nonetheless, the typicality of the responsibilities of judicial office has found expression in the requirement of judicial impartiality,[67] the essence of which is neutrality.[68] The Court has qualified impartiality as the absence of prejudice or bias.[69] In principle, a judge's personal impartiality must be presumed until there is proof to the contrary.[70] The Court has distinguished two tests to establish judicial impartiality, a subjective one and an objective one. While the former test seeks to ascertain the personal conviction of a judge, the latter one determines whether a judge offers guarantees sufficient to exclude any legitimate doubt.[71] In relation to the

---

63 Ibid.
64 Ibid.
65 Ibid, para. 65.
66 *Altin v. Turkey* (Appl. no. 39822/98 ECtHR, 6 April 2000), p. 5. *Wille v. Liechtenstein* (Appl. no. 28396/95 ECtHR, 28 October 1999), para. 42: 'Accordingly, the status of civil servant obtained by the applicant when he was appointed President of the Liechtenstein Administrative Court did not deprive him of the protection of Article 10.' However, the special status of public officials might imply a more limited interpretation of rights. Cf. the application of Article 6(1) which specifically reads '*civil* rights and obligations' (emphasis added). For example, the Court declared Article 6(1) to be inapplicable in *Pitkevich v. Russia* (Appl. no. 47936/99 ECtHR, 8 February 2001): 'The Court observes that the judiciary, while not being part of the ordinary civil service, is nonetheless part of typical public service. A judge has specific responsibilities in the field of administration of justice which is a sphere in which States exercise sovereign powers. Consequently, the judge participates directly in the exercise of powers conferred by public law and performs duties designed to safeguard the general interests of the State,' p. 8.
67 In this section, independence is not addressed as this element rather refers to the institutional context whereas the judge's personal attitude is more relevant to this study, see Van Dijk and others (2006), p. 613; M. Kuijer, *The blindfold of Lady Justice: judicial independence and impartiality in light of the requirements of Article 6 ECHR* (PhD Universiteit Leiden, Wolf Legal Publishers, Nijmegen 2004), pp. 203 and 303.
68 As stated by Kuijer: 'The essence of impartiality is [better] captured by "neutrality", in the sense of detachment, open mindedness and objectivity, or "equidistance" from the parties to the case and from the subject-matter of the dispute', Kuijer (2004), p. 303.
69 *Piersack v. Belgium* (Appl. no. 8692/79 ECtHR, 1 October 1982), see also ibid, p. 304.
70 *Hauschildt v. Denmark* (Appl. no. 10486/83 ECtHR, 24 May 1989), para. 47. *Le Compte, van Leuven and De Meyere v. Belgium* (Appl. nos. 6878/75, 7238/75 ECtHR 23 June 1981), para. 58.
71 *Piersack v. Belgium*, (ECtHR 1982), para. 30; *Hauschildt v. Denmark* (ECtHR 1989), para. 46.

objective test, the Court has underscored the vital importance of judicial impartiality by pointing out that judicial impartiality is concerned with safeguarding the confidence of the public – and, in the case of criminal proceedings, of an accused – in the courts in a democratic society, In this regard, the Court has equally stated that 'appearances may be of a certain importance'.[72]

At least three subjects can be discerned amongst the cases concerning judicial impartiality: membership of religious organizations, religious activities and public statements.[73] Two cases in the first category were the similar cases of *N.F. v. Italy* and *Maestri v. Italy*[74] dealt with by the Court in 2001 and 2004 respectively. The applicants in both cases were judges who had been members of the Freemasonry. The membership proved to impede their career from developing further; disciplinary sanctions for membership were, for instance, imposed on both of the applicants. The cases are mainly relevant for the purpose of the present study because they include indications on the possibly legitimate reasons for introducing limitations on judges' personal freedoms. The reasoning of the Government in both cases implied that Italian legislation aimed at safeguarding the trust, consideration and prestige of the judiciary.[75] The Freemasons had become subject to guidelines passed by the National Council of the Judiciary in 1990 in view of the 'particularly strong hierarchical and mutual bond' they imposed on their members. This bond caused anxiety over 'delicate problems as regards observance of the values enshrined in the Italian Constitution',[76] including that judges are beholden to the law alone.[77] The guidelines not only safeguarded the obligation of loyalty to the Constitution and the impartial and independent exercise of judicial activity, but they also aimed to prevent undermining citizens' confidence in the judiciary due to the loss of credibility. In the end, the Court found a violation of the freedom of association (Article 11) for the simple reason

---

See also Kuijer (2004), pp. 304, 309 ff. The subjective approach is more relevant in the context of this research.

72 *Hauschildt v. Denmark* (ECtHR 1989), para. 48. See also Kuijer (2004), p. 304. The importance of appearance is corroborated by other cases, such as *Pitkevich v. Russia* (ECtHR 2001), '... an opinion by a judge concerning the morality of a party may justify an appearance of bias by the judge', p. 12. *Piersack v. Belgium*, (ECtHR 1982): '... the public are entitled to fear that he [public prosecutor] does not offer sufficient guarantees of impartiality' (a violation of Article 6(1) was found).

73 This shows that impartiality is a notion closely intertwined with neutrality, which can also be distinguished in political and religious neutrality.

74 *N.F. v. Italy* (Appl. no. 37119/97 ECtHR, 2 August 2001) and *Maestri v. Italy* (Appl. no. 39748/98 ECtHR, 17 February 2004).

75 A relevant provision in this regard was Article 18 of Royal Legislative Decree no. 511 of 31 May 1946, stating that any judge who 'fails to fulfil his obligations or behaves, in the performance of his duties or otherwise, in a manner which makes him unworthy of the trust and consideration which he must enjoy or which undermines the prestige of the judiciary' will incur a disciplinary sanction, e.g. *N.F. v. Italy* (ECtHR 2001), para. 15.

76 Ibid, para. 18.

77 Ibid.

that the law was not sufficiently clear. This finding rendered an examination of the requirements for justification unnecessary. Therefore, the cases cannot be taken as generally precluding limitations on judges' membership of religious organizations. But it is certain that when states would envisage such limitations, they should be sure to provide a proper legal basis for them. Thus, in general, the typical character of the judicial function in itself cannot be taken to justify limitations.

The applicant in the previously mentioned case of *Pitkevich v. Russia* was evidently found to have carried out religious activities while carrying out her public function. The activities included proselytizing colleagues, recruiting people for the church and praying in the courtroom.[78] The Court found her complaint that her freedom under Article 10 was violated to be manifestly ill-founded. It considered that she had not been dismissed because of mere membership of a church or expression of her views in private.[79] In other cases, the test *in concreto* applied by the Court in establishing a violation of a judge's personal freedom is evident from how it assesses alleged breaches with the freedom of expression. A distinction is made between statements within and outside the court. As to the latter statements, the Court verifies detriment to the impartiality and independence of the judiciary by assessing whether statements concern facts or value judgments.[80] On a different note, judges enjoy more freedom to make academic statements.[81]

5.3.4 Educational neutrality

A significant number of cases are situated against the background of education. They are not all purely Article 9 cases; for example, cases have been brought on grounds of Article 9 read in conjunction with Article 14. Additionally, cases have regularly referred to Protocol 2, Article 1 which lays down the freedom of education. The next section discusses cases that most easily fit into the mould of the study, namely those concerning the neutrality of educational staff.

5.3.4.1 Educational staff's neutrality

Chronologically, but perhaps also content-wise, it is sensible to start with *Dahlab v. Switzerland*[82] decided in 2001. The application had been submitted by a state school teacher wearing a headscarf. Although it was 'just' an inadmissibility decision, the

78 *Pitkevich v. Russia* (ECtHR 2001), p. 12.
79 Ibid, p. 13.
80 See e.g. *Kudeshkina v. Russia* (Appl.no. 29492/05 ECtHR, 26 February 2009), p. 19.
81 *Wille v. Liechtenstein* (ECtHR 1999), para. 65 ff.
82 *Dahlab v. Switzerland* (ECtHR 2001).

Court made some quite substantive statements. It should be noted that the decision provoked a wave of reactions in scholarly literature.[83]

The applicant, Ms Dahlab, had already been working for some months at a Swiss State primary school, when she converted to Islam and decided to wear a headscarf. After wearing the headscarf for approximately four years she was summoned by the Director General of Primary Education and asked to stop wearing the headscarf because of the incompatibility with the Public Education Act. When this request was issued in a formal ruling, the case escalated to proceedings before the Federal Court, which dismissed her appeal in an elaborate decision with a great emphasis on the importance of the strict denominational neutrality of the State school system. This principle had been referred to by the domestic courts from the outset.[84] The extensive decision of the Federal Court contained a number of considerations on the neutrality principle, which were integrally included in the decision of the Court.

According to the Federal Court, the denominational neutrality principle is coupled with the separation of church and state and with the secular character of the state.[85] It considered that the neutrality principle was aimed at the protection of the religious beliefs of pupils and parents as well as at religious harmony. In addition, the Federal Court interwove this main line of argument with other arguments of gender equality, the danger of provocation or conflict and the special responsibility incumbent on Ms Dahlab as both a teacher and a civil servant. In assessing the proportionality of the decision of the Director-General, it weighed the public interest of ensuring denominational neutrality against the applicant's individual freedom to manifest religion. In conceding that the principle of neutrality is not absolute, the Federal Court described the principle as giving consideration 'to all conceptions existing in a pluralistic society'. A subsequent paragraph seems to imply that the Federal Court likened neutrality to secularism, which 'seeks to preserve individual freedom of religion and to maintain religious harmony in a spirit of tolerance'. After having highlighted the special role of public education and of teachers, it implied that the

---

83 Scholarly analyses sometimes evaluated the *Dahlab* case in conjuction with the 2005 *Şahin* case (discussed *infra*, Section 5.3.3.2), e.g. A. Vakulenko, 'Islamic Dress in Human Rights Jurisprudence: A Critique of Current Trends' (2007) 7 (4) *Human Rights Law Review* who notes that the 'unfailing belief that liberal orders are gender-neutral ignores ... feminist critique that exposes liberalism as itself deeply insribed with hidden but pervasive signs of male dominance', p. 733; Evans points to the lack of evidence of proselytism, C. Evans, 'The Islamic Scarf in the European Court of Human Rights' (2006) 4 *Melbourne Journal of International Law*, p. 13. Additionally, she points to the inconsistency of the Court in applying two stereotypes to women, that of victim and that of aggressor, ibid, pp. 20-21. Another point of criticism concerned the lack of evidence of proselytism, e.g. J. Temperman, 'State Neutrality in Public School Education: An Analysis of the Interplay Between the Neutrality Principle, the Right to Adequate Education, Children's Right to Freedom of Religion or Belief, Parental Liberties, and the Position of Teachers' (2010) 32 (4) *Human Rights Quarterly*, p. 894.
84 *Dahlab v. Switzerland* (ECtHR 2001), p. 2.
85 Ibid, p. 4.

applicant's headscarf might risk religious harmony. In so doing, it casually qualified the headscarf as difficult to reconcile with gender equality.[86]

The Court included a large part of the national proceedings in its decision. Although it finally found the application to be manifestly ill-founded,[87] it nonetheless took the trouble of verifying the justification criteria of Article 9(2).[88] In establishing no fewer than three legitimate aims[89] pursued by the state, it highlighted the protection of the rights and freedoms of others when assessing whether the interference was necessary in a democratic society. The Court explained the rights and freedoms of others as referring to the right to be taught in a context of denominational neutrality. The essential consideration of the Court for its final finding can be reduced to its qualification of the headscarf. It accepted that 'it is very difficult to assess the impact that a powerful external symbol such as the wearing of a headscarf may have on the freedom of conscience and religion of very young children'. It then made the following statement, the controversy of which justifies its citing in full:

> it cannot be denied outright that the wearing of a headscarf might have some proselytizing effect, seeing that it appears to be imposed on women by a precept which is laid down in the Koran and which, as the Federal Court noted, is hard to square with the principle of gender equality. It therefore appears difficult to reconcile the wearing of an Islamic headscarf with the message of tolerance, respect for others and, above all, equality and non-discrimination that all teachers in a democratic society must convey to their pupils.[90]

The Court considered that the national authorities had not overstepped their margin of appreciation and concluded that the application was manifestly ill-founded.

In addition to this contested case, there have been admissibility decisions against Turkey, which have not given as much cause for debate. Then again, the principle of *laïcité* figured prominently in these cases, and as proved by the previously discussed cases involving students, this principle provides the state with a strong argument to justify limitations. This may hold even more true, considering that these admissibility decisions concerned educational staff.

In 2006, the Court declared the application in *Kurtulmuş v. Turkey*[91] to be inadmissible. As an economy professor at Istanbul University, the applicant had

---

86 Ibid, p. 7.
87 Whereas formally only judgments address merits, there may be quite large sections of the reasoning dedicated to the merits in an inadmissibility decision, e.g. Viljanen (2003), p. 8.
88 The criteria are assessed on the basis of the following questions: does the interference have a legal basis; does it pursue a legitimate aim; and is it necessary in a democratic society? E.g. Van Dijk and others (2006), p. 340 ff.
89 Viz, the protection of the rights and freedoms of others; public safety; and public order.
90 *Dahlab v. Switzerland* (ECtHR 2001), p. 13 (emphasis added).
91 *Kurtulmuş v. Turkey* (Appl. no. 65500/01 ECtHR 24 January 2006).

to comply with dress regulations precluding her from wearing the headscarf. In disregarding these regulations, she had become subject to disciplinary proceedings as a result of which she was finally dismissed. She complained that the dress regulations in general and the dismissal in particular violated her rights under Articles 8, 9 and 10 of the Convention.

In coming to its decision that the application was manifestly ill-founded, the Court mainly relied on earlier case law. It took together a host of previously articulated principles in finding that Turkey had not overstepped its margin of appreciation in imposing the dress regulations on university professors. The Court considered the special status of public officials in finding it acceptable that the state subjected them, by virtue of their status, to an obligation of discretion in publicly manifesting their religion.[92] The Court complemented this obligation with a duty of loyalty to the constitutional principles of the state, of which the principle of *laïcité* was particularly important in the instant case.[93] The regulations of the universities envisaged upholding this principle by requiring public officials to have a neutral appearance. In a later similar complaint, *Fatma Karaduman v. Turkey*,[94] lodged by a secondary school teacher the Court confirmed its approach. It very briefly dealt with the application in referring to previous cases and declaring the complaint manifestly ill-founded.

While the line of cases involving the principle of neutrality thus seems rather consistent, another case shows that the Court has not in every situation accepted neutrality-based arguments as justifying limitation. Such exceptions can be illustrated by a discussion of the case of *Ivanova v. Bulgaria*.[95] It must be pointed out though that the facts in this case significantly differed from those in the other cases. Most importantly, the applicant did not complain about being subject to dress regulations but about being dismissed on the basis of her religion; she was a member of the unregistered religious organization called Word of Life. The Government claimed to have dismissed the applicant as a swimming pool manager at the River Shipbuilding and Navigation School because she did not meet the newly amended requirements for the post.[96] Additionally, it argued that any limitations imposed on the applicant's

---

92 '... it is legitimate for a State to impose on public servants, on account of their status, a duty to refrain from any ostentation in the expression of their religious beliefs in public ...', ibid, p. 5.

93 'It is that principle, and not objections to the way a person dresses as a result of his or her religious beliefs, that is the paramount consideration underpinning the rules.' Additionally, the Court refers to *Vogt*, para. 59, ibid, p. 6.

94 *Karaduman and Tandoğan v. Turkey* (Appl. nos 41296/04 et 41298/04, ECtHR, 3 September 2008).

95 *Ivanova v. Bulgaria* (Appl. no. 52435/99 ECtHR, 12 July 2007).

96 While she had been appointed to this post for an indefinite period, a new principal arrived after her appointment who had changed the roster of posts. This followed the preparation of a list of posts without job descriptions which included the applicant's post, while her post with job description had been on the roster of posts for years. It became clear during the domestic proceedings that the new principal had changed the job description and requirements which had later been approved by

religious freedom were justified by the secular nature of the system of education in Bulgaria.

The Court noted the lengthy submissions on the secular nature of the system of education and the references to proselytism made by the Government. However, the Court also remarked that no evidence had been provided in support of such proselytism.[97] Moreover, the Court deemed the submissions of the Government to be 'ambiguous and contradictory'[98] with respect to its lengthy submissions on the alleged proselytism on the one hand and the denial that the applicant's dismissal had anything to do with her religious beliefs on the other. The Court instead considered that the sequence of events strongly pointed to a causal link between the various events, which resulted in the applicant's dismissal. Subsequently, the Court elaborately canvassed the facts, mentioning *inter alia* the ongoing negative media comments on Word of Life, the inquiries by the Prosecutor and the National Security Service into the religious activities of the school staff and, most importantly, the meeting between the Educational Inspector and his deputy and the applicant and a colleague where the last two were asked to resign or to renounce their faith. All in all, in placing the sequence of the events against the general background of an increasingly intolerant policy towards Word of Life, the Court concluded that the applicant's dismissal appeared 'to have resulted directly from the implementation of that policy'.[99] Accordingly, her right to freedom of religion was violated.

5.3.4.2 Students' neutrality

The issue of students' neutrality has mainly emerged against two states, Turkey and France. By no accident both adhere to a strict interpretation of state neutrality. Indeed, their interpretation of state neutrality boils down to an exclusive one, being labelled as secularism. Turkish legislation concerning religious symbols in educational institutions was adopted relatively early in time. It was in 1993 that the Commission decided simultaneously on the admissibility of two similar applications under Article 9. The respective applicants, Ms. Senay Karaduman and Ms. Bulut,[100] were female students at universities in Ankara. When they had completed their studies they did not receive their diplomas because the passport photos they had handed in for their diplomas depicted them with a headscarf. They complained that the requirement that the diploma needed a picture with them bareheaded violated Article 9.

---

the Ministry. The applicant, however, had not been informed of this change. See for the facts ibid, paras. 7-22.

97 Ibid, para. 82.

98 Ibid.

99 Ibid, para. 85.

100 *Senay Karaduman v. Turkey* (Appl. no. 16278/90 ECnHR, 3 May 1993); *Lamiye Bulut v. Turkey* (Appl. no. 18783/91, ECnHR 3 May 1993).

The Commission started with a statement, which has been regularly reiterated in its case law, that Article 9 does not always guarantee the right to behave according to religious precepts in the public sphere. Moreover, not every act inspired or motivated by religion or belief is protected under Article 9. Subsequently, the Commission established that the university regulations, to which the applicants had subjected themselves in choosing to pursue their studies at this university, aimed at 'preserving the "republican", and hence "secular", nature of the university'.[101] The Commission then placed the importance of *laïcité* against the background of the national context in noting that there was a danger of pressure on students who did not practise the majority religion. This fear of fundamentalist pressure was underscored in the next paragraph, where the Commission considered universities adhering to *laïcité* to guard against fundamentalist movements meddling in the public order of universities and infringing on others people's consciences. It was thus clear for the Commission, as was evident from following paragraphs as well, that the principle of *laïcité* and the ensuing dress regulations were of importance in safeguarding the rights and freedoms of others. Finally, the Commission added that the sole objective of a certificate was to testify to a student's professional capacities and was not meant for the attention of the larger public. Accordingly, the photo on the certificate served to identify the student and was not meant to enable a student to manifest his or her religion or belief. The Commission concluded that the regulations contested did not interfere with the freedom of religion thus rendering the complaint manifestly ill-founded.[102]

Years of relative quietness concerning dress regulations in Turkish universities were rudely interrupted by the *Leyla Şahin* case. The case echoed the previously mentioned *Dahlab* case in containing comparable elements and in equally causing controversy.[103] The complaint was lodged in 1998, alleging that university dress regulations violated the applicant's right to freedom of religion, and ended with a Grand Chamber ruling in 2005. On the basis of the facts, the case seemed to be exemplary for the gradually increased unrest concerning religious dress at universities in Turkey. In 1998, the University of Istanbul had sought to end this unrest by adopting a circular, which precluded students from wearing the headscarf and students with beards from being admitted to lectures, courses or tutorials. As a result of this circular, the applicant had been refused access to a written examination, after which disciplinary proceedings followed.

---

101 E.g. *Senay Karaduman v. Turkey* (ECnHR, 1993), p. 7.

102 Ibid, p. 8.

103 Cf *supra* n 83. Cumper and Lewis point to the flaws of the Court's reasoning. Specifically, they observe that 'the language of autonomy ... may not be adequate to explain the obligation on the wearer of *hijab*, P. Cumper and T. Lewis, '"Taking religion seriously"? Human rights and *hijab* in Europe – Some problems of adjudication' (2009) 24(2) *The journal of law and religion*, p. 615. In Dutch debate see e.g. T. Loenen and A. Terlouw, 'De ondraaglijke zwaarte van de hoofddoek: het EVRM bevestigt dat een hoofddoekverbod aan de Turkse universiteiten geoorloofd is (2006) 31(2) *NJCM-Bulletin: Nederlands tijdschrift voor de mensenrechten.*

The applicant submitted to the Court that the ban on wearing the Islamic headscarf at university constituted an unjustified interference with her right to freedom of religion, in particular, the right to manifest her religion. The Chamber had concluded that the interference with Article 9 was justified. In doing so, it considered the interpretation of secularism as advanced by the Government compatible with the underpinning values of the Convention and found the measure necessary for the protection of democracy in Turkey.[104]

The Grand Chamber followed the Chamber in assuming that the regulation in question constituted an interference with the applicant's right to manifest her religion. Furthermore, it considered the regulation to be prescribed by law and to pursue the legitimate aims of protecting the rights and freedoms of others and of protecting public order. In assessing the final requirement of justification, namely whether the interference was necessary in a democratic society, the Grand Chamber first extensively went over the general principles. It set out the paramount importance of the freedom of thought, conscience and religion as one of the foundations of democratic society. However, it reiterated that Article 9 did not protect every act motivated or inspired by a religion or belief. The necessity of imposing restrictions might precisely be informed by the need to reconcile the interests of various religious groups. The role of the State in this reconciliation was to be 'a neutral and impartial organiser of the exercise of various religions, faiths and beliefs'.[105] In the view of the Court, the maintenance of pluralism and democracy required concessions on the part of (groups of) individuals.

A large part of the discussion of the general principles was dedicated to the margin of appreciation. The Grand Chamber considered that the role of the decision-making body must be given special importance in 'questions concerning the relationship between State and religions'.[106] As regards regulating the wearing of religious symbols in educational institutions, the Grand Chamber noted the diversity of approaches taken by national authorities, which accordingly justified a wider margin of appreciation. It further referred to the previously discussed *Karaduman* and *Dahlab* cases. It cited the controversial passage in the latter case portraying the headscarf as a 'powerful external symbol' and questioning the possible proselytising effect, 'seeing that it appeared to be imposed on women by a religious precept that was hard to reconcile with the principle of gender equality'.[107] The Grand Chamber also mentioned that the Court had noted in these cases that 'wearing the Islamic headscarf could not easily be reconciled with the message of tolerance, respect for others and,

---

104 *Leyla Şahin v. Turkey* (ECtHR [Chamber], 2004), para. 106.
105 *Leyla Şahin v. Turkey* (ECtHR [Grand Chamber] 2005), para. 107.
106 Ibid, para. 109.
107 Ibid, para. 111.

above all, equality and non-discrimination that all teachers in a democratic society should convey to their pupils'.[108]

In applying the general principles to the instant case, the Grand Chamber followed the Chamber ruling in that upholding the principle of secularism might be considered 'necessary to protect the democratic system in Turkey'.[109] Its endorsement was made all the more clear by the verbatim citation of a substantial part of the Chamber's judgment on this point. The judgment linked the dress regulations to the protection of the rights and freedoms of others and the maintenance of public order. A particular factor taken into account was that the majority of the population adhered to the Islamic faith. In view of the increasing political significance of the headscarf, the Grand Chamber regarded the imposition of limitations as 'meeting a pressing social need'. This was corroborated by the presence of extremist political movements. The Grand Chamber continued:

> it is the principle of secularism ... which is the paramount consideration underlying the ban on the wearing of religious symbols in universities. In such a context... it is understandable that the relevant authorities should wish to preserve the secular nature of the institution concerned and so consider it contrary to such values to allow religious attire ...[110]

In addressing the final point of proportionality between the means and the legitimate aim, the Grand Chamber considered that Muslim students were free within limits to manifest their religion in accordance 'with habitual forms of Muslim observance'.[111] Furthermore, it took into account that the process leading up to the implementation of the circular had taken several years during which continued dialogue took place. Having thus found the measure to be proportional, the Court concluded that Article 9 had not been violated.

The reasoning in the *Leyla Şahin* judgment has been followed in subsequent years. For instance, the complaint in *Köse v. Turkey* in 2006, lodged by pupils of secondary schools and their parents, that a directive prohibiting the headscarf violated their religious freedom was found to be manifestly ill-founded. The consistency of the approach chosen by the Court was further corroborated by cases against France. By now, there are a fair number of instances concerning pupils who want to wear religious symbols at state schools. In 2004, France adopted a law prohibiting pupils from wearing conspicuous religious symbols at state schools.[112] Both before and

---

108 Ibid.
109 Ibid, para. 114.
110 Ibid, para. 116.
111 Ibid, para. 118.
112 In 2004, France adopted a law precluding pupils at State primary and secondary schools from wearing conspicuous religious symbols. The aim of the law was the safeguard of the principle of *laïcité*. It did not take long before the first cases were brought to court and in 2008, the Court dealt

after 2004, cases have been lodged with the Court. Obviously, the adoption of the domestic law has not gone unnoticed in the observations of the Court. That said, the thrust of the approach of the Court is the same. For example, in the case of *Dogru v. France*[113] of 2008, the Court judged that measures prohibiting a pupil from wearing a headscarf during physical education did not violate Article 9. The dispute went back to 1999 when the applicant was a secondary school pupil who was finally expelled for not complying with the duty of assiduity. This duty had been laid down in the Education Act and required pupils, amongst other things, to attend compulsory classes. Furthermore, the school which the applicant attended, had stipulated rules including the prohibition on conspicuous religious symbols.[114]

In assessing the compatibility of the ban on headscarves with the applicant's right to freedom of religion, the Court took a broad view on the legal basis. Apart from the specific provision in the Education Act, the Court took notice of the principle of secularism as it had developed in the French context. Moreover, it deemed an opinion of the *Conseil d'Etat* dating back to 1989 and which also concerned a schoolgirl wearing a headscarf, to constitute part of the legal basis for the measure in question. That opinion first set out what conditions the wearing of religious symbols at state schools had to meet in order to conform to the principle of secularism. In so doing, it had created leeway for schools to prohibit such symbols.

The Court relied on a wide range of its previous cases in determining that the interference was necessary in a democratic society. It noted that the school rules applied to all pupils without distinction. Additionally, the Court explained that that the purpose of the measure was to uphold secularism. In line with its previous case law, it attributed the state with a wide margin of appreciation in affairs concerning religion and state. Finally, it found that the state had still undertaken a balancing exercise between the interests involved. Relevant factors for this balancing exercise were the attempts of the school to enter a dialogue and the fact that the ban on the headscarf was limited to the sports class.[115]

A number of cases[116] were instituted around the same period, namely the beginning of the school year 2004-2005 when the consequences of the previously mentioned 2004 law took effect. They basically concerned the same complaint and have been dealt with in the same way by the Court. That said, it should be noted that a novel aspect of these cases is that some concerned alternative modes of dress which

---

with a range of applications arising from the 2004 law. These cases, as well as the background and content of the law are addressed in Chapter 6.

113 *Dogru v. France* (Appl. no. 27058/05 ECtHR, 4 December 2008).
114 Ibid, paras. 23-25.
115 Ibid, para. 74 ff.
116 The Court dismissed all cases in similar decisions on 30 June 2009: *Aktas v. France* (Appl. no. 43563/08), *Bayrak v. France* (Appl. no.14308/08), *Gamaleddyn v. France* (Appl. no. 18527/08), *Ghazal v. France* (Appl. no.29134/08), *J. Singh v. France* (Appl. no. 25463/08) et *R. Singh v. France* (Appl. no. 27561/08).

might not directly qualify as religious symbols. For instance, the case of *Gamaleddyn v. France* concerned a schoolgirl wearing a bonnet. The Court has decided all of these cases to be inadmissible.[117]

5.3.4.3 Neutrality of the educational curriculum and environment

As early as 1976, the Court made some statements indirectly bearing on the neutrality of state schools in *Kjeldsen, Busk Madsen and Pedersen v. Denmark*.[118] Three sets of parents had submitted a complaint against Denmark objecting to integrated sex education at State primary schools. Such education was the result of many years deliberation on whether such a topic should be a compulsory part of the curriculum. From 1970 onwards, integrated sex education had been included in the amended State Schools Act. In principle, pupils could not be exempted from sex education, except for a few subjects. The applicants' complaint primarily invoked the violation of the right to education as enshrined in Article 2 of Protocol 1, which also covers parents' rights to education and teaching in conformity with their own religious and philosophical convictions. Additionally, the applicants alleged a breach of Articles 8, 9 and 14 of the Convention.[119]

The reason why the case is interesting for the study in hand is not so much because of the finding of the Court that the disputed legislation was not in violation of the Convention, but because of the statements of the Court concerning the interpretation of Article 2 of Protocol 1. To begin with, it shows that cases concerning religious freedom in education have sometimes been dealt with primarily or even exclusively under Article 2 of Protocol 1. That said, such cases may also be adjudicated on under Article 14 in conjunction with Article 9.[120]Additionally, the statements of the Court in the *Kjeldsen and others* case have proved their relevance in being reiterated in subsequent rulings of the ECHR bodies such as in the case *Folgerø and others v.*

---

117 E.g. *Gamaleddyn v. France* (2008), para. 3. It is interesting to note that Bikramjit Singh, a Sikh, has brought an individual communication before the UN Human Rights Committee, complaining about the same issue. It has appeared that when ruling on the same issues, the Human Rights Committee might strongly diverge from the Court, e.g. in the *Ranjit Singh* case, Human Rights Committee (102nd session) Views Communication no. 1876/2000, 27 September 2011. This case concerned a Sikh who complained about being compelled to take off his turban for an ID-photograph and can be compared with the case *Shingara Mann Singh v. France* (ECtHR, Appl. no. 24479/07, 13 November 2008). Whereas the Human Rights Committee found a violation of the ICCPR, the Court did not find a violation of the ECHR. A similar contrast has already been found with regard to a school ban on headscarves, cf. *Hudoyberganova v. Uzbekistan*, (82nd session) Views Communication 931/2000, 5 November 2004, see also J. Temperman (2010), p. 886.

118 *Kjeldsen, Busk Madsen and Pedersen v. Denmark* (Appl. nos. 5095/71; 5920/72; 5926/72 ECtHR, 7 December 1976).

119 Ibid, para. 46.

120 Cf. *Grzelak v. Poland* (Appl. no. 7710/02 ECtHR, 15 June 2010).

Norway.[121] In this case, parents who were members of the Norwegian Humanist Association complained that their children could only obtain a partial exemption from the subject 'Christianity, religion and philosophy'. One of the statements of the Court which has proven its value concerned the emphasis on the crucial role of State teaching for safeguarding the possibility of pluralism in education, the interest of which is the preservation of the democratic society.[122] Furthermore, the provision of private education may be a relevant factor in determining whether the State safeguards such pluralism.

Additionally, parents' religious and philosophical convictions, which need to be respected, should be interpreted broadly. In the instant case, parents' objections to sex education fell within the scope of such convictions. Later cases included objections to corporal punishment, and pacifist beliefs.[123] As previously mentioned, the Court has in the later *Case of Campbell and Cosans* further specified formal criteria for views qualifying as religious and philosophical convictions, namely those attaining 'a certain level of cogency, seriousness, cohesion and importance'.[124] Moreover, the state should take care to respect these not only with regard to religious instruction but also with regard to other instruction. As a matter of fact, the duties of the state under Article 2 of Protocol 1 extend to any function which the state assumes in relation to teaching and education. While in the instant case the function concerned a form of instruction, later cases pertained to mandatory participation in a parade, and to disciplinary measures.[125]

The duty of the state to respect parents' views does not alter the fact that the setting and planning of the curriculum fall in principle within the competence of the state.[126] Moreover, the state is not prevented from imparting, through teaching or education, information or knowledge of a directly or indirectly religious or philosophical kind. This was clear in the *Folgerø* case in which knowledge about Christianity represented a greater part of the curriculum at issue.[127] However, in doing so the state 'must take care that information or knowledge included in the curriculum is conveyed in an objective, critical and pluralistic manner'.[128] Most importantly, the Court makes it utterly clear that the State is precluded from pursuing 'an aim of indoctrination

---

121 *Folgerø and others v. Norway* (Appl. no. 15472/02 ECtHR, 29 June 2007).
122 *Kjeldsen, Busk Madsen and Pedersen v. Denmark* (1976), para. 50. Cf. *Folgerø and others v. Norway* (ECtHR, 2007), para. 84.
123 See the *Campbell and Cosans* (ECnHR 1982) and the cases *Valsamis v. Greece* (Appl. no. 74/1995/580/666 ECtHR, 18 December 1996) and *Efstratiou v. Greece* (Appl. no. 77/1996/696/888 ECtHR, 18 December 1996) respectively.
124 *Campbell and Cosans v. United Kingdom* (ECnHR 1982), para. 36.
125 *Valsamis* and *Efstratiou* (ECtHR, 1996) and *Campbell and Cosans* cases (ECnHR 1982) respectively.
126 *Kjeldsen, Busk Madsen and Pedersen v. Denmark* (ECtHR 1976), para. 53. Cf. *Folgerø and others v. Norway* (ECtHR, 2007), para. 84.
127 *Folgerø and others v. Norway* (ECtHR, 2007), paras. 17 ff. and 45.
128 *Kjeldsen, Busk Madsen and Pedersen v. Denmark*, para. 53.

that might be considered as not respecting parents' religious and philosophical convictions'.[129] A possible mechanism for a state to avoid breaching this standard is by providing the possibility for parents and pupils to be exempted from a particular subject When doing so however, a state should make sure that making use of such an exemption is not made unreasonably complicated.[130] The standard of above all avoiding indoctrination has been applied in subsequent cases as well.[131]

In finding the state not to be overstepping its limits against the background of these general principles, the Court also took into account that parents remained free to enlighten and advise their children and that they retained the alternative option to send their children to private schools or to instruct them at home. Parents' freedom to enlighten and advise their children also weighed heavily in the balance in finding whether their right under Article 2 of Protocol 1 was violated in *Valsamis v. Greece* and *Efstratiou v. Greece*.[132] Briefly, these cases concerned the question whether a suspension imposed on a school pupil who did not want to attend compulsory school parades because of her Jehovah's Witness belief contravened Article 2 of Protocol 1. Although the Court showed its surprise 'that pupils can be required on pain of suspension from school … to parade outside the school's precincts on a holiday',[133] it found that the suspension did not contravene Article 2 of Protocol 1. Particular factors were that the Court did not consider the parade to offend the applicant's pacifist convictions to an extent amounting to a violation of Article 2 of Protocol 1. On the contrary, it considered that such events served both pacifist objectives and the public interest. Furthermore, the Court took into account the limited duration of the suspension.[134]

An element of the educational environment, which is of particular pertinence to this study, is the use of symbolism in the school building. In the recent case of *Lautsi v. Italy*,[135] the Grand Chamber dealt with the question whether the display of a crucifix within the classroom of state schools was compatible with the requirements of Article 2 of Protocol 1 and Article 9 of the Convention. Such display emanated from a compulsory duty incumbent on primary state schools, which had been codified in several decrees. The applicant's viewpoint was that the crucifixes violated the secular character of the state and her secular beliefs. The case has sparked a furious debate both on the role of the Court in general and on religious symbolism at

---

129 Ibid.
130 *Folgerø and others v. Norway* (ECtHR, 2007), para. 97 ff.
131 E.g. *Angeleni v. Sweden* (Appl. no. 10491/83, ECnHR 3 December 1986). It has been argued that the standard is rather general and is subject to pitfalls. Carolyn Evans for instance has argued that the standard has become quite high for the applicant to show actual indoctrination instead of potential indoctrination, see p. 95.
132 Referred to *supra* note 123.
133 *Valsamis v. Greece*, para. 31 and *Efstratiou v. Greece*, para. 32.
134 *Valsamis v. Greece*, paras. 31-32 and *Efstratiou v. Greece*, paras. 32-33.
135 *Lautsi and others* (ECtHR [Grand Chamber] 2011), *supra* n. 21.

schools in specific.[136] The ruling was given in a period when the Court was already subject to critical scrutiny. The debate ensuing from the case added to this scrutiny and undeniably had a political flavour.[137] Furthermore, it is striking that the Chamber and the Grand Chamber came to conclusions which can be called contrasting at the least.[138]

Both the Chamber and the Grand Chamber made reference to general principles previously articulated in the cases mentioned. Additionally, they both left no doubt as to the predominantly religious, more specifically Christian, character of the crucifix. Be that as it may, their further application of these principles diverged to the extent that they came to opposite rulings: whereas the Chamber considered the display of crucifixes as violating Article 2 Protocol 1 and Article 9 of the Convention,[139] the Grand Chamber did not. The Chamber referred to the state's duty to refrain from imposing religions, to uphold confessional neutrality in public education and to ensure the educational pluralism, which is essential to the preservation of democratic society. In its view, the 'compulsory and highly visible presence of crucifixes in classrooms' might well clash with the applicant's secular convictions as well as be 'emotionally disturbing' for pupils of non-Christian religions or those who professed no religion.[140] The Chamber was of the opinion that the negative freedom of religion extended to practices and symbols expressing a religion or belief. Moreover, it could not see how the display of a crucifix could serve the educational pluralism essential for the preservation of democratic society.

The Grand Chamber likewise reiterated the state's duty of neutrality and impartiality. Nonetheless, it also stated that the diverse national practices of Contracting States give rise to a wide margin of appreciation to states in ensuring compliance with the Convention. Accordingly, in line with previous statements, the setting and planning of the curriculum fell within the competence of the state, as also did the choice to impart through teaching or education information or knowledge of a directly or indirectly religious or philosophical kind. Again, the Court stressed the absolute limit to be the prohibition on pursuing an aim of indoctrination.[141]

---

136 E.g. 'Special Issue: The Lautsi Case' (2011); McGoldrick (2011).

137 As McGoldrick states: 'The political response to the Chamber's judgment in *Lautsi* is without precedent in European human rights terms. It caused a storm of political controversy in Italy and elsewhere in Europe, (2011), p. 470.

138 This came as a surprise to some experts. In an article which evaluated the Chamber ruling, Andreescu and Andreescu believed 'it unlikely for the Grand Chamber to change the initial decision. This impression is shared by other experts ...', G. Andreescu and L. Andreescu, The European Court of Human Rights' Lautsi Decision: Context, Contents, Consequences (2010) 26(9) *Journal for the Study of Religions and Ideologies*, p. 65.

139 Ibid, paras. 30-32 contain the Chamber's judgment.

140 Ibid, para. 31.

141 Ibid, paras. 60-61.

In applying the general principles to the facts of the case, the Grand Chamber followed the broad definition of state functions as mentioned in Article 2 of Protocol 1 and considered the decision to display symbols within the school to fall within these functions. Neither the Chamber nor the Grand Chamber gave a definite view on the effect of the crucifix. However, the difference between the two lay in how they assessed the possibility of the crucifix inappropriately influencing the applicant and pupils. Whereas the Chamber let the uncertainty decide in favour of the applicant, the Grand Chamber did the reverse. The lack of evidence of the influence of the display of a religious symbol on classroom walls on pupils precluded a reasonable assertion on the effect on young persons whose convictions were still in the process of being formed. The Grand Chamber did find it 'understandable that the first applicant might see in the display of crucifixes in the classrooms of the State school formerly attended by her children a lack of respect on the State's part for her right to ensure their education and teaching in conformity with her own philosophical convictions'.[142] Nonetheless it found her 'subjective perception' in itself insufficient to establish a breach of Article 2 of Protocol no. 1.[143]

The Grand Chamber further argued this viewpoint by elaborating on the margin of appreciation. Whilst the state had taken the angle of approaching the crucifix as a tradition, the Court established that the decision whether or not to perpetuate a tradition fell in principle within the margin of appreciation of the respondent State. In assessing whether or not the state exceeded this margin, the Grand Chamber reiterated that the visibility of the majority religion was not in itself sufficient to denote a process of indoctrination. To corroborate this finding it also put forward 'that a crucifix on a wall is an essentially passive symbol',[144] which did not have the same influence as didactic speech or participation in religious activities. In finding this, it disagreed with the Chamber, which qualified the crucifix as a powerful external symbol capable of inappropriate influence. This qualification was taken from a previous case involving a teacher wearing a headscarf.[145] The Grand Chamber denied a parallel since the facts of the previous case were entirely different, such as that the Islamic headscarf was worn while teaching. It further placed the visibility of the crucifix in schools in perspective by pointing to two other factors. The first one was that the presence of crucifixes was not associated with compulsory teaching about Christianity. The second one was that the Italian school environment was open to other religions, in that religious dress or symbols were allowed, and that non-majority religious practices were celebrated. Finally, the Court concluded by referring again

---

142 Ibid, para. 66.
143 Ibid.
144 Ibid, para. 72.
145 *Dahlab v. Switzerland* (ECtHR 2001) *supra* n. 21.

to the parent's right to enlighten and advise her children.[146] All these factors led the Court to conclude that there had been no violation in the present case.

5.4 OTHER VALUES

While the cases described in the previous sections contained explicit references to state neutrality, they also hinted that state neutrality is bound up with other values, which can be said to be inherent to a public official's special status. Values which can be singled out are loyalty and authority. Whereas at first sight they are more or less associated with a specific function, they can be considered applicable to all functions. Moreover, they are not strictly separate but rather closely entwined notions. The present section briefly discusses cases in which the special status of public officials was considered, but not so much looking at state neutrality but at the other values.

5.4.1 Loyalty

The discussion of *Kurtulmuş v. Turkey* in the previous section showed how the principle of *laïcité* was coupled with the professor's duty of loyalty to this principle. In making this connection, the Court referred to *Vogt v. Germany*,[147] a seminal case on a teacher's freedom of expression. The case was accordingly dealt with under Article 10, but as it is nonetheless exemplary of a state schoolteacher's rights, it is relevant to the main research question of the present study.

The applicant, Ms. Vogt was a secondary school teacher with the status of civil servant. In Germany, civil servants were at that time subject to a duty of loyalty, which was enshrined in its domestic law. The applicant had been dismissed because she was alleged to have breached her duty of loyalty by her membership of the German Communist Party. Allegedly, the party's pursuit of 'anti-constitutional aims' was incompatible with a civil servant's duty of loyalty to the Constitution.[148] The contextual significance of this duty was clarified by substantive passages of German legislation and case law included in the Court's judgment. Loyalty entails that civil servants 'will at all times uphold the free democratic constitutional system within the meaning of the Basic Law'. As a consequence their 'membership of parties or organisations that oppose the constitutional system ... shall ... as a general rule lead to a conflict of loyalty'.[149] According to a Federal Constitutional Court judgment of 1975 the aim of civil servants' loyalty is to enable the state administration to accomplish its tasks in an 'adequate, effective and prompt manner'. Civil servants

---

146 *Lautsi and others* (ECtHR [Grand Chamber] 2011), paras. 71-75.
147 *Vogt v. Germany* (ECtHR 1995), *supra* n. 10.
148 Ibid, para. 20.
149 Ibid, para. 30.

must thus be 'united and loyal' and furthermore perform duties 'faithfully' and be 'thoroughly dedicated to the State and the Constitution'.[150] They have to be 'prepared to identify with the idea of the State which the official has to serve and with the free democratic constitutional order of that State based on the rule of law and social justice'.[151] Such identification entails that a civil servant 'approves the State … and the existing constitutional order as it is in force and that he or she recognises that they merit protection, bears witness to them accordingly and is active on their behalf'. Therefore, they should 'dissociate themselves unequivocally from groups and movements that criticise, campaign against and cast aspersions on that State'.[152]

In assessing whether the safeguard of loyalty constituted a legitimate aim, the Court noted that 'a number of Contracting States impose a duty of discretion on their civil servants'.[153] It understood the duty of loyalty in this case to be 'founded on the notion that the civil service is the guarantor of the Constitution and democracy'.[154] The Court found this duty of discretion to be legitimate for the state, on account of the status of civil servants.

In applying the general principles to the case though, the Court found a violation of Article 10. Two important factors brought it to its decision. First of all, the Court was struck by the 'absolute nature of the duty [of loyalty]'.[155] The duty required every civil servant to renounce unambiguously all groups and movements deemed inimical to the Constitution.[156] Moreover, the duty was incumbent on the person of the civil servant whether in a private or an official capacity. The second factor was that the duty did not apply as strictly in other Contracting States. Apart from these features of the German duty of loyalty, the Court looked at a few specific factors in assessing the proportionality of the measure. To begin with, the Court considered the measure of dismissal very severe, taking into account the effect on her reputation, on her livelihood and the difficulty of finding another job in the civil service.[157] Furthermore, the Court pointed out that her post did not 'intrinsically involve any security risks'. This would only be the case if 'she would take advantage of her

---

150 Ibid, para. 34.
151 Ibid.
152 Ibid.
153 Ibid, para. 51.
154 Ibid.
155 Ibid, para. 59.
156 It is remarkable that the application of the loyalty principle to all civil servants was considered to be too absolute by the Court, as it had previously accepted an absolute duty of neutrality in cases against Turkey and France, see *Kurtulmuş v. Turkey*, *supra* n. 91. It appears to be crucial that these two countries adhere to a constitutional principle of *laïcité*.
157 The Court noted that in Germany teaching posts outside the civil service are scarce. Consequently, secondary school teachers 'will almost certainly be deprived of the opportunity to exercise the sole profession for which they have a calling, for which they have been trained and in which they have acquired skills and experience', *Vogt v. Germany* (ECtHR 1995), para. 60.

position to indoctrinate or exert improper influence in another way on her pupils during lessons',[158] of which there was no indication.

Notwithstanding the fact that the Court did not accept loyalty in the *Vogt* case as justifying the applicant's dismissal, it has accepted the possibility of loyalty imposing limitations on public officials. On several occasions the Court has reiterated that a democratic state can require its public officials to be loyal to the fundamental principles on which it is founded.[159] This entails that when a state has constitutionally enshrined the principle of *laïcité,* the duty of loyalty can be expected to strengthen the duty of public officials to comply with this principle. Indeed, this was the case for instance in *Kalaç v. Turkey*,[160] where the applicant had been compelled to retire as he had 'manifested his lack of loyalty to the foundation of the Turkish nation, namely secularism, which it was the task of the armed forces to guarantee'.[161] This consideration allows states to adopt disciplinary regulations for their armies. In the *Pellegrin* case, the Court made clear that because the holders of public service posts 'wield a portion of the State's sovereign power', the State has a legitimate interest in requiring of them 'a special bond of trust and loyalty'.[162] The Court later confirmed the specific rationale for imposing a duty of loyalty in making a clear distinction from the private sector, where a similar duty of loyalty does not apply.[163]

The limits to which a state can require public officials to testify to their loyalty were clear in *Buscarini and others v. San Marino*,[164] in which the applicants were members of parliament. In order to be installed they had to take a pledge including a reference to the 'Holy Gospels'. The Government argued that this reference was not so much religious as it was historical and social and that the oath was necessary as a pledge of loyalty to republican values. The oath carried 'the need to preserve public order, in the form of social cohesion and the citizens' trust in their traditional institutions'.[165] Notwithstanding this line of argument, it took the Court only a few paragraphs to rule that the oath on the Gospels violated the applicants' rights under Article 9 as it was 'tantamount to requiring two elected representatives of the people to swear allegiance to a particular religion'.[166] The Court noted that the particular

---

158 Ibid, para. 60.
159 *Kurtulmuş v. Turkey* (ECtHR, 2006). See also *N.F. v. Italy* (ECtHR, 2001). para. 59. This has been reiterated in subsequent cases, e.g. in the comparable case of *Volkmer v. Germany* (Appl. no. 39799/98 ECtHR, 22 November 2001) (albeit it in an admissibility decision), p. 9.
160 Cf. *Kalaç v. Turkey* (Appl. nos. 61/1996/680/870 ECtHR, 23 June 1997); *Usta v. Turkey* (Appl. no. 390/70/97 ECtHR, 4 June 2002), *Engel v. the Netherlands* (Appl. nos. 5100/71; 5101/71; 5102/71; 5354/72; 5370/72 ECtHR, 8 June 1976); *Tepeli and others v. Turkey*, Appl. no. 31876/96 11 ECtHR, 11 September 2001).
161 *Kalaç v. Turkey* (ECtHR 1997), para. 25.
162 *Pellegrin v. France* (Appl. no. 28541/95 ECtHR, 8 December 1999), para. 66.
163 *Sidabras and Džiautas v. Lithuania* (Appl. nos. 55480/00 and 59330/00 ECtHR, 27 July 2004).
164 *Buscarini v. San Marino* (Appl. no. 24645/94 ECtHR, 18 February 1999).
165 Ibid, para. 36.
166 Ibid, para. 39.

feature of representation was of relevance as it might precisely entail 'representing different views of society'.[167] In sum, Article 9 protects an individual from being compelled to swear allegiance to a particular religion. Moreover, the Court made clear in the case *Alexandridis v. Greece*, that the right to manifest a religion or belief includes a negative aspect which is the right not to be forced to reveal religion or belief; this includes not having to act in such a way that a religion or belief can be inferred.[168]

5.4.2 Authority

In the *Vogt* case, the Court mentioned authority as a special feature of a teacher's function. It noted:

> since teachers are figures of authority to their pupils, their special duties and responsibilities to a certain extent also apply to their activities outside school.[169]

The relevance of authority for teachers in particular is enhanced by the possibility that they might take advantage of their position to indoctrinate pupils. This possibility was judged to be reality in the *Volkmer* case,[170] which was clearly distinct from the *Vogt* case. The applicant, a teacher, had asked one of his pupils to attend a conference on ecology organized by church groups.[171] The Court considered this to be at odds with the aspect of authority, and thus agreed with the domestic court. The teacher's request was deemed to be using the pupil as an instrument to spy on political opponents.[172] Equally, though more implied, authority played a role in the *Dahlab* case. The Court emphasized the important role played by teachers. It stated:

> Their mere conduct may have a considerable influence on their pupils; they set an example to which pupils are particularly receptive … Teachers are both participants in the exercise of educational authority and representatives of the state …[173]

Apart from considering authority in relation to a public official's individual person, the Court has also interpreted authority to apply more broadly to the whole of a public function. In *N.F. v. Italy*, the Court bracketed authority with impartiality in finding

---

167 Ibid.
168 *Alexandridis v. Greece* (Appl. no. 19516/06 ECtHR, 21 February 2008), para. 38. See also *Dimitras and Others v. Greece* (no. 2) (Appl. nos. 34207/08 and 6365/09 ECtHR, 3 November 2011).
169 *Vogt v. Germany* (ECtHR, 1995), para. 60.
170 *Volkmer v. Germany* (ECtHR, 2001), p. 11.
171 Ibid, p. 10.
172 Ibid, p. 11.
173 *Dahlab v. Switzerland* (2001), p. 6.

these values a legitimate aim in limiting judges' freedoms.[174] In the instant case, the state had adopted domestic legislation involving the imposition of disciplinary sanctions in order to uphold the authority of the judiciary.[175] In the admissibility decision in *Kudeshkina v. Russia*, the Court underscored the relevance of upholding the authority of the judiciary.

5.5 VOLUNTARY OBLIGATIONS

As previously argued, on a conceptual level, public officials can be said to possess a special status, which is corroborated by a particular legal status in national systems. That said, limitations have also been examined from the point of view that public officials have voluntarily accepted an employment relation. Accordingly, they may be said to have accepted certain obligations inherent to their position. This point of view has been further endorsed by the line of case law turning on 'particular regimes'. This line of case law concerns the choice of individuals to subject themselves voluntarily to a particular regime as well as to relinquish that regime.

5.5.1 Contractual arrangements

In 1981 the Commission dealt with an admissibility decision on a public official's contractual duties in *X. v. United Kingdom*.[176] In this case, the applicant, a Muslim teacher, wanting to attend Friday prayers during contractually agreed working hours, complained that Article 9 had been violated. The applicant had already worked at six different schools within the Inner London Education Authority (ILEA), most of the time as a supernumerary teacher. The third school he worked at disagreed with the teacher attending the mosque on Friday, which finally resulted in the teacher resigning from his function.[177]

 The Commission observed that it was a matter of dispute whether the applicant's attendance at Friday's prayers in the mosque constituted a necessary part of his religious practice.[178] However, the Commission emphasized that an individual needed to take into account his particular professional or contractual position in exercising his freedom to manifest religion.[179] The Commission observed that it was because of

---

174 *N.F. v. Italy* (ECtHR 2001), the impartiality aspect of the judiciary is addressed in Section 5.3.3.
175 Ibid, para. 16. The Court established that Article 11 ECHR had been violated on the ground that the interference was not prescribed by law.
176 *X. v. United Kingdom* (ECnHR 1981).
177 Ibid. The facts can be found in paras. 1-17. He did so, because he preferred to resign over accepting part-time employment, which had been offered to him. However, after an eight-month period of unemployment he reapplied to the ILEA to take up its offer of a part-time teaching post, see para. 17.
178 Ibid, para. 6.
179 Ibid.

his contract, which the applicant had accepted of his own free will, that he could not attend Friday prayers. Moreover, it did not consider that he was 'required by Islam to disregard his continuing obligations vis-à-vis the ILEA'.[180] The Commission looked at some additional factors as well, such as that the applicant had not previously disclosed during the first six years of his employment that he might require time off to observe his religious duties.[181] The Commission concluded that there had been no interference with the applicant's freedom of religion under Article 9(1) of the Convention.

This approach, namely letting the contractual duties prevail, was confirmed in *Konttinen v. Finland*.[182] This time, a Seventh Day Adventist who was an employee of the State Railways wished to refrain from working on the Sabbath, which caused him to leave early from his Friday shift at certain times of the year. He was dismissed, after having left early from his Friday shift six times without authority.[183] When examining whether such a dismissal would constitute an interference with Article 9 ECHR, the Commission needed only a few paragraphs to find the complaint manifestly ill-founded. Again, it emphasized the acceptance of the obligation to observe the rules concerning working hours, the refusal of which was grounds for his dismissal.[184] Moreover, the Commission explicitly considered that 'the applicant was free to relinquish his post', which in the view of the Commission is 'the ultimate guarantee of his right to freedom of religion'.[185] This combination of voluntarily complying with contractual duties and the possibility of freely relinquishing those duties has regularly recurred in ECHR case law. Another case which has confirmed that dismissing someone who refuses to work on rest days does not fall under the protection of Article 9 is *Stedman v. UK*.[186] In this case, the Commission also emphasized that an applicant's religious convictions had thus not been the reason for dismissal, by considering that the refusal to work had been the basis for dismissal.[187]

Finally, the Court more or less stated in *Kosteski v. the former Yugoslav Republic of Macedonia*[188] that requests to be exempted from contractual obligations might

---

180 Ibid, para. 9.
181 Ibid, para. 14.
182 *Konttinen v. Finland* (ECnHR 1996).
183 Ibid, p. 2.
184 Ibid, p.7.
185 Ibid, p. 7.
186 *Stedman v. United Kingdom* (Appl. no. 29107/95 ECnHR, 9 April 1994). Although the case did not directly concern a public function inherent to the state, the Commission considered that 'if a violation of one of those rights and freedoms [in the Convention] is the result of non-observance of that obligation in the domestic legislation, the responsibility of the State is engaged', para. 1. In the same vein, the case concerned an employee in a private agency, but the Commission stated: '... had the applicant been employed by the State and dismissed in similar circumstances, such dismissal would not have amounted to an interference with her rights under Article 9 para. 1'.
187 Ibid.
188 *Kosteski v. "The Former Yugoslav Republic of Macedonia"* (Appl. no. 55170/00 ECtHR, 13 April 2006).

qualify as concerning a 'privilege'.[189] The applicant worked in a public utility company and had been fined twice for unauthorized absence. He claimed to have been absent to celebrate a Muslim holiday and started proceedings before the domestic courts complaining that he had been discriminated against because of his religious beliefs. In dismissing his complaint, the courts established that he had not only breached the disciplinary rules but he had also failed to adduce convincing evidence that he was indeed a Muslim.[190] After having reiterated that not every act motivated or inspired by a religion or belief is protected, the Court stated that it was not persuaded that his absence from work was 'a manifestation of his beliefs in the sense protected by Article 9'.[191] Subsequently, the Court addressed his complaint of interference with the inner sphere of belief in that he was required to prove his faith. While conceding that the State should not sit in 'judgment on the state of a citizen's inner and personal beliefs', the Court did not consider it 'oppressive or in fundamental conflict with freedom of conscience' to require 'some level of substantiation' when an employee sought exemption from working obligations.[192]

5.5.2 Particular regime

The line of cases revolving around the concept of 'particular regime'[193] is in part closely connected to the line of cases based on contractual arrangements, but the concept of 'particular regime' is also applied in a broader sense and emerges mainly in two types of cases: those in the context of the military and those concerning educational institutions. In these two types of cases, the emphasis is not so much on contractual arrangements having the effect of restricting the scope for religious manifestation, but rather on the existence of 'regimes'. The gist of this argument is that in voluntarily entering a particular regime an individual accepts the possible imposition of certain restrictions on his rights.[194]

A case in the military category is *Yanasik v. Turkey*, which is certainly not the only case against Turkey involving the military where a similar line of reasoning has been applied; this is mainly due to the previously discussed principle of strict secularism in Turkey.[195] The applicant was a cadet at the Ankara Military Academy and had been

---

189 Ibid, para. 39.
190 Ibid, para. 36.
191 Ibid, para. 38.
192 Ibid, para. 39.
193 See also N. Blum, *Die Gedanken-, Gewissens- und Religionsfreiheit nach Art. 9 der Europäischen Menschenrechtskonvention* (Duncker & Humblot, Berlin 1990), p. 133 ff.
194 As mentioned *supra* n 12, see also Van Dijk and others (2006), p. 345. It should be noted that the concept of 'particular regimes' or more generally the 'doctrine of inherent limitations' is not incontestable. One of the points of criticism is that inherent restrictions run counter to the non-discrimination principle as recognized under Article 14, see ibid.
195 *Yanasik v. Turkey* (Appl. no. 18783/91 EcnHR, 3 May 1993).

expelled on the ground of participation in fundamentalist activities. His claim before the Commission alleged the violation of various provisions of the Convention including Article 9 ECHR.[196] In assessing the admissibility of this claim, the Commission set out by reiterating that not every act which was motivated or influenced by a religion or belief constituted a practice protected by Article 9. Furthermore, it took the view that an officer cadet 'submitted of his own accord to military rules' by enrolling at a military academy. Such rules might also entail 'limitations on cadets' freedom to practise their religion as to time and place'. This would still leave cadets free to perform their religious duties within the limits imposed by the requirements of military life. The Commission underscored that military discipline, by its very nature, implied the 'possibility of placing certain limitations on the rights and freedoms of members of the armed forces which could not be imposed on civilians'.[197] The Court has followed this basic principle for army discipline established by the Commission in similar cases since, using nearly identical words.[198]

Additionally, as has already become implicitly evident from the previous discussion of the education cases, the same principle *mutatis mutandis* figured in these cases, being applied to pupils or students as well as to teachers or professors.[199] In the *Senay Karaduman* case, the Commission noted in addition that 'in choosing to pursue his studies at a secular university, a student submits himself to the university regulations'.[200] In the *Dahlab* case the Court had included a statement of the Federal Court considering that 'civil servants are bound by a special relationship of subordination to the public authorities, a relationship which they have freely accepted'.[201] In assessing the claim, the Court did not make explicit reference to this argument, but it might be thought that the Court had implicitly respected the argument when it considered that the Geneva authorities had not exceeded their margin of appreciation.

In addition to the free will with which an individual has entered a particular regime, his possibility of relinquishing that regime can further substantiate the finding that Article 9 has not been interfered with. In the *Knudsen* case the two reasons were taken together in the finding that a clergyman within a State church system had accepted certain obligations towards the State, and that he was free to relinquish office. The Commission regarded this 'as the ultimate guarantee of his

---

196 Ibid, p. 24.
197 Ibid.
198 Namely in e.g. *Kalaç v. Turkey* (ECtHR 1997), para. 28; *Usta v. Turkey* (ECtHR 2002), p. 5.
199 In this regard, it may be interesting to point out that the dissenting opinion of Judge Tulkens in the *Şahin* case pointed out the difference that in her view exists between teachers and pupils in the following wording: 'As [teachers and all public officials] have voluntarily taken up posts in a neutral environment, the position of pupils and students seems to me to be different.', see *Leyla Şahin v. Turkey* (ECtHR [Grand Chamber] 2005), dissenting opinion, para. 7.
200 *Senay Karaduman v. Turkey* (ECnHR, 1993), p. 7.
201 *Dahlab v. Switzerland* (ECtHR 2001), p. 3.

right to freedom of thought, conscience and religion'.[202] In the previously mentioned case of *X. v. UK*, the Commission observed as well that 'the applicant remained free to resign if and when he found that his teaching obligations conflicted with his religious duties'. In so doing, it referred to *X. v. Denmark*[203] in which the Commission had stated it more boldly by asserting that 'the freedom of religion of servants of a State church is exercised at the moment they accept or refuse employment as clergymen, and their right to leave the church guarantees their freedom of religion in case they oppose its teachings'.[204]

The possible implications of the 'particular regime'-concept became clear indirectly in the case *Francesco Sessa v. Italy*.[205] In this case, a lawyer complained about a judge's refusal to adjourn a hearing which was scheduled on a Jewish holiday. The Court was 'not convinced' that fixing the date of the hearing on a Jewish holiday and refusing to adjourn this hearing could be understood as a limitation in terms of Article 9.[206] Even if such a limitation would be assumed to have been imposed, the Court estimated it to be justified.

5.6 APPLICATION OF THE CONCEPTUAL MODEL

As previously explained, the study examines the ECHR case law in order to identify the minimum human rights standards which a policy on religious symbols should respect. Most possibly, these minimum standards pose boundaries to the arguments in favour of limiting the freedom of public officials to manifest their religion or belief by displaying religious symbols. After all, unlike the arguments against such limitations, these arguments encroach on the religious freedom of public officials.

The presentation of case law has provided an initial impression of how state neutrality has played a role in cases relevant to religious symbols in public functions. The present section takes an evaluative approach in looking at the case law from the perspective of the conceptual model. It aims at finding to what extent the points of contention can be retrieved from case law. In so doing, it attempts to identify the factors which the supervisory bodies have taken account of in taking a position regarding points of contention. Where relevant, the analysis also notes certain additional points. Before addressing the points of contention, the section first briefly

---

202 *Knudsen v. Norway* (Appl. no. 11045/84 ECnHR, 8 March 1985), p. 257. This was also stated in *Konttinen v. Finland* (ECnHR 1996), para. 1 of the Law in the Proceedings before the Commission. Reiteration in *Stedman v. United Kingdom* (ECnHR 1994).

203 *X. v. Denmark* (Appl. no. 7374/76 ECnHR, 8 March 1976), para. 11.

204 Ibid, para. 1.

205 *Francesco Sessa v. Italy* (Appl. no. 28790/08 ECtHR, 3 April 2012). At the time of writing, a request for referral to the Grand Chamber was pending.

206 Ibid, para. 37.

discusses what conception of the basic concepts and dynamics in the conceptual model can be derived from case law.

5.6.1 Dynamics of neutrality

Initially, neutrality figured in the case law on a more general level in relation to religious communities. This concept was shaped in such a way as mainly requiring the state to refrain from interfering in disputes between religious communities. In later cases, the supervisory bodies gradually developed neutrality into a more positive obligation. Accordingly, states could be required to take on a more active stance in furthering neutrality. This resounds with the conceptual idea that the state should actively provide an arena in which individuals can prosper, in part by being able to pursue a religion or belief of their choosing. It can be derived from the cases discussed that, throughout the whole period, all three core duties distinguished can be recognized to a greater or lesser extent.

Obviously, the very nature of the Convention shapes how the actors and their mutual relations within the model are looked at. An inherent implication of the Convention is that the individual merits protection of his rights against interference by the state. The Convention grants this protection to everyone, including those with a 'special' status like public officials.[207] That said, such protection is not unconditional, as it is not for any individual. Accordingly, just like other individuals, public officials can be limited in the exercise of their individual rights. A standard formula to limit the scope of religious manifestations is that 'not every act inspired by religion or belief gets protected under the Convention'.[208] Thus, a symbol first has to qualify as manifesting a religion or belief in terms of Article 9. Another aspect often emphasized is that the freedom of religion does not protect at all times the right to manifest religion or belief *in public*. Indeed, the distinction between the private and public sphere is relevant for the imposition of limitations. It is not difficult to imagine that manifesting religion or belief while exercising a public function might be limited by virtue of the public character of the function.

5.6.2 Neutrality of the state towards the public official

The previous chapters explained that the two points of contention regarding the relation between the state and the public official revolved around equal treatment and personification. The argument that a policy pursuing equal treatment of public officials not only leaves room for, but even requires prohibiting them from displaying religious symbols, is informed by a formal conception of equality. It is this conception

---

207 *Konttinen v. Finland* (ECnHR 1996); *Vogt v. Germany* (ECtHR 1995).
208 E.g. *Leyla Şahin v. Turkey* (ECtHR [Grand Chamber] 2005), para. 105.

that encroaches on public officials' religious freedom, rather than a substantive conception. The latter would after all specifically take into account any disparate impact which such a policy might have on particular groups. In light of this larger encroachment, the question is whether this conception has been endorsed within the ECHR framework. In the same vein, the argument that, in personifying the state, the public official is to refrain from manifesting his religion or belief underlies the limitation of his religious freedom. Accordingly, it should be examined to what extent the supervisory bodies have endorsed these arguments. Generally, it can be stated that there have been cases supporting each line of argument. As such, the limitation of public officials' freedom to manifest religion or belief based either on a formal equal treatment argument or on a personification argument do not necessarily contravene the Convention.

The previous sections have shown that two lines of case law are relevant for the point of equal treatment. The first one is based on the contractual duties by which an individual is bound when taking on a function. Naturally, public officials may have a special status in terms of employment law For instance, they may be subject to different rules of dismissal. Nonetheless, it is submitted that the thrust of the contractual duty line of case law may be relevant to the limitations of public officials' freedoms. This thrust is that contractual duties can justify religious manifestations being limited. The cases discussed mainly concerned religious activities conflicting with work schedules which had been agreed on at the outset of the employment. The contractual duties approach can be related to the broader perspective of the second line of case law based on the particular regime approach.

The 'particular regime' approach implies that, in entering a particular regime, an individual implicitly consents to the requirements of this regime, even when this means that these requirements encroach on his individual rights. This line of reasoning has mostly been applied in cases involving the military or education. In emphasizing an individual's voluntary compliance with the limitations of a particular regime, the ECHR bodies have accepted the legitimacy of such limitations. This is even more the case when they have found that an individual has the possibility of relinquishing that regime. In sum, in considering whether such a regime is applicable and capable of limiting individuals' rights, the ECHR bodies have looked at:

1. whether individuals chose to become part of the regime;
2. whether they truly had a choice; and
3. whether they were aware beforehand of the possible limitations.

Additionally, two things mitigate the particular regime approach. Firstly, it often went hand in hand with a constitutionally enshrined principle of secularism. Secondly, the ECHR bodies still paid regard to whether ample room for religious practice remained, so a blanket ban on religious manifestation does not emanate from the particular regime approach. In other words, contextual factors were looked at.

The point of personification can be discerned in the case law in favour of the position that public officials can be seen personifying the state. Public officials have been described as representatives of the state on numerous occasions.[209] More specifically, the supervisory bodies have considered it appropriate for a state to require public officials to have and testify to a certain allegiance to the state, for instance by way of a duty of loyalty. Such a duty can be an inherent condition of employment in public functions seeking to protect the general interest.[210]

It must be noted that such a duty holds specifically true in the case of civil servants, whose position can be said to differ significantly from the public officials examined in this study. Furthermore, some of the key cases involving loyalty concerned the question of political neutrality, which is charged with a different meaning from religious neutrality. Nonetheless, loyalty has been coupled with religious neutrality as well. In principle, the supervisory bodies have been critical towards too absolute an implementation of a duty of loyalty. For example, in the *Vogt* case, the Court found the German Government to have violated Article 10 by imposing a duty of loyalty on civil servants without having regard for specific factors such as the task being undertaken. On the other hand, the Court had less regard for such specific factors in the *Dahlab* case. The difference between the two cases is probably caused by the fact that the *Vogt* case concerned membership of a political party and the *Dahlab* case the wearing of the headscarf. In terms of proportionality, the supervisory bodies seem to ascribe less weight to having to take off a religious symbol than being limited in membership or activities.

5.6.3 Neutrality of the public official towards the citizen

The points of contention determining the interpretation of neutrality of the public official towards the citizen mainly turned on the safeguard of the citizen's rights, namely his right to equal treatment and his right to freedom of religion or belief. The position favouring limitations on the right of public officials to display religious symbols argued that such display might jeopardize the citizen's rights by conveying bias and possibly exerting improper influence. The points of contention have figured in the case law and appear to have been looked at in line with the above position.

The *Dahlab* case provides an exemplary instance of how the Court has dealt with these points of contention. The applicant's display of a religious symbol was assessed as to its impact on her relation with the pupils. Despite an intricate reasoning by the

---

209 E.g. *Dahlab v. Switzerland* (ECtHR 2001).
210 *Sidabras and Džiautas v. Lithuania*, (ECtHR, 2004). The Court reiterated that the requirement of an employee's loyalty to the State was an inherent condition of employment with State authorities responsible for protecting and securing the general interest, para. 57.

Court, it would not be too far-fetched to construe this line of reasoning as follows: a public official's neutrality towards the citizens may require the former to refrain from displaying a religious symbol. Basically, the Court inferred the effect of the headscarf on other individuals' right to equal treatment to be potential and indirect. It began by establishing that a headscarf 'appears to be imposed on women by a precept which is laid down in the Koran'.[211] This imposition brought the Court to find the headscarf 'hard to square' with the 'principle of gender equality'. It concluded this line of reasoning by stating 'it appeared difficult to reconcile the wearing of the headscarf with the message of … respect for others and, above all, equality and non-discrimination'.[212] In sum, in attributing a specific significance to the headscarf the Court rendered the symbol itself as incompatible with equality. Evidently, the wearing of such a symbol becomes similarly incompatible with equality. Additionally, the Court did not rule out that the headscarf might have a proselytising effect. It couched this possible effect in cautious terms, including a double negative and qualifying terms, in stating that 'it cannot be denied outright that the wearing of a headscarf might have some kind of proselytising effect'.[213]

It should be noted that the applicant's specific role as a teacher coupled with the relatively young age of the pupils were relevant for the outcome of this case. In other words, the decision cannot be applied with certainty to all public officials in all circumstances. It was pertinent that the applicant had the role of an exemplar for her pupils who were so young that they were found to be possibly vulnerable to external influences, especially those exerted by their teacher. Additionally, it is not clear how other contextual factors contribute in particular to the assessment of the proportionality of the measure. In the *Dahlab* case, the Court appeared to disregard that for years there had been no complaints about the teacher's headscarf or her performance in general. In addition, it did not examine to what extent the school environment or the curriculum could possibly compensate for the influence, if any, of the headscarf. However, it did look at such factors in other cases like the *Vogt* case or the later *Lautsi* case.

It should not be forgotten that contextual factors were significant for the Court in inferring that teachers displaying religious symbols might jeopardize pupils' rights and freedoms. Obviously, the domestic law was important. Additionally, it mattered that the manifestation in question was a headscarf and that the pupils were of a certain age. The *Ivanova* case, for instance, had already shown that the Court could strike a different balance of the factors in play.[214] It did not lightly accept limitations created by the applicant's membership of a religious organization. In the same vein,

---

211 *Dahlab v. Switzerland* (ECtHR 2001), p. 13.
212 Ibid.
213 It is remarkable how the Court deals differently with the lack of evidence in this case and in the *Lautsi* case, see also McGoldrick (2011), p. 487.
214 *Ivanova v. Bulgaria* (Appl. no. 52435/99 ECtHR, 12 April 2007).

in cases involving judges, such as the *Pitkevich* case, the Court emphasized that the applicant's impartiality should be presumed until there was proof to the contrary.[215]

5.6.4 Neutrality of the state towards the citizen

In the debate, arguments pointing to the relation between the state as an abstract entity and the citizen concerned the question as to how the state could best convey that it was equally available for all citizens. Briefly, two positions were put forward. One position argued that the state should reflect society in its diversity. By contrast, the other position was in favour of distance between the state and society: the latter could thrive in diversity but the former should be without colour so as to express its non-commitment to a single conviction. It would appear that the task of the supervisory bodies does not, in principle, equip them to promulgate a position regarding these points of contention. After all, their main task is to supervise the compatibility of domestic measures with the Convention. They do not, indeed should not, determine for instance how states should apply and interpret neutrality.[216] With that in mind, some observations can be made with respect to the points in question.

Before an evaluation of these observations is made, a comment is called for regarding the relation of the public official displaying a symbol to the image of the state. A preliminary question would be whether such a display would be capable in the first place of conveying the image of the state. In a way, this question can be related to the previous point of personification. It should therefore not be too surprising that the supervisory bodies have not rejected altogether a connection between a public official displaying a religious symbol and neutrality of the state. The *Dahlab* case again illustrates this point. What may be seen as remarkable is that the Court has not considered a crucifix hanging on a school wall as representing the state to a larger extent than a headscarf on a teacher's head. On the contrary, by underscoring that the headscarf was worn 'while teaching', the Court suggested the headscarf would therefore bear more on the task of teaching. However, it did not mention that a person wearing the headscarf exercises her personal rights, whereas a school displaying a crucifix could not rely on such rights. Nor did it suggest that the crucifix might be seen as more representative than the headscarf of how the state presents itself towards citizens. In sum, the 'image of the state' has certainly been found to find expression through the personal manifestation by public officials.

It is certain that the Court has called on states to *act* as a 'neutral and impartial organiser'.[217] This duty may entail that states are precluded from taking sides in disputes between religious communities. Additionally, the Court has linked the duty

---

215 *Pitkevich v. Russia* (ECtHR 2001).
216 As Judge Bonello eloquently implies in his dissenting opinion in the case of *Lautsi and others* (ECtHR [Grand Chamber] 2011)*,* para. 2.2.
217 See e.g. M.D. Evans (2009), p. 44, referring to *Metropolitan Church of Bessarabia v. Moldova.*

of neutrality to values of tolerance, pluralism and broadmindedness.[218] However, it has not been equally explicit on any possible implications for the image of the state. In other words, the Court has not commanded states to convey a plural image. Indeed, in accepting both exclusion and selective religious visibility, the image of the state does not seem decisive concerning whether the state upholds neutrality. Moreover, it should be kept in mind that neutrality is not necessarily an objective in and of itself. This emerges from the *Hauschildt* case that concerned the role of the judiciary. The Court explicitly considered the importance of the interest to inspire the public and the accused with confidence in the courts.[219] In other words, it is by creating this confidence that an image is preferred to be either blank or inclusive.

In quite a number of cases, the Court has accepted that a version of neutrality excluding religion can expressly serve to safeguard values of tolerance and pluralism. This is especially so when the state has implemented secularism as a constitutional principle and even more so when there are societal developments carrying the risk of religious radicalisation and extremism. On the other hand, the Court also seems to have accepted that a non-equitable visible representation by way of religious symbols, such as a crucifix, in State schools does not necessarily violate neutrality. Either way, it considers contextual factors that might outweigh the possibility that the display or exclusion of religious symbols might violate neutrality.[220] Such factors might include room for parents to educate their children according to their own insight, room to manifest religion or belief in other ways than by displaying a symbol, or room in general to display religious symbols.

For the relation between the state and the citizen, the other point of contention concerned the separation of church and state. While the Court has been unequivocal on democracy as the only political model that is compatible with the Convention, it has been less prescriptive on church–state models. As such, a variety of church–state models are compatible with the ECHR, including models with a strict version of secularism banning religion from public institutions. Consequently, a state requiring public institutions to be secular does not as such breach the Convention. Yet again, the circumstances of the case remain important for measures taken within such a model to be actually compatible with the Convention.

5.7 CONCLUSION

The present chapter has conducted an analysis of the ECHR case law in order to find out the minimum human rights standards which Member States have to meet when interfering with the freedom of religion or belief. In so doing, this chapter

---

218 E.g. *Leyla Şahin v. Turkey* (ECtHR [Grand Chamber] 2005), para. 108.
219 *Hauschildt v. Denmark* (ECtHR 1989), para. 48.
220 Cf. *Lautsi and others v. Italy* (ECtHR [Grand Chamber] 2011), paras. 74 and 75.

has specifically examined how state neutrality has been considered as justifying limitations on public officials to manifest their religion or belief by displaying symbols. One of the challenges in assessing limitations on the freedom of public officials to display religious symbols emanates from the indivisibility of the bringing about of state neutrality. More specifically, looking for the justification of limitations on public officials' freedom to display religious symbols also touches on the protection of citizens' religious freedom. The present chapter has found that, in the context of the Convention, state neutrality may justify but does not necessitate limitations on public officials' freedom to display religious symbols. Due to the wide margin of appreciation, states have a good deal of leeway to impose limitations. At the same time, although case law cannot serve to find general rules, it does point to some relevant factors to be taken into account when imposing such limitations. The wide margin of appreciation does not mean that anything goes.

Case law has confirmed that the point of departure remains that the public official can rely on his individual rights and freedoms, including the right to freedom of religion or belief. At the same time, the case law has shown that public officials' special status is relevant for the ways in which limitation of this freedom may be justified. To begin with, the protection of public officials' rights does not prevent a state from imposing conditions on holding a position in public service. When such conditions, for instance dress requirements, effectively result in restricted access, they can still be compatible with the Convention. Moreover, the supervisory bodies have accepted that contractual duties or particular regimes may preclude Article 9 from applying altogether. Limitations on the freedom to manifest religion or belief which are inherent to such particular regimes have been more likely to be accepted when these regimes were also entwined with constitutional principles like secularism.

When Article 9 does apply, the freedom to manifest religion or belief can obviously still be limited. Technically, it first has to be established that a particular religion or belief and a particular religious manifestation fall within the ambit of Article 9. In practice, however, the supervisory bodies have usually given little consideration to this point and have moved on to assessing the justification for limitations. The grounds for such limitations do not include state neutrality. Rather, state neutrality has been gradually developed as a general principle by the supervisory bodies of the Convention. With respect to limitations, they have mostly been read into the rights and freedoms of others. In assessing whether the requirements for the justification of limitations have been met, the supervisory bodies have generally focused on the question whether an interference was necessary in a democratic society. As has already been said, the wide margin of appreciation has appeared to leave a good deal of leeway to states and consequently more divergence has been allowed to creep in as regards the limitations on religious symbols. That said, the supervisory bodies have still looked at the proportionality of interference concerning which three findings can be pointed out regarding the issue of religious symbols in public functions.

Firstly, it should be noted that in comparison with other religious manifestations, being required to refrain from displaying religious symbols is not considered a far-reaching breach of an individual's religious freedom. Secondly, it was striking that the Court has paid attention to the type of religious symbol and the way in which it is displayed in order to determine the proportionality of prohibiting such a symbol. Thirdly, on the basis of these facts in combination with other contextual factors such as the age of pupils, the Court has presumed a religious symbol to have a particular effect.

Although the supervisory bodies have acknowledged in case law that the appearance of public services should not undermine public trust, they have not made specific statements as to how states should foster a neutral image which is in tune with the Convention. Clearly, the supervisory bodies have indicated how states are expected to act neutrally with regard to for instance religious communities, but they have not made such indications as to the neutral appearance of a state. As the *Lautsi* case illustrated, such reservation on the part of the Court may be caused by the risk of flying into the face of the domestic discretion of states. It is indeed an arduous task for the Court to make statements on the neutral appearance of states which vary enormously, as already shown, within Europe. The next two chapters deal with the two divergent systems included in this study, beginning with the French system.

CHAPTER 6
FRANCE

6.1 INTRODUCTION

In religion-related matters, France is seen as exemplifying an uncompromisingly exclusionary stance towards religion.[1] This image runs the risk of being too one-sided and stigmatizing France. Then again, governmental initiatives on the face veil, *laïcité*, and nationality do not help much in bringing across a more nuanced image of France. Indeed, the very reason for including France in this study is that France is positioned on the 'exclusive' end of the spectrum regarding religious symbols. What is more, the French approach has been a source of inspiration to Dutch proponents of limitations on religious symbols in public functions. Nonetheless, to the extent possible in being written by an outsider, this study attempts to avoid the pitfall of rigidly putting France in a box. The main question of this chapter is:

> How is state neutrality considered in the French context to justify and/or necessitate limitations on public officials in the judiciary, the police and public education to manifest their religion or belief by displaying symbols?

The present chapter begins with a mainly descriptive account of the relevant elements of the French context. More specifically, it explores the French context by briefly going over the elements, which also have been examined for the Netherlands. Accordingly, it first looks at religious freedom, the position of religion in the public sphere and state neutrality in France. Subsequently, it elaborates on public officials' freedom to manifest their religion or belief by wearing symbols in each of the three public functions being considered. It briefly explores which relevant issues have specifically emerged in French debate. Finally, it places the central issue against the background of the French context in making use of the conceptual model.

---

1   E.g. I. Rorive, 'Religious symbols in the public space: in search of a European answer.' (2009) 30(6) *Cardozo Law Review*, p. 2670; J. Temperman, *State-Religion Relationships and Human Rights Law: Towards a Right to Religiously Neutral Governance* (Martinus Nijhoff Publishers, Leiden/Boston 2010).

6.2 RELIGION IN FRANCE

This section revolves around the same notions as were discussed in the Dutch context. In French discourse, these notions are interconnected with each other, even more than in Dutch discourse. Therefore, the following subsections inevitably show some overlap.

6.2.1 Religious freedom

Protection of religious opinions was included in the fundamental text of the French Revolution, the 1789 Declaration of human and civic rights (*Déclaration des droits de l'homme et du citoyen*, hereinafter: 1789 Declaration).[2] Although the 1789 Declaration goes back more than two centuries, it is still relevant today. The present Constitution affirms the commitment of the French people to the rights proclaimed in the 1789 Declaration.[3] Furthermore, three things which are typical for the French approach to rights are illustrated by the 1789 Declaration.

First of all, individuals' liberty and equality before the law[4] were included in the first provision of the 1789 Declaration. This underscores the significance attributed to these rights, then and today. What is more, the definition of these rights at the time has been important for how they have been interpreted right up to the present time. Article 4 of the 1789 Declaration defines liberty as 'anything, which is not harmful to any other'.[5] Equality before the law ensues from the view that the law is the expression of the general will and must therefore be *similar* for everyone.[6] A second characteristic of the 1789 Declaration is that the origin of these rights was not explicitly traced back

---

2   Déclaration des droits de l'homme et du citoyen (1789 Declaration). An English translation can be found through e.g. the website of the Conseil Constitutionnel <www.conseil-constitutionnel.fr/ conseil-constitutionnel/root/bank_mm/ anglais/cst2.pdf>. The original text of Article 10: 'Nul ne doit être inquiété pour ses opinions, même religieuses, pourvu que leur manifestation ne trouble pas l'ordre public établi par la Loi.'

3   The Preamble of the Constitution states: 'Le peuple français proclame solennellement son attachement aux Droits de l'Homme et aux principes de la souveraineté nationale tels qu'ils ont été définis par la Déclaration de 1789....' The 1789 Declaration has been granted constitutional status by the Constitutional Council.

4   Article 1 of the 1789 Declaration reads: 'Les hommes naissent et demeurent libres et égaux en droit ....'

5   Article 4 of the 1789 Declaration reads: 'La liberté consiste à pouvoir faire tout ce qui ne nuit pas à autrui.'

6   Article 6 of the 1789 Declaration reads: 'La loi est l'expression de la volonté générale. ... Elle doit être la même pour tous ....' Additionally, it implied equal eligibility to public functions: 'Tous les citoyens, étant égaux à ses yeux, sont également admissibles à toutes dignités, places et emplois publics, ...' Equality has thus long since been an integral part of French constitutional and legal doctrine, see also D. McGoldrick, *Human Rights and Religion: The Islamic Headscarf Debate in Europe* (Hart Publishing, Oregon 2006), p. 41. The idea of the general will has been elaborated extensively by Jean-Jacques Rousseau, see J.-J. Rousseau, *Du contrat social* (Flammarion, Paris 1992), see in particular Livre II, p. 50 ff..

to a divine source, which would not have been uncommon for that period of time.[7] This omission illustrates the strained relations with religion and the church at the time, the legacy of which can still be seen today.[8] A final particularity of the French approach to rights, which may not be evident from the 1789 Declaration, is the role of the state in relation to individual rights. Usually, rights are understood as legal guarantees against the state. In France, however, rights have been considered as being guaranteed through the state.[9] It must be said though that the attribution of this very power to the state derives from the people. As mentioned before, the law binding the state is seen as expressing the general will. Indirectly, the state thus remains subject to this will.[10]

The period after the outbreak of the French Revolution was marked by contradictory developments. On the one hand, the 1801 Concordat between Napoleon and Pope Pius VII established an uneasy peace between the state and the Catholic Church.[11] On the other hand, division between the proponents and opponents of the Catholic Church kept growing, to the extent that the division has been labelled the War of the Two Frances.[12] When the opponents gained ground at the end of the nineteenth century, they managed to pass a seminal piece of legislation: the 1905 Law on Separation of Church and State (*Loi du 9 décembre 1905 concernant la séparation des Eglises et de l'Etat*, hereinafter: 1905 Law). This Law linked the protection of freedom of conscience to the separation of church and state, besides codifying some important arrangements. Examples of such arrangements were the end to state funding of religious communities, and the property assignment of religious buildings to the state.[13] The 1905 Law was a landmark in the legal protection of freedom of conscience. In the first provision, it straightforwardly declared that 'the Republic ensures freedom of conscience'.[14] Today, legal protection of the freedom of

---

7   Although the Preamble of the 1789 Declaration mentions the Supreme Being, it does not explicitly qualify the Supreme Being as the author, unlike the 1776 American Declaration of Independence which referred to the Creator as endowing men with rights, see J. Baubérot, 'The Place of Religion in Public Life: the Lay Approach', in: T. Lindholm, W. Cole Durham Jr. and B.G. Tahzib-Lie (eds), *Facilitating Freedom of Religion or Belief: a Deskbook* (Nijhoff, Leiden 2004), p. 442.

8   The 1795 Constitution can likewise be considered as deriving from the people, see McGoldrick (2006), p. 35.

9   E.g. M. Troper, 'Constitutional Law' in G.A. Bermann and E. Picard (eds), *Introduction to French law* (Kluwer Law International, Alphen aan den Rijn 2008), p. 16; D. Lyon and D. Spini. 'Unveiling The Headscarf Debate' (2004) 12(3) *Feminist Legal Studies*, p. 335, McGoldrick (2006), p. 44.

10   This is still the case today, see Troper in Bermann and Picard (eds) (2008), p. 4.

11   See McGoldrick (2006), p. 35.

12   J. Baubérot, *Histoire de la laïcité en France* (Que sais-je? 2nd edn Presses Universitaires de France, Paris 2004), p. 31. Reality of course went beyond this simple antagonism: differences within both groups also existed, and several generations, nuances and contexts must be distinguished, see G. Bedouelle and J.P. Costa, *Les laïcités à la française* (Politique d'aujourd'hui, Presses Universitaires de France, Paris 1998), p. 38.

13   Article 2 and Title II respectively.

14   Article 1, original text: 'La République assure la liberté de conscience. Elle garantit le libre exercice

conscience can also be found in Article 1 of the present Constitution of 1958. Apart from making explicit the laic character of the Republic, this provision declares that '[France] respects all beliefs'.[15] The Constitutional Council has confirmed freedom of conscience to be a fundamental principle.[16]

A brief remark on the term 'freedom of conscience' is in order. The terminology does not seem to be accidental and instead appears to be typical for French discourse. Freedom of conscience refers mainly to the *forum internum* of the freedom of religion. While there has been some debate on the specificity of the freedom of conscience vis-à-vis the freedom of opinion,[17] the former has been presented as being a form of the latter. The freedom of religion in terms of manifestation is aligned with the freedom of expression.[18]

Although the Constitution thus includes the freedom of conscience, it does not include a further catalogue of fundamental rights, in contrast with other countries.[19] It only establishes that statutes can lay down civil rights and fundamental guarantees.[20] Nonetheless, fundamental rights are given effect by international human rights conventions, the major ones of which France is a party to.[21] French law attributes self-executing force to the norms of international human rights instruments: once an international treaty has been published in the Official Journal, individuals can rely on it in court.[22] European and international treaties and agreements prevail over national legislation, whether enacted before or after that legislation.[23] Furthermore, as an EU

---

des cultes sous les seules restrictions édictées ci-après dans l'intérêt de l'ordre public.'

15 Article 1, original text: 'La France est une République indivisible, laïque, démocratique et sociale. Elle assure l'égalité devant la loi de tous les citoyens sans distinction d'origine, de race ou de religion. Elle respecte toutes les croyances. Son organisation est décentralisée.' For the legislative history of the constitutional principle of laïcité, e.g. H. Prélot, 'Définir juridiquement la laïcité' in G. Gonzalez (ed), *Laïcité, liberté de religion et Convention européenne des droits de l'homme* (Droit et justice edn Nemesis - Bruylant, Brussels 2005), p. 116 ff.

16 Conseil Constitutionnel, 23 November 1977, Décision no. 77-87 DC <www.conseil-constitutionnel.fr>.

17 E.g. D. Lochak, 'For intérieur et liberté de conscience' in Centre universitaire de recherches administratives et politiques de Picardie (ed), *Le for intérieur* (Presses Universitaires de France, Paris 1995), pp. 183-184.

18 E.g. V. Saint-James, 'La liberté religieuse du fonctionnaire' (2005) 12 *La Semaine Juridique - Administrations et Collectivités Territoriales*, p. 1143.

19 N. Guimezanes, *Introduction au droit français* (2ⁿᵈ edn Nomos, Baden-Baden 1999), p. 64.

20 Article 34 of the Constitution.

21 For instance, France ratified the ECHR on 3 May 1974, See Chart of signatures and ratifications on the website of the ECtHR, on <conventions.coe.int/Treaty/Commun/QueVoulezVous.asp?NT=005 &CL =ENG>.

22 Although the courts decide whether the convention is directly applicable when an individual invokes it. The only limitation on self-execution is the common-sense limitation that the treaties must be ratified or approved by the French Government, see M. Saxena, 'The French Headscarf Law and the Right to Manifest Religious Belief' (2007) in 84 (5) *University of Detroit Mercy Law Review*, p. 784. Additionally, the Constitutional Court can be requested to verify whether a treaty is consistent with the French Constitution.

23 Article 55 of the Constitution determines: 'Les traités ou accords régulièrement ratifiés ou approuvés

Member State, France is bound to implement the various EU Equality Directives. While the implementation of these directives has not been without difficulties,[24] non-discrimination norms are inevitably gaining importance, although the norms are still scattered throughout various sources.[25] In general, it can be established that France adopts a repressive approach towards discrimination mainly by means of criminal law and employment law.[26] In 2004, France showed its commitment to combating discrimination by assigning an independent administrative authority with this task: *Haute Autorité de Lutte contre les Discriminations et pour l'Égalité* (HALDE).[27] This body was responsible for fighting all forms of discrimination and it also dealt with individual complaints. In March 2011, a new law transferred the competences of HALDE to a new institution called the Defender of Rights (*Défenseur des droits*).[28] While HALDE has had considerable impact on the public debate, it remains to be seen whether the Defender of Rights will have a comparable impact.[29] On a legal level, it should be noted that disputes turning on religious freedom have been adjudicated on the basis of the freedom of religion or belief or state neutrality rather than on anti-discrimination norms.[30]

Like the Netherlands, France has not remained free from societal changes which have affected the protection of religious freedom. These changes also relate to religion as a sociological factor and to the demography of the French population. With regard to the first point, the Catholic Church has been confronted with a process of internal secularization while the previously strong antipathy to the Catholic Church has abated. Otherwise, a more general trend of secularization can be observed; for instance, the younger people tend to abandon religion.[31] France has also witnessed demographic

---

ont, dès leur publication, une autorité supérieure à celle des lois, sous réserve, pour chaque accord ou traité, de son application par l'autre partie.'

24   In 2007, France received a reasoned opinion of the European Commission that it had not transposed Council Directive 2000/43/EC of 29 June 2000 (Racial Equality Directive) correctly, see European Union Agency for Fundamental Rights, 'Annual Report' < fra.europa.eu>, p. 19.

25   See for the proper implementation of the Racial Equality Directive Loi no 2008-496 du 27 mai 2008 portant diverses dispositions d'adaptation au droit communautaire dans le domaine de la lutte contre les discriminations (Journal Officiel de la République Française (JORF), 28 May 2008).

26   F. Curtit, 'Egalité vs. non-discrimination. Primauté du principe d'égalité en droit français' in M. Hill (ed), *Religion and discrimination law in the European Union. La discrimination en matière religieuse dans l'union européenne* (Institute for European Constitutional Law, University of Trier, Trier 2012), p. 150.

27   See also F. Gaudu, 'Labor Law and Religion' (2009) 30(507) *Comparative Labor Law & Policy Journal*, p. 525.

28   French Constitution, Article 71-1, see <www.defenseurdesdroits.fr>. See also Curtit in Hill (ed) (2012), p. 148.

29   Ibid.

30   Curtit in Hill (ed) (2012), p. 154.

31   See E. McCaffrey, 'The Return of Faith and Reason to Laïcité: Régis Debray and "le fait religieux"' (2005) 16(3) *French cultural studies*, p. 281. Although she also points out that religious belief itself has not been eclipsed, see, p. 274. Here, reference can also be made to the increasing interest

change in the form of considerable waves of immigrants[32] during the 20th century, prompted by labour needs and decolonization. While during World War I and after World War II, these waves mainly came from neighbouring countries, later on they came from predominantly Muslim countries in the Maghreb.[33] Consequently, these later waves of immigration mainly brought Islam with them.[34] France had already been acquainted with this religion through colonization in the nineteenth century,[35] which had not exactly entailed a positive association with Islam.[36]

The French Government has responded variably to immigration; sometimes it had a liberal policy[37] and at other times it tightened its policy.[38] The response of the Government as well as the immigrants' expectations has had an influence on the accommodation of religious practices. Initially, neither party had thought that the immigrants would stay permanently. Accordingly, the immigrants did not make any

---

in Buddhism and the emergence of personal spirituality, see F.M. Gedicks (2006), 'Religious Exemptions, Formal Neutrality, and *Laïcité*' (2006) 13(2) *Indiana Journal of Global Legal Studies*, p. 484.

32 Since the 19th century immigration had been maintained at a high level due to a declining population, which then made the import of foreign labour necessary during a period of industrialization, see R. Zauberman and R. Lévy, 'Police, minorities, and the French Republican ideal' (2003) 41(4) *Criminology*, p. 1069. Costa-Lascoux points out that at that time France was an immigration country but, unlike the United States, it did not turn into an immigrants' nation. Immigrants became part of the national community. This resounds with France's intention to become a diverse and heterogeneous immigration country, but not a multi-ethnic society, see J. Costa-Lascoux, 'Het individu en de godsdienstvrijheid beschermd. *Laïcité* en burgerschap in Frankrijk' in M. ten Hooven and T.W.A. de Wit (eds), *Ongewenste goden: de publieke rol van religie in Nederland* (Sun, Amsterdam 2006), pp. 152-153.

33 J.S. Fetzer and J.C. Soper, *Muslims and the State in Britain, France, and Germany* (Cambridge University Press, Cambridge 2005), p. 63. For a period during the 1920s, France was the number one host country in the world to immigrants, see Zauberman and Lévy (2003), p. 1069.

34 Although other religions have also emerged, such as Buddhism, see e.g. J. Baubérot, who refers to the rise of Buddhism in France, which is capable of a certain degree of expression in the public sphere, see Baubérot in Lindholm, Cole Durham Jr. and Tahzib-Lie (eds) (2004), p. 449.

35 Fetzer and Soper (2005), p. 63.

36 The historic colonial bonds and the way in which the Algerian War of Independence had been waged has imbued the French perception of Islam, see e.g. Fetzer and Soper (2005), p. 64.

37 Especially towards the immigrants coming from neighbouring countries, see J.E. Jenkins, *West Africans in Paris: an assessment of French immigration policies in the 1960s and 1970s* (VDM Verlag Dr. Müller, Saarbruecken 2008), p. 19. Also at the end of the 19th century and the beginning of the 20th century, many immigrants came from Europe. The origin of these immigrants favoured their integration. For many of them, it was relatively easy to learn the language and often they were also Catholics, Bedouelle and Costa (1998), p. 227. During the 1970s, immigration numbers greatly increased because of the oil crisis of 1974, see Bedouelle and Costa (1998); Zauberman and Lévy (2003), p. 1070 and Fetzer and Soper (2005), p. 64. See p. 65 for the efforts made by the Immigration Minister in both trying to bribe and force immigrants to return.

38 Fetzer and Soper (2005), p. 64 The first efforts to start limiting immigration date back to the 1930s. Measures were connected to the economic situation and rising xenophobia. See also E.R. Thomas, *Immigration, Islam and the Politics of Belonging in France. A Comparative Framework* (University of Pennsylvania Press, Philadelphia 2012), p. 78 ff.

real effort to have their religious needs met[39] and the Government did not make any real attempt to meet these needs either.[40] When in response to the limitations imposed on immigration during the 1970s immigrants decided to stay permanently,[41] France was faced with the challenge of how to accommodate the immigrants' needs in a more structured way.[42] This challenge ensued amongst other things from the different way in which immigrants dealt with religious practice. For instance, while not all French Muslims were practising believers, as a whole they did appear to practise their religion more actively than French Catholics.[43] The French approach to accommodating immigrants' religious needs cannot be seen separately from its approach towards citizenship. Therefore, the next section briefly explains this approach.

6.2.2 State–citizen relation

The way in which France construes citizenship and the relation between the individual and the state is essential for how France deals with religious minorities. To begin with, the concept of the state is powerful in French thought, which thinks of the state as nearly tangible.[44] The very basis for the conception of the state is the ideology of

---

39 Fetzer and Soper (2005), p. 64.

40 L. Michalak and A. Saeed, 'The Continental Divide: Islam and Muslim Identities in France and the United States' in N. AlSayyad and M. Castells (eds), *Muslim Europe or Euro-Islam: Politics, Culture, and Citizenship in the Age of Globalization* (Lexington Books ; [etc.], Lanham, MD 2002), p. 157.

41 Before that period, many immigrants had remained mobile between France and their country of origin. The measures tightening immigration caused them to fear that they would not be let back into France once they wanted to return, see Zauberman and Lévy (2003), p. 1070. This time they brought over their family members, Fetzer and Soper (2005), p. 64.

42 A factor complicating integration of immigrants at that time was the collapse of the economy, which increased the levels of unemployment among immigrant workers. This was contrary to the experience of the immigrants who came in the interwar period and right after the war, who benefited from important integrative mechanisms such as education, see Zauberman and Lévy (2003), p. 1070-7071. Kastoryano identifies Islam as constituting a two-fold challenge, albeit to *laïcité* (but which can be related to France's church–state arrangement as well): Muslims constitute a minority and Islam has a public expression, see R. Kastoryano, 'French secularism and Islam: France's headscarf affair' in T. Modood, A. Triandafyllidou and R. Zapata-Barrero (eds), *Multiculturalism, Muslims and Citizenship: a European Approach* (Routledge, London 2006), p. 62.

43 E.g. Fetzer and Soper (2005), p. 77. Willa endorses the observation that Muslims may be less observant than generally assumed, by referring to research results showing that the number of Muslims who actually practise their faith is small, although the source he relies on dates back to 1985, see J.P. Willaime, '*Laïcité* et religion en France', in G. Davie and D. Hervieu-Léger (eds), *Identités religieuses en Europe* (La Découverte, Paris 1996), p. 169.

44 Influential sociologists and lawyers have helped in shaping this conception of the state, see for a historical account, J. Terrier. 'The idea of a Republican tradition: Reflections on the debate concerning the intellectual foundations of the French Third Republic.' (2006) 11(3) *Journal of political ideologies*, p. 299 ff.

Republicanism,[45] which posits definite premises on the state and the individual, three of which can be mentioned as having an impact on how immigrants are dealt with.

First of all, one of the ideals emanating from the French Revolution characterizes individuals as citizens who have a direct link with the state without any groups acting as an intermediary. What is more, the formation of groups based on ethnicity, culture or any other common trait, which has been labelled as *communautarisme*,[46] is looked at with disfavour. French discourse regards *communautarisme* as a force undermining national cohesion.[47] In order to foster such cohesion, French discourse instead emphasizes that national identity should prevail over individual characteristics of any kind.[48] Access to citizenship is seen as the best means to accomplish integration of immigrants;[49] French nationality is obtained on the principle of *jus soli*.[50] The French approach of integrating immigrants has been labelled as assimilation,[51] which emphasizes that subordinating their individual characteristics to national identity could be seen as giving up their cultures of origin.[52] It must be noticed though that such assimilation exclusively applies to those trying to obtain French nationality.[53]

The second premise of Republican theory is that it does not recognize the concept of minorities, whether conceptually, politically or legally.[54] This is connected to the aversion to the already mentioned *communautarisme*. Consequently, when ratifying

---

45 See also S. Poulter, 'Muslim Headscarves in Schools: Contrasting Legal Approaches in England and France' (1997) 17(43) *Oxford Journal of Legal Studies*, p. 50.

46 This is again a French term for which there is no exact English equivalent.

47 E.g. the report Rapport du groupe de travail, présidé par A. Rossinot, 'La laïcité dans les services publics' (2006), p. 8.

48 Poulter (1997), p. 50 and McGoldrick (2006), p. 42. See also Costa-Lascoux who discusses this distinction between citizenship and (personal) identity, Costa-Lascoux in Ten Hooven and De Wit (2006), pp. 156-157. As Terrier also emphasizes, France is the archetype of a civic nation. This means that nationality is formed by the decision to form a nationality, which is a decision made by the corporate will, see Terrier (2006), p. 290.

49 McGoldrick (2006), p. 44. See also Zauberman and Lévy (2003), p. 1066. A book about nationality, immigration and citizenship is e.g. P. Weil, *Qu'est-ce qu'un français? Histoire de la nationalité française depuis la Révolution* (revised edn, Gallimard, 'Folio Histoire', Paris, 2005); translated in English: C. Porter (tr), *How to be French. Nationality in the Making since 1789*, Durham, De University Press, 2008.

50 See Zauberman and Lévy (2003), p. 1079. The first law on *jus soli* dates back to 1851, see Costa-Lascoux in Ten Hooven and De Wit (2006), p. 152.

51 Kastoryano in Modood, Triandafyllidou, Zapata-Barrero (eds) (2006), p. 62. See also L. Molokotos Liederman, 'Pluralism in Education: the display of Islamic affiliation in French and British schools' (2000) 11(1) *Islam and Christian-Muslim Relations*, p. 113.

52 Michalak and Saeed in AlSayyad and Castells (eds) (2002), p. 155.

53 E.g. *Code civil*, Article 21-4, which lays down the competence of the Government to bar an individual from obtaining French nationality for failing to assimilate. Original text: 'Le Gouvernement peut s'opposer par décret en Conseil d'Etat, pour … défaut d'assimilation, … à l'acquisition de la nationalité française par le conjoint étranger …'.

54 McGoldrick (2006), pp. 43 and 48. Kastoryano in Modood, Triandafyllidou, Zapata-Barrero (eds) (2006), p. 62.

the International Covenant on Civil and Political Rights, France declared Article 27 on the protection of minorities' identity to be inapplicable.[55] Some commentators have pointed to particularities of French language as typifying the French approach, such as the lack of hyphenated identities[56] or the lack of a proper equivalent of the term 'ethnicity'.[57] It is true that French public statistics disregard ethnicity or religion of the population.[58] Nonetheless, it should be noted that, in practice, French policy has not remained free from recognizing minorities. For instance, the state negotiates with religious groups, dietary requirements are accommodated and religious holidays other than the official ones are recognized.[59]

The third point of the French Republican ideology is connected to the second one. If there were to be any individual feature taken into account in discussions of migration and citizenship, it would be religious identity rather than ethnic identity.[60] Evidently, despite its controversial role, religion at least had a significant role during French history. Therefore, religion is a concept which French discourse is more at ease with than the concept of ethnicity.[61] This focus on religion entails for instance viewing Muslims as one group, regardless of their ethnic background. However, the French Muslims come from parts as various as North Africa and Turkey,[62] and they do not see themselves as one group. The various immigrant groups do not cooperate that much with each other either,[63] although many Muslim organizations have been established.[64] It is reasonable to suppose that such diffusion has not been beneficial to immigrants' emancipation.

---

55 The text of the reservation reads 'In the light of article 2 of the Constitution of the French Republic, the French Government declares that article 27 is not applicable so far as the Republic is concerned.' To be found on the website of the UN Treaty Collection <treaties.un.org >.

56 Michalak and Saeed in AlSayyad and Castells (eds) (2002), p. 154 and Kastoryano in Modood, Triandafyllidou, Zapata-Barrero (eds) (2006), p 62.

57 *Ethnie* is associated with tribes. See Michalak and Saeed in AlSayyad and Castells (eds) (2002), p. 154.

58 Zauberman and Lévy (2003), p. 1066.

59 McGoldrick (2006), p. 50. Furthermore, during the 1950s and 1960s France introduced quotas for Algerians for specific positions. In addition, some policies are indirectly aimed at minorities, such as the designation of 'educational priority zones', see E.S. Langan, 'Assimilation and Affirmative Action in French Education Systems.' (2008) 40(3) *European education*, pp. 51 and 52.

60 Michalak and Saeed in AlSayyad and Castells (eds) (2002), p. 151. Otherwise, immigration-related problems have been looked at through the lens of socio-economic problems, Zauberman and Lévy (2003), p. 1083.

61 See e.g. Michalak and Saeed in AlSayyad and Castells (eds) (2002), p. 151. The headscarf affair attested to the French uneasiness with the notion of race, see Molokotos Liederman (2000), p. 112.

62 E.g. SOPEMI (Système d'observation permanente des migrations), 'Immigration et présence etrangère en France en 2010' Secretariat Général à l'Immigration et à l'Intégration Ministère de l'Intérieur, de l'Outre-Mer, des Collectivités Territoriales et de l'Immigration (Paris) <www.immigration.gouv.fr> under Ressources - Etudes et documents.

63 Michalak and Saeed in AlSayyad and Castells (eds) (2002), p. 160. See also McGoldrick (2006), pp. 54-55.

64 These organizations did not really cooperate either. It was not until 2003 that one representative

171

After this brief discussion of the particular French approach to the state–citizen relation, the next section examines the state–religion relation. While it cannot do full justice to the ever-complex dynamics of history, it focuses on highlighting some aspects of importance for the study.

6.2.3 The position of religion in the public sphere

Before the Revolution, state and church had been involved in bitter conflict for centuries.[65] During the French Revolution, more extreme forms of secularism had emerged; a civil religion was even proclaimed.[66] Despite moderate forces, the Revolution indirectly aimed at reducing the influence of the Catholic Church. The Revolution aspired to end the legal arrangements, including privileges, of the Catholic Church which were in place during past centuries (*Ancien Régime*).[67] When the more moderate forces which were anticlerical[68] rather than antireligious gained ground, they gradually managed to eradicate religious influence from the domain

---

body, the Conseil français du culte musulman, was established, see Fetzer and Soper (2005), p. 91.
65 Ibid, p. 34.
66 See Willaime in Davie and Hervieu-Léger (eds) (1996), p. 158. That the supporters truly aspired to a religion was evident from the instauration of ceremonies such as Festival for the Goddess of Reason, see Fetzer and Soper (2005), p. 69. See also J. Baubérot, 'Secularism and French Religious Liberty: A Sociological and Historical View' (2003) 2 *Brigham Young University Law Review*, p. 460. In addition, a Republican calendar was introduced, see Willaime in Davie and Hervieu-Léger (eds) (1996), p. 162. Generally, the French Enlightenment proved to be more radical than the British or German Enlightenment, which only sought an enlightened religion, see Baubérot in Lindholm, Cole Durham Jr. and Tahzib-Lie (eds) (2004), p. 442.
67 McGoldrick (2006), p. 34. Or in Baubérot's words: 'the French Enlightenment proved more radical' in its conflict with the Catholic Church, Baubérot in Lindholm, Cole Durham Jr. and Tahzib-Lie (eds) (2004), p. 442. He has equally pointed out that modernity in France proceeded against faith, in contrast with Protestant countries where religion has been 'integral to the emergence of modernity', p. 441. See also O. Roy, *Secularism confronts Islam* (G. Holoch (tr) Columbia University Press, New York, N.Y. 2007), p. viii. Willaime in Davie and Hervieu-Léger (eds) (1996), p. 156. As Fetzer and Soper note: 'Even in the largely "post-Christian" Western Europe, France stands out in the extent to which it has become thoroughly secularized', Fetzer and Soper (2005), p. 77. F. Messner, P.H. Prélot, J.M. Woehrling (eds), *Traité de droit français des religions* (LexisNexis Litec, 2003), p. 87.
68 See D. Saunders, 'France on the knife-edge of religion: commemorating the centenary of the law of 9 December 1905 on the separation of church and state' in G.B. Levey and T. Modood, *Secularism, religion and multicultural citizenship* (Cambridge University Press, Cambridge 2009), p. 78 and Willaime in Davie and Hervieu-Léger (eds) (1996), p. 156. On p. 155 he quotes Alain Boyer, who remarked that the literal meaning of *laïcité* confirms this, since a laic is the one who is not a priest. See also McGoldrick (2006), p. 35. This remark has also been made by Bedouelle and Costa, see Bedouelle and Costa (1998), p. 9. Another point is that although foreign evaluations in particular of the French church system are not too positive in relation to religious tolerance, Robert states that the French regime is by no means hostile to but rather tolerant of religion, see J. Robert, 'Religious Liberty and French Secularism' (2003) *Brigham Young University Law Review*, p. 639. P. Weil, 'Why the French laïcité is liberal' (2008-2009) 30(6) *Cardozo Law Review*, p. 2703.

of the state by the end of the nineteenth century.[69] The beginnings of removing the influence of the church were made in the field of education. As a matter of fact, education was at the heart of the political project of realizing national integration.[70] It had a fundamental role in the laic state in conveying Republican values such as individualism and equality and a sense of citizenship;[71] teachers had an essential role in implementing this endeavour.[72] Pupils were encouraged to use the faculty of reason, which enabled them to critically question belief.[73]

In 1833, a law (*loi Guizot*) established state primary education and in 1850, another law (*loi Falloux*) extended state education to a secondary level.[74] In the 1880s, the then Education Minister, Jules Ferry, introduced several laws, secularizing or laicizing[75] education. The law of 28 March 1882 envisaged the laicization of education and introduced moral and civic instruction.[76] This instruction was to be mandatory whereas the state school was to be free and *laïque*.[77] The law also provided for one additional free day per week in order to allow parents to have their children instructed in religion.[78]

As mentioned, in 1905 the Law on the separation of church and state was adopted.[79] Apart from underscoring respect for the freedom of conscience, it included

---

69 See e.g. Willaime in Davie and Hervieu-Léger (eds) (1996), pp. 153-154.
70 C. Lelièvre, 'The French model of the educator state.' (2000) 15(1) *Journal of education policy*, p. 5. This article also makes the suggestion that even during the 'Ancien Régime' around the 18th century there were projects of public instruction or national education. Furthermore, the school has provided the battleground for the conflict of the two Frances, see McGoldrick (2006), p. 77 and Saunders in Levey and Modood (eds) (2009), p. 61.
71 See e.g. McGoldrick (2006), pp. 77-78, Langan (2008), p. 49. For two centuries education has also been the most discordant area as to *laïcité* of the state, see Bedouelle and Costa (1998), p. 91 and Saunders in Levey and Modood (eds) (2009), p. 61. Willaime in Davie and Hervieu-Léger (eds) (1996), p. 161. Kastoryano in Modood, Triandafyllidou, Zapata-Barrero (eds) (2006), p. 61. Commission de réflexion sur l'application du principe de laïcité dans la République, 'Rapport au President de la République' (Paris 2003) (Stasi Report) to be found e.g. on the website <www. ladocumentationfrancaise.fr>, para. 4.2.
72 J.R. Bowen, 'Why Did the French Rally to a Law Against Scarves in Schools?' (2008) 68 *Droit et société*, p. 38. Langan (2008), p. 50.
73 See e.g. McGoldrick (2006), p. 76. See also Baubérot (2003), p. 461. See also McCaffrey (2005), p. 283.
74 See Saunders in Levey and Modood (eds) (2009), p. 61.
75 These laws implemented *laïcité*, which will be explained further in Section 6.4.2. The word 'secularizing' might appear to be a poor equivalent, but is nonetheless used here since *laïcité* has not yet been explained.
76 Instead of the previous moral and religious instruction, see G. Haarscher, *La laïcité* (Que sais-je? Vendôme Impressions, Vendôme 2004), p. 28.
77 Baubérot, *Histoire de la laïcité* (2004), p. 47. Private education and even education at home remained.
78 Article 2, see also Bedouelle and Costa (1998), p. 93.
79 This was not done without long and fierce debate, see for a detailed description of the build-up to the law, the Report of the Council of State on *laïcité* (2004), p. 256 ff.

the separation of church and state by stipulating: 'the Republic does not recognize, remunerate or subsidize any religion'.[80] Additionally, the provision identified the main budgetary consequences, entailing above all the exclusion of expenses concerning religion from the budget of the state. The 1905 Law confirmed the dissociation of citizenship and religious adherence; thus religion lost its function of officially socializing citizens. Additionally, the Law ended public support for religious communities; from then on, religious communities were neither recognized nor financed or supported by the state. More generally, the 1905 Law was an important part of a gradual evolution which made France cease to define itself as a Catholic nation.[81] It has been pointed out, though, that it would be too simplistic to merely regard the Law as removing religion from the public sphere. Rather, the separation of church and state has been considered a way for the state to support and control religious institutions.[82] More specifically, separation of church and state in France has been regarded as protecting the state from the excesses of religion.[83]

Some aspects of current practice confirm that the separation of church and state should not be interpreted too rigidly. Firstly, the strictness of the separation should be put into perspective.[84] More specifically, there may be more room for financial mutual ties than suggested at first sight. For example, strictly speaking, the 1905 Law leaves room for the state to subsidize (non-religious) activities which happen to take place in religious buildings. In the same vein, the state can pay religious ministers when they perform a service for the general public.[85] In addition, the state can provide financial support for the maintenance of religious buildings from before 1905 as well as for chaplaincies. Secondly, the church–state arrangement does not apply to the region of Alsace-Moselle.[86] Since this study looks at the predominant French discourse, it leaves this region aside. Thirdly, as described before, the contemporary social context

---

80 Article 2, original text: 'La République ne reconnaît, ne salarie ni ne subventionne aucun culte'.

81 Stasi Report (2003), Première Partie, para. 1.1.

82 See Bowen (2008), p. 40. After 1905, the sentiments against the Church eased. In addition, France has made a distinction between religion and sect, so in fact it has strictly been engaged in developing distinctions among religions, Gedicks (2006), p. 484.

83 As opposed to the United States, where the wall of separation seeks to protect religion from the excesses of the state, see T.J. Gunn, 'Under God but Not the Scarf: The Founding Myths of Religious Freedom in the United States and Laïcité in France' (2004) 46 *Journal of Church & State*, p. 9. The Stasi Commission has emphasized the mutuality of the separation, see Stasi Report (2003), p. 13.

84 Commission nationale consultative des droits de l'homme (CNCDH), 'La laïcité aujourd'hui' (2003), Fiche 2, para. 3. Nonetheless, Robert puts forward the view that the previously formally recognized religions, the Catholic Church, the Reformed Church, the Lutheran Church and Judaism, are still de facto recognized, see Robert (2003), p. 647.

85 Robert, p. 641. See also M. Troper, 'Sovereignty and laïcité' (2009) 30(6) *Cardozo Law Review*, p. 2563. See also Bowen (2008), p. 41.

86 E.g. Willaime in Davie and Hervieu-Léger (eds) (1996), p. 155. It still has a Concordat system. See for a comparison between the laic laws of France and the concordatarian laws of Alsace, J.M. Woehrling, 'Réflexions sur le principe de la neutralité de l'état en matière religieuse et sa mise en oevre en droit français' (1998) 101 *Archive de sciences sociales des religions*.

is rather different from the one in 1905. The role of the Catholic Church has changed, as has religion as a sociological factor and the demography of the French population. Therefore, as can be imagined, the implementation of the separation of church and state has faced contemporary challenges, at some points resulting in accommodation, which may be interpreted as being incompatible with the separation. The recognition of religious holidays other than the official ones has already been mentioned. Another example of accommodation is providing chaplaincy service to citizens in public institutions who are precluded from normally manifesting their religion or belief, such as prisoners.[87]

Anyhow, no discussion of the contemporary religion–state relation in France can be had without mentioning the principle of *laïcité*. Article 1 of the Constitution qualifies the French Republic as *laïque*.[88] Whereas the complexity of this paramount principle is evident from the numerous monographs written on it,[89] the next section attempts to highlight some important aspects.

6.2.4 State neutrality

French discourse has invariably entwined *laïcité* and neutrality, although the way in which it has conceptualized the precise link between those two concepts varies.[90] The former notion is complex in terms of conceptualization as well as of definition. It begins with the difficulty of translating the principle in English. Basically, no English translation can actually fully cover the purport of this principle,[91] although 'secularism' or 'secularity'[92] has been offered as an equivalent, poor as it may be. In line with the specificity of the French term, the purport has been abstractly explained as the specifically French understanding of the proper place and function of religion within the state.[93] Is *laïcité* exclusively French?[94] Strictly speaking, it is

---

87   E.g. R. Schwartz, *Un siècle de laïcité* (Le point sur, Berger-Levrault, Paris 2007), p. 109 ff.
88   Original text of Article 1: 'La France est une République indivisible, laïque, démocratique et sociale.'
89   E.g. Baubérot, *Histoire de la laïcité* (2004) and Bedouelle and Costa (1998).
90   In referring to Article 1 of the Constitution, Prélot has put forward the view that *laïcité* needs to be interpreted in the light of equality and respect for religious beliefs, which implies the confirmation of the religious neutrality of the state, see Prélot in Gonzalez (ed) (2005), p. 120. See also Saint-James (2005), para. 13. Stasi Report (2003), para. 1.2.1. G. Peiser, *Droit administratif général* (23rd edn Dalloz, Paris 2006), p. 151. See also CNCDH Report (2003), p. 15.
91   See e.g. McGoldrick (2006), p. 38; Gunn (2004), p. 8; Gedicks (2006), p. 475. Baubérot offers the term 'laicism', see Baubérot, in Lindholm, Cole Durham Jr. and Tahzib-Lie (eds) (2004), p. 441.
92   J.P. Willaime, 'European Integration, Laïcité and Religion' in L.N. Leustean and J.T.S. Madeley (eds), *Religion, Politics and Law in the European Union* (Routledge, Abingdon, 2010), p. 20.
93   McGoldrick (2006), p. 38.
94   Bedouelle points out that although *laïcité* is nowhere else experienced as in France, other countries, such as Belgium, Italy, Spain or Portugal, are familiar with similar debates, Bedouelle and Costa, p. 3.

not: other countries have also implemented *laïcité*, be it by imitation or export.[95] Furthermore, the ideas associated with *laïcité* resound in other states, such as in the United States, where the notion of the wall of separation between church and state is crucial.[96] Therefore, French discourse has used the term French singularity[97] rather than French exception.[98] Apart from the contested specificity of the principle, its nature is multifold. Whereas it is often understood as a political notion,[99] or a political and legal pact,[100] it has also been explained as encompassing other dimensions, such as a historical and philosophical one.[101] In any event, particular premises underlie the principle relating to a particular non-religious vision on the good, the world and man.[102] It has been stated that *laïcité* is most of all an ideal, rather than a legal norm.[103] Furthermore, it has been considered as being closely connected to other values, such as freedom of conscience, legal equality between spiritual and religious options and neutrality of the political power.[104]

---

95 E.g. in Turkey, where it is labelled with the related term 'laiklik'. See also Baubérot, who refers to research being done on Mexican and Quebec *laïcité*, see Baubérot, *Histoire de la laïcité* (2004), p. 116 and J. Baubérot, *Laïcité 1905-2005, entre passion et raison* (Seuil, Paris 2004), p. 10.

96 Although it has been suggested that the US is not a laic country, since it lacks the underlying ideological conviction of a non-religious vision of man and the world, see Willaime in Davie and Hervieu-Léger (eds) (1996), p. 156, and paragraphs below on *laïcité*.

97 Conseil d'Etat Report (2004), p. 359. It is not the concept as such which is unique, but rather its extensive codification. See also CNCDH Report (2003), Fiche 2, para. 2. Willaime highlights four 'singular' characteristics of France such as the strongly ideological nature of the problem of the influence of philosophical conceptions and political critiques of religions; and the more pronounced affirmation of the supremacy of the state and its influence on civil life, Willaime in Leustean and Madeley (eds) (2010), p. 19.

98 E.g. Lelièvre (2000), p. 8 and McCaffrey (2005), p. 274.

99 Saxena (2007), p. 769.

100 Saunders in Levey and Modood (eds) (2009), p. 69.

101 Roy (2007), p. 34. Cf. Costa-Lascoux, who has distinguished philosophical and democratic aspects, and has labelled *laïcité* as an organizational principle, a moral conception of responsibility, a constitutional principle and a way of thinking and acting, Costa-Lascoux in Ten Hooven and De Wit (2006), pp. 157-158.

102 As Gedicks points out, the conception of the good in France is more substantive than that in the United States, Gedicks (2006), p. 476. The Stasi Commission also acknowledges that *laïcité* in fact translates as a conception of the common good, see Stasi Report (2003), introduction. Willaime in Davie and Hervieu-Léger (eds) (1996), p. 156. In a way, *laïcité* itself seems at times to have taken on almost a religious connotation, see for instance the phrasing of the oath taken by judges. And, as noted, during the Revolution some tendencies of secularism were so strong as to proclaim it a civil religion.

103 Rossinot Report (2006), p. 3.

104 Ibid, introduction. In para. 1.1. the Stasi Report also relates *laïcité* to wider values of respect and living together. See also Conseil d'Etat, 'Réflexions sur la laïcité. Considérations générales. Un siècle de la laïcité.' (2004), to be found on the website of the Conseil d'Etat <www.conseil-etat.fr>, p. 272, ff., which also mentions respect for pluralism.

The actual term '*laïcité*'[105] first appeared at the end of the nineteenth century during the first stage of *laicization* of the state in the context of public education.[106] Its long legacy notwithstanding, the exact meaning of *laïcité*[107] remains debatable and no formal definition has been officially established or generally accepted.[108] Be that as it may, two common elements can be identified. Firstly, *laïcité* concerns the separation of state and religion.[109] Such separation has been specified to mean the restraint of the state in recognizing and subsidizing any religion[110] and in exercising any religious power, while the churches are restrained in exercising political power.[111] Secondly, free exercise of religion is seen as inherent to *laïcité*. What is more, guaranteeing freedom of conscience is often considered to constitute the very rationale of the principle of *laïcité*.[112]

While the principle as it stands is thus already difficult to grasp, it is made even more so by the changing context.[113] Like this context, the principle has not stopped evolving.[114] The ongoing debate notwithstanding, the acceptance of the principle as

---

105 It is to be distinguished from 'laïcisme', which term had already been in existence since 1842 to describe a doctrine aiming at giving institutions a non-religious character, see Bedouelle and Costa (1998), p. 10.
106 See McGoldrick (2006), p. 38 and Bedouelle and Costa (1998), p. 10.
107 See Fetzer and Soper (2005), p. 71.
108 Saxena (2007), p. 769. McGoldrick expresses the difficulty of defining *laïcité* thus: '*laïcité* is a complex and ambiguous concept, and there has been an intense French debate as to its meaning and application in different contexts', McGoldrick (2006), p. 41. It is not an unequivocal concept and has inspired several conceptions, ranging from unitary to more pluralist ideas, see Bedouelle and Costa (1998), pp. 2, 6.
109 Roy referred to by Bowen (2008), p. 37. *Laïcité* is translated as a certain version of separationism between religion and state, see Fetzer and Soper (2005), p. 69.
110 See e.g. definition in Le Grand Robert, referred to in Fetzer and Soper (2005), p. 73: *Laïcité* could more appropriately be understood as free exercise of religion where the State neither recognizes nor subsidizes any religion. Or even more generally: separation of civil society and religious society, see Saxena (2007), p. 769.
111 'le principe de separation de la societé civile et de la societé religieuse, l'état n'exercant aucun pouvoir religieux et les eglises aune pouvoir politique', see Bedouelle and Costa (1998), pp. 11, 13-14.
112 E.g. McGoldrick (2006), pp. 39 and 65. Baubérot, *Histoire de la laïcité* (2004), p. 117. Bedouelle and Costa (1998), p. 3; Stasi Report (2003), para. 1.2.2; Gedicks (2006), p. 476, referring to Gunn. Strictly, Gunn speaks of the state protecting itself, (2004), p. 9. Many, mostly non-French, scholars do not emphasize this element of *laïcité*, which may explain why the assessment of *laïcité* outside France is not always that positive. See e.g. Baubérot, *Histoire de la laïcité*, p. 116 ff. More generally, *laïcité* outside France is rarely associated with religious tolerance, whereas within France this is more likely to occur. Although of course, within France as well, there are debates on the various interpretations of *laïcité*, see e.g. Molokotos Liederman (2000), p. 110.
113 See Kastoryano in Modood, Triandafyllidou, Zapata-Barrero (eds) (2006), p. 61. Baubérot, *Laïcité 1905-2005, entre passion et raison* (2004), p. 9. Fetzer and Soper (2005), pp. 73-76.
114 See Bedouelle and Costa (1998), p. 213. In a way, a more open *laïcité* has arisen, but then probably in comparison with its original meaning, see P. Birnbaum, 'On the secularization of the public square: Jews in France and in the United States' (2009) 30(6) *Cardozo Law Review*, p. 2441. However, at

such is uncontested. To put it another way, there is consensus on the usefulness of the term.[115] Furthermore, the underlying principles are not called into question.[116] So it is that these days as well, *laïcité* has remained the cornerstone of French society.[117]

Inextricably linked with *laïcité*, though not codified, is the principle of neutrality, which encompasses the idea that the public service should be neutral. Additionally, it has been identified to comprise two aspects, a positive one and a negative one. The former aspect of neutrality requires the state to allow for religious pluralism. Accordingly, the state provides various socio-cultural trends access to broadcasting. Furthermore, it makes a budget available for chaplaincy services in for instance hospitals and prisons.[118] This aspect emphasizes neutrality rather as a right for citizens than as a duty for public officials. The negative aspect precludes the state in its dealings with individuals from taking into account their opinions, be they religious or political. Moreover, the state should take care not to favour one (form of) religion over another (form of) religion. This aspect of neutrality generally takes the form of abstention: the state should not display religious symbols and should not take a position regarding religion or belief in school curricula.[119] Furthermore, this aspect of neutrality bars public officials' from manifesting their religion or belief altogether. This holds true for all public officials. In this way, neutrality is understood as affording a double protection. On the one hand, it protects public officials against the state, and on the other hand, it protects citizens making use of a public service – or, when literally translated from French, 'users'[120] – against public officials.[121] The next section discusses in more detail the implications which the principle of neutrality has for public officials' freedom to wear religious symbols.

---

the same time, the schism is between moderate and strict adherents to *laïcité*, Willaime in Davie and Hervieu-Léger (eds) (1996), p. 163. Cf. J. Lagreé and P. Portier (eds) *La modernité contre la religion? Pour une nouvelle approche de la laïcité* (Presses Universitaires de Rennes, Rennes 2005) which departs from a more extensive interpretation of *laïcité*, p. 8. The latest developments seem to point to the advantage of the latter. See also Stasi Report (2003), p. 50 ff.

115 See McGoldrick (2006), p. 41; CNCDH Report (2003), p. 15; Stasi Report (2003), p. 9.

116 CNCDH Report (2003), p. 17. See also Willaime in Davie and Hervieu-Léger (eds) (1996), p. 163.

117 See Ibid, Conseil d' Etat Report (2004), CNCDH Report (2003). Also e.g. Gunn (2004), p. 10, p. 10.

118 J. Berthoud, 'La neutralité religieuse du fonctionnaire' (2005) 12 *Semaine Juridique - Administrations et Collectivités Territoriales*, p. 1143.

119 Ibid.

120 Again, English seems to lack in grasping the exact purport of the specific French term 'usager' which is aimed at those citizens making use of public services. To avoid confusion, this chapter mainly uses 'citizen' instead of 'user' save in occasional cases.

121 N. Kada, 'Service public et religion: du renouveau du principe de neutralité' (2004) 5 *L'actualité juridique - Fonctions publiques*, p. 250.

6.3 Public officials' freedom to display religious symbols

As stated, the principle of neutrality applies to the whole public service in France. In French discourse, the concept of public service speaks for itself,[122] in that its specificity in relation to the private sector is uncontested as is the applicability of specific principles. Public service comprises public officials with a permanent position,[123] both appointed and contracted, on the central level, the local level and in the hospital sector. While statutes include general provisions on public officials,[124] the legal regime applicable to each public service can vary.[125] A point worth noting is that magistrates fall under a separate regime.[126]

Three principles have been recognized as fundamental ones for the public service: continuity, mutability and equality.[127] The last principle is pertinent for this study, as it imposes an obligation on public officials to treat those dealing with the public services identically in identical situations.[128] Traditionally, the principle of equality is considered to be the basis of the duty of neutrality, in such a way that the latter has acquired the status of the fourth principle of public service.[129] While initially neutrality mainly applied to the domain of public education,[130] it was later extended to apply to all public functions.

---

122 E.g S. Salon and J.C. Savignac (eds), 'La fonction publique; documents réunis et commentés', (La Documentation Française, Paris 1999), pp. 2-3. As observed by a British scholar: 'La notion de service public est une conception originale du droit français.', see J. Bell, 'Le service public: l'expérience britannique' (1997) *L'actualité juridique - Fonctions publiques*, p. 130.

123 In principle, public officials are recruited for a lifelong career, during which they progressively pass through the public service hierarchy, see A. Claisse, and M.C. Meininger, 'Fonctions publiques en Europe', in Salon and Savignac (eds) (1999), p. 5.

124 L. Rouban, *La fonction publique* (La Découverte, Paris 1996), p. 4. See also Loi no. 83-634 du 13 juillet 1983 portant droits et obligations des fonctionnaires: Loi dite loi Le Pors. The general status of public officials is further specified in four titles, which in fact constitute separate laws, loi Le Pors Article 4. See also Constitution, Article 34.

125 Peiser (2006), p. 148. The 1983 law comprises four titles which basically constitute separate laws for the different categories of public officials.

126 As do members of the military, for that matter. See *infra*, Section 6.3.1.

127 These principles have been articulated by the French legal scholar Louis Rolland, see A. Ondoua, 'Le service public à l'épreuve de la laïcité: a propos de la neutralité religieuse dans les services publics' (2006) 12 *Droit Administratif*, para. 20. Continuity means that public officials should respond in a continuous manner to the needs of citizens. Mutability means that the public service should adapt according to the circumstances and evolution of the needs, see Ch. Stoffaës, 'Services publics, question d'avenir', in Salon and Savignac (1999), p. 4; Peiser (2006), pp. 150-151 and Guimezanes (1999), pp. 104-105. The public service is regarded as benefiting the general interest, See Peiser (2006), p. 146.

128 Zauberman and Lévy (2003), p. 1080 ff.

129 Ondoua (2006), para. 20.

130 Berthoud (2005), p. 1145.

As a corollary of their participation in public service, public officials are subject to the duty of neutrality.[131] Consequently, their personal convictions are neutralized, which implies that public officials should completely refrain from expressing or manifesting beliefs in religious matters.[132] This prohibition extends to conduct and to verbal expressions as well as dress.[133] In fact, it concerns any sign, either one which could be interpreted as a sign of adherence to a particular religion or belief, or one which could be considered to be critical.[134] In other words, for the safeguard of neutrality the appearance of neutrality is essential.[135]

Apart from not differentiating between religious expressions, the duty of neutrality also does not differentiate as to particular aspects of a public function, such as whether the public official actually comes into contact with other individuals or whether he wears a uniform.[136] Additionally, the duty of neutrality applies to any public official regardless of his function. The Council of State (*Conseil d'Etat*) clearly confirmed this in its opinion in *Mademoiselle Marteaux* in 2000.[137] Miss Marteaux was a teacher who had been dismissed from a school for wearing a headscarf. One of the questions which the tribunal dealing with the teacher's request to annul her dismissal had submitted to the Council of State concerned the extent to which the duty of neutrality should be further specified regarding the specific public function at stake. The Council of State explicitly established that neutrality should not be differentiated depending on the public function in question.

The underlying aim of neutrality is to avoid at any time that any individual who enters into contact with the public service might think that the public official lacks impartiality.[138] At the same time, it is regarded as safeguarding the public official's freedom of conscience, as it is also effective in the relation of the state with public officials. The underlying line of reasoning is as follows. In being neutral, the state is absolutely precluded from recruiting or assessing individuals on the basis of their religion or belief. In 1954, the Council of State gave a ruling on this in the *Barel* decision.[139] In this decision, it made clear that such a bar served to guarantee equal access for individuals to public services.[140] Apart from being seen as guaranteeing

---

131 Ibid, p. 1142.
132 Ibid, p. 1144.
133 Stasi Report (2003), para. 2.2. See also McGoldrick (2006), p. 73. In reality, accommodation has taken place, see McGoldrick, p. 75.
134 Berthoud (2005), p. 1144.
135 Ibid, para. A.2. Stasi Report (2003), para. 2.2. As also determined by the Conseil d'Etat, 3 May 2000, *Mlle Marteaux*, Avis no. 217017.
136 McGoldrick (2006), p. 73 and 75. Stasi Report (2003), para. 2.2.
137 CE, *Mlle Marteaux* (2000).
138 Berthoud (2005), p 1144. The rights and freedoms of the citizens of public services are protected, see L. Favoreu, *Droit des libertés fondamentales* (3ʳᵈ edn Dalloz, Paris 2005), p. 158.
139 CE, *Barel*, 28 mai 1954, Rec. Lebon, p. 308.
140 E.g. Zauberman and Lévy (2003), p. 1081. See also Guimezanes, p. 124; Bedouelle and Costa (1998), pp. 118-119. Equal access to public functions had been laid down in the 1789 Declaration,

equal access, neutrality is seen as preserving public officials' freedom of conscience, a right that is considered fully available to them, just like other rights such as the freedom of opinion.[141] Above all, public officials are considered to be citizens whose rights cannot be set aside by principle. Accordingly, they are entitled for instance to take leave for religious holidays.[142] However, the exercise of the freedom of religion or the freedom of expression in terms of externalisation is evidently deemed to collide with the duty of neutrality. Just as evidently, it is the former, which needs to make way for the latter. The French perception of neutrality implies neutral appearance.[143]

It is by taking on a public function that public officials are considered as voluntarily subjecting themselves to the duty of neutrality. This is corroborated by the fact that the duty of neutrality only applies within their function. In principle, outside their function, public officials are free to have and to manifest their religion or belief. However, they need to do so without prejudice to the proper functioning of public service; they are still subject to a less strict obligation of taking care not to undermine the image of public service.[144] Since principle of neutrality applies uniformly to all public services, the three public functions examined in this study are in principle subject to the same policy. Nevertheless, the next sections briefly go over a few specificities.

Article 6 and confirmed in the general law on the status of public officials. See Gaudu (2009), p. 517. In reality, it turns out that the principle of equal access is not complied with effectively. For this reason, the Minister concerned adopted in cooperation with HALDE a Charter to promote equality in the public service, see E. Woerth, A. Santini and Schweitzer, Charte pour la promotion de l'égalité dans la fonction publique, 2 December 2008 found on the website of the Ministère de la Réforme de l'Etat, de la décentralisation et de la Fonction Publique <www.fonction-publique.gouv.fr>. Previously, a report on diversity in the public service was published see D. Versini, 'Rapport sur la diversité dans la fonction publique', (Paris, 2004).

141 See loi Le Pors, Chapitre 1, Article 6: 'La liberté d'opinion est garantie aux fonctionnaires. This is also according the principle of citizenship, implying that public officials are in principle entitled to individual rights and freedoms', see Anicet le Pors, in Salon and Savignac (1999), pp. 11-12. See also Favoreu (2005), p. 102-103. See the Module Territoire. Le haut fonctionnaire et le fait religieux, p. 12: 'Les fonctionnaires bénéficient comme les autres citoyens de la liberté de conscience.' The principle of equality has been confirmed by the Constitutional Council on 18 September 1986 (86-217). Certes, les fonctionnaires et agents publics bénéficient, comme les autres citoyens, de la liberté de conscience affirmée notamment par les textes constitutionnels, see Berthoud (2005), p. 1143. Saint-James (2005), p. 1.

142 Kada (2004), p. 256. Berthoud (2005), p. 1144.

143 Kada (2004), p. 254.

144 The obligation of restraint (in French 'obligation de réserve') compels the public official to avoid, in all circumstances, conduct which undermines the image of the public service in the conception of those making use of the public services.

6.3.1 Judicial officers' freedom to display religious symbols

The general principles of equality and neutrality are reflected by the judicial principles of independence and impartiality. The principle of judicial independence has been explicitly enshrined in Article 64 of the Constitution,[145] which also includes the principle of irremovability.[146] Impartiality has been guaranteed in the Code on the Judicial Organization (*Code de l'organisation judiciaire*, hereinafter: the JO Code),[147] which governs the organization of the judiciary. This organization lies primarily with the Minister of Justice; justice is a public service rendered in the name of the French people.[148] The Minister of Justice recommends magistrates who have been trained at the National Legal Service College[149] to be appointed by the President. When appointed, a magistrate takes an oath, swearing to fulfil his functions well and in good faith.[150] No exemption from this oath is possible and no alternative oaths or promises are available. The status of magistrates[151] is slightly different from that of public officials; it is not determined by the laws on public officials' general status,[152] but by a specific order of 1958.[153] This order specifies the general principles, such as the one of irremovability: it determines in Article 4 that judges cannot be suspended or removed by the political authorities except where the law has so prescribed.[154] The principle guarantees the independence of the judiciary from citizens, other judges

---

145 See 1958 Constitution, Article 64: 'Le Président de la République est garant de l'indépendance de l'autorité judiciaire ...' (The president of the Republic guarantees the independence of the judicial power).

146 'Les magistrats du siège sont inamovibles.'

147 Code de l'organisation judiciaire, Article L111-5, créé par Ordonnance no. 2006-673 du 8 juin 2006 JORF 9 June 2006, Article 1: 'L'impartialité des juridictions judiciaires est garantie par les dispositions du présent code et celles prévues par les dispositions particulières à certaines juridictions ainsi que par les règles d'incompatibilité fixées par le statut de la magistrature.'

148 See website of the Ministry of Justice, on <www.justice.gouv.fr/index.php?rubrique=10031& ssrubrique= 10032>. This is evident for instance from the revolutionary vision that judges would be subject to the laws which express the general will (*volonté generale*). P. Langbroek, 'Het beheer van rechters en gerechten', inaugural speech, 30 October 2009, original text: 'In de Franse revolutionaire ideologie werden rechters gezien als instrumenten bij de tenuitvoerlegging van de wet'. p 7.

149 Individuals participate in a 'concours' to obtain entrance to the Ecole Nationale de la Magistrature. An exception to this is the recruitment of judges of the Conseil d'Etat who are selected from the National School of Administration or by external appointment.

150 Original text: 'Je jure de bien et fidèlement remplir mes fonctions, de garder religieusement le secret des délibérations et de me conduire en tout comme un digne et loyal magistrat.'

151 The term *magistrats* applies to the judges in the judicial order. The term *juges* applies to the judges in the administrative order. The third group of judicial professions is that of '*les auxiliaries de la justice*', that is to say the other actors who make the administration of justice possible, such as lawyers, see e.g. Guimezanes (1999), p. 48-49. They are not included in the scope of this research.

152 Dadomo and Farran, *The French legal system* (2nd edn Sweet & Maxwell, London 1996), p. 142.

153 Ordonnance no. 58-1270, Article 6.

154 On the basis of the 'principe de l'inamovibilité' (the principle of irremovability), Ordonnance no. 58-1270, Article 4. See also the Constitution, Article 64.

and public authorities.[155] The principle of non-liability, protecting the judiciary from damage claims, further strengthens the independence of the judiciary.[156]

Other provisions of the order specify the impartiality of the judiciary. For instance, they state functions and professions which are incompatible with a judicial function. In any case, a magistrate is precluded from holding a(nother) public function, expect when derogation is allowed. Otherwise, administrative and political functions, such as Member of Parliament, are explicitly mentioned as incompatible with the judicial function.[157] Additionally, the order lays down a more general duty of loyalty precluding any political deliberation in the judiciary; such a duty comprises a prohibition on political demonstration, which is incompatible with their obligation of restraint.[158] Further guarantees of judicial impartiality and independence are provided by the possibility for a judge to voluntarily withdraw or for a litigant to challenge a judge's authority.[159] The order does not include provisions concerning religious activities, although one provision seems to emphasize that religion belongs to the private sphere. Article 6 stipulates that the personal files on magistrates should not include any information on their religious and political activities and opinions.[160]

The JO Code also incorporates provisions concerning the judicial robe.[161] It includes a table outlining the judicial costume for the various judicial officials on various occasions.[162] More specifically, the costumes differ depending on whether judges are sitting in a normal session or in a ceremonial session. In olden days the judicial robe, in resembling the royal robe, expressed the idea that the king delegated his power to adjudicate to the judiciary. Nowadays, the judicial robe symbolizes uniformity and the equality of the judges composing the tribunal and their judicial duty.[163] The robe is black or red – depending on the type of judge and session – and is optionally covered with a black cloak; in addition, the costume may be completed with a sash, a cap and bands.[164] In principle, judicial officials are compelled to wear a robe.

As briefly mentioned, the duty of neutrality incumbent on public officials has not been codified. *A fortiori*, such a duty has not been laid down for the judiciary

---

155 Guimezanes (1999), p. 50; Dadomo and Farran (1996), p. 145.
156 Ordonnance no. 58-1270, Article 11-1. This does not apply in cases of abusive conduct. And individuals can bring claims against the state, Dadomo and Farran (1996), p. 147.
157 See Ordonnance no. 58-1270, Articles 8-9.1.1.
158 See Ordonnance no. 58-1270, Article 10.
159 Dadomo and Farran (1996), p. 149.
160 Ordonnance no. 58-1270, Article 6: 'Le dossier du magistrat … ne peut y être fait état ni de ses opinions ou activités politiques, syndicales, religieuses ou philosophiques, ni d'éléments relevant strictement de sa vie privée.'
161 Code de l'organisation judiciaire, Article L111-5, créé par Ordonnance no. 2006-673, Article 1.
162 Tableau des costumes et insignes. Magistrats de la Cour de Cassation et Membres du Parquet près ladite Cour, T. 101.
163 See the website of the Ministry of Justice, on <www.ca-paris.justice.fr/index.php?rubrique=11126>.
164 Images can be found on <www.ca-paris.justice.fr/index.php?rubrique=11126&ssrubrique=11127>.

either,[165] except for the principles of impartiality and independence. Nevertheless, as described, the prohibition for public officials on the wearing of religious symbols can be presumed to apply to the judiciary. Recently, allegedly in the face of perceived challenge to this prohibition, there has been some debate about consolidating the duty of neutrality in the form of legislation. This debate is briefly addressed in Section 6.4.1 of this chapter.[166] The exclusion of religious symbols tends to be equally applicable to other actors in the courtroom, such as lawyers and jurors.[167]

6.3.2 Police officers' freedom to display religious symbols

In the same way that the judiciary is subject to the law which expresses the general will of the people, the police exercise authority by virtue of protecting the people. Accordingly, this authority should serve the benefit of all. The organizational structure of the French police breaks down into a military and a civil part, the latter of which is the focus of the study. Additionally, the civil part comprises a national[168] as well as a local branch.[169] The former branch is under national government control. The latter branch falls to the prefect and the mayor and it has very limited prerogatives.[170]

Police officers are public officials.[171] The Professional Code of the National Police (*Code de déontologie, Décret n° 86-592 du 18 mars 1986 portant code de déontologie de la police nationale* hereinafter: Professional Code)[172] prominently mentions that in carrying out its tasks, the National Police respects the 1789 Declaration, the constitution

---

165 S. Gaboriau, '*Laïcité* et Justice', in H. Pauliat (ed), *Services public et religions: les nouvelles frontières de l'action publique*, (Presses Universitaires de Limoges, Limoges 2006), p. 116.

166 Ibid, 'La liberté religieuse s'arrête à la toge du juge.', p. 117.

167 See McGoldrick (2006), p. 74. This is corroborated by a newspaper article in *Le Nouvel Observateur*, see 'Une jurée remplacée pour port du voile', 1 December 2003, on: <tempsreel.nouvelobs.com/societe/20031124.OBS0225/une-juree-remplaceepour-port-du-voile.html>. That said, Gaboriau has stated that she is aware of cases where jurors have sat while wearing a headscarf, see Gaboriau in Pauliat (ed) (2006), p. 118. Furthermore, she personally favours a case-by-case approach because in her view jurors essentially differ from judges. People are not juror by choice but are compelled to serve as jurors on the basis of a civic duty. Such a civic duty also implies that jurors do not represent the state, but incur their duties by virtue of being citizens.

168 See for a historical and organizational description of the French police e.g. A.M. Ventre, 'Les polices en France' (2002) 102 Pouvoirs. Revue française d'études constitutionnelles et politiques, p. 31 ff.

169 The mandate of the municipal police is laid down in the Code général des collectivités territoriales. Article L2212-1 determines that the mayor is in charge of the municipal police. Article L2212-2 determines that the municipal police aims to ensure good public order, public safety, public security, and public health ('La police municipale a pour objet d'assurer le bon ordre, la sûreté, la sécurité et la salubrité publiques'). The provision further specifies the tasks.

170 Zauberman and Lévy (2003), p. 1082.

171 Ibid.

172 Code de déontologie, Décret no. 86-592 du 18 mars 1986 portant code de déontologie de la police nationale.

and international law.[173] French citizens are guaranteed equal access to the police.[174] In addition, the Professional Code explicitly stipulates some duties for national police officers, which ensue from their exemplary function. For example, Article 7 lays down a duty of loyalty to the republican institutions. This provision also includes what may be interpreted as a translation of the duty of neutrality in requiring the police officer to have 'absolute respect for persons, regardless of their nationality or origin, their social condition or their political, religious or philosophical convictions'.[175] Otherwise, police officers are automatically subject to the general duty of neutrality and the ensuing prohibition on religious symbols. In 2005, the police uniform was revised.[176] Contrary to other countries, no discussion concerning possible inclusion of religious symbols appears to have arisen at all. French newspapers have reported on the practice in other states of including religious symbols in the police uniform, but this practice does not seem to have inspired the French approach to follow suit.[177] That is not to say that the policy in place has remained entirely uncontested. In 2010, a police officer had to appear before the disciplinary board of the police for refusing to take off her headscarf.[178] Nonetheless, such incidents have not altered the formal policy, which is to adhere to the principles of *laïcité* and neutrality in consistently prohibiting police officers from displaying religious symbols.

---

173 Article 2, original text: 'La police nationale s'acquitte de ses missions dans le respect de la Déclaration des droits de l'homme et du citoyen, de la Constitution, des conventions internationales et des lois.'

174 Article 3, original text: 'La police nationale est ouverte à tout citoyen français satisfaisant aux conditions fixées par les lois et règlements.' Also concerning recruitment, see Zauberman and Lévy (2003), pp. 1080-1081.

175 Original text: 'Le fonctionnaire de la police nationale est loyal envers les institutions républicaines. Il est intègre et impartial: il ne se départit de sa dignité en aucune circonstance. ... Il a le respect absolu des personnes, quelles que soient leur nationalité ou leur origine, leur condition sociale ou leurs convictions politiques, religieuses ou philosophiques.' Although the reality shows that the police are quite aware of ethnic differences, see Zauberman and Lévy (2003), p. 1073.

176 Lettre d'information des service de l'Etat, on <www.meuse.pref.gouv.fr/lettre/article.php?article=81>.

177 For instance, in February 2009, several articles appeared concerning the Norwegian Government's plan to allow headscarves for police officers, e.g. 'Foulard islamique dans la police norvégienne', in *Les Echos* (5 February 2009) and 'Norvège. La directrice de la police norvégienne, Ingelin Killengreen, a annoncé que les femmes de police musulmanes pourraient porter le foulard islamique', in *La Croix* (6 February 2009); 'Le port du hijab dans la police agite la Norvège', *La Libération* (16 February 2009); 'Norvège. Le gouvernement revient sur l'autorisation du voile dans la police', *La Croix* (12 February 2009).

178 <www.lefigaro.fr/actualite-france/2010/02/05/01016-20100205ARTFIG00015-police-une-contractuelle-refuse-d-oter-son-voile-.php.>; <www.france24.com/fr/20100204-policiere-voile-islamique-comparaitre-conseil-discipline-fonctionnaire-paris>.

6.3.3 State school teachers' freedom to display religious symbols

Section 6.2.3 mentioned the essential role of the Ferry laws in the laicization of education. Subsequent to these laws, a law was introduced in 1886 by one of Ferry's successors, René Goblet.[179] This law was specifically aimed at laicizing the teachers at state schools. Since the state has taken on the organization of education, it has extensive control,[180] extending to the curriculum,[181] recruitment and remuneration of personnel. State schools account for the majority of education, which is almost free of charge. Since 1959, the *loi Debré* has further shaped the principle of neutrality by enabling schools to entertain various degrees of liaison with the state, depending on the extent of privileges and obligations.[182] Confessional schools are for the most part Catholic ones.[183] Whereas Muslims are in theory eligible to receive state funding for their private schools, there is currently not a single funded Muslim state school.[184] In September 2003, the first Muslim secondary school, privately funded, was founded.[185]

Even today, it is beyond doubt that state schoolteachers in primary and secondary education are subject to a duty of strict neutrality.[186] Teaching personnel at universities are in principle also bound to observe *laïcité*.[187] The Council of State has underscored the specificity of the position of university professors, requiring the freedom of

---

179 In a way, the *Goblet* law can be considered as following up on Ferry's legislative project. In a report on this project, Jean-Baptiste Ferrouillat argues fervently in favour of *laïque* teachers. He points to the danger of having religious teachers at *laïque* schools, where there is no more place for religion. In his view, this creates the risk of having teachers who have two superiors: the state and the divine. Were a conflict between the two superiors to arise, these teachers would be more inclined to obey the divine superior, see the website of the French *Sénat* <www.senat.fr/evenement/archives/D42/loi1886.html>.

180 Through the Ministry of National Education and the Ministry of Higher Education and Research. Agricultural education falls under the Ministry of Agriculture and certain ministries have their own secondary and higher institutions to educate future personnel. Otherwise, certain tasks can be delegated to the local level.

181 This is strongly associated with Jacobin ideals, see Poulter (1997), p. 54. See also McGoldrick (2006), p. 78. It has been said that the centralization arose from such a political need in the 19th century, see Lelièvre (2000).

182 See Bedouelle and Costa (1998), pp. 96 and 99.

183 See e.g. C. Glenn, 'Historical Background to Conflicts over Religion in Public Schools' (2004) 33 *Pro rege*, p. 6.

184 The first Muslim school ever to obtain simple contract status was a school at Ile de la Réunion, see Fetzer and Soper (2005), p. 85, and A. Haquet, L'enseignement privé musulman dans une République laïque', (2009) 3 *Revue française de droit administratif*, p. 518. In 2009, there were still no more than five Muslim schools, p. 515.

185 Lycée Averroes in Lille, see e.g. 'Douze élèves bien sages pour le premier lycée musulman', *Libération* (3 September 2003) on <www.liberation.fr/societe/0101452998-douze-eleves-bien-sages-pour-le-premier-lycee-musulman>.

186 This rule is even said to have been settled by a wide consensus in French society, see Gaudu (2009), p. 516.

187 The Education Code (*Code de l'Education*) also lays down *laïcité* for higher education.

expression and the independence of personnel to be guaranteed.[188] The rule that public education including its teaching personnel should be laic has nowadays been laid down in Article 141-5 of the Education Code (*Code de l'Education*).[189] Article L 141-3 echoes the Ferry law in allowing parents one day a week to let their children – who attend primary education – follow religious instruction.[190] Since 2004, pupils have been equally subject to a prohibition on wearing conspicuous religious symbols,[191] which has been inserted into Article L 141-5-1. The background to this law is further discussed in Section 6.4.2.

Neutrality precludes teachers from manifesting religion or belief during their function. Their religion or belief alone cannot bar their access to a position.[192] Moreover, neither can a teacher's private activities in principle be a reason for refusal of employment.[193] Although neutrality and its specific requirements have been considered self-evident, it has been contested by teachers wearing religious symbols. At times, this has led to court cases. The judicial approach taken, on both lower and higher levels, has been consistent and straightforward. The previously mentioned case of *Marteaux* in 2000[194] before the Council of State is a seminal ruling which confirms that a strict duty of neutrality applies to teachers. As previously touched on, the tribunal dealing with Ms. Marteaux's request had submitted three questions to the Council of State. Basically, these questions concerned the extent to which the duty of neutrality should be further specified regarding the specific public service or particular task at stake. Additionally, a question addressed the specific nature of the religious symbol in question. The Council of State established that the strictness of the duty of neutrality precluded it from being differentiated as to type of public service or type of function. Accordingly, it confirmed the wearing of a headscarf or any other conspicuous religious symbol to be a grave fault leading to sanctions. It did find, however, that the severity of the sanction depends on the circumstances including the conspicuous nature of the symbol. Although subsequent to this ruling, disputes on wearing religious symbols, notably the headscarf, have continued, there has been no

---

188 Favoreu (2005), p. 917.
189 Article L 141-5 reads: 'Dans les établissements du premier degré publics, l'enseignement est exclusivement confié à un personnel laïque.'
190 'Les écoles élémentaires publiques vaquent un jour par semaine en outre du dimanche, afin de permettre aux parents de faire donner, s'ils le désirent, à leurs enfants l'instruction religieuse, en dehors des édifices scolaires.'
191 Loi no. 2004-228 du 15 mars 2004 encadrant, en application du principe de *laïcité*, le port de signes ou de tenues manifestant une appartenance religieuse dans les écoles, collèges et lycées publics.
192 In an early decision (*Abbé Bouteyre*) in 1912, the *Conseil d'Etat* decided that a clergyman registered for a philosophy examination had rightfully been excluded from the list. However, later decisions such as the *Barel* case appear to have abandoned that line, in explicitly ruling that someone's opinion alone cannot be the basis of refusal for recruitment.
193 CE, 28 April 1938, *Dlle Weiss*. Although such activities need to be within the boundaries drawn by the duty of reserve.
194 CE, *Mlle Marteaux* (2000).

alteration of the judicial approach. In general, for the past decade, religion in general and religious symbols in particular in various contexts have provoked heated debate. The next section has selected three issues of debate which are relevant to this study.

6.4 DEBATE IN FRANCE

As mentioned, the importance of the principles of *laïcité* and state neutrality are uncontested. Nevertheless, there has been debate on public officials' freedom to wear religious symbols. In part such debate was instigated by individual claims. Additionally, some legislative developments have taken place, in the form of bills consolidating the current practice. Two other issues are addressed as well. One of them marks a relatively early stage of dispute in the 1980s when pupils started to claim the right to wear a religious symbol (most of the time Muslim pupils with a headscarf).[195] Although this issue concerns pupils instead of teachers, it cannot be left aside altogether. As an integral part of the developing debate on religion in public, it is revealing as regards the French approach.[196] Furthermore, it seems to have served as a catalyst in the comprehensive debate which later on came to be directed at public service as well. The second issue that cannot be left aside due to its importance for the French debate on religious symbols is the face veil and the efforts to ban the wearing of the face veil in public.

6.4.1 State neutrality in public service

In spite of or perhaps precisely because of the uncontested status of state neutrality within the public service, it has not been explicitly codified.[197] A need for such codification, or at least for consolidation of the principles of *laïcité* and neutrality, emerged around the start of the twenty-first century. This need sprang from intensifying debate on the meaning and scope of these principles, which were perceived to be increasingly undermined. It is difficult to precisely pinpoint the reasons for this perception. Somehow, there was a shared feeling that *communautarisme* was increasing, *laïcité* and neutrality were challenged, and individual claims were growing.[198] These claims have been highly publicized in the media. Some of them,

---

195 Fetzer and Soper suggested that the question of Muslim schoolgirls wearing a headscarf is by far the most controversial issue, see Fetzer and Soper (2005), p. 78.
196 It has been considered essential for French thinking about citizenship and immigration issues, see E.R. Thomas, 'Competing Visions of Citizenship and Integration in France's Headscarves Affair' (2000) 8(2) *Journal of European Area Studies*, p. 168.
197 See also Stasi Report (2003), p. 55. Haut Conseil à l'Intégration (HCI), 'Projet de charte de la laicite dans les services publics. Avis à Monsieur le Premier ministre', (Paris 2007), on <www.hci.gouv.fr>, p. 32.
198 E.g. Rossinot Report (2006), which speaks of an increase in *communataurisme* and the appeal of nationalism, p. 3; HCI Rapport (2007), p. 12. C. Durand-Prinborgne, 'Autour du projet de charte

concerning the public service, have also been dealt with in court. They concerned state schoolteachers, as well as an official of the Labour Inspectorate[199] and a hospital employee. Most, if not all of the cases, concerned the wearing of a headscarf.[200] A significant case, already referred to, was the *Marteaux* opinion of the Council of State.[201] This ruling reaffirmed the indivisibility of the duty of neutrality. Subsequent cases with similar facts therefore seemed to have little chance of leading to a ruling favourable for the claimant.[202]

Meanwhile, contention concerning religious dress and symbols in the judiciary had also emerged and in 2003 a parliamentary question concerning this issue[203] was submitted to the Minister of Justice. In response, the Minister of Justice referred to the duty of impartiality, precluding the judiciary from showing 'any manifestation which is hostile to the principle or form of the Government of the Republic' and 'any demonstration of a political nature, which is incompatible with the restraint which their functions impose on them'.[204] He proposed explicitly that regardless of the motivation, the wearing of dress or the adoption of attitudes, which are incompatible

de la laicite dans les services publics', (2007) 14 *Actualité Juridique Droit Administratif*, who establishes a 'set of social and legal facts which have affected and are affecting the functioning of the public service on a polemic basis', p. 722. McGoldrick (2006) p. 73. See Stasi Report (2003), para. 3.2.

199 *M. Ben Abdallah c. Ministres des Affaires sociales et de l'Equipement*, see e.g. E. Kolbert, 'Le port du foulard islamique dans l'exercice de la fonction publique', Conclusions sur Cour administrative d'appel de Lyon, 19 November 2003 in *Revue Française de Droit Administratif* (2004), p. 588 ff.

200 An exception was a case of a teacher who was accused of dealing partially with the Second World War in placing too much emphasis on the Shoa, see 'Accusée de consacrer trop de temps à la Shoah, une professeure d'histoire suspendue à Nancy' in *Le Monde* (1 September 2010) on <www.lemonde.fr/societe/article/2010/08/31/accusee-de-consacrer-trop-de-temps-a-la-shoah-une-professeure-d-histoire-suspendue-a-nancy_1405083_3224.html>.

201 CE, *Mlle Marteaux* (2000).

202 Such as the case involving a Ph.D. student who was also a teaching assistant at the University of Toulouse. While giving tutorials, she wore a headscarf and was dismissed for that reason in 2009. She instituted proceedings against the university with the administrative tribunal in Toulouse (Tribunal Administratif de Toulouse). On 14 April, the judge decided not to suspend the dismissal. See e.g. D. Delarue, 'Discrimination raciste et neutralité religieuse des fonctionnaires', on <amitie-entre-les-peuples.org/spip.php?article665>.

203 See question écrite no. 07652 de M. Michel Charasse, published in the *Journal Officiel Sénat*, 22 May 2003, p. 1648 and réponse du Ministère de la justice, published in the *Journal Officiel Sénat*, 16 December 2004 also on <www.senat.fr>, p. 2916.

204 '[les magistrats se voient interdire] "toute manifestation d'hostilité au principe ou à la forme du Gouvernement de la République" et "toute démonstration de nature politique incompatible avec la réserve que leur imposent leurs fonctions".'

with the exercise of the function, can justify disciplinary proceedings.[205] That would also apply to a magistrate who refused to wear his robes.[206]

Subsequent to this question, a bill on specifically an obligation of neutrality for the judiciary was submitted and presented on 24 June 2003.[207] The bill drew attention to the fact that the legislation in place did not contain specific provisions on the respect for *laïcité* and neutrality of the public services of the judiciary. Therefore, it proposed the insertion of such a provision into the 1958 Regulation on the status of the magistrature.[208] It would further explicitly impose a duty on judges 'to abstain from any manifestation of religious adherence or proselytism'.[209] This tendency to consolidate the duty of neutrality by legislation took place for the public service as a whole.

The run-up to such general consolidation witnessed the installation of various committees to conduct in-depth examinations resulting in a number of reports, three of which can be considered as the most important ones. Two of them[210] concern the duty of neutrality in public service in particular: the 2006 Report on *laïcité* in the public service by a working group presided over by André Rossinot (Rossinot Report) and the 2007 Recommendation on the Project of a Charter of *laïcité* in public service (Charter Recommendation) by the High Council of Integration[211] (*Haut Conseil à l'Intégration*).

Having consulted the relevant actors, the Rossinot Report drew two main conclusions. Firstly, it established that it was necessary for the law to guarantee the principle of *laïcité* more effectively. Secondly, it concluded that public action should focus on explaining as well as informing and educating about *laïcité*. One of the specific proposals ensuing from these conclusions was the explicit codification of the duty of neutrality incumbent on public officials.[212]

---

205 'l'adoption - quel qu'en soit le motif - de tenues vestimentaires ou d'attitudes incompatibles avec l'exercice des fonctions est de nature à justifier l'engagement de poursuites disciplinaires. [Il en va, évidemment, de même pour l'hypothèse dans laquelle un magistrat refuserait le port de son costume d'audience.]'

206 Although, on some occasions, judges are allowed not to wear their robes, as is the case with a magistrate in a juvenile court, see Gaboriau in Pauliat (ed) (2006), p. 116.

207 Proposition de loi organique visant à garantir le respect de la laicité et de la neutralité du service public de la justice Sénat (2002-2003) 364.

208 L'ordonnance du 22 décembre 1958 relative au statut de la magistrature.

209 Article 10-1, original text: 'Le corps judiciaire assure sa mission dans le respect des principes de neutralite et de la laïcité. Dans l'exercice de leurs fonctions, les magistrates, les juges et les jurés d'assises, ainsi que les agents du service public de la justice, s'abstiennent de toute manifestation d'appartenance religieuse ou prosélytisme.'

210 The third report concerned religious symbols in public education and is discussed in depth in the next section.

211 HCI Report (Paris, 2007).

212 Rossinot Report (2006), p. 49.

As is clear from its title, the Charter Recommendation specifically focused on *laïcité* in public service in being part of the numerous contemporary reflections on that principle.[213] Like previous committees, it came to its findings after having heard dozens of experts. Basically, it presented the concrete text of the Charter in explaining the background and scope of the text. It proposed a text consisting of a preamble and two parts concerning public officials and citizen-users of the public service respectively. In submitting the text, the High Council of Integration underscored its non-binding and pedagogic character.[214]

The then Prime Minister followed up on the report on 13 April 2007 by sending a letter to his cabinet comprising a Charter of *laïcité* in the public service (*Charte de la laïcité dans les services publics*), which was clearly informed by the Charter recommendation.[215] According to the Prime Minister, the objective of this Charter was to 'remind the public officials and citizens of public services what their rights and obligations are, in order to contribute to a good functioning of the public service'.[216] The Charter explicitly reiterated that every public official has a duty of strict neutrality. Additionally, every public official should treat all persons equally and respect their freedom of conscience. When a public official manifests his religion or belief during the exercise of this function he commits a grave violation of his obligations.[217]

In 2008, a bill was submitted to Parliament concerning a prohibition on public officials wearing religious dress and symbols.[218] In referring to the 2004 Law on religious symbols at state schools, which is further discussed in the next section, the bill underlined the readiness to affirm the importance of *laïcité*. It regretted that the legislature had not extended the scope of application of the 2004 Law. After

---

213 It can be considered as a follow-up to one of the many recommendations of the Stasi report, which had already recommended in 2004 that legislation be adopted to enshrine the obligation of neutrality for public officials. It appears to favour a Charter of *laïcité* which should serve as a guide. It also considers the insertion of a duty of neutrality for public officials to be opportune, see Stasi Report (2003), p. 55 ff. This recommendation resounds in the speech of President Chirac, who considers a Code of *laïcité* desirable, see 'Discours prononcé par M. Jacques Chirac, Président de la République, relative au respect du principe de *laïcité* dans la République', Palais de l'Elysée (17 December 2003), on the website of the Presidency of the Republic, see: <www.elysee.fr>.

214 Charter Recommendation, pp. 41-43.

215 'Charte de la *laïcité* dans les services publics', no. 52009/SG (13 April 2007).

216 Original text: 'Rappeler aux agent publics comme aux usagers des services publics quells sont leurs droits et leurs devoirs à cet égard pour contribuer au bon fonctionnement des services publics', p. 12.

217 Original text: 'Tout agent public a un devoir de stricte neutralité. Il doit traiter également toutes les personnes et respecter leur liberté de conscience. ... Le fait pour un agent public de manifester ses convictions religieuses dans l'exercice de ses fonctions constitue un manquement à ses obligations', pp. 32-33.

218 Proposition de loi visant à interdire le port de signes ou de vêtements manifestant ostensiblement une appartenance religieuse, politique ou philosophique à toute personne investee de l'autorité publique, chargée d'une mission de service public ou y participant concurremment, F. Hostalier and others, no. 1080 (22 July 2008) to be found on <www.assemblee-nationale.fr>

suggesting that the principle had continued to be undermined since 2004, the bill proposed to clearly prohibit persons vested with public authority from conspicuously displaying any garment or symbol manifesting religion or belief.[219] It was clear from the formulation of the bill that the scope of subjects addressed was quite large. For example, the second provision extended the prohibition on garments or symbols to persons in a public building, thus including citizens, when such garments or symbols would provoke or be at odds with human dignity.[220] The bill clearly exemplified the endeavours to prohibit the explicit display of religious or political symbols. It confirmed the French take on religious symbols in the public sphere. At the same time, it could also be interpreted as seeking to fill a legal void.

That said, at the time of writing, the bill does not appear to have passed the stage of first reading in the Parliamentary Assembly. In other words, it has thus far not materialized into legislation.[221] The so far unsuccessful attempt at codification does not alter the unambiguous application of the principles of *laïcité* and neutrality to the public service. These principles have commonly not been considered to apply to those making use of public services; in the context of this study, they concern litigants, pupils and so forth. In 2004, France attracted much international attention when it adopted a law prohibiting pupils at state schools from wearing religious symbols. In France, it also caused debate, because it seemed as if the law was a breach of the clear distinction between public officials and citizens.

6.4.2 Conspicuous religious symbols at state schools

Although France made the headlines internationally in 2004 for prohibiting pupils at state schools from wearing religious symbols, the issue goes back much further.[222] One particular incident in October 1989 is commonly referred to as having incited national debate on religious symbols at state schools.[223] At that time, three Muslim pupils wanted to wear a headscarf in school and were subsequently suspended from a state secondary school in Creil, a suburb of Paris.[224] Initially, a compromise had been

---

219 'Le port de tenues ou de signes manifestant ostensiblement une appartenance religieuse, politique ou philosophique est interdit à toute personne investie de l'autorité publique et à toute personne chargée d'assurer une mission de service public ou y participant concurremment. ...'
220 'Le port de tenues ou de signes manifestant ostensiblement une appartenance religieuse, politique ou philosophique est interdit dans l'enceinte des établissements dans lesquels est exercée une activité de service public, s'ils appellent à la provocation ou s'ils sont contraires à la dignité humaine.'
221 To be found on <www.assemblee-nationale.fr/13/dossiers/signes_autorite.asp>.
222 Fetzer and Soper suggest that the question of Muslim schoolgirls wearing a headscarf was by far the most controversial issue, see Fetzer and Soper (2005), p. 78.
223 E.g. Conseil d'Etat Rapport (2004), p. 338. See also H. Chérifi, 'Application de la loi du 15 mars 2004 sur le port des signes religieux ostensibles dans les établissments d'enseignement publics' (Ministère de l'éducation nationale de l'enseignement supérieur et de la recherche, Paris 2006), to be found e.g. on <ladocumentationfrancaise.fr>, p. 30.
224 See for a recapitulation of the events e.g. Fetzer and Soper (2005), p. 78 ff; McGoldrick (2006),

arrived at allowing the girls to wear the headscarf at school, as long they took it off in class. This compromise was broken when the girls later on demanded to wear it in class too.[225] In the end, the case was settled when the schoolgirls decided to revert to the previously concluded compromise.[226] The circumstances of the case and the domestic context at the time probably allowed for the incident to trigger an enormous national debate.[227]

In this debate, both the Minister of National Education[228] and the Council of State[229] took the position that the wearing of religious symbols was in itself not incompatible with the principle of *laïcité*, in so far as it constituted religious manifestation.[230] Be that as it may, the Council of State qualified this position in its Advice (1989 Advice) by identifying three sets of criteria, which could preclude pupils from wearing religious symbols, either individually or collectively. Firstly, the nature, context and character of the symbols mattered; if these symbols were conspicuous, campaigning or protesting they were not permitted.[231] Secondly, if symbols constituted an act of pressure, provocation, proselytism or propaganda, they could be prohibited.[232] Finally, limitation was considered possible if the symbols undermined other interests, which included the pupil's or someone else's dignity, liberty, health or safety and the normal functioning of the public service.[233] These earlier headscarf affairs invoked concerns

---

p. 65 ff. In general, it has mostly been the headscarf which has significantly fuelled the debate, Bowen (2008), p. 44. Molokotos Liederman (2000), pp. 109, 111.

225 They possibly did so because of support by human rights groups and the Catholic Cardinal of Paris, see Fetzer and Soper (2005), p. 78.

226 While one of the girls decided to do so after negotiations with key players, the other two only did so after intervention by the King of Morocco. In general, Islamic and immigrant organizations played a significant role in the affair, see McGoldrick (2006), p. 67.

227 The context clarifies why this incident aroused such high emotions, see ibid, pp. 65-66. See also Bowen (2008), p. 42 and Thomas (2000), p. 169 ff.

228 His approach was not widely supported and created deep controversy even in his own party, see McGoldrick (2006), p. 68.

229 Conseil d'Etat, Avis 'Port du foulard islamique', 27 November 1989, no. 346893, retrieved from the website of *Revue de l'Actualité Juridique Française*, <www.rajf.org>, Section 1. This Advice was at the request of Lionel Jospin, possibly to deflect attention, see McGoldrick (2006), p. 69, or to 'calm the situation', see Poulter (1997), p. 58.

230 The Conseil d'Etat ruled in its 'Avis': 'Il résulte de ce qui vient d'être dit que, dans les établissements scolaires, le port par les élèves de signes par lesquels il entendent manifester leur appartenance à une religion n'est pas par lui-même incompatible avec le principe de laïcité, dans la mesure où il constitue l'exercice de la liberté d'expression et de manifestation de croyances religieuses.', Section 1, last paragraph.

231 '... par leur nature, par les conditions dans lesquelles ils seraient portés ..., ou par leur caractère ostentatoire ou revendicatif ...'. Translation taken from McGoldrick (2006), p. 69.

232 ' ... un acte de pression, de provocation, de prosélytisme ou de propagande ...'. Translation taken from ibid, p. 69.

233 '... porteraient atteinte à la dignité ou à la liberté de l'élève ou d'autres membres de la communauté éducative, compromettraient leur santé ou leur sécurité, perturberaient le déroulement des activités d'enseignement et le rôle éducatif des enseignants, enfin troubleraient l'ordre dans l'établissement

about public order,[234] and the pupils claiming the right to wear a headscarf were considered to violate their duty of assiduity. The Council of State left application of limitations based on these criteria to the schools.[235]

The Advice of the Council of State was consolidated in a Ministerial Circular (*Circulaire*, hereinafter: 1989 Circular) of 12 December 1989.[236] This 1989 Circular elaborated more explicitly on the criteria justifying limitations on religious symbols.[237] In particular, it concluded that pupils had to refrain from wearing any conspicuous symbol which aimed at promoting a religious belief.[238] Again, the 1989 Circular intended no more than to provide a guide for schools and teachers.[239] In so doing, it also outlined the steps to be taken in case of a dispute.[240]

Despite the directions in the 1989 Advice and 1989 Circular, variations in interpretations continued,[241] and claims continued to be brought before the Council of State, which were most of the time decided in the claimant's favour.[242] An example of such a decision was the *Kherouaa* decision which confirmed that *laïcité* in itself was not incompatible with pupils wearing religious symbols.[243] In response to the persisting unrest,[244] another ministerial circular was issued on 20 September 1994 (*Circulaire du 20 septembre 1994*, hereinafter: 1994 Circular).[245] In making

---

ou le fonctionnement normal du service public.' Translation taken from ibid, pp. 69-70.

234 Ibid, p. 66. This was also confirmed in the Stasi Report (2003), see, p. 58.

235 It stated that disciplinary matters should be governed by local school rules in light of local conditions, see Poulter (1997), p. 59.

236 Circulaire du 12 décembre 1989, (Education nationale, Jeunesse et Sports), *Laïcité*, port de signes religieux par les élèves et caractère obligatoire des enseignements, found on the website of the National Assembly, see <www.assemblee-nationale.fr>.

237 Clothing should not impede physical education or other practical activities. The requirements of security and health can also entail limitations.

238 'Ainsi, les élèves doivent se garder de toute marque ostentatoire, vestimentaire ou autre, tendant à promouvoir une croyance religieuse.', para. 1, p. 2. 'Tout jeune doit être respecté dans sa personnalité. … le jeune doit apprendre et comprendre que le respect de la liberté de conscience d'autrui appelle de sa part une réserve personnelle', para. 1, p. 2.

239 As the Circular states: 'je tiens à vous donner les orientations et les indications qui vous aideront à mettre en oeuvre, … le principe de *laïcité*' (I am anxious to give you the advice and information which will assist you in implementing the principle of *laïcité*), introduction, p. 1.

240 Circular, pp. 2-3. First and foremost, dialogue had to be initiated.

241 E.g. Fetzer and Soper (2005), pp. 79-80.

242 E.g. McGoldrick (2006), p. 71. Many courts decided in the same way, see e.g. Fetzer and Soper (2005), p. 81.

243 CE, *K.*, 2 November 1992, no. 130394; CE, *époux A.*, 20 October 1999, no. 181486. See also McGoldrick (2006), p. 71.

244 More generally, a tendency of increasing religious demands seemed to arise among Muslim students. Furthermore, an incident in 1993 reignited the debate, see e.g. McGoldrick (2006), p. 72. Finally, the wider international context, such as the resistance groups in Algeria, also contributed to the reversal, see Bowen (2008), p. 43.

245 Circulaire du 20 septembre 1994 (Circulaire Bayrou) relative au port de signes ostentatoires dans les établissements scolaires 1994.

explicit the distinction between conspicuous and discreet symbols, the 1994 Circular proposed to prohibit the former category of symbols.[246] A new surge of controversy around religious symbols, notably the headscarf, emerged around the beginning of the twenty-first century.[247] Schoolgirls were excluded from their classes, protests emerged, and the Muslim headscarf was again the object of scrutiny.[248]

President Chirac decided to establish a commission (*Commission de réflexion sur l'application du principe de laïcité dans le république*, hereinafter: Stasi Commission). He assigned the Stasi Commission the task of thoroughly examining the application of the principle of *laïcité* in the French Republic.[249] After having held interviews with people ranging from teachers to politicians and religious representatives as well as having paid visits to several other European countries,[250] the Stasi Commission presented its findings on 11 December 2003. The Stasi Report left no doubt about the incontestable importance of *laïcité* as the cornerstone of the Republican pact, despite the dynamic nature of the principle. At the same time, the Stasi Commission observed that recent developments attested to increasing encroachments on the principle of *laïcité*.[251] In response to these encroachments in particular, and to integration

---

246 Such prohibition would take effect by inserting the following text into the internal regulations of schools: 'Le port par les élèves de signes discrets, manifestant leur attachement personnel à des convictions notamment religieuses, est admis dans l'établissement. Mais les signes ostentatoires, qui constituent en eux mêmes des éléments de prosélytisme ou de discrimination, sont interdits. ...' (The wearing of discreet signs by pupils, manifesting their personal belonging to particularly religious convictions is permitted at school. But conspicuous signs, which in themselves constitute elements of proselytism or discrimination, are prohibited), see the annex of the Bayrou circular. See also Saxena (2007), p. 780. Again, the circular was understood to target headscarves, see Poulter (1997), p. 61.
247 Bowen (2008), p. 43. In addition, some trends in that period contributed to the re-emergence of the headscarf controversy, such as the new wave of anti-Semitism in Western Europe, the strong Islamophobia after 9/11 and the expansion of the EU, see Saxena (2007), p. 767. A new affair in March 2002 reignited the debate, see Bowen (2008), pp. 44-45.
248 Led by the right-wing political leader Le Pen, a large part of French society came to perceive the headscarf as a symbol of Muslim conspiracy and extremism. It was seen as a provocative symbol of Muslim identity in the neutral and secularized public sphere, see L. Barnett, 'Freedom of Religion and Religious Symbols in the Public Sphere' (Parliament of Canada, Ottawa 2011) Background paper no. 2011-60-E on <www.parl.gc.ca>, p. 31.
249 The commission was established on 3 July 2003, see Stasi Report (2003), introduction. The mandate did not explicitly mention the issue of headscarves, see Saxena (2007), p. 776. However, presumably the tussle about headscarves was an unofficial trigger for this report, see Bowen (2008), p. 46. What is more, some authors even consider the importance of the report to lie solely in the issue of headscarves and assess the report as being strikingly short on this issue, see Gunn (2004), p. 17.
250 The methods and approach have been contested in the sense that the objectivity of the report may have been affected, see e.g. Bowen (2008), p. 48. Otherwise, the testimonies of principals who were struggling with their responsibility to decide on and to motivate exclusion of religious symbols appeared crucial for the Stasi Commission in perceiving a need for legal exclusion, Thomas (2000).
251 For instance, it has been undermined in the public sector. The wearing of conspicuous religious signs has troubled public order in schools, see Stasi Report (2003), p. 40 ff.

problems in general, the Stasi Commission made recommendations on a variety of issues. Such recommendations involved accommodating religious needs, such as employing Muslim chaplains in the army and the prisons, making religious holidays such as Yom Kippur and Eid into festivals at all schools and establishing a national school of Islamic studies.[252] Be that as it may, the report has become primarily known for its recommendation to explicitly prohibit conspicuous religious symbols at state schools.

Public and political opinion soon closed ranks in underscoring the need for such a prohibition.[253] And so it was that in a little over three months after the Stasi Report the prohibition became a fact; the Act prohibiting dress or symbols with which pupils conspicuously manifest their religious adherence (2004 Act) was adopted on 15 March 2004.[254] It established the prohibition on religious symbols in the following words:

> Dans les écoles, les collèges et les lycées publics, le port de signes ou tenues par lesquels les élèves manifestent ostensiblement une appartenance religieuse est interdit.

Two months later, a Ministerial Circular (2004 Circular), replacing previous ones, further clarified the 2004 Act.[255] The 2004 Circular explained conspicuous religious symbols to mean symbols 'which can immediately be recognized as denoting the belonging to a religion';[256] it mentioned headscarves, yarmulkes or excessively large crucifixes as examples. Yet again, contention did not stop with the passing of the law.[257] To begin with, an appeal was lodged against the 2004 Circular. The Council of State dismissed the appeal, judging the 2004 Circular to be in accordance with the

---

252 Ibid, p. 69.
253 See McGoldrick (2006), p. 83. Even before the Report, key figures had expressed their preference for a law banning Muslim headscarves, such as Prime Minister Raffarin, see Gunn (2004), p. 7. Public opinion had already swung firmly behind a new law even before the Report was issued, see Bowen (2008), p. 50 and Gunn (2004), p. 7. On the politicians, see Bowen, p. 49. However, it has also been pointed out that teachers were divided and that many doubted the effectiveness of a new law, see Bowen (2008), p. 47.
254 Loi no. 2004-228 (2004). The vote was overwhelming: 494 in favour, 36 against in the National Assembly. In the Senate, a similarly large majority of 276 (20 against) voted in favour of the law, see Gunn (2004), p. 7. Although the law was phrased neutrally in aiming at religious signs, public debate focused on the headscarf, see Lyon and Spini (2004), p. 334.
255 Circulaire du 18 mai 2004 relative à la mise en oeuvre de la loi no. 2004-228 du 15 mars 2004 encadrant, en application du principe de *laïcité*, le port de signes ou de tenues manifestant une appartenance religieuse dans les écoles, collèges et lycées publics (*Journal Officiel*, no. 118, 22 May 2004), p. 9033, texte no. 10.
256 Article 2.1, original text: 'Les signes et tenues qui sont interdits sont ceux dont le port conduit à se faire immédiatement reconnaître par son appartenance religieuse …'. See also McGoldrick (2006), p. 92.
257 See for details on the application of the 2004 Act, Chérifi Report (2006).

European Convention on Human Rights. Additionally, quite a number of claimants affected by the law instituted proceedings. These proceedings went to the Council of State, which ruled in line with the 2004 Act. According to these rulings, it was the conspicuous nature of religious symbols, which caused them to be prohibited, be they a headscarf, a kippah or a large crucifix.[258] What is more, there have been decisions where garments which in themselves would probably not have qualified as conspicuous religious symbols, such as bandanas or bonnets, have nonetheless been considered to be prohibited symbols.[259] The motivation given was that these garments were clearly worn for religious reasons.[260] These cases have been pursued to the European Court of Human Rights, which has declared all of them to be inadmissible.[261]

In the years following the 2004 Act, debate persisted on related issues as well. More specifically, situations arose after 2004 in which it was not clear how *laïcité* and the 2004 Act applied. For example, there have been instances where women wearing a headscarf participated in a (compulsory) language course, which was provided in state school buildings. As a consequence, the question emerged whether these women could be compelled to take off their headscarf. Quite a number of these cases have come before HALDE, which has mostly ruled in favour of these women.[262] Nevertheless, some have interpreted *laïcité* in such a way as to apply to the school buildings, thus precluding these women from wearing religious symbols. Similar discussions have taken place regarding mothers accompanying pupils on school

---

258 E.g. CE, 5 December 2007, *M.S.*, décision no. 285394, para. a), original text: '... sont en revanche interdits, ... les signes ou tenues, tels notamment un voile ou un foulard islamique, une kippa ou une grande croix, dont le port, par lui-même, manifeste ostensiblement une appartenance religieuse...'

259 E.g. ibid, where the applicant wore a *keski*, a subturban. In CE, 5 December 2007, *Mdlle G.*, décision no. 295671, the applicant wore a bandana. Some schools have allowed the bandana, see, p. 92. See also F. Dieu, 'Le Conseil d'État et la laïcité négative' (2008) 13 *La Semaine Juridique Administrations et Collectivités territoriales*, paras. 36 and 46.

260 Gemie questions the consistency of this line of reasoning by giving examples like Rasta dreadlocks. When a white kid wears these, he suggests, he would probably be seen as a trendy fashionista. By contrast, a black kid would be deemed to wear them for religious (Rastafarian) reasons, see S. Gemie, 'Stasi's Republic: the school and the "veil", December 2003 - March 2004' (2004) 12(3) *Modern & Contemporary France*, p. 393.

261 E.g. *Gamaleddyn c. France* (ECtHR, Appl. no. 18527/08, 30 June 2009), cf. *supra* n. 261; E. Deceaux, 'Chronique d'une jurisprudence annoncée: laïcité française et liberté religieuse devant la Cour européenne des droits de l'homme' (2010) 21(82) *Revue trimestrielle des droits de l'homme*, p. 262 ff.

262 E.g. *Délibération relative au refus par un organisme public de formation d'accès à une formation se tenant dans les locaux d'un lycée public au motif qu'elle porte le foulard islamique*, (no. 2008-167, 1 September 2008). The HALDE has been consistent in condemning such expulsions as unjustified discrimination, exception for situations where the applicant wore a face veil, e.g. *Délibération relative à une demande de consultation de l'ANAEM sur la compatibilité de l'interdiction du port de la burqa dans le cadre d'une formation linguistique obligatoire en vertu d'un contrat d'accueil et d'intégration (CAI)* (no 2008-193, 15 September 2008). HALDE opinions can be found on <www.droitdesreligions.net>.

trips.[263] While there have thus been voices arguing in favour of extending *laïcité*, there have equally been voices in favour of a more open version of *laïcité*.[264]

Apart from the competing interpretations of *laïcité*, those aiming at excluding religious symbols from the public sphere seem to be gaining ground. It was noted that the prohibition on pupils wearing religious symbols could be considered as an extension of *laïcité*. In the same vein, a recent prohibition on the face veil could be considered as extending the reason and territorial scope for prohibiting religious symbols. On a legal level, over time, the Council of State seems to have embraced a negative version of *laïcité*.[265] French discourse in this issue thus relies on a different angle of approach – state neutrality is not at stake. Nonetheless, it has been so much at the forefront of French debate that it cannot be completely left aside. The next section deals briefly with the face veil prohibition.

6.4.3 Face veils in public

Like the issue of religious symbols at schools, the issue of face veils has cropped up throughout Europe. That said, France was the first European state to adopt a general prohibition on the wearing of face veils in public.[266] The roots of French debate can be tracked down to 2008 when the Council of State gave a decision on a nationality request by a Moroccan woman wearing a face veil.[267] The Council of State stated that the (radical) practice of wearing a face veil was incompatible with the essential values of the French community, especially gender equality. While this decision in itself managed to prompt debate, President Sarkozy gave an additional impetus to national debate when he declared in Parliament in June 2009 that the burqa was not welcome in France. The very next day, the French Parliament established a committee headed by André Gerin (*La mission d'information sur la pratique du port du voile intégral sur le territoire national*, hereinafter: the Gerin Committee) to investigate the practice of face veils. The Gerin Committee presented its findings, the Gerin Report, in January 2010. One of the main conclusions was that the legislation in force did not (yet) offer a basis for prohibiting the face veil. That said, the majority of the Gerin Committee was in favour of such a prohibition and accordingly the Gerin Report strongly recommended the adoption of a parliamentary resolution confirming

---

263 The HALDE has decided that measures imposing a headscarf ban on mothers constitute unjustified discrimination, see *Délibération relative au principe de la laïcité concernant une interdiction de port de signes religieux pour les accompagnateurs de sorties scolaires* (no. 2007-117, 14 May 2007).

264 See Fetzer and Soper (2005), pp. 75 and 84; Lyon and Spini (2004), p. 341; Saxena (2007), pp. 814-822.

265 Dieu (2008), para. 46.

266 Although the first, it has not remained the only one. In April 2011, Belgium followed suit. The Netherlands has been working on a bill for years now which is envisaged to become law in 2013. See Chapter 2.

267 CE, 27 June 2008, *Madame M.*, décision no. 286798.

the Republican values. On 11 May 2010, Parliament unanimously accepted such a resolution.

Subsequent to the Gerin Report, several parliamentary bills, as well a Government bill, were drafted. As to the latter bill, the Council of State gave its (requested) advice in March 2010 (2010 Advice). Although the Council of State considered the face veil to be contrary to gender equality, it clearly advised against a general prohibition. Like the Gerin Committee, the Council of State did not find a solid legal basis for such a prohibition. It should be noted that, unlike the prohibition on religious symbols at state schools, the prohibition on face veils could not be based on *laïcité* because it was envisaged to apply to public space where *laïcité* does not apply. The wide scope of application was a reason for the Council of State to describe the prohibition as an unjustified infringement on individual rights. Contrary to the 2010 Advice, the Government pursued its plans for a general prohibition, which passed the test of the Constitutional Council.[268] The Government brought the law on the grounds of public order coupled with the values of French society. On 11 April 2011, the Act banning the face veil (2011 Act) entered into force.[269] Like the 2004 Act, the 2011 Act illustrated how limitations on religious manifestations were imposed on citizens. In principle, this development represented a breach with the traditional French approach which had hitherto applied a clear distinction between public officials and citizens making use of the public service.[270] Indeed, Ministerial Circulars issued in March 2011 exclusively addressed the application to citizens.[271] Furthermore, the 2011 Act extended the scope of application even beyond public institutions to public space.

---

268 The Constitutional Council said that the bill did not strike an unfair balance between protecting public order and safeguarding constitutionally protected rights, see Conseil Constitutionnel, 7 October 2010, *Décision Loi interdisant la dissimulation du visage dans l'espace public*, no. 2010-613 DC, to be found on <www.conseil-constitutionnel.fr>.

269 E.g. A. Gerin and E. Raoult, 'Rapport d'information fait en application de l'article 145 du Règlement au nom de la mission d'information sur la pratique du port du voile intégral sur le territoire national' (Assemblée nationale, Paris 2010).

270 The French approach has usually emphasized the fact that citizens come from the 'outside' and only intend to make use of the public service. Accordingly, it could not endanger public order or the proper functioning of the public service when citizens would display religious symbols. In contrast, individuals hold the position as a public official by virtue of representing a public collectivity which is constitutionally bound by *laïcité*. In being neutral, they also convey an impartial image, L. Lainé, 'Liberté religieuse des agents territoriaux et obligation de neutralité religieuse' in J. Fialaire (ed), *Liberté de culte, laïcité et collectivités territoriales* (LexisNexis Litec, 2007), p. 16.

271 Circulaire d'application du 2 mars 2011 (JORF no. 0052, 3 March 2011), p. 4128. The question of public officials wearing face veils is not in the least envisaged. Surely, it is simply inconceivable that a public official would cover her face with a face veil in view of the neutrality of public service.

Chapter 6

6.5 APPLICATION OF THE CONCEPTUAL MODEL

6.5.1 Dynamics of neutrality

It has been shown that the typically French conception of neutrality cannot be seen separately from the long struggle between church and state. This struggle has strongly imbued the French take on religion in general and on the church in particular. The fact that *laïcité* was effectuated first in the field of education goes to show that the eradication of religion at the time served to create a secular form of instruction based on other values than religious ones. On a more general level, safeguarding neutrality of the state was achieved by laicising the state. In other words, it is by absolutely eliminating the visibility of religion from what is considered part of the state that the core duties of state neutrality are fulfilled. Indeed, the French context is also known for implementing neutrality in a mainly exclusive version. In ensuring its policies to be neutral, the French state mainly applies a standard of formal neutrality in classifying religion or belief as irrelevant categories.

Having been dissociated from religion, the French state actively endorses Republican ideology. As the name already conveys, this ideology attributes a dominant role to the state, which is conceived as a strong, nearly tangible actor. Consequently, those taking on a function within public service are considered as incurring duties in conformity with the image of the state. In their relation with citizens, these public officials are expected to bring across this alignment with the state. The apparent disappearance of the public official's private person may suggest that the public official can be omitted from the triangle of actors, thus reshaping the triangle to a straight line between state and citizen. This would rightly underscore the personification of the state, which the public official is to convey towards the citizen. When the public official is considered as the actor representing the state towards citizens he no longer appears to be primarily an individual bearing rights. At the same time, the relation between the state and the public official is not irrelevant in the French conception. While considering it self-evident that the public official forgoes his freedom to manifest religion or belief, this conception accepts that he still has freedom of conscience. Moreover, it remains useful to distinguish the relation between the public official and the citizen from the relation between the state and the citizen. In accordance with the indivisibility of French citizenship, citizens have a direct connection with the state without intermediary groups. Therefore, the triangle as such remains intact, but its inner dynamics is typical of the French conception of state neutrality.

One of the things which is typical of the French conception of neutrality is that all public officials alike assume an absolute duty of neutrality, as a corollary of the uniformity of the public service. For instance, a judge as well as a secretary in court as well as the cleaner in the court building incur the duty of neutrality. All those working in public service are precluded from manifesting their religion or belief by

200

displaying religious symbols. Accordingly, the model of actors and dynamics applies identically to all public functions, irrespective of the type of public function or of the tasks exercised. The complete abstraction of the characteristics of the actors or relations is consistent with the idea that it is the visibility of religious symbols as such which is problematic, irrespective of when and by whom such symbols are displayed.

6.5.2 Neutrality of the state towards the public official

At first sight, the French take on the relation between the state and the public official accords with the general image of how France deals with religion. The point of equal treatment appears to be interpreted according to a formal version of equality: a uniform policy applies for all public officials without regard for the actual effects on their religious freedom. Additionally, it turns out that the state absorbs the individual person of the public official: by taking on a public function, an individual becomes the state and accordingly incurs the duties of the state. This general image captures the gist of the French approach. However, it does not address the underlying reasons for and nuances of this approach, which can be considered as revolving around two relevant factors: the construction of religious freedom and the rationale of the absolute duty of neutrality.

It has already been said that French discourse primarily emphasizes religious freedom as the freedom of conscience, which protects the *forum internum*. French discourse considers this freedom to remain unaffected, even for public officials. Accordingly, public officials are considered as remaining free to have any religion or belief. They can freely communicate on their religion or belief with their colleagues and they can request leave for religious holidays. This occurs on a voluntary basis and the state in its turn is not allowed to intrude into public officials' freedom of conscience. For example, the personal files of public officials do not include information on their personal opinions, including religious ones. With regard to their freedom of conscience, the individuality of public officials can be said to remain intact.

This freedom is clearly considered as separate from the freedom to manifest religion or belief. The latter freedom is considered as inherently incompatible with the principle of *laïcité* and neutrality, which are incumbent on the state and the public service respectively. It is by voluntarily taking on a position in public service that a public official subjects himself to these principles. As well as not affecting his freedom of conscience, the duty of strict neutrality is not considered to be in violation of the public official's individual rights as it only applies during his working hours. Outside his office, a public official is considered free to manifest his religion or belief, although he is still subject to an obligation of restraint, albeit a less strict one. This regime is viewed as leaving sufficient room for enjoying religious freedom.

The rationale of strict neutrality corroborates this view. This rationale is informed by how the actors are assumed to relate to one another. Such assumptions are made *in abstracto* and probably emanate from the Republican ideology. The powerful conception of the Republican state coupled with the idea that public officials personify the state makes it likely that these officials should only embody the Republican ideology. The duty of strict neutrality is seen as offering a two-fold protection. On the one hand, it protects the public official against the state and on the other hand, it protects the citizen from the public official. Strict neutrality is considered as guaranteeing that public officials' freedom of conscience and right to equal access are safeguarded. French discourse emphasizes that state neutrality prevents the state from assessing a public official's religion or belief, either at the time of his entry into public service or during his career development. In the same vein, the requirement that public officials renounce the manifestation of their religion or belief is seen as consolidating the protection afforded to them. By refraining from such manifestations, public officials avoid making themselves susceptible to being assessed on the basis of their religion or belief.

The absoluteness of the duty of neutrality resounds with the abstractness of the assumptions underpinning strict neutrality. This combination of absoluteness and abstractness allows for a uniform application of neutrality to the whole of public service. Accordingly, the uniform limitation of public officials' freedom to manifest religion or belief is capable of disregarding the type of function altogether. As said, differentiation is made neither between the different public functions nor between different types of functions within one and the same public function. For example, a judge is in principle subject to the same limitations as a state schoolteacher, and the secretary working at a state school is also bound by the duty of neutrality. The specific factors which may be considered as shaping the actors and their relations do not come into play for the application of neutrality. Because they are all in the service of the state, they equally conform to the duties inherent to such service.

The formal equality underlying the policy of the French state raises the question whether it unequally affects particular individuals or groups thus resulting in differential treatment. It can be considered remarkable that the policy of exclusion applies identically to the whole of public service including functions as diverse as judges and schoolteachers. On the other hand, the uniformity of the French policy concerning access to public functions and the limitation on religious manifestation makes it straightforward to get the policy across. Without having to take notice of exceptions or other reservations to the policy, the state can communicate that any individual should refrain from manifesting religion or belief when pursuing any position within the public service. *A contrario*, it conveys that if someone wishes to wear religious symbols during work, he should not aspire to a public function. According to the French line of reasoning, the policy leaves an individual's religious freedom unharmed. After all, individuals are not, nor can they be, barred from access to public service solely on the basis of their religion or belief. It is the active manifestation of their religion or belief by displaying symbols, which would preclude them from entering public service. As said, this is also for the benefit of the very protection of public officials. By not actually seeing religious manifestations, the state is expected not to discriminate against public officials on the basis of their religion or belief.

6.5.3 Neutrality of the public official towards the citizen

In the French model, a public official who displays religious symbols is assumed to convey bias and to pose a risk of proselytizing the citizen. These assumptions justify the strictness of the duty of neutrality. Additionally, they account for the abstract application of this duty. Three factors can be pointed to as explaining these implications of neutrality: the conception of the state as a strong entity and hence the dominant role of public officials vis-à-vis citizens; the importance of citizens' perception; and the religious character of symbols.

To begin with the first factor: the conception of the strong state coupled with the idea that public officials personify the state logically results in the idea that public officials are powerful actors in relation to citizens. Accordingly, the French conception deems it necessary that citizens are protected against public officials. It is the safeguard of citizens' equality, which is the very source of the public official's duty of neutrality. What is more, neutrality is emphasized as conferring a right on citizens rather than imposing an obligation on public officials. By abstaining from manifesting religion or belief, public officials themselves show they are not concerned with citizens' opinion, religion or belief. Being neutral automatically implies appearing neutral or *a contrario* appearing neutral gives the impression of being neutral. Only complete abstention from displaying religious symbols is thought of as the proper way to avoid any doubts on the citizen's side about the public official's neutrality.

The last point implies the decisive role of citizens' perception. The possible risk that public officials displaying religious symbols may cause citizens to question the officials' neutrality is assumed to exist *a priori* and *in abstracto*. In other words, it is deemed irrelevant which capacity the citizen possesses or which relation he has with the public official. The uniform and abstract application anticipates the possible perception of citizens and could be seen as choosing to be on the safe side. Differential treatment may naturally remain a possibility but it is assumed that it is less likely to occur due to the exclusion of religious symbols. A legitimate question is whether a self-fulfilling prophecy is at work here. In an environment where religious symbols are completely excluded, any religious symbol is likely to stand out more. What does this mean for those perceiving such a symbol?

French history shows how religion has come to be loaded with pejorative connotations as a consequence of a fierce struggle between state and church. In the discussions on religious symbols, the (attributed) religious character of symbols seems to make them controversial. As the 2004 Act on conspicuous religious symbols at state schools illustrated, it is accepted that there may be a connection between religious symbols and proselytism. Early on in the discussions within the school context, it was the (assumed) proselytizing character of religious symbols which justified them being prohibited. Again, this *a priori* assumption as to the possible effect of religious symbols justified the general exclusion of such symbols. At the same time, the specification 'conspicuous' should not be overlooked. The 2004 Act emphasized that discreet symbols such as crucifixes and the hand of Fatima (*hamsa*) were still allowed. Most probably, conspicuous is equated with visible which is in line with the premise that it is the visibility of religious symbols which poses a threat to neutrality in possibly conveying bias or having a proselytizing effect. The emphasis on conspicuousness has not entirely circumvented the question of determining which symbols should be seen as conspicuously religious. As the cases concerning for instance bonnets and hats showed, some garments and symbols which are not particularly known for being religious have been attributed a religious character nonetheless. In sum, the conspicuousness of a symbol may be objectively established, but the religiosity of a symbol remains difficult to determine.

It should also be noted that the degree of conspicuousness might leave some room for leeway for authorities. To illustrate, the Council of State opinion in the *Marteaux* case left no doubt that no differentiation was possible regarding the type of public function or duties. But the Council of State did consider 'the nature and degree of the conspicuous character of a religious symbol' may be relevant for determining the precise consequences. It thus seems that the allegedly proselytizing character of a religious symbol is related to the degree of conspicuousness of the symbol.

6.5.4 Neutrality of the state towards the citizen

It has become clear by now that French discourse portrays the state as a strong, monolithic and *laïc* entity. As such, the state has been disconnected with society on a conceptual level. In a way, the French conception of the relation between state and society can be related to its outlook on three spheres representing varying degrees of private and public. The private sphere is where individuals are entirely free to have and to manifest their religion or belief. They can display any religious symbol, they can attend their religious community and they can partake in religious activities. Perhaps this sphere constitutes an essential element of what may be seen as 'French society'. When individuals partake in public service as citizens, they could be said to move in the public sphere. In that sphere, the French citizenship model impacts on their scope of individual freedoms. Although they remain individuals with in principle full enjoyment of their rights and freedoms, their capacity as citizens prevails. That is to say that they might be subject to limitations on their freedom to manifest religion or belief when this is necessary, for instance to safeguard the proper functioning of the public service. Additionally, their personal opinion is irrelevant for obtaining rights attached to their citizenship. Furthermore, formal policies do not recognize minorities in the sense that the individual characteristics which distinguish them from the majority are considered irrelevant, although accommodation does take place in practice. Individuals who represent the public service as public officials may be considered to be in the state sphere where strict limitations on their individual freedoms may apply. Pursuant to the French view on state and society, the state is not likely to mirror society in representative terms. The French take on the relation of the state with society does not envisage a state which intentionally includes recognizable characteristics for individuals in that society. Rather than legitimizing the state, the visibility of such characteristics would be seen as potential sources of division.

The area of education illustrates nicely that the state is not meant to correspond to the composition of society. Being at the heart of the Republican ideology, schools are considered as creating a space where Republican values can be fostered. The primary mission of schools is to turn young individuals into citizens. As a bearer of state authority, the teacher is entrusted with this mission. In pursuing this mission, he should refrain from anything incompatible with this mission, such as manifesting his personal religion or belief. These and other personal characteristics are deemed irrelevant to and probably deflecting from his function as a teacher. Accordingly, as explained previously, the teacher is expected not to show these personal characteristics.

It is by this exclusive neutrality that the state seeks to protect citizens from undue influence by the state, be it by way of its representatives or directly. The state only incorporates and conveys Republican values, eschewing any other values. The creation of a blank space, free from religious or ethnic characteristics has been emphasized as the best way to pursue the Republican project, which in its turn is best suited to guarantee individuals' rights. This is closely connected to the idea that personal features in the public domain are more likely to be a source of division and unequal treatment, perceived or not.

The separation of church and state is part and parcel of the principle of *laïcité* and as such equally informs how neutrality of the state towards the citizen is shaped. Especially in light of the historical relation with the Catholic Church, part of the neutrality of the state towards citizens revolves around the separation of church and state. In other words, the separateness of the state is also in relation to the Church. In being *laïc*, the state upholds its neutrality towards citizens.

6.6 CONCLUSION

The French stereotype has been confirmed in that the French context typically shows how a formal version of state neutrality has been implemented. Without taking account of the actual effects, neutrality applies to the public service as a whole in absolutely excluding the display of religious symbols. In the French conception, limitations on public officials' religious freedom are not only justified but also necessitated by state neutrality. This chapter has attempted to find the underlying reasons for this conception. It appeared that state neutrality is part and parcel of the constitutional principle of *laïcité*, which is firmly rooted in French history and the outlook on state–religion relations. The historical dimensions of the principle partly explain why it carries so much value. In focusing on the arguments brought forward to substantiate that state neutrality justifies and/or necessitates limitations on public officials' religious freedom, this study has analysed French discourse on the basis of the model developed in Chapter 4. In order to explain how the conceptual model is shaped in French discourse four findings can be pointed to.

Firstly, it has been commonly emphasized in French discourse that state neutrality should be seen as protecting citizens rather than as limiting public officials. In other words, citizens' interests and rights are paramount. This is also shown by the fact that the citizens' perception is the standard in considering banning public officials from wearing religious symbols. The mere risk that this perception may lead to the feeling of being treated differentially or being proselytised justifies the absolute prohibition on public officials wearing such symbols. Secondly, the link between the public official and the state is such that the former is considered as personifying the latter. Such personification equates public officials' actions with actions by the state. Accordingly, individual public officials automatically assume the duties incumbent on the state as being their duties. The state is emphasized to embody Republican values and thus public officials are to convey Republican values, forgoing any expression of personal characteristics. However, French discourse does not consider that public officials lose their individuality altogether. On the contrary, as a point of departure it emphasises public officials' freedom of conscience. Thirdly, it appeared that the conception of religious freedom partly explains why the prohibition on religious symbols is not considered as violating public officials' individual rights. Their freedom of conscience is seen as clearly separate from the freedom of religious manifestation. The latter is seen as evidently making way for the duty of neutrality, which public officials voluntarily incur by exercising a public function. What is more, if they were to manifest religion or belief, this might be seen as undermining their impartiality. One might even argue that it would undermine their impartiality and that appearance reflects on public officials' judgment. The state obligation of neutrality is seen as rightfully applying uniformly and generally, without regard for proportionality as to particular characteristics of public officials exercising their function. Another aspect of the typical French conception of religious freedom is that proselytism is not considered part of religious freedom. As Chapter 5 demonstrated, the right to manifest religion or belief includes the right to convince others of your religion or belief and to attempt to convert others, as also confirmed in ECHR case law. In this chapter, it came to the fore that French discourse looks negatively on anything which has the slightest potential to qualify as proselytism. Fourthly, French discourse draws a strict division between public officials and citizen-users of public services. In principle, no limitations on citizens' religious freedom apply, including their freedom to manifest religion or belief. Moreover, their rights are considered to be safeguarded by the strict duty of neutrality limiting public officials' religious freedom.

This has also been a significant factor in the tendency to extend the scope of *laïcité*, which has come to limit state school pupils' religious freedom as well. This tendency has led to prohibiting religious symbols, which qualify as conspicuous. This qualification could not prevent the difficulty in determining when something can be considered to be a conspicuous religious symbol; even determining the religious character mostly remains a conundrum. Garments which are commonly not known for their religiosity, such as caps or hats, have nonetheless been excluded, because they were suspected of being worn for religious motives.

As a matter of fact, the difficulties of qualifying a symbol as a conspicuous religious symbol demonstrate the more general problem that the French approach is not free from contention, although at first sight it may seem so appealing for its straightforwardness. While the boundaries in the French policy seem crystal-clear, persistent claims show that it cannot avoid the question where the boundaries can really be drawn. The extension of *laïcité* to pupils also exemplifies this constant search for boundaries. Related questions are whether the strict duty of neutrality applies to public officials alone, or to public buildings as well, or perhaps to any context where a public interest can be discerned.

Despite the ongoing contention, the French approach also illustrates that it is self-reinforcing. More specifically, the ongoing contention seems in no way to have provided a reason for considering a change of policy or enhancement of accommodation. On the contrary, the formal response, on a political and a legal level, is to consolidate the French approach. The more incidents seem to occur, the more adamant the calls for such consolidation appear to become. As announced, the next chapter will turn to how the English approach grapples with the question of state neutrality and religious symbols in public functions.

CHAPTER 7
ENGLAND

7.1 INTRODUCTION

Like France, England cannot entirely escape being branded with stereotypical ideas. Unlike France, though, the stereotype of England is that it is inclusive towards religion.[1] This stereotype is borne out by the knowledge that judges can wear turbans or that police officers can wear headscarves. Indeed, Chapter 1 mentioned that France and England are considered as representing the extremes of a spectrum regarding the approach towards religion. By virtue of being such extremes they inspire the debate in the Netherlands. Whereas the French approach serves the argument in favour of excluding religious symbols from public functions, the English approach helps in arguing against such exclusion. Along the same lines as Chapter 6 did as regards France, the present chapter carries out an in-depth examination of how the issue plays out within the English context. Like the previous chapter, it aims at going beyond the stereotypical image; it seeks for the underlying reasons underpinning the English conception of neutrality and the relation of this conception to religious symbols in public functions. The main question of the present chapter is as follows:

> How is state neutrality considered in the English context to justify and/or necessitate limitations on public officials in the judiciary, the police and public education to manifest their religion or belief by displaying symbols?

---

1   As Parekh proposes: '… acceptance of the diversity of dress in a multicultural society is a good indicator of whether or not the latter is at ease with itself'. A quick glance at English society reveals that the diversity of religious dress accepted is relatively broad, from which it may be concluded that English multicultural society is quite at ease with itself, B. Parekh, *Rethinking multiculturalism. Cultural diversity and political theory,* (MacMillan's, Palgrave 2000), p. 243. See e.g. D. McGoldrick, *Human Rights and Religion: The Islamic Headscarf Debate in Europe* (Hart Publishing, Oregon 2006), p. 173. Poulter also considers that conventional political discourse tends to portray England in this manner, S. Poulter, 'Muslim Headscarves in Schools: Contrasting Legal Approaches in England and France' (1997) 17(43) *Oxford Journal of Legal Studies*, p. 44. This image is put into perspective by e.g. Modood who distinguishes between the period before and after the events of 9/11. According to him, the Government had sought to emphasize the plural and dynamic character of British society until 2001, T. Modood, *Multiculturalism: a Civic Idea* (Polity, Cambridge 2007), p. 10. In 2000, a commission published a report in which it was considered that England was at a turning point in history. It submitted that England could either become 'narrow and inward-looking' or it could develop as a community of citizens and communities, see the Commission on the Future of Multi-Ethnic Britain (Chair: Bikhu Parekh) 'The Future of Multi-Ethnic Britain' (London, 2000).

This chapter contains the same components as the previous chapter on France. That is to say that it first explores the English context by looking at religious freedom, the position of religion in the public sphere and state neutrality in England. Subsequently, it elaborates on public officials' freedom to manifest their religion or belief by displaying symbols, for each public function. After briefly examining which relevant debates have taken place specifically in the English context, the chapter closes by assessing the points of contention on the basis of the conceptual model.

7.2 RELIGION IN ENGLAND

7.2.1 Religious freedom

As a preliminary note, it may be good to bring to mind one of the distinctive features of the English constitutional framework: there is no constitution in the form of a single legal document providing for the basis of state power. Instead, the constitution can be considered to derive from a variety of legal and extra-legal rules and practices.[2] What is more, these rules are expectations of proper conduct rather than legal rules in the strict sense.[3] The supremacy of Parliament is telling for the relative importance of the Constitution in the English context.[4] While a written constitution has been lacking, a written catalogue of rights has long been lacking as well.[5] It could be said that the British tradition has relied on a tolerance-based approach rather than on a rights-based approach.[6]

In this light, it might be seen as particularly remarkable that the United Kingdom was one of the first states to ratify the European Convention on Human Rights (hereinafter: ECHR or Convention). Moreover, it accepted the jurisdiction of the European Court of Human Rights (hereinafter: ECtHR or Court) at a very early stage.

---

2 P.W. Edge, *Legal Responses to Religious Difference* (Kluwer Law International, The Hague/London/New York 2002), p. 75.
3 Ibid, p. 76. As an example, he mentions the royal prerogative of pardon, p. 165.
4 That is to say that 'an Act of Parliament can change any law, produce any result, and cannot be challenged on legal grounds due to its disregard for fundamental rights or constitutional values', see ibid, p. 77. See also M. van Noorloos, *Hate Speech Revisited* (PhD Universiteit Utrecht, Intersentia, Antwerp, 2011), p. 282.
5 J.S. Fetzer and J.C. Soper, *Muslims and the State in Britain, France, and Germany* (Cambridge University Press, Cambridge 2005), p. 35. A specific enforcement mechanism was also lacking, see Edge (2002), p. 78.
6 E.g. M. Freedland and L. Vickers, 'Religious Expression in the Workplace in the United Kingdom' (2009) 30(3) *Comparative labor law & policy journal* and J.G. Oliva, 'Religious Symbols in the Classroom: A Controversial Issue in the United Kingdom' (2008) 20(3) *Brigham Young University Law Review*, pp. 877-878; S. Knights, 'Approaches to Diversity in the Domestic Courts: Article 9 of the European Convention on Human Rights' in R. Grillo and others (eds), *Legal Practice and Cultural Diversity* (Ashgate, Farnham [etc.] 2009), p. 285.

The ECHR as such did not become part of the domestic legal order[7] and had relatively little impact on the law or legal debate in England.[8] The impact of the Convention on the domestic legal order was effected by national courts which took the Convention into account. Furthermore, it gave an impetus to several pieces of legislation on rights.[9] An Act worth mentioning is the 1998 Human Rights Act[10] (hereinafter: HRA or Human Rights Act) enacted in 2000.

The Human Rights Act enabled rights enshrined in the ECHR to form the basis of a domestic legal challenge.[11] Instead of constituting a full-fledged human rights catalogue, the Human Rights Act primarily aimed at incorporating the guarantees of the Convention.[12] Accordingly, it introduced a few innovations into the English legal order which were intended to enhance compatibility with the Convention. For example, the Human Rights Act introduced a new principle for statutory interpretation: 'so far as it is possible to do so, primary and subordinate legislation must be read and given effect in a way which is compatible with the Convention'.[13] Additionally, it created structures for reducing the likelihood of new legislation which would be contrary to the Convention.[14] Finally, the Human Rights Act expanded the possibilities for judicial review on the basis of the Convention.[15] On a conceptual level, the Human Rights Act has been noted to mark the shift in considering religious freedom as a positive right instead of a negative right.[16] Be that as it may, the Human Rights Act can be said to have had relatively little bearing on the way in which legal questions concerning religious manifestations have been adjudicated.

---

7   See e.g. Edge (2002), p. 77.
8   D. McClean, 'United Kingdom' in M. Hill (ed), *Religion and discrimination law in the European Union. La discrimination en matière religieuse dans l'union européenne* (Institute for European Constitutional Law, University of Trier, Trier 2012), p. 334.
9   R.J. Walker and others, *Walker & Walker's English legal system* (9th edn Oxford University Press, Oxford 2005), p. 149.
10 To be found on <www.legislation.gov.uk>.
11 Walker and others (2005), p. 149. Oliva (2008), pp. 883-884. The Human Rights Act was the first explicit statement of fundamental rights within the United Kingdom, Edge (2002), p. 77.
12 Edge (2002), p. 78. As he notes, before the Human Rights Act, there was no explicit statement of fundamental rights within the UK. Rights were protected by normal laws.
13 Human Rights Act 1998, Section 3(1), see also Edge (2002), p. 79. Although the rule is not absolute and has its limitations, it is nevertheless a potent one.
14 Edge (2002), p. 81.
15 Ibid, p. 83. Walker and others (2005), p. 163. The Act takes a functional approach to the term 'public authority'; a body is qualified as a public authority on the basis of how public its tasks are. See also Freedland and Vickers (2009), p. 602. Oliva (2008), p. 883.
16 Oliva (2008), p. 883. He had pointed out that originally, in keeping with the common law tradition, freedom of religion was perceived as a negative right, p. 879.

The non-discrimination norms implementing the EU Equal Treatment Directives[17] have proved more effective in that regard.[18] Until 2010, these norms had been scattered over the 2003 Employment Equality (Religion or Belief) Regulations[19] and the Equality Act 2006. The Equality Act 2010 joined together the provisions on religion and belief discrimination.[20] Generally, the emergence of a whole legal framework concerning religion was innovative in itself compared with the previous modest regulation.[21] The tolerance-based approach has now undoubtedly shifted to a rights-based approach.[22] This 'juridification' of religion[23] was remarkable in two other respects.

Firstly, it provided a solid basis to challenge discrimination on religious grounds, which did not exist before. Anti-discrimination law had developed in a piecemeal manner and in English law there is not a broad non-discrimination principle.[24] Secondly, it marked an extension of the focus on race to religion as a ground on which discrimination was prohibited. Initially, the protection of ethnic or religious minorities – which partly overlap – was primarily based on race.[25] Particular manifestations had obtained protection not because they were characterized as religious but because they were worn by particular ethnic groups.[26]

---

17 Specifically, Council Directive 2000/78/EC of 27 November 2000 establishing a general framework for equal treatment in employment and occupation 2000/78/EC, to be found on <eur-lex.europa.eu>.

18 This is demonstrated by the fact that cases brought on the ground of Article 9 ECHR have not been successful, whereas the one successful case concerning religious symbols was brought on the basis of non-discrimination law, see R. Sandberg, *Law and Religion* (Cambridge University Press, Cambridge 2011), p. 110. Section 7.4.3 further elaborates on this difference in outcome.

19 At the time, the Regulations had already caused controversy, see for the detailed legislative history T. Edmonds, and J. Lourie, 'Employment Equality Regulations: Religion and Sexual Orientation' (House of Commons, London 2003) Research Paper no. 03/54. See also Freedland and Vickers (2009), p. 601; A. Blair and W. Aps, Blair and Aps (2005)(2005) 17(1-2) *Education and the Law*, p. 15.

20 R. Sandberg, 'A Uniform Approach to Religious Discrimination? The Position of Teachers and Other School Staff in the UK' in M. Hunter-Henin (ed), *Law, Religious Freedoms and Education in Europe* (Cultural Diversity and Law, Ashgate, Farnham [etc] 2011), p. 327; McClean in Hill (ed) (2012), p. 337.

21 Sandberg in Hunter-Henin (ed) (2011), pp. 327 and 332.

22 Sandberg (2011), p. 192.

23 Term used by Sandberg in Hunter-Henin (ed) (2011), p. 330.

24 Blair and Aps (2005), p. 9.

25 E.g. S. Vertovec and A. Rogers, *Muslim European Youth: Reproducing Ethnicity, Religion, Culture* (Ashgate, Aldershot [etc] 1998), p. 62. See also Poulter (1997), p. 63. Cf. Parekh Report (2000), p. 240.

26 It has been suggested that this emphasis on race rather than on religion can even be related to the Protestant versus Catholic culture, see Blair and Aps (2005), p. 10. See also L. Molokotos Liederman, 'Pluralism in Education: the display of Islamic affiliation in French and British schools' (2000) 11(1) *Islam and Christian-Muslim Relations*, p. 112. Otherwise, following the example of American (sub) culture may have influenced religious minorities in emphasizing their racial rather than their religious identity, T. Modood, 'The Place of Muslims in British Secular Multiculturalism' in

The evolvement of (the protection of) religious freedom in contemporary English society can be compared to similar processes in the Netherlands and France. Developments related to the societal role of religion and to the impact of immigration have had their bearing on the changes in the legal framework of religion. The Anglican Church is formally still the established church, but England has not remained unaffected by secularization. On a legal level, this found expression in the way in which the law was adjudicated and in the minimal legal protection of religion.[27] On a social level, it is perhaps paradoxical in light of the establishment of the Church to find that England has become considerably secularized, which shows from a decline in terms of church membership and attendance.[28] That said, the significance of belief for individuals has not abated.[29] Moreover, as in the Netherlands and in France, religion has assumed renewed political importance by the increasing claims of religious minority groups, notably Muslims.[30] Immigration has been an important factor for the presence of these groups in England too.

The influx of religious minorities can be traced back to the 1950s and 1960s.[31] The immigrants differed in several respects, such as their origin. The immigration waves were partly composed of immigrants from the colonies and the New Commonwealth,[32] including migrants from South Asia as a result of the partition of India.[33] In addition to their geographically diverse background, the immigrants adhered to a variety of religions ranging from Islam to Hinduism and Sikhism.[34] Moreover, the immigrants'

N. Alsayyad and M. Castells (eds) *Muslim Europe or Euro-Islam: Politics, Culture, and Citizenship in the Age of Globalization* (Lexington Books ; [etc.], Lanham, MD 2002), p. 118 ff.

27 Sandberg in Hunter-Henin (ed) (2011), p. 329.
28 Fetzer and Soper (2005), pp. 35-36. G. Davie, 'Croire sans appartenir: le cas britannique' in G. Davie and D. Hervieu-Léger (eds), *Identités religieuses en Europe* (La Découverte, Paris 1996), p. 176. A. Bradney, 'Religion and Law in Great Britain at the End of the Second Christian Millennium' in P. Edge and G. Harvey (eds), *Law and Religion in Contemporary Society: Communities, individualism and the State* (Ashgate, Aldershot [etc.] 2000), p. 18.
29 See e.g. Sandberg in Hunter-Henin (ed) (2011), p. 330.
30 T. Modood, 'British Muslims and the politics of multiculturalism' in T. Modood, A. Triandafyllidou and R. Zapata-Barrero (eds) (2006), *Multiculturalism, Muslims and Citizenship: a European Approach* (Routledge, London 2006), p. 37. Modood in AlSayyad and Castells (eds) (2002), p. 121.
31 At that time, the immigration numbers increased dramatically. Before that, the first Sikhs and Muslims had already arrived in England, albeit in small numbers, see S. Poulter, *Ethnicity, Law and Human Rights: The English Experience* (Clarendon Press, Oxford 1998), p. 277. Fetzer and Soper (2005), p. 26.
32 Poulter (1998), p. 3. Modood in AlSayyad and Castells (eds) (2002), p. 115. C. Joppke, *Multiculturalism and Immigration: a Comparison of the United States, Germany, and Britain* (European University Institute, Florence, 1995), p. 35. He also notes that in this period 'Britain refashioned itself from a "civic nation" to an "ethnic nation", in which membership became defined by birth or ancestry'.
33 Poulter (1998), p. 281. Fetzer and Soper (2005), p. 26.
34 J. Baubérot, 'The Place of Religion in Public Life: The Lay Approach' in T. Lindholm, W. Cole Durham Jr. and B.G. Tahzib-Lie (eds), *Facilitating Freedom of Religion or Belief: A Deskbook* (Martinus Nijhoff Publishers, Leiden 2004); Modood in AlSayyad and Castells (eds) (2002), p. 113.

educational background varied from unskilled to professional.[35] Like most governments, the British Government has varied its immigration policy. Whereas it initially administered a policy of granting Commonwealth inhabitants access to all the rights and privileges of British citizenship,[36] it tightened its immigration policies from the 1960s onwards.[37] As in other countries, neither the Government nor the immigrants initially anticipated the latter's permanent settlement in England. The British Government did not take steps in order to protect the immigrants from being discriminated against on the basis of religion.[38] Immigrants for their part did not make any claims for protection and practised their religion in the confines of their private sphere or adjusted themselves to the dominant norms in the public sphere.[39] Such claims arose at the moment when the immigrants settled more permanently.[40] Religious minorities institutionalized their faith and they began to manifest their religion more openly.[41] Moreover, they started making efforts to enhance legal protection of their religious manifestations.[42] Some of these efforts did result in larger protection; other efforts were unsuccessful. The Sikh struggle for recognition to wear the turban in public is a successful example, which is regularly referred to.[43]

Fetzer and Soper (2005), p. 26. Poulter (1998), p. 281. The remainder of this section seems to focus on Sikhs and Muslims, but that is rather because these two groups were most prominent in issues concerning religious dress.

35 Fetzer and Soper (2005), p. 26, Poulter (1998), pp. 281-282 and 291, Modood in in AlSayyad and Castells (eds) (2002), p. 113. Among the latter group were originally South-Asian political refugees who were expelled from African countries as a result of policies of 'Africanization'.

36 Fetzer and Soper (2005), p. 27. It has been suggested that this policy was aimed at white colonial subjects and did not anticipate that these rights and privileges would also be given to the many non-white residents of the Commonwealth.

37 Ibid, pp. 4 and 28-29. Joppke (1995), pp. 34-37. Joppke qualifies the British immigration policy as exceptionally restrictionist, p. 34. Like the white-oriented immigration anticipated, it has been suggested that the restrictions introduced were inspired by anxiety about non-white immigration, see S. Kiliç, 'The British Veil Wars' (2008) 15(4) *Social politics: international studies in gender, state, and society*, p. 436.

38 A common justification is to point out England's long tradition of religious tolerance, which makes special guarantees redundant, see Poulter (1997), p. 73. Other possibilities offered were the failure to see or acknowledge that minority religions differed from mainstream religion and the expectation of the immigrants' return to their home country, see Fetzer and Soper (2005), pp. 27 and 30.

39 For example, Sikhs shaving their beards and taking off their turbans, see e.g. Fetzer and Soper (2005), pp. 27 and 31. See also Poulter (1998), p. 284. In society, they met with suspicion and apprehension and the reality left them being refused employment and accommodation because of their appearance. Moreover, some public figures were also of the opinion that they should adjust their appearance in order to integrate into society.

40 Poulter has also pointed out that 'faced with continued prejudice, discrimination ... from sections of the majority community, many members of the ethnic minority communities are responding by emphasizing their distinctive religious and cultural identities', Poulter (1998), p. 10.

41 For instance, Sikhs stopped shaving their hair and beards and taking off their turbans, see Poulter (1998), p. 285. Fetzer and Soper (2005), pp. 27 and 31.

42 Fetzer and Soper (2005), p. 31.

43 Poulter (1998), p. 285.

Muslims' efforts in extending the laws of blasphemy to protect Islam failed.[44] In any event, it is clear that the upshot of immigration is a diverse population with divergent ethnic and religious backgrounds.[45] It is not hard to see that such diversity presents the English state with the inevitable challenges regarding its relation with citizens.

7.2.2 State–citizen relation

Like France, England has received a great number of its immigrants from former colonies. Accordingly, the attitude towards immigrants and the ensuing willingness to accommodate their needs were influenced by colonial history. In comparison with the French fiercely negative colonial-related association with Muslims, England had a relatively positive perception of both the Sikhs[46] and the Muslims[47] as a result of the colonial mutual experiences. The English policy has been generally characterized as fairly open to the demands of accommodation.[48] This open attitude resonated with the multiculturalist principle underlying the English immigration model,[49] for which assimilation was not the leading strategy. The way in which the English had governed their colonies could be seen as illustrative for the English approach. The English had left the local chiefs in charge and the local laws and customs in force through the principle of indirect rule.[50] The rejection of assimilation and the implementation of

---

44   In the end, the laws on blasphemy were abolished altogether, and came to be replaced by new Acts on religious offences, treating Christianity the same as other religions, see Modood in AlSayyad and Castells (eds) (2002), p. 44. See on the state funding of Islamic schools in Britain, Molokotos Liederman (2000), p. 107. Also Kiliç (2008), p. 442. On blasphemy, Fetzer and Soper (2005), p. 37. See Sandberg (2011), p. 135 ff.

45   In 2001, there were about 1.6 million Muslims, 471,000 Indian Hindus, and 307,000 Indian Sikhs in the UK, see National Statistics online, <www.statistics.gov.uk>, under 'People and Places' > Identity.

46   Sikhs have not failed to refer to these experiences if they could use them to their advantage. For example, when arguing in favour of an exemption for Sikh turbans for public transport employees, a Sikh applicant referred to the possibility for Sikh soldiers to wear the turban in the British army In so doing, he somewhat sarcastically raised the question that if Sikhs could die in their turbans, why could they then not work for Britain in them?, see Poulter (1998), p. 286.

47   For almost a century up to Indian independence, sympathy, mutual respect and trust existed between British soldiers and Sikh soldiers, see ibid, pp. 279 and 282. It has further been suggested that 'the British inherited a positive image of Islam because of their experiences in Muslim parts of the Empire', see Fetzer and Soper (2005), pp. 26-27.

48   Ibid, p. 4. Liberal multiculturalism has dominated civil society since the 1980s, see Kiliç (2008), p. 438. See also P. Lewis, 'Between Lord Ahmed and Ali G: Which Future for British Muslims?' in W.A.R. Shadid and P.S. van Koningsveld (eds), *Religious Freedom and the Neutrality of the State: the Position of Islam in the European Union* (Peeters, Leuven 2002), p. 130. In addition, the pluralist nature of public policy is also evident from the possibility for financial support by the state to support minority cultures, see Poulter (1998), pp. 64-65. This is confirmed in the context of education, see Molokotos Liederman (2000), p. 113.

49   Fetzer and Soper (2005), p. 30.

50   Joppke (1995), p. 38. Poulter (1998), p. 40.

an approach of integrating minorities by letting them retain their cultural, religious and ethnic customs resounded in the immigration policy.[51] Additionally, the English attitude has made their citizenship model fundamentally different from the French one. Unlike France, England explicitly recognizes the existence and the value of communities, be they religious, ethnic or cultural.[52]

That said, England has afforded variable protection to identity markers. As mentioned previously, religion has long gone unprotected on a legal level.[53] Instead, legislation has primarily focused on ethnicity as a ground for protection against discrimination.[54] The Sikhs' and Jews' emancipation in English society has been attributed to their recognition as an ethnic minority.[55] By contrast, the failure of Muslims to be accommodated in a number of respects has been explained by the failure to be recognized as an ethnic minority.[56]

The position of religion in the public sphere is recognized as influencing how a state copes with religious diversity. The previous chapters described how the Netherlands and France have both implemented a separation of church and state, although they differ as to the strictness with which they have done so. England contrasts with both of them because it has an established church. The next section briefly reviews the position of religion in the public sphere in England, with the proviso that it is confined to highlighting the aspects that are considered important for this study.

---

51 Evidently, reality is more nuanced than this. More specifically, British policy encompasses both assimilationist and multiculturalist tendencies. But the overall approach is commonly accepted as being multiculturalist. Poulter (1998), pp. 46, 48 and 49. In a theoretical analysis of the appropriate state response to ethnic diversity in Western Europe, he identifies the dichotomy as assimilation versus cultural pluralism, ibid, pp. 48 and 49. Modood offers a nuanced explanation of multiculturalism requiring support for two conceptions of equality which each can be seen as more assimilationist and multiculturalist, see Modood in AlSayyad and Castells (eds) (2002), p. 115

52 B. Parekh, 'The future of multi-ethnic Britain. Reporting on a report' (2001), 362 *The Round Table* (2001), p. 695.

53 It must be observed that the argument of religious freedom did figure in the debates initiated by the Sikhs, see Poulter (1998), pp. 293, 297, 321. The exemption law finally enacted, relieving Sikhs from the duty to wear a motorcycle helmet, exempted 'any follower of the Sikh *religion* while he is wearing a turban' (italics added).

54 Ibid, pp. 303-304.

55 See *Mandla and another v Dowell Lee and another* (UKHL 7, 1982), see also Poulter (1998), p. 322. One of the effects of this success was that a large part of the Sikh community rededicated themselves to orthodox practice, ibid, pp. 286-287.

56 Modood in Modood, Triandafyllidou and Zapata-Barrero (2006) p. 38. Muslims have not been recognized as a race, see T. Modood, 'Establishment, multiculturalism and British citizenship' (1994) 65(1) *Political Quarterly*. p. 57. The lack of protection poses serious questions about their religious identity, see Kiliç (2008), p. 440. Although they have not been the only group falling outside the scope of the Act, Oliva (2008), p. 880.

7.2.3 The position of religion in the public sphere

The Anglican Church has been the formally established Church of England for more than five centuries.[57] This long establishment does not mean that it has entirely steered clear of debate. Of course, England has had its own long history of religious conflicts, including violent religious intolerance and discrimination.[58] From the sixteenth century onwards, however, limited and piecemeal toleration of religions other than the established Church of England increased.[59] Especially towards the end of the nineteenth century a strong divide emerged between Liberals in favour of state neutrality between religious groups and Conservatives defending religious establishment.[60] Some voices in the former group even advocated a purely secular state free from any religious influence. Being in the minority, however, these voices had to give way to the majority tendency among the Liberals to favour extension of privileges to other churches.[61] The Liberal activity[62] did seem to precede a reduction of the privileges of the established church and the easing of the restrictions on religious minorities.[63] Whether this led the debates to fade throughout the twentieth century cannot be established as a fact, but the Catholic–Protestant divide in party politics was not nearly as prominent as it was in the century before.[64]

Whereas the political powers and privileges of the Church have been progressively diluted,[65] remnants of its privileged position can still be recognized today.[66] An obvious one is that twenty-four senior bishops and two archbishops still sit by right in the House of Lords.[67] Another one is that the monarch is also the head of the

---

57 The Church of England was established in the middle of the sixteenth century, see Fetzer and Soper (2005), pp. 32-33.

58 See for a concise historical account J. Rivers, *The Law of Organized Religion. Between Establishment and Secularism* (Oxford University Press, Oxford 2010). Sandberg in Hunter-Henin (ed) (2011), p. 329.

59 Sandberg in Hunter-Henin (ed) (2011), p. 329.

60 Fetzer and Soper (2005), p. 33. See also P. Weller in P. Edge and G. Harvey (eds), *Law and Religion in Contemporary Society: Communities, individualism and the State* (Ashgate, Aldershot [etc.] 2000), p. 54.

61 Fetzer and Soper (2005), p. 33.

62 The Liberals were not necessarily anticlerical, just as the Conservatives were not necessarily committed to the privileges of the Anglican Church, see ibid, p. 33.

63 Ibid, pp. 33-34.

64 Ibid, p. 33.

65 The debate continued in moderate form, and a large part of it was conducted within the Church, see Weller in Edge and Harvey (eds) (2000), p. 54.

66 For some of these remnants, see also Parekh (2000), p. 257. Also Kiliç (2008), p. 442. In an early article, Modood has briefly listed some of the privileges and disabilities see Modood (1994), p. 53. As pointed out by Weller in Edge and Harvey (eds) (2000), p. 56.

67 Fetzer and Soper (2005), p. 34. L. Vickers, 'Religion and Belief Discrimination and the Employment of Teachers in Faith Schools' (2009) (4) *Religion and Human Rights*, p. 146.

Church.[68] In the field of education in particular, the Anglican Church still possesses a privileged position.[69] It must be pointed out that despite this position the Anglican Church is not part of the state.[70] As a consequence, it is not a public body and as such also does without specific privileges of the state; on the other hand, it does not incur specific obligations either.

In previous centuries the debate was mostly characterized by discrepancies between rival groups within Christianity.[71] The contemporary controversies surrounding the position of the Anglican Church have shifted to include non-Christian groups.[72] As such, the dispute has become part of the wider debate on the position of these groups. Moreover, minorities' claims shed a different light on previously unquestioned norms and practices. For example, the Rushdie affair, which raised pertinent questions on the freedom of expression, blasphemy and Islam,[73] exposed the privileged position of Christianity with respect to the laws of blasphemy.

The Rushdie affair also illustrated that it is not so much establishment in itself,[74] which Muslims or other non-Christians turn against, as it is the disadvantages emanating from this system.[75] One of the criticisms was that the policy of the state fell short of being consistently secular or neutral towards religions.[76] It has been pointed out that religious minorities have evaluated establishment in itself positively in the sense that establishment has recognized the valuable role that religion can

---

68 See Act of Settlement 1701. Under this Act, the monarch must pledge to uphold Protestant Christianity, Weller in Edge and Harvey (eds) (2000), p. 61. See also Edge (2002), p. 186.

69 Weller in Edge and Harvey (eds) (2000), p. 61.

70 Molokotos Liederman (2000), p. 106. This is corroborated in the context of the obligations incumbent on church authorities with respect to the Human Rights Act. It has been ruled that a parochial church council of the Church of England is not a public body under the Act, see the case of *Cantlow v. Wallbank* before the House of Lords, referred to by Oliva (2008), p. 884.

71 Fetzer and Soper (2005), p. 33.

72 See Weller in Edge and Harvey (eds) (2000), p. 55.

73 See for a description of the events, e.g. Parekh (2000), p. 295 ff. Elaine Thomas points out that the affair 'also sparked a rich and revealing debate in Britain about the nature of political membership [of e.g. Muslims]', E.R. Thomas, *Immigration, Islam and the Politics of Belonging in France. A Comparative Framework* (University of Pennsylvania Press, Philadelphia 2012), p. 204.

74 Indeed, establishment has not been considered in itself to be incompatible with the freedom of religion or religious equality, e.g. Parekh (2000), p. 260. See also C. Evans and C.A. Thomas, 'Church-State Relations in the European Court of Human Rights' (2006) (3) *Brigham Young University Law Review.*

75 Fetzer and Soper (2005), p. 32.

76 Ibid, p. 38.

play in public.[77] Accordingly, rather than imposing limitations, it is creating space for religious minorities to experience their religion in public as well.[78]

In keeping with its previously mentioned open attitude towards religious minorities' claims for accommodation,[79] the state has generally acted with a willingness to modify the relations between public institutions.[80] Some practices have been gradually modified to correspond more with the composition of the population of contemporary society. That such modification takes time is illustrated by the long-pending plans to have the House of Lords represent other religions than that of the Church of England.[81] In 2000, a report recommended reserving the right to seats in the House of Lords not only to the bishops but to allot at least five of them to representatives of non-Christian communities.[82] In 2011, the discussion on the reform was still ongoing. The representation of other faiths in Parliament had still not passed the stage of discussion, as testified to by a Library Note published at the end of 2011.[83] In other words, the efforts to change arguably archaic practices in order to reflect contemporary reality do not swiftly come to fruition. Nonetheless, they reflect the underlying will to further neutrality towards religions.

7.2.4 State neutrality

The English legal system has not expressly articulated a principle of state neutrality.[84] Nonetheless, it is generally accepted that the state should be religiously neutral,

---

77 Ibid, p. 38. Modood has conducted specific research on the established church and the stance of religious minorities, and dryly observes that he has not come across one article by a non-Christian which argues against establishment, see Modood (1994), p. 61. What is more, religious minorities have even emphasized the importance of a link between religion and state, Modood in AlSayyad and Castells (eds) (2002), p. 126. His observations are endorsed by Weller in Edge and Harvey (eds) (2000), p. 56.

78 See Weller in Edge and Harvey (eds) (2000), p. 56. This is in conformity with the traditional characteristic of Anglican establishment not to preclude public space for other Christian denominations, see Lewis in Shadid and Van Koningsveld (eds) (2002), p. 132. Fetzer and Soper (2005), pp. 57-61.

79 E.g. Fetzer and Soper, p. 38.

80 Fetzer and Soper (2005), p. 34.

81 Which are part of the general reform of the House of Lords which generally can be said to progress very ponderously.

82 Fetzer and Soper (2005), pp. 34-35. The original Wakeham Report can be retrieved through: <www.archive.official-documents.co.uk>.

83 M. Purvis, 'House of Lords, Library Note, Religious Representation' (25 November 2011), no. LLN 2011/036, to be found on <www.parliament.uk>, under 'Parliamentary business' > Publications & records > Research publications > Research briefings > House of Lords: Religious Representation - Lords Library Note.

84 J. Bell, 'Le service public: l'expérience britannique (1997) L'actualité juridique - Fonctions publiques, p. 136.

notwithstanding the establishment of the Anglican Church.[85] The rule of law and the principle of equality before the law have been taken to imply state neutrality. Furthermore, rather than entailing exclusion of religion or belief, neutrality in the English context has been interpreted as reflecting the full citizenry of society, thus conveying the message of equality.[86] Otherwise, public service has been seen to embrace particular ethics, labelled as the 'public service ethos'.[87] Efforts to grasp the concept of public service ethos have not been without their difficulties. Nonetheless, they have led to identifying it as an amalgam of principles including impartiality,[88] which is mostly seen as a primary value.[89]

Three specificities of the English system might explain why a principle of neutrality has not been made explicit. In stating the obvious, one would first point to the legal tradition of generally not codifying legal principles. Perhaps just as obvious is the point that explicit neutrality as it has been shaped in France would sit uneasily with the system of establishment. Finally, unlike the French discourse, the English discourse does not have a solid conception of the state or of public service. The next section considers the English conception regarding public service, and in particular public officials' freedom to display religious symbols, both on a general level and on the level of the specific public functions.

7.3 PUBLIC OFFICIALS' FREEDOM TO DISPLAY RELIGIOUS SYMBOLS

Public service has not been legally defined in English law, although it is an important notion in political discourse.[90] Still, political discourse has mainly focused on the governance of public service and not so much on the existence of public service itself. The fluidity of the concept is also evident from the lack of a clear distinction from the private sector.[91] Additionally, the public employment sphere has not been identified as a formally secular one or even as neutral as to religion and non-religion.[92] The idea

---

85 Cf. Vickers (2009), p. 144.
86 Ibid, p. 145.
87 It emerged in the mid-nineteenth century, e.g. J. Rayner and others, 'Public Service Ethos: Developing a Generic Measure' (2010) *Journal of Public Administration Research and Theory*, p. 28.
88 Ibid, p. 28.
89 E.g. R. Plant (Lord Plant of Highfield), 'A Public Service Ethic and Political Accountability' (2003) 56 (4) *Parliamentary Affairs*, p. 564.
90 Bell (1997), p. 130.
91 Freedland and Vickers (2009), p. 599. Bell, p. 131. The modern perception of public service concerns those activities which are decided on by a public authority and provided to the public in the general interest. Traditionally, private actors have also been considered as able to provide such activities. The fuzzy distinction also speaks from the way legal claims are dealt with. More specifically, recent cases have twice been paired even though the separate cases took place in the public sector and the private sector respectively, *infra* subsection 7.4.1 and 7.4.2.
92 Freedland and Vickers, p. 599. In their article, they juxtapose tolerance with multiculturalism as, in their perception, the former requires less from the state towards minorities than the latter, which

of tolerance has had more impact than secularism. While a general rule concerning public officials and their freedom to display religious symbols does not apply to the whole of public service, specific rules may be identified in relation to the specific public functions.[93]

7.3.1 Judicial officers' freedom to display religious symbols

There is no integral legal framework applicable to all courts.[94] On the contrary, as a result of the piecemeal development of the English legal system, the rules governing the procedure and jurisdiction of the courts are scattered throughout statutes, court rules and the like, which seem to be under constant revision.[95] Another element adding to the confusion is the debate on judges' constitutional position in relation to the limits of their authority, more specifically on whether or not they are 'servants' of the Crown.[96] Suffice it to say that they derive their authority from the Crown and swear allegiance to the Crown.[97] Accommodation has been made precisely with regard to the oaths sworn on taking office. It is possible to take a religious oath,[98] as well as to make a secular affirmation[99] for both the oath of allegiance and the judicial oath. What is more, Hindus, Jews, Sikhs and Muslims can take oaths specific to their religions.[100]

---

aims for full equality, ibid, p. 600.

93 Bell (1997) points out that each public service has been organized by its own laws, p. 131.

94 Walker and others (2005), p. 230.

95 Ibid, p. 229.

96 The fact of their appointment being technically by the Queen and their payment out of the Consolidated Fund points to an affirmative answer to this question. On the other hand, in the exercise of their office, judges cannot be controlled by either Parliament or the executive, as judicial independence is a fundamental principle of English law, see ibid, p. 304.

97 Lord Chancellor and Secretary of State for Justice, The Governance of Britain: Judicial Appointments, 2007, no. Cm 7210, p. 25.

98 Oath of allegiance, original text: 'I, [name], do swear by Almighty God that I will be faithful and bear true allegiance to Her Majesty Queen Elizabeth the Second, her heirs and successors, according to law.' Judicial oath, original text: 'I, [name], do swear by Almighty God that I will well and truly serve our Sovereign Lady Queen Elizabeth the Second in the office of [function], and I will do right to all manner of people after the laws and usages of this realm, without fear or favour, affection or ill will.' See <www.judiciary.gov.uk> Under ' Judges and the constitution'.

99 Affirmation of allegiance, original text: 'I, [name], do solemnly sincerely and truly declare and affirm that I will be faithful and bear true allegiance to Her Majesty Queen Elizabeth the Second Her Heirs and Successors according to Law.' Judicial affirmation, original text: 'I, [name], do solemnly sincerely and truly declare and affirm that I will well and truly serve our Sovereign Lady Queen Elizabeth the Second in the office of [function], and I will do right to all manner of people after the laws and usages of this Realm without fear or favour affection or ill will.' See <www.judiciary.gov.uk> under 'Judges and the constitution'.

100 Members of the Hindu faith will omit the words 'I swear by Almighty God' and substitute the words 'I swear by Gita'. Members of the Jewish faith use the oaths above although some may wish to affirm. Members of the Muslim faith will omit the words 'I swear by Almighty God' and substitute

Despite the indistinctness of the legal framework for the judiciary, the principles of impartiality and independence apply to the whole of the judiciary.[101] To enhance the latter principle, the appointment process was revised by the Constitutional Reform Act 2005. This Act transferred the task of appointing judges from the Lord Chancellor to the independent Judicial Appointments Commission.[102] The revised procedure significantly constrains the role of the executive in the appointments process. Through an intricate procedure, which envisages several stages of cooperation between the Commission and the Lord Chancellor, vacancies of a judicial office to which the Act applies are filled. Separate procedures apply for Justices of the Supreme Court.[103]

The principles of impartiality and independence in principle do not encompass an explicit limitation on judicial officials' religion or belief. The judicial oath and the ethical obligation to declare any interests are considered as guarantees for the impartiality of the court.[104] There has been debate, though, on the judiciary and Freemasonry which became discredited in the 1990s. Allegations were made that the Freemasonry had unduly influenced the criminal justice system, concerning decisions, promotions and appointments.[105] As a result, political forces pushed for public declaration of membership of the Freemasonry bringing the Government in 1998 to a policy initiative requiring new employees of *inter alia* the judiciary and the police to make such a declaration.[106] By asking judges to voluntarily declare membership, a register was created.[107] In practice though, the request was not complied with sufficiently and in the end, the upheaval surrounding the Freemasonry died away.

---

the words 'I swear by Allah'. Members of the Sikh faith will omit the words 'I swear by Almighty God' and substitute the words 'I swear by Guru Nanak'.

101 See <www.judiciary.gov.uk> under 'Judges and the constitution'. The principle of independence and impartiality is foremost an unwritten constitutional principle, which was enshrined in an Act with the reform in 2006. However, this in no way implies that the Act is necessary for it to be a principle. Illustrative of the British scepticism towards written rules is a statement by the Lord Chief Justice who in an interview said: 'It will be a sorry day when we have to rely on a written Act of Parliament for independence'. At the same time, previous cases have at times demonstrated that the judicial attitude is one of neutrality towards belief but hostility towards the practices that come with alien beliefs, see Bradney in Edge and Harvey (eds) (2000), pp. 19, 24. Of course, the principle also affects the British legal order by reason of its being enshrined in the ECHR.

102 Which was established in 2001, following the Peach report. Its status is that of a Non-Departmental Public Body. The members of the Commission are appointed by the Queen on the advice of the Lord Chancellor, see pp. 22-23. See also Lord Chancellor and Secretary of State for Justice, 'The Governance of Britain: Judicial Appointments' (The Stationary Office, London 2007) to be found on <www.official-documents.gov.uk>, pp. 22-23.

103 Ibid, pp. 23-24.

104 Edge (2002), pp. 181 and 185.

105 Home Affairs Committee Report (1997), vol. I, pp. v-vi.

106 Edge (2002), pp. 179-180. See Home Affairs Committee Report (1997), which recommends that 'judges ... should be required to register membership of any secret society', referred to in the follow-up report 'Freemasonry in Public Life' (1998-1999) para. 2.

107 Edge (2002), p. 180.

The Freemasonry affair illustrates that despite the lack of general limitations on judges' religious freedom, discussion may emerge on the compatibility of religious or philosophical membership with the judicial function.[108] That said, the Freemasonry affair appeared to revolve primarily around the assumed corruptive influence of such membership rather than the membership in itself.[109] To put it another way, it was not so much problematic that Freemasonry was a belief, but rather that the content of the belief seemed to imply putting fellow members before other people.

That there is a need for further specification of what judicial impartiality and independence entail may be inferred from the Guide to Judicial Conduct (Guide). A working group of judges set up by the Judges' Council first published this Guide in 2004.[110] As a guide, the document primarily intends to offer assistance to judges[111] in leaving room for interpretation. The introduction puts forward that standards of conduct are informed by the particularity of the judiciary and its considerable power.[112]

The Guide refers to the internationally adopted Bangalore Principles of Judicial Conduct,[113] which emphasize the essential significance of the appearance of propriety for the performance of all the judge's activities.[114] It underscores the importance of appearance by stating: 'judges should always take care that their conduct, official or private, does not undermine ... the public appearance of independence'.[115] Notably, this statement specifically speaks of 'conduct', which seems to aim at a judge's acts rather than his appearance. The rules concerning judicial impartiality equally determine that 'a judge should strive to ensure that his or her conduct, both in and out of court, maintains and enhances the confidence of the public, the legal profession and litigants, in the impartiality of the judge and of the judiciary'.[116] The subsequent rules lay down what this conduct might be: extrajudicial activity, political activity and expression of views.[117] The standard for measuring confidence in the judiciary is the 'perception which the fair-minded and informed observer would have'.[118]

---

108 Ibid, p. 179.
109 Freemasonry in Public Life (1998-1999), paras. 32 and 34.
110 See foreword to the Guide to Judicial Conduct (Judges' Council 2004, supplemented in 2006 and 2008) to be found at <www.judiciary.gov.uk> under 'About the judiciary > Governance of the Judiciary > Guide to Judicial Conduct.
111 Guide to Judicial Conduct (2004), p. iv.
112 Ibid, pp. 1-2.
113 Bangalore Principles of Judicial Conduct, adopted by the Judicial Group on Strengthening Judicial Integrity, and revised at the Round Table Meeting of Chief Justices (The Hague, 2002). In 2006 they were adopted by ECOSOC Resolution 2006/23, e.g. in the UN Official Documents System Search <www.un.org/en/documents/ods>.
114 Guide to Judicial Conduct (2004), p. 4.
115 Ibid, p. 7.
116 Ibid, p. 9.
117 Ibid, pp. 9-10.
118 Ibid, p. 11.

It is thus clear that the judiciary incurs a particular responsibility to uphold judicial impartiality and independence and to retain public confidence. However, this responsibility does not preclude judges from relying on rights and freedoms available to all citizens.[119] The search for a balance between the requirements of judicial office and the legitimate demands of the judge's personal and family life[120] are evident from the next section:

> A judge, like any other citizen, is entitled to freedom of expression, belief, association and assembly, but in exercising such rights, a judge shall always conduct himself or herself in such a manner as to preserve the dignity of the judicial office and the impartiality and independence of the judiciary.[121]

As to the impact of judicial impartiality and independence on court dress, no specific rules have been defined regarding religious symbols. The English court dress in principle does not exclude such symbols. Typically, the English court dress is associated with wigs.[122] While these wigs have been part of judicial dress for a long time, they have been practically abolished with the reform of court dress in October 2008. In civil and family law cases in particular, court dress was simplified. Consequent on this change, a practice direction was handed down by the Lord Chief Justice.[123] The direction determines that judges need to wear a gown in specified situations. This may vary according to the type of court, the type of judge and the type of case.[124] Court dress in the criminal jurisdiction remained unaltered. Otherwise, it may be good to note that the lay magistrates, as well as tribunal panel members and those district judges who sit in the magistrates' courts are at any rate dressed in business attire.[125]

The question remains as to what the above implies for judges' freedom to display religious symbols. In practice, there have been Sikh judges from 1982[126] onwards. One of them is a High Court judge.[127] They have worn their turbans in court without problems. That said, these instances do not necessarily represent a broad practice of

---

119 Ibid, p. 19.
120 Ibid.
121 Ibid, p. 23. Cf. Article 4.6 of the Bangalore Principles (2002).
122 English court dress can be traced back to medieval times, when it was fashionable to wear robes and wigs, see <www.judiciary.gov.uk>, under 'About the judiciary' > Court dress > History of court dress.
123 Ibid, under 'About the judiciary' > Court dress.
124 Ibid, under 'About the judiciary' > Court dress > History of court dress.
125 Ibid, under 'Roles, types and jurisdiction'.
126 'Sitting In Judgement', at *BBC News* (7 August 2002) on <news.bbc.co.uk/2/hi/programmes/hardtalk/ 2179368.stm>.
127 Rabinder Singh is the judge sitting with a turban in the High Court, see: 'Rabinder Singh, Q.C.: Britain's First Turbaned High Court Judge', at *Sikh Times (*24 March 2003) on <www.sikhtimes.com/bios_032403a.html>. He was appointed in 2011, see: <jac.judiciary.gov.uk/274.htm>

the manifestation of religious symbols within the judiciary. The judiciary in practice still rather seems to lack ethnic or religious diversity, which reduces the possibility of or need for explicitly allowing for religious symbols.[128] Nevertheless, there are some indications that accommodation regarding religious symbols within the judiciary is not necessarily dismissed out of hand. To begin with, there do not seem to have been fierce debates on whether limitations on the freedom of the judiciary to wear religious symbols should be imposed. Admittedly, such a lack of debate could also be attributed to the currently small presence of religious minorities in the judiciary. But it is telling that the appointment of Sikh judges did not provoke much debate either. Another indication is the established practice of barristers displaying religious symbols. There is no impediment for barristers to display religious symbols.[129] Of course, it can be argued that barristers have a different role from judges. The fact that barristers represent one party instead of having to be impartial like judges may create more room for personal expressions. It appears, though, that jury members are equally able to wear religious symbols without problems.[130] A final indication is that the way in which religious symbols in the courtroom generally are dealt with is indicative of how religious symbols worn by judges might be looked upon. Individual instances illustrate that judges sometimes do take issue with religious symbols within the courtroom, but they are usually eager to emphasize that they are certainly not religiously intolerant. For example, a Rastafarian attending a trial was arrested in 2002 for refusing to take off his hat on the basis of religious reasons.[131] Later on, the judge hastened to emphasize that he did not mean to 'disparage Rastafari or Rastafarianism'.[132] A garment which is capable of provoking quite strong reactions is the face veil, especially the *niqab*. Even so, the policy urges judges to adopt a respectful and accommodative approach.

At the end of 2006, an immigration tribunal was adjourned when the appellant's lawyer refused to remove her face veil.[133] No precedent to decide on this issue was

---

128 L. Barmes and K. Malleson, 'The Legal Profession as Gatekeeper to the Judiciary: Design Faults in Measures to Enhance Diversity' (2011) 72 (2) *The Modern Law Review*.

129 In the Bar News it was announced in 2001 that 'the Lord Chief Justice had indicated that there is no objection to members of the Bar varying the usual dress in court for religious reasons', see 'Court dress' (2001) (139) *Bar News*, p. 10.

130 As can be gathered from a news item on a juror who was sued for contempt of court for listening to music under her headscarf, see 'Juror accused over music in court' at *BBC News* (10 July 2007) on <news.bbc.co.uk/2/hi/uk_news/england/london/6287226.stm>.

131 'Apology demanded in "Rasta hat" row', at *BBC News* (29 May 2002), see <news.bbc.co.uk/2/hi/uk_ news /england/2015209.stm>.

132 'Judge "regrets" Rasta row', at *BBC News* (30 May 2002) on <news.bbc.co.uk/2/hi/uk_news/england/ 2016325.stm>.

133 'Row over face veil halts tribunal', at *BBC News* (8 November 2006) on <news.bbc.co.uk/go/pr/fr/-/2/hi/uk_news/england/staffordshire/6127572.stm>. See also N. Bakht, 'Objection, Your Honor! Accommodating Niqab-Wearing Women in Courtrooms', in R. Grillo and others (eds), *Legal Practice and Cultural Diversity* (Ashgate, Farnham [etc.] 2009), p. 115.

available and after deliberation the chief of the tribunal advised the judiciary to use their discretion to allow legal advisers and solicitors to wear the Islamic veil.[134] At the same time, the Lord Chief Justice had asked the Judicial Studies Board's Equal Treatment Advisory Committee to issue guidelines on the use of veils by all people involved in court cases.[135] As a result, the Equal Treatment Bench Book (Bench Book) was published a few months later. While including more detailed considerations, it implicitly stipulated that there is room for allowing veils.[136] The guidelines of the Bench Book emphasized inclusiveness as well as the importance of specific circumstances. They were based on the starting point of room for diversity and of willingness to accommodate different practices.[137] One of the reasons for such inclusiveness is that the system of justice must be, and must be seen to be, inclusive and representative of the whole community. Accordingly, the Bench Book urged that as many people as possible should be enabled to participate in and engage with judicial processes.[138] The weight of specific circumstances requires the judge to take context-sensitive decisions regarding face veils in the courtroom. In taking such decisions, the judge should be guided by the interests of justice.[139] Accordingly, in balancing whether a woman can be required to take off her face veil, a judge should assess the extent to which seeing her face is relevant.[140] Obviously, this assessment is partly informed by the role of the wearer. The ensuing recommendation is liberal in that the wearing of face veils is generally expected to raise no objections.[141] Even for the role of the judge, the Bench Book does not unequivocally rule out that the face veil can be worn, although it leaves the definitive decision to the Lord Chief Justice or other appropriate members of the senior judiciary.[142] In all cases, when a judge decides that a face veil should be removed, he should justify this decision.

---

134 'Lawyers "can wear veils in court"', at *BBC News* (10 November 2006) on <news.bbc.co.uk/go/pr/fr/-/2/hi/uk_news/6134804.stm>.

135 Ibid.

136 It laid down that 'forcing a woman to choose between her religious identity and taking part in a court case could have a "significant impact on that woman's sense of dignity" and could serve to "exclude and marginalize her"'. Moreover, 'it should [never] be assumed without good reason that it is inappropriate for a woman to give evidence in court wearing the full veil', see 'Muslim veil "allowed in courts"', at *BBC News* (24 April 2007) on <news.bbc.co.uk/go/pr/fr/-/2/hi/uk_news/england/staffordshire/6588157.stm>.

137 Judicial Studies Board, 'Equal Treatment Bench Book' (2010), to be found through the website of the Judicial Studies Board on <www.judiciary.gov.uk/publications-and-reports/judicial-college/Pre+2011/equaltreatment-bench-book>, p. 3-18/1.

138 Equal Treatment Bench Book (2010), p. 3-18/2.

139 Ibid.

140 The Equal Treatment Bench Book envisages a distinction of three situations: a) seeing her face is useful or important; b) seeing her face is essential; c) seeing her face may not be of any relevance, ibid, p. 3-18/2-3.

141 As can be derived from several statements for instance: 'In many cases, there will be no need for a woman to remove her *niqab* ', see ibid, p. 3-18/6.

142 Although it does point out that it may be exactly here where 'the wearer is providing the face of

Judges who fail to comply with the Bench Book can generally expect to be reprimanded. In mid-2007, a magistrate walked out of a courtroom because the defendant, charged with criminal damage, wore a face veil.[143] He was formally reprimanded, and obliged to follow further training so as to ensure that he would follow the appropriate judicial guidelines and procedures.[144] His later explanations disclosed that 'he is supportive of different faiths and cultural traditions and acknowledges and regrets his action could be misinterpreted'.[145] It can also be derived from news reports that the main motivation for his conduct stemmed from concerns about the defendant's identity. This motivation was in principle in line with the recommendations of the Judicial Studies Board, that any consideration concerning the wearing of the *niqab* should be functional.[146] But it is not difficult to imagine that his action in walking out of the court did not show the sensitivity he should have displayed or the requirement to explain properly the motivation behind his request to her to remove the *niqab*. The apparent willingness for accommodation of the face veil, even within the courtroom, seems to indicate a general sensitivity for religious symbols. Although it is understood that policy tends to be more idealistic than reality,[147] the above instance demonstrates how policy can pervade practice.

As demonstrated by the incidents just described, there is not a dominant discourse advocating limitation on religious dress and symbols in the judiciary. It can be gathered from these incidents that the issue is not wholly uncontested, but when it comes to the formal policy, the approach towards religious dress and symbols is relatively inclusive. Moreover, it would seem as if the judiciary itself is also wary of being seen as religiously intolerant.[148] It can be seen as significant that the face veil is considered as most likely to raise questions concerning religious symbols and then still mostly for reasons of visibility.[149] *A contrario*, it can be deduced that other

justice' [by which] 'the question of the transparency of justice might be said most obviously to come into play', see ibid, p. 3-18/3.
143 'Magistrate walks out in veil row', at *BBC News* (29 June 2007) on <news.bbc.co.uk/go/pr/fr/-/2/hi/uk_ news/england/manchester/6254506.stm>.
144 'Veil row magistrate reprimanded', at *BBC News* (8 January 2008) on <news.bbc.co.uk/go/pr/fr/-/2/hi/uk _news/england/manchester/7177455.stm>.
145 'Magistrate walks out in veil row' (2007).
146 Equal Treatment Bench Book (2010), p. 3-18/2. Interestingly, when the defendant's case was taken up by another female district judge, the defendant did take off her veil and gave evidence from behind a screen, see 'Veil row magistrate reprimanded', (2008).
147 In 2012, a Muslim juror with a face veil was removed from the jury, see 'Muslim juror removed from jury after refusing to take off veil', *Telegraph* (20 March 2012).
148 As it is with attitudes and opinions, research is faced with the challenge to look beyond socially acceptable ones. For instance, Davis and Vennard demonstrated that when ethnic minority magistrates faced instances of possible racism, such racism was so subtle in nature that it was not easy to establish, G. Davis and J. Vennard, 'Racism in Court: The Experience of Ethnic Minority Magistrates', (2006) 45 (5) *The Howard Journal*, pp. 490 and 497.
149 Equal Treatment Bench Book (2010), p. 3-18/1.

examples of religious symbols are considered less problematic. The willingness to accommodate is underlined by the statement that the starting point should be the choice made by the person in question.[150] Overall, it can be seen that the guidelines advocate a pragmatic approach from this starting point rather than a principled one.[151]

7.3.2 Police officers' freedom to display religious symbols

In England and Wales, policing is for the most part organized on the level of forty-three local police forces, which perform the bulk of investigatory and law enforcement work.[152] These forces are not only composed of full-time police officers – constables – but also of part-time police officers as well as of civilian staff. Constables hold office under the Crown, although they are not Crown servants or employees of the Chief Constable.[153] Loyalty to the Queen is attested to by police officers when taking office; the wording of the oath was laid down in the 2002 Police Reform Act.[154] Contrary to the judicial oath, only one oath is available which has no regard for religion or belief. The 2002 Police Reform Act, together with other Acts, concerns the structure and organization of the police.[155] Additionally, special regulations lay down further rules governing officers' employment.[156]

Such regulations may stipulate certain limitations on police officers' activities in order to uphold their impartiality. For instance, the 2003 Police Regulations determine that a police officer should 'abstain from any activity which is likely to interfere with the impartial discharge of his duties or which is likely to give rise to the impression amongst members of the public that it may so interfere'. This provision continues by articulating an even more concrete limitation, which is that 'they shall not take

---

150 Ibid, p. 3-18/2.
151 Ibid, p. 3-18/1: It is qualified as a 'general guidance' which is designed to 'assist judges'. It emphasizes that it is for the judge to decide according to the circumstances which steps would be appropriate. Moreover, it concedes that it is not possible to give advice here on any specific situation or to give model answers, ibid, p. 3-18/2.
152 Walker and others (2005), p. 384. Other organizations which perform law enforcement functions in addition to the local police forces are left out of this study.
153 Ibid, p. 389.
154 Section 83 determines: 'I, [Officer's Name] of [Police Service] do solemnly and sincerely declare and affirm that I will well and truly serve the Queen in the office of constable, with fairness, integrity, diligence and impartiality, upholding fundamental human rights and according equal respect to all people; and that I will, to the best of my power, cause the peace to be kept and preserved and prevent all offences against people and property; and that while I continue to hold the said office I will to the best of my skill and knowledge discharge all the duties thereof faithfully according to law.'
155 The latest Acts, the Police Act and the Police Reform Act, date from 1997 and 2002 respectively. See Walker and others (2005), p. 386.
156 Namely the Police Regulations 2003 SI 2003/527 and the Police (Conduct) Regulations 2004, SI 2004/645, referred to in ibid, p. 389.

any active part in politics'.[157] The emphasis is clearly on police officers' activities; accordingly, it is their conduct rather than their appearance which is scrutinized as to their compatibility with the impartiality of the police.[158] At the same time, it is sufficient for such activities to give rise to the impression of partiality to be limited or even prohibited. The perception of the general public is the standard to determine whether such impression is justified.

The Secretary of State can issue codes of practice and make regulations for the use of equipment.[159] Specifically as to dress regulations, the Secretary of State can determine 'the circumstances in which and the conditions subject to which uniform and equipment is to be issued by the police authority to a member of a police force of the rank of constable or sergeant'. In so doing, he may confer discretion on the police authority to further determine the rules concerning uniform.[160] As a result, the more specific rules on police uniform are adopted on a local level. Such rules can explicitly leave room for the diverse needs of all staff.[161] This has resulted for instance in the gradual introduction of the headscarf in an increasing number of forces.[162] The wearing of the turban had already been accepted for quite some time,[163] although it has not yet been allowed for firearms officers.[164] In sum, police officers are allowed to manifest their religion or belief by displaying special symbols or wearing special garments with their uniform. What is more, it is not uncommon to have uniformed services operating a tailoring service for staff in a uniformed role to make reasonable adjustments to the uniform.[165]

---

157 Police Regulations 2003, Regulation 6, Schedule 1, para. 1.

158 Like the judiciary, the police was subject to an inquiry in relation to the Freemasonry. As explained in the previous paragraph, suspicions concerning corruption arose, which did not have to do so much with the 'religious' character of the Freemasonry, but rather with its secrecy and with the suspicion of conflicts of interest and of power abuse, see Report of the Home Affairs Committee 'Freemasonry in the Police and the Judiciary' (House of Commons, 1997), to be found on <www.publications.parliament.uk>, under 'Parliamentary business' > Publications and Records > Committee Publications > All Select Committee Publications > Commons Select Committees > Home Affairs. See also 'Freemasons – moral guardians or centre of corruption?', at *BBC News* (5 March 1998) on <news.bbc.co.uk/2/hi/uk_news/57463.stm>.

159 As determined e.g. in the Police Reform Act 2002, see Walker and others (2005), p. 387.

160 Police Regulations 2003, Article 45.

161 Such as the Metropolitan Police Service Dress Code and Appearance Policy and Standard Operating Procedure Equality Impact Assessment (2008) Policy Version 1, to be found on <www.met.police.uk>, under 'About us' > Policies and reports > policies.

162 As early as 2001, the Metropolitan Police decided to introduce the headscarf into the police uniform for Muslim women, see C. John, 'Police hope for Muslim head start', at *BBC News* (24 April 2001) on <news.bbc.co.uk/2/hi/uk_news/1294417.stm>. See also e.g. 'Police adopt uniform *hijab*' (31 January 2009), at *ThisisLeceistershire.co.uk* <www.thisisleicestershire.co.uk/news/Police-adopt-uniform-*hijab*/article-660197detail/article.html>.

163 Parekh (2000), p. 244.

164 'Sikh police want ballistic turban', at BBC News (8 May 2009) on: <news.bbc.co.uk/2/hi/uk_news/8039921.stm>. Efforts to have the turban accepted in this part of the police service have failed.

165 Metropolitan Police Service Equality Impact Assessment (2008), question 4(i).

In addition, the police have some mechanisms in place to monitor equality such as Equality Impact Assessments.[166] Such assessments are shared with stakeholders including religious groups.[167] The aim of such assessments is to take account of equality legislation, in the context of which certain strands have been defined; it is considered good practice to include religion or belief.[168] In complying with equality legislation, the police can go to some lengths to accommodate police officers' individual needs regarding religion or belief.[169] The impact of the Dress Code Policy on employees is also taken into account in assessing equality in the police force. Apart from observing the attention of policies to diversity needs, the assessments can also be critical in pointing out that uniform policies may still negatively affect equality of opportunity, when health, safety or duty of care must take precedence.[170]

It should be emphasized that the picture of diversity with the police is not all rosy. With respect to those policed as well as those policing, discrimination on the basis of ethnicity, religion or belief is still far from having been excluded.[171] Nonetheless, this brief exploration goes to show the efforts made by the police in preserving plurality, accommodating religious needs and raising awareness and sensitivity.

7.3.3 State school teachers' freedom to display religious symbols

The local authorities bear responsibility for implementing the policy for state education and state schools.[172] The funds for state schools are provided for through national taxation. Religious state schools account for over a third of the total number

---

166 Ibid.

167 Ibid, question 4(v).

168 Ibid, question 1. See also Association of Chief Police Officers (ACPO), Home Office (HO) and the Association of Police Authorities (APA), 'The Employment Monitoring Duty. Guidance for the police service in England, Wales and Northern Ireland' (2006), p. 4, to be found on <www.apa. police.uk>, under 'Publications'.

169 Monitoring may indicate for instance that police officers adhere to the Jedi religion, see 'Force is strong for Jedi police', at *BBC News*, (16 April 2009) on <news.bbc.co.uk/2/hi/uk_news/scotland/ glasgow_and_west/8003067.stm>. While it should be noted that registering as a Jedi has also occurred as a form of protest against monitoring religion, it goes to show that the police do not automatically bypass this when ensuring conformity with anti-discrimination legislation. This may result in giving pagan police officers time off to enable them to celebrate pagan holidays, see 'Pagan police allowed to take Halloween and summer solstice off work', at *Telegraph* (16 July 2009) on: <www.telegraph.co.uk/news/newstopics/howaboutthat/5842330/Pagan-police-allowed-to-take-Halloween-and-summer-solstice-off-work.html>.

170 Metropolitan Police Service Dress Code and Appearance Policy and Standard Operating Procedure Equality Impact Assessment, question 4(iii).

171 Case before the Employment Tribunal, Manchester, involving Gurmeal Singh, who was requested to take off his turban and not appropriately accommodated. Also another case, involving a Sikh woman, see: <www.personneltoday.com/articles/2009/07/27/51548/sikh-pc-wins-met-police-discrimination-tribunal-case.html>.

172 Molokotos Liederman, p. 106, footnote 9.

of schools.[173] Church of England or Roman Catholic schools constitute the majority of faith schools in the maintained sector.[174] Most Muslim children attend state or faith schools.[175] It is apparent from the high representation of Christian schools among the faith schools that Christianity has enjoyed a privileged position in the English education system as a consequence of the historical importance of the church for schools.[176] Originally, many schools in the maintained sector started as church foundations. Their religious character continues to be reflected in the schools.[177] What is more, no part of the modern education system can be qualified as secular.[178] Since 1997, religions other than Christianity have been able to set up a faith school.[179] Muslims succeeded rather recently in having Muslim schools funded, albeit not in a great number. For them, education has been a focal point of tension with the state. They realized the significance of education for their children to be successful in British society, but they were at the same time concerned about education possibly undermining their own religious values.[180]

In principle, state school teachers can display religious symbols. At any rate, general limitations do not apply and where the local authorities have a say in determining the dress policies, they seem to refrain from imposing limitations on teachers' dress. The lack of contention concerning state school teachers wearing religious symbols is corroborated by the lack of legal disputes. Apart from one reported case, in which a teaching assistant had lodged a complaint before an employment tribunal, the most prominent legal disputes in the context of religious dress and symbols at schools have involved pupils, whose religious dress or symbols do not comply with the school uniform policy in force. The next section discusses both the case involving the teaching assistant as well as some of the cases involving pupils. The latter cases are included because they can be helpful in giving an impression of English discourse on religious dress and symbols in the educational context. Therefore, some remarks concerning the legal regulation of religious symbols for pupils should be made.

In general, a policy of wearing school uniforms is in place at English schools. The school uniform policies are regulated on a local level in line with the rather decentralized nature of the school system. As a result, local authorities or schools are

173 McGoldrick (2006), p. 174. Vickers (2009), p. 138.
174 Blair and Aps (2005), p. 3.
175 McGoldrick (2006), p. 176.
176 The predominant importance of Christianity was confirmed by the Government which introduced a new requirement in the Education Reform Act 1988 that the compulsory act of worship at state schools must be of a wholly or mainly Christian character, see Blair and Aps (2005), p. 2. Weller in Edge and Harvey (eds) (2000), p. 61.
177 Blair and Aps (2006), p. 1; Vickers (2009), p. 141.
178 Blair and Aps (2006), p. 2.
179 Ibid, p. 3.
180 Fetzer and Soper (2005), p. 38.

authorized to determine school uniform policies.[181] In adopting such policies, local school governors are bound to conform to national anti-discrimination legislation.[182] Generally, school uniform policies have been accommodative towards pupils of minority religions.[183] Echoing the wave of religious revival in the 1960s,[184] pupils claimed their right to wear religious dress. The response to such claims has generally been to regulate and accommodate them.[185]

The Guidance to schools on school uniform and related policies (Guidance) adopted by the (former) Department for Children, Schools and Families testifies to such accommodation. It puts forward that 'a school should ensure that its school uniform policy is fair and reasonable'.[186] More specifically, it recommends the governing body to engage with the parties involved in consultations on the proposed school uniform policy; community leaders representing minority religious groups are explicitly mentioned.[187] Moreover, another recommendation advises the careful consideration of any request to vary the policy to meet the needs of any individual pupil to accommodate their religion or belief.[188] An explicit recommendation to accommodate states: 'it may be possible for many religious requirements to be met within a school uniform policy'; accordingly, 'a school should act reasonably in accommodating religious requirements'.[189] On the other hand, the Guidance acknowledges that a school will also need to weigh the concerns of different groups and that it may not be possible to accommodate all.[190] It explicitly provides that the freedom to manifest a religion or belief is not infinite and that limitations can be imposed when justified.[191]

In sum, neutrality in state education seems to be compatible with including religious symbols in school uniform. It should be emphasized though that the rationale for school uniform is mainly informed by discipline, not so much by neutrality.[192] One may link neutrality to one of the aims of the uniform policies, namely the need to

---

181 As can be derived from the *Begum* case in the House of Lords (*infra* n. 242), see McGoldrick (2006), p. 201. See also Department for Education, 'School Uniform. A Guide for Head Teachers, Governing Bodies, Academy Trusts, Free Schools and Local Authorities' (2012), p. 1, to be found on <www.education.gov.uk/schools/leadership/schoolethos/b0014144/schooluniform>.

182 McGoldrick (2006), p. 178.

183 Concerning Muslim pupils, see Fetzer and Soper (2005), p. 42.

184 See Section 7.2.1.

185 McGoldrick (2006), p. 178. Liederman (2000), p. 113. Education is one of the areas where a policy of cultural pluralism has been conducted, see Poulter (1998), p. 19.

186 Guidance, para. 4

187 Ibid, para. 4.

188 Ibid, para. 4.

189 Guidance, para. 18-19.

190 Guidance, para. 4.

191 Guidance, para. 20.

192 Guidance, paras. 1 and 22. See also Blair and Aps (2005), p. 16; Molokotos Liederman (2000), p. 110.

preserve the internal cohesion of the school community and harmony among pupils. Nevertheless, neutrality is rather given effect to by possibilities such as a provision to opt out of religious education.[193]

Thus far, the description of the English approach towards religion-related matters has painted a relatively pluralist picture. Policy documents cherish values like tolerance, pluralism and respect. England is no exception though in not having reality respond one hundred per cent to policy. In the real world, even in England, sentiments of religious and racial intolerance cannot be fully eradicated.[194] Specifically as regards Islam, it goes without saying that the events of 9/11 in New York and more specifically those of 7/7 in London have not done much good for the image of Islam and Muslims in England.[195] In other words, it would be a mistake to think that England has steered clear of debate in religion-related matters. The following section addresses some of the debate by highlighting some prominent legal claims.

7.4 DEBATE IN ENGLAND

A goodly number of religion-related debates have taken place in England during the past few decades and the media have had a part in making such debates public.[196] The emergence of these debates seems to contrast with the previously mentioned liberal approach in England towards religion-related issues. Of course, a certain dissonance between policy and practice is not too astonishing a phenomenon. The debates discussed in the following subsections shed further light on what this dissonance consists of in English discourse.

Two things are remarkable about the English debate. Although Islam has had some prominence in the debates, Christianity has certainly caused controversy as well. In part, this is the upshot of the light which the advent of new religions has cast on established religions.[197] Additionally, it has been asserted that Christianity is increasingly unfairly treated, whereas other religions find more willingness of accommodation. The dismissal of some Christians' claims was taken to corroborate this point and caused indignation, which was exemplified by an open letter of Church officials to the *Daily Telegraph*.[198] Another thing worth mentioning is the divergence in outcome of cases lodged. It has been submitted that essential for the outcome is

---

193 Blair and Aps (2005), p. 16.
194 See Modood in AlSayyad and Castells (eds) (2002), p. 114
195 Oliva (2008), p. 885; Modood in Modood, Triandafyllidou and Zapata-Barrero (eds) (2006), p. 39, but arguably, anti-Muslim sentiments can be traced back further to the end of the Cold War, see Molokotos Liederman (2000), p. 106.
196 As Sandberg notes: 'In twenty-first century Britain, the interaction between law and religion is rarely far from the headlines.', Sandberg (2011), p. 1.
197 Cf. Chapter 2, Section 2.4.1.
198 'The religious rights of Christians are treated with disrespect', *Telegraph* (28 March 2010). See also McClean in Hill (ed) (2012), p. 339.

whether the claim has been put forward on the basis of a discrimination claim or on the basis of a human rights claim.[199] The following subsections further elaborate on both things.

The debates are presented according to their pertinence for the central issue. The first subsection begins by discussing three different claims involving a public official. The second subsection deals with two claims which mirror two of the public officials' claims although strictly speaking they belong to the private sector. Thirdly, as in the chapter on France, debates on pupils' claims to wear religious symbols cannot be left out because of the importance they have for the general approach to religious symbols.

7.4.1 Public officials and religious manifestations

There is no such thing as a general principle of neutrality applicable to public service in England, by virtue of which public officials are generally subject to a prohibition on religious manifestation. Accordingly, unlike in France, the starting point in England is that public officials enjoy freedom to manifest their religion or belief. That said, limitations can be imposed on this freedom, provided they are justified. The insignificance of neutrality shows from the three cases discussed in this section. It becomes apparent that the limitations in question have mostly been imposed to pursue aims other than neutrality. The cases further corroborate that not only Muslim but also Christian manifestations have been the subject of dispute. Additionally, all three cases have been lodged on the basis of a discrimination claim and moreover all have been unsuccessful thus far, albeit for different reasons.

The first one of these cases, chronologically speaking, was pursued up to the Employment Appeal Tribunal in 2007.[200] The claimant, Ms. Azmi, was a teaching assistant at a junior school with children ranging from seven to eleven years old.[201] She had been employed as a bilingual support worker whose task was focused on pupils' learning and welfare; it was her job to assist in the educational activity specifically for children from ethnic minority backgrounds, who constituted an overwhelming majority of the pupils.[202] The school had adopted a uniform policy, which allowed for various religious garments. When applying for the job and during her training, the claimant had worn a black tunic and headscarf without her face

---

199 Cf. Sandberg (2011), p. 110. Howard attributes more importance to how the proportionality test is applied, see also E. Howard, *Law and the Wearing of Religious Symbols: European bans on the wearing of religious symbols in education* (Routledge, Abingdon 2012), p. 162.

200 *Azmi v. Kirklees Metropolitan Borough Council* (Mr Justice Wilki, EAT 434, 30 March 2007).

201 I.e. the Headfield Church of England (Controlled) Junior School. As expounded above, many of the state schools are operated via the church but financed through the state. The defendant in this case was thus Kirklees Metropolitan Council, see *Azmi case* paras. 3-4.

202 The facts are derived from the case, ibid, paras. 1-39. Ninety-two per cent of the pupils were Muslim and of minority ethnic origin, ibid, paras. 3-4.

being covered. It was not until the first week of the term that she made a request to either wear a face veil, specifically a *niqab*, when working with male teachers or be exempt altogether from working with male colleagues.[203] Her request was taken into consideration by the school staff which dismissed the latter option after deliberation. As regards the former option, the school director sought advice from the education department of the Metropolitan Council and allowed the claimant to wear the face veil pending the receipt of advice.[204] This advice was issued, after a few meetings and observation sessions, and argued against wearing the face veil.[205] Subsequent to this advice, the school director and the claimant had many exchanges vis-à-vis the matter, by telephone and letter.[206] Because the claimant did not intend to comply with the advice, she was suspended from school in the end, subsequent to which she lodged an appeal with the Employment Tribunal. The Tribunal dismissed her appeal, as did the Employment Appeal Tribunal. Moreover, in finding that indirect discrimination had taken place, both Tribunals deemed the discrimination to have been justified.

Two things came to the fore in the considerations of the Employment Appeal Tribunal. Firstly, the extensive description of the facts disclosed in detail that the school had not immediately and inflexibly turned down the claimant's request to wear a face veil. On the contrary, the school turned out to have gone to great lengths to see how her request could be reconciled with a proper exercise of her function. Secondly, the approach of the school was based on practical considerations. The objections of the school to the claimant's face veil were not based on principled reasons related to her function or to the significance of the face veil. The arguments adduced against her wearing the veil were rather of a practical or performance-related sort.[207] The school claimed, also on the basis of observations, that when she wore the veil, she was more difficult to hear, had less contact with the pupils and was overall quieter herself. In sum, the approach of the school had shown regard for the claimant's interest and it had sought empirical substantiation of its objections against the face veil. This careful and sensitive approach of the school certainly weighed in its favour before the Tribunals.

The facts of the second case, the *Ladele* case,[208] differed as to context and as to the nature of the religious manifestation in question. The claimant, Ms. Ladele, had been a registrar for the London Borough of Islington since 2002. The disputed religious manifestation was the claimant's objection to officiating at registrations of civil partnerships between same-sex couples on the grounds of her Christian belief

---

203 Ibid, paras.8-9.
204 Ibid, para. 12.
205 Ibid, para. 18.
206 Ibid, paras. 19-29.
207 Freedland and Vickers (2009), p. 614.
208 *Lillian Ladele v. The London Borough of Islington* (Master of the Rolls Lord Justice Dyson and Lady Justice Smith, Civ 1357 EWCA, 15 December 2009).

that marriage is 'a union of one man and one woman for life'. Such civil partnerships had been made possible by the entry into force of the Civil Partnership Act in 2005, in other words in the course of the claimant's employment as a registrar. The claimant considered it to be 'contrary to God's instructions' to 'take active part in enabling same-sex unions to be formed'. Although she had indicated this to her line manager, before the entry into force of the Civil Partnership Act, the latter decided later on that the civil partnership duties would have to be shared out between all existing registrars. During the first few months after the entry into force of the Act, the claimant managed to avoid having to officiate at civil partnerships by swapping with her colleagues. It was only after two of her colleagues, who were gay, complained that the claimant's conduct victimized them that the situation caused a problem.

As a direct result, the claimant's line manager declared the claimant's conduct in breach of Islington's equality and diversity policy. As an indirect result, a sequence of exchanges between the claimant and her employer ensued, leading up to formal disciplinary proceedings against the claimant on the ground that 'she had refused to carry out work in relation to the civil partnership service solely on the grounds of sexual orientation of the customers of that service'. When dismissal loomed for the claimant, she lodged a claim with the Employment Tribunal, complaining of discrimination and harassment. The Tribunal found in her favour, but this decision was quashed by the Employment Appeal Tribunal to which Islington had appealed. The Court of Appeal agreed with the findings of the Employment Appeal Tribunal and accordingly dismissed the claimant's appeal.

This case is typical in two respects which echo the discussion conducted in the Netherlands.[209] First of all, rather than a claimant wanting to display a religious symbol, this case is characterized by a claimant seeking exemption from a professional duty. It may be argued that this duty had been modified in the course of her employment. Whereas she first expected to register marriages between men and women alone, the Civil Partnership Act 2004 added to her duties by requiring her to register civil partnerships between same-sex couples. Moreover, she was to perform this duty as an employee of a public body. Indeed, the Court of Appeal considered that registering civil partnership was a secular activity which she had to carry out under the auspices of a secular, public body.[210] Secondly, the conscientious objection at issue had been argued to effectively result in discrimination against others, on the basis of sexual orientation. According to the plea of the respondent, fighting discrimination was an important if not the primary reason for requiring the claimant to fulfil her registration duties for civil partnerships as well.[211] The Court of Appeal considered this to be a proportionate means to achieve the legitimate aim of fighting discrimination.[212]

---

209 See Chapter 2, Section 2.4.2.
210 Ibid, paras. 52, 70.
211 Ibid, para. 46.
212 Ibid, para. 52.

The third case, the *Chaplin* case,[213] also involved a Christian claimant, Ms. Chaplin, who had been working as a nurse in the National Health Service for thirty years. The religious manifestation concerned here though was her wish to visibly wear a crucifix at work. According to the claimant, she had been wearing the crucifix throughout all her years as a nurse during which it had never been a problem. The introduction of a new uniform still did not pose problems, until she was asked to remove her crucifix. The reason for this request was the safeguard of safety and security. She wished to pin the crucifix to the outside of her uniform and refused to remove the crucifix or to pin it inside her uniform, as she felt this would violate her faith. She lodged a discrimination claim with the Employment Tribunal which turned down her complaint.

Although strictly speaking this case concerns a public official as well, the reasons for asking the claimant to remove her crucifix seem to be primarily informed by safety and security. In other words, similar to the *Azmi* case, the respondent based the plea on pragmatic considerations. The question could be asked why the crucifix came to be considered contrary to safety and security requirements, if the nurse's contention that she had worn it without problems during all the years before was correct. Additionally, it could be asked whether the reasons of safety and security were really in play. Judging on the basis of the sheer amount of facts available, the claimant had made seemingly reasonable proposals to pin the crucifix to her uniform or to use a magnetic clasp of her necklace, but these proposals were rejected by the hospital. Leaving doubts on the measures aside, it appears in any event that the Tribunal found that the respondent had acted reasonably. Ms. Chaplin's intention to appeal did not take effect because such an appeal was not expected to have any prospect of success, in light of the Court of Appeal's judgment in the earlier and widely publicized *Eweida* case, which is further discussed in the following subsection.

7.4.2 Employees and religious manifestations

The almost certain lack of success for Ms. Chaplin in pursuing her case further on a national level was expected on the basis of the similarity of the facts with the *Eweida* case.[214] This is one of the reasons for further discussing the latter case although strictly speaking the case falls within the private sector.[215] Moreover, three other reasons justify a more elaborate discussion of the case. Albeit a private company today, British Airways had been a state company for years. Conceptually speaking, (the reputation of) the company still remains significant for the state. Secondly, the case

---

213 *Chaplin v. Royal Devon & Exeter NHS Foundation Trust* (Case no. 17288862009 ET, 6 April 2010).
214 McClean in Hill (ed) (2012), p. 341.
215 Sandberg mentions four indirect discrimination cases which have been of significance for the question of religious dress and symbols worn by employees, see Sandberg in Hunter-Henin (ed) (2011), p. 339.

was widely publicized and caused heated debate on the display of religious symbols. Accordingly, it is revealing on the English approach to the display of religious symbols in public. Thirdly, the final judgment on a domestic level considered the ban on the cross to be justified. It seems to contrast with the previously described pluralist policy and thus arouses curiosity as to the reasons underlying this decision. The facts can be summarized as follows.

The claimant, Ms. Eweida, worked as a member of the check-in staff of British Airways. The airline had a uniform policy, which prohibited employees from visibly wearing jewellery. It envisaged an exemption for items which met a 'mandatory scriptural requirement' whereby they could not be concealed under the uniform. Such an exemption was still only given with the approval of the management.[216] As a devout Christian, the claimant wished to visibly wear a necklace with a cross.[217] While conceding that such display was not an article of her faith, she considered this to be a personal expression of her faith. The dispute between the claimant and the defendant culminated in a national news row. The claimant had brought her case to the Employment Tribunal before which she alleged that she had been discriminated against and had been subject to harassment.[218] Her claim was dismissed because the Tribunal did not find that she had suffered a disparate disadvantage and, even if she had, that the measure causing this disadvantage was justified.[219] The Employment Appeal Tribunal upheld the decision of the Employment Tribunal, subsequent to which the claimant went to the Court of Appeal.[220] In departing from some of the conclusions drawn by the Employment Tribunal, the most important of which was that no direct discrimination had taken place, the Court of Appeal restricted its examination to the question of indirect discrimination. After dealing with the exact interpretation of the Employment Equality (Religion or Belief) Regulations 2003, it judged that indirect discrimination had not taken place either. One of the questions for interpretation was whether indirect discrimination in terms of Regulation 3 could be established when a single individual had been affected.[221] The Court of Appeal decided that it could not and in doing so also took into account that the visible display did not appear to be a requirement of the Christian faith. The dispute was clearly a matter of principle to the claimant. Although British Airways had in the meantime adapted its policy so as

---

216 *Ms. N. Eweida v. British Airways PLC*, (Mr. Justice Elias, UKEAT, no. 0123/08/LA, 20 November 2008), para. 2.
217 Remarkably, this is emphasized by the Tribunal to be different from a crucifix, cf. para. 1.
218 So, contrary to most cases involving pupils, this case was based on anti-discrimination law.
219 Eweida (UKEAT, 2008), paras. 16-17.
220 *Eweida v. British Airways* ([2010] EWCA, Civ 80).
221 She did so by proposing that 'persons' in Regulation 3 (1)(b)(i) could mean one individual. Furthermore, she asserted that '*would* put at a disadvantage' could be interpreted to 'aggregate the individual with an entirely hypothetical peergroup to whom the same disadvantage is to be attributed'. Lord Justice Sedley rejected both interpretations, although he qualified her submission as 'extremely able', see para. 10.

to allow employees to visibly wear a cross, the claimant, together with Ms. Chaplin, lodged a joint application at the European Court of Human Rights which at the time of writing was at an early stage.[222]

The Court of Appeal remarked at the outset that the case had generated substantial media attention. Therefore, it seemed to have felt compelled to clarify any misunderstandings on what the case was about. Apparently, the case touched on delicate questions. Not uncommonly for religious freedom cases, it dealt with the question whether the manifestation in question could be qualified as a religious manifestation. This remains a sensitive exercise for lawyers, requiring them to walk a fine line in not entering the theological area too deeply. In principle, judges are precluded from making assessments on the contents of religious tenets or requirements. The Court of Appeal nonetheless concluded on the basis of evidence put before the Tribunal[223] that it did not appear to be a requirement of Christianity to display a cross. Obviously, it was helpful that the claimant herself had conceded that this display was a personal choice.[224] The precise interpretation of the Regulation also preoccupied the Court of Appeal. This is no wonder in light of the relatively brief existence of the Regulations. Furthermore, their ongoing dynamics was revealed by the upcoming Equality Bill which, to Lord Justice Sedley's appreciation, was commented on by counsel for the claimant.[225] In that regard, the case is probably also an important precedent for the interpretation of anti-discrimination law in England.

In the same way that the *Eweida* case resembled the *Chaplin* case as to the facts, the *McFarlane* case[226] was not 'dissimilar' to the *Ladele* case. In a procedural as well as in a material respect, it closely followed the latter case, which can be taken as demonstrating the relatively unimportant distinction between the public and the private sector. Whereas Ms. Ladele was a registrar working for a London Borough, Mr. McFarlane was a counsellor with a private federation providing relationship counselling services. He objected to counselling same-sex couples when sexual issues arose, because he believed '… that it follows from Biblical teaching that same-sex sexual activity is sinful and that he should do nothing which endorses such activity'.[227] At one point, he asked to be exempted from counselling same-sex couples where issues of psycho-sexual therapy were involved. When the employer refused to grant him such an exemption, a sequence of communications and discussion ensued which finally resulted in his dismissal. Subsequent to an unsuccessful internal appeal, he went to the Employment Tribunal complaining of discrimination, harassment, unfair

---

222 *Eweida v. United Kingdom* (Appl. no. 48420/10), *Chaplin v. United Kingdom* (Appl. no. 59842/10), a Chamber hearing has been scheduled on 4 September 2012.
223 *Eweida v. British Airways* (EWCA, 2010), para. 8.
224 Ibid, paras. 8-9, 37.
225 Ibid, para. 40.
226 *McFarlane v. Relate Avon Ltd* ([2010] EWCA, Civ 880).
227 Ibid, para. 4.

and wrongful dismissal. All of his claims were materially dismissed, subsequent to which he pursued an appeal on the grounds of discrimination and unfair dismissal. With reference to the *Ladele* case, the Employment Appeal Tribunal dismissed these claims, which was endorsed by the Court of Appeal. Because of the similarity in facts between the two cases, they 'cannot sensibly be distinguished'. Accordingly, Lord Justice Laws briefly concluded that 'there is no more room here than there was there for any balancing exercise in the name of proportionality'.

Referring to the *Ladele* case would have enabled a 'short route to the resolution of this application'. Nonetheless, Lord Justice Laws allowed for a witness statement by Lord Carey of Clifton, in part out of respect for the latter's senior position in the Church. The witness statement made a vigorous plea in the claimant's favour. It can be seen as reflective of the formerly mentioned indignation among Christians who feel increasingly disadvantaged. Basically, Lord Carey called for more judicial sensibility on religious issues. He detected 'a disparaging attitude to the Christian faith and its values'. In his view, a specialist panel with an expert view on religious rights should properly deal with the 'lack of knowledge about the Christian faith' shown by the judges assigned to the case. Lord Justice Laws resolutely brushed aside this statement in finding it misplaced and implying matters which were never stated as such by the judges. In the same vein as the *Eweida* and *Chaplin* cases, the *McFarlane* and *Ladele* cases have resulted in applications before the European Court of Human Rights, which were equally pending on the time of writing.[228]

This section has demonstrated that despite multiculturalist policies, England has not steered clear from debate. As stated previously, there has also been debate regarding pupils wearing religious symbols at schools. Although the reasons for contention did not directly concern state neutrality, this debate is relevant for understanding the English discourse on religious symbols.

7.4.3 Pupils and religious symbols

As in France, schools in England have grappled with religious symbols and their struggle is central to the last debate discussed. The discussion includes cases which have been essential for the policy on religious symbols for pupils when they happened to have taken place in non-state education as well. As mentioned previously, dress policies at schools have been generally liberal.[229] The headscarf has barely created

---

228 *Ladele v. United Kingdom* (Appl. no. 51671/10), *McFarlane v. United Kingdom* (Appl. no. 36516/10), which have been scheduled in the same Chamber hearing on 4 September 2012.

229 The emphasis is on 'generally', which does not preclude the existence of some schools having more restrictive policies in place. This can be seen in the case of *Sarika Singh* (*infra* n. 251), for instance, where no religious dress was allowed at her school.

a stir, certainly in comparison with France.[230] Apart from a few exceptions,[231] it has simply been allowed even at state-run schools.[232] Other religious garments, such as the *salwar kameez*,[233] a long tunic-like dress, have been equally incorporated into the school uniform; it is not uncommon for these to match the school uniform, for instance by their colour.[234] For a long time, only the Sikh turban had managed to create something which resembled a debate.

The turban figured in the seminal case *Mandla v. Dowell Lee*[235] in the 1970s. The importance of the case lies in its implications for the recognition of Sikh dress requirements. The main plaintiff in the case was a schoolboy, Gurinder Singh Mandla, who had been refused admission to a private school because he wore a turban and had long hair. In the end, his case was heard by the House of Lords. The Lords' broad interpretation of 'ethnic group' which took account of shared customs, beliefs and traditions made their decision historic. According to this interpretation, Sikhs were from then on considered to constitute an ethnic group. This was legally significant because they now could now rely on protection by the Race Relations Act 1976. In line with this judgment, Sikhs have been allowed to wear their turbans and other appropriate dress at school.[236]

The beginning of the 21st century witnessed a surge of pupils' claims concerning a variety of religious symbols at schools. In 2006, the House of Lords heard the case of Shabina Begum who wanted to wear a *jilbab* for religious reasons;[237] the *jilbab* is a Muslim plain dress reaching to the ankles and with long sleeves. This garment had not been included in the school uniform policy, in contrast with the headscarf or *salwar kameez*.[238] Until that moment, the policy had met the religious needs of the pupils,

---

230 As also confirmed by a detailed review of the news articles between 1989 and 1998 in Molokotos Liederman (2000), p. 108. See also Kiliç (2008), pp. 434 and 444.

231 E.g. in 2003, when a school in Luton banned all headgear. Subsequent to an announcement of legal action to be taken by the Commission for Racial Equality and to political pressure, it reversed the ban, see: McGoldrick (2006), p. 179.

232 Fetzer and Soper (2005), p. 41; Poulter (1998), p. 43.

233 There were some bans in the 1960s, which were challenged by pupils. At least one of these disputes was resolved to the advantage of the pupil. It is not entirely clear whether this holds true for all disputes, but it can be derived from the conclusion of McGoldrick that the *shalwar kameez* at some point ceased to pose a problem, see McGoldrick (2006), p. 177.

234 See also Molokotos Liederman (2000), p. 107.

235 *Mandla and another v Dowell Lee and another*, House of Lords, [1983] 2 AC 548, [1983] 1 All ER 1062, [1983] 2 WLR 620, [1983] IC R 385, [1983] IRLR 209, (46 MLR 759, 100 LQR 120, [1984] CLJ 219), 28 February, 1, 2, 24 March 1983. He lodged the case with his father.

236 See Poulter (1998), p. 4.

237 [2006] UKHL 15, 22 March 2006.

238 See for a brief summary of the facts McGoldrick (2006), p. 179 ff; G. Davies, 'Banning the Jilbab: Reflections on Restricting Religious Clothing in the Light of the Court of Appeal in SB v. Denbigh High School. Decision of 2 March 2005' (2005) 1 *European Constitutional Law Review*, p. 512; Oliva (2008), p. 886 ff; Kiliç (2008), p. 445 ff. and E. Howard, 'School Bans on the Wearing of Religious Symbols: Examining the Implications of Recent case Law from the UK' (2009) 4 (7)

seventy percent of whom were of Bangladeshi or Pakistani origin. A practically equal percentage qualified as Muslim.[239] In response to the pupil's insistence on wearing the *jilbab*, the school informed her that she could not enter the school unless she wore the standard school uniform. Claiming that she had been excluded from the school, Begum began judicial review proceedings, going all the way up to the House of Lords.

Along the way, Begum's claims were consecutively dismissed, recognized and finally dismissed. Underlying these opposing rulings were divergent perspectives. For instance, the High Court departed from the school uniform policy and it considered that Begum's decision alone and not her religious beliefs had led to her 'exclusion'.[240] In contrast, the Court of Appeal began with Begum's position as an individual right-holder.[241] In having a procedural outlook,[242] it pointed out that the school had not followed the proper statutory procedure for excluding her from education. It opined that the school should have taken a rights-based approach.[243] Contrary to the High Court, the Court of Appeal did consider Begum's religious beliefs to constitute the ground of exclusion, whereby the school had failed to adduce proper justification.[244] Before the House of Lords, the school referred to the ECHR judgment in the case of *Şahin v. Turkey*.[245] In so doing, it put forward some aspects leading to a ruling favourable for the school in the said case. Accordingly, it mentioned that it was a secular school, and it referred to the social cohesion, which the policy aimed at preserving, in reinforcing this claim, by referring to extremist pressures at school.[246] At this stage, the Secretary of State for Education and Skills had joined the school in the proceedings,[247] in endorsing most of the arguments advocating an objective proportionality test in the context of the Human Rights Act, as opposed to the procedural one defended by the Court of Appeal.[248] The House of Lords decided in favour of the school in finding primarily that Begum's freedom to manifest her

---

Religion and Human Rights, p. 16 ff. See also the arguments of the Denbigh school during the proceedings, which pointed out that it had engaged students' wishes, McGoldrick (2006), p. 181.

239 In adopting its policy, Denbigh High School had sought advice as to whether its policy offended against the Islamic dress code. It got independent advice that limiting the wearing of a *jilbab* did not offend against the Islamic dress code, see McGoldrick (2006), p. 181.

240 Formally, she had never been excluded, ibid, pp. 181 and 190.

241 Ibid, pp. 182 and 189.

242 Davies (2005), p. 514.

243 Ibid p. 514. McGoldrick (2006), pp. 185 and 186.

244 McGoldrick (2006), p. 185.

245 *R (on the application of Begum (by her litigation friend, Rahman)) v. Headteacher and Governors of Denbigh High School* (Lord Bingham of Cornhill, Lord Nicholls of Birkenhead, Lord Hoffmann, Lord Scott of Foscote and Baroness Hale of Richmond, UKHL 15, 22 March 2006), paras. 22 ff. This study discusses the *Şahin* case in Chapter 5.

246 McGoldrick (2006), p. 191.

247 Ibid.

248 Ibid, pp. 191-192.

religion had not been interfered with and, in the alternative, if interference was to be assumed, it was justified. The decision of the House of Lords has not remained uncontested. Nonetheless, it has proved to be of importance for subsequent decisions, such as the High Court decision in the *Playfoot* case in 2007.

This decision concerned a schoolgirl's[249] request for judicial review. The schoolgirl, Lydia Playfoot, had attended a maintained non-denominational school, which had explicitly excluded jewellery from the school costume. She wore a so-called purity ring as a symbol of her commitment to celibacy before marriage, which was part of her faith. After having worn the ring for a year, she was told not to wear it anymore because it did not comply with the uniform policy. Over time, the dispute escalated with the imposition of a disciplinary sanction. The claim brought before the High Court was, like the *Begum* claim, based on Article 9 ECHR. Accordingly, the High Court was first faced with the question whether the claimant's wish to wear a purity ring constituted a religious manifestation in terms of Article 9 ECHR. The subsequent questions were whether the prohibition on wearing it interfered with her freedom of religion and whether this interference was justified.

In heavily relying on the *Begum* case, the sitting judge dismissed the claim. He ruled negatively on all three questions. To begin with, the judge did not consider the purity ring to constitute a religious manifestation. In referring to the *Begum* case as well as to ECHR case law, he established that the ring was not intimately linked to her belief in celibacy. To his mind, the ring was not a religious manifestation in terms of Article 9 ECHR.[250] Although he thus found that Article 9 ECHR was not engaged, he nonetheless also examined whether the claimant's right to freedom of religion had been interfered with and whether such interference justified. He rejected the claim that interference had taken place, on the basis of two reasons: the claimant's voluntary compliance with the school uniform policy by attending the school and the availability of alternatives, for instance the possibility of displaying other items to express her belief or the possibility of attending another school. Finally, even if the policy would have interfered with her rights, it would still be justified in the judge's opinion. The judge considered the policy to pursue legitimate aims, to allow for reasonable exceptions and to have taken into account proportionality.

The impact of the *Begum* decision was also clear from another case brought before the High Court. The claimant was a schoolgirl wanting to wear a face veil, the *niqab*, at a girls' grammar school, having reached puberty at that time.[251] Her three older sisters had been able to wear the *niqab* at the same school. However, the

---

249 *R. (on the application of Playfoot) v. Governing Body of Millais School* (Mr Deputy Judge Michael Supperstone Q.C., 1698 (Admin) EWHC, 16 July 2007).

250 Ibid, para. 38 ii).

251 *R (on the application of X (by her father and litigation friend) v. The Headteachers of Y School, The Governors of Y School* (Mr Justice Silber, 298 EWHC, 16 July 2007). The facts described can also be derived from the case summaries in Kiliç (2008), pp. 446-447 and Howard (2009), pp. 18-19.

school policy had been revised in the meantime and no longer included the *niqab*. Consequently, she was told that she would be excluded from school unless she were to take off her *niqab*. She claimed that the policy violated her right to manifest religion under Article 9 ECHR. Mr Justice Silber dismissed her claim, referring to the line taken in the *Begum* case. Firstly, he emphasized that the claimant could have attended another school, which precluded her right under Article 9 ECHR from being interfered with.[252] The non-interference notwithstanding, the judge also established that even if interference were to be assumed, it was justified. In so doing, he took into account in some detail several grounds of justification. Two other grounds adduced by the claimant in arguing violation of Article 9 ECHR were dismissed as well.[253]

Not much later, the High Court received another complaint, which again concerned a schoolgirl, Sarika Watkins-Singh, wishing to wear a religious symbol considered incompatible with the school uniform policy. This time, the symbol in question concerned a steel bangle worn for religious reasons; the bangle, *kara*, is one of the items worn by Sikhs.[254] The case turned out differently in comparison with the former claims, in that it was successful. It took Mr Justice Silber about twice as many pages of judgment, at the outset of which he very explicitly limited his decision to this particular case. He emphasized that 'this judgment is fact-sensitive and it does not concern or resolve the issue of whether the wearing of the Kara should be permitted in the schools of this country'. That said, what were the reasons for this seemingly opposite outcome?

The most important or at least most striking difference from the other cases is the different legal framework applied in the *Watkins-Singh* case. Contrary to the previous claims, this claim was not argued under the Human Rights Act or the ECHR but under the Race Relations Act and discrimination law. Accordingly, the judge examined whether the claimant had suffered a particular disadvantage and whether such disadvantage could be objectively justified. In establishing the former point, the judge heard an expert witness and applied a test, which was less strict than the one applied in the other cases. He found it sufficient that the claimant attached exceptional importance to wearing the *kara*.[255] With regard to the second point, Mr Justice Silber confirmed the claimant's contention that it was not the uniform policy as such but the refusal of the defendant to grant an exemption which had to be justified. In determining the justification, Mr Justice Silber emphasized the discreet nature

---

252 *X* case (2007), para. 40.
253 Mr Justice Silber dismissed the claim made by the claimant that she had a legitimate expectation that she would be allowed to wear the *niqab* and that she could reasonably expect the same policy to apply to her as had applied to her sisters.
254 *R (on the application of Sarika Angel Watkins-Singh (A child acting by Sanita Kumari Singh, her Mother and Litigation Friend) v. The Governing Body of Aberdare Girls' High School* (Mr Justice Silber, 1865 EWHC, 29 July 2008).
255 Ibid, para. 61.

of the bangle. To his mind, this clearly contrasted the case at hand with previous cases, which concerned conspicuous symbols such as the *niqab*.[256] The rest of his reasoning made it clear that he considered the *kara* to be an exceptional symbol, which accordingly carried little risk that allowing the *kara* would cause others to raise claims to display religious symbols. He emphasized that an important obligation rested on the school in fostering tolerance for other religions. In addition to finding the decision of the school not to grant an exemption to the claimant from its uniform policy to constitute indirect discrimination, the judge established moreover that the school had not fulfilled important obligations under the Race Relations Act. This can be taken to demonstrate the recognition of Sikhs as an ethnic group.

The above cases go to show that, despite the generally liberal character of uniform policies, claims for displaying religious symbols which are incompatible with these policies have not been accommodated at all times. Moreover, claims alleging violation of claimants' individual rights have been dismissed most of the time. It is striking, at the least, that the one claim which did succeed was based on non-discrimination law and the Race Relations Act. Although this does not yet justify the general statement that non-discrimination claims are more likely to succeed than human rights claims, it will certainly be something to take into account for future claimants.[257] Be that as it may, all decisions emphasize their facts-based nature. The courts have emphasized time and again that their decision is limited to the facts of the case and that they are not called on to judge generally on religious symbols at schools.[258]

7.5 APPLICATION OF THE CONCEPTUAL MODEL

7.5.1 Dynamics of neutrality

The lack of an explicitly formulated principle of neutrality should not be taken to imply that neutrality is irrelevant in the English context. As in the Dutch context, neutrality can be derived from other principles such as the rule of law and equality before the law. The establishment of the church in England does not exempt the English state from being neutral in its dealings with citizens. That said, the Anglican Church has played a role in accepting the visibility of religion in the public sphere. Furthermore, it has helped to create room for a variety of religions by which neutrality is upheld. Even-handedness has proved to be a guiding concept for doing so. In other words, in offering religions and beliefs the scope for being observed in public, the state has taken care to avoid disparity.

---

256 Ibid, para. 77.
257 Sandberg (2011), p. 110.
258 Howard stresses that it is not so much the test applied which matters but rather the rigour with which the proportionality test is applied, Howard (2012), p. 162.

Contrary to the French conception of the state and public service, English discourse does not draw on an image of the state as a strong actor. Neither is the public service looked on as a uniform entity. As a result, those taking on a function within the public service are not considered as entering a clearly defined professional realm with univocally applicable rules. In the same vein, they are not seen as personifying 'the state'. Accordingly, their individual being can easily remain a separate actor conceptually in the model. Because there is not a uniform conception of the public service, there is room for varying the triangle of actors per function. Moreover, their mutual dynamics becomes more important in understanding how neutrality plays out against the English background. With regard to the specific issue of religious symbols in public functions, it could be derived from case law that neutrality is not necessarily the primary concept. For example, in the *Chaplin* case, the argument of the hospital was not so much that the applicant could not display a cross because she represented the National Health Service; instead, other considerations such as safety prevailed in applying a balancing test to assess the limitation.

7.5.2 Neutrality of the state towards the public official

It is precisely·through the principle of equality before the law that neutrality assumes meaning. Unlike in France, there is not an a priori, formal and uniform limitation on individuals' freedom to manifest religion or belief when taking on a function within the public service. In part, this is related to the lack of a uniform conception of the public service in the first place. Additionally, the absence of such a limitation is also informed by how rights are interpreted for public officials as well.

An important consideration for implementing an equal treatment policy is creating diversity throughout public service.[259] The idea of public officials mirroring society is clearly held high. It is in this way that they merit legitimacy, not by representing an abstract, distanced authoritative entity. Accordingly, public officials who manifest personal preferences, like religious ones, are not automatically considered to act in contravention of neutrality. Of course, it is conduct rather than appearance which serves as a standard to qualify neutrality.[260] For instance, special limitations applicable to the judiciary as well as to the police concern political activities.[261] Apart from relating to actual activities, these limitations are in place in the official sphere as well as in the private sphere. In other words, (certain categories of) public officials can be subject to integral limitations on political activities. Specifically, for the judiciary

---

259 Cf. in relation to the judiciary Barmes and Malleson (2011), p. 258.
260 This holds true as well for professions in the private sector; it is rather a rule of employment law that an employee's conduct should not negatively impact on his profession or the company he works for, see e.g. *Pay v. Lancashire* (EAT, [2004] ICR 187).
261 Cf. the rules concerning civil servants and their freedom to engage in political activities, see Chapter 5, Section 5.3.2.

there is at least a very strong expectation that judges should not have any political affiliation let alone carry out any political activity. In general, scrutiny of judges focuses on conduct instead of on appearance.

The emphasis on public officials' conduct equally impacts on the extent to which public officials may be considered to personify the state. In order to argue that a public official personifies the state, one first has to establish what the state signifies. As previously described, the 'state' does not have a well-defined meaning in English discourse. In any event, it falls short of being a very strong entity. More specifically, the absence of a uniform conception of public service makes each public function stand in its own and be subject to its own rules. The indistinctive character of the public sector precludes public officials from personifying a clear entity. Therefore, it is difficult to make a general statement on the implications which taking on a public function may have for individual freedoms.

Indeed, the indistinctiveness of the public sector resounds on the level of the individual public official. English discourse does not indicate a clear distinction between a public official's public and private capacity. Although there is some notion of the public function having a special character, it does not seem to be based on the public–private distinction. In other words, the taking on of a public function by an individual is not perceived as causing that individual to automatically shed his personal capacity; a public official's public and personal capacity are not seen as mutually exclusive.

This view can be found across all three public functions. All three of them allow for religious symbols to a greater or lesser extent. This practice seems to indicate that visible manifestations of religion or belief by public officials are not considered incompatible with their public capacity. This can be interpreted in two ways: either the visibility of private characteristics in public officials' public capacity is not deemed problematic or no clear qualification of private or public is made regarding for instance religion or belief.

7.5.3 Neutrality of the public official towards the citizen

The emphasis on conduct rather than on appearance is also of pivotal importance for the points of contention concerning the relation between the public official and the citizen. As previously explained, the position arguing that a public official encroaches on a citizen's rights by displaying religious symbols hinges strongly on his *appearance* of bias. It considers that by displaying such a symbol, a public official may give the impression of being biased towards the citizen. The English approach does not seem to relate bias to appearance but to conduct. Accordingly, displaying religious symbols is in itself not seen as undermining neutrality. In other words, citizens' perception is not automatically taken as inferring bias when seeing public officials displaying religious symbols. The emphasis on conduct comes to the fore for example in the Guide to Judicial Conduct, the very title of which is telling. In the Guide, the importance of appearance has been mentioned. However, such appearance concerns the possible impact of judges' conduct on the appearance of the judiciary as a whole. No specific limitations on religious symbols have been laid down or even argued by reference to others' rights. The English outlook on citizens' perception is equally entwined with the two other factors pointed to as shaping neutrality between the public official and the citizen: the conception of the state and hence the role of public officials vis-à-vis citizens and the religious character of symbols.

The lack of a uniform conception of public service in English discourse precludes a uniform rule directing all public officials how to behave or to appear towards citizens; no integral duty of neutrality is incumbent on public officials. Insofar as neutrality may be spoken of, it can be said to derive from the principle of equality before the law. The observance of the principle of equality is also established on the basis of conduct. In the same vein, conduct is in principle paramount for verifying violation of citizens' religious freedom, for instance by way of proselytizing acts. Accordingly, the point of proselytism in relation to symbols has played a minor role. To the extent that it has even emerged in English discourse, it has only done so in the context of education and only on the side of one party. In the *Begum* case, for instance, the school had advanced that allowing the *jilbab* might jeopardize other pupils' rights in exerting pressure on them to wear it as well. An implicit assumption on the garment in question is its image of representing more extremist movements of religion.[262] This is also illustrative for how the religious character of symbols is taken to play out.

In principle, the mere fact of symbols being attributed with a religious meaning is not considered problematic in English discourse. The by now classic and significant example is the appointment of Sikh judges who wear their turbans in court. The turban does not seem to have raised questions regarding the judges' ability to be unbiased towards litigants. The same holds true for the other public functions. Quite a number of police forces have created the possibility for police officers to wear religious symbols. This recent modification of the police uniform does not seem to have raised any doubts or even discussion on whether the wearers of religious symbols would be able to safeguard their neutrality. Religious symbols worn by state schoolteachers do not seem to have caused suspicion either as to the teacher's ability to remain neutral. The act of displaying a religious symbol is not seen as necessarily diminishing a public official's neutrality any more than the act of taking off a religious symbol is considered to distance a public official from his religion or belief. English discourse points out that public officials taking off religious symbols does not preclude them from still holding their religion or belief.[263]

---

262 This argument is refuted by Davies, who casts serious doubts on how substantiated such suggestions are, see Davies (2005), p. 520.
263 Ibid, p. 526.

Another factor reinforcing the effect of the three previously mentioned factors is the weight of specific circumstantial factors to which both guidelines and case law testify. To the extent possible, these factors are measured on the basis of empirical evidence instead of on the basis of assumptions. The *Azmi* case clearly illustrates this approach. It was examined to what extent the face-covering character of the *niqab* could jeopardize pupils' rights. This question was answered with the help of observations of her teaching. Only when the observations showed that the *niqab* affected Ms Azmi's performance as a teaching assistant and hence the learning of the children,[264] was the request to remove the *niqab* made more pressingly. The detailed and arguably careful manner in which the school dealt with Ms Azmi's request illustrates that her interest was not automatically assumed to make way for the interests of her pupils. Instead, a reconciliation of their interests was looked for. Such a balancing test has equally been incorporated in the Guidance on school uniforms. The Guidance emphasizes the need for careful deliberation of accommodation, not only of the interests of the majority but also of an individual's interest. Similarly, the approach to *niqabs* shown by the courts illustrates that they do not advocate an absolute prohibition beforehand but promote a balancing test in the situations that occur. Removal of the *niqab* is not necessarily considered as the most preferable of possible measures.[265] Furthermore, the approach to *niqabs* illustrates that it is not so much the religious aspect of the *niqab* as the face-covering aspect, which may pose problems. Apart from that, the risk that the *niqab* may raise questions as to the judge's impartiality has been viewed in light of the possibility for a judge to recuse himself or be challenged.[266] In sum, regarding the *niqab*, the evidence of identity problems seems to underlie limitations rather than assumptions on the impact of religious symbols.

7.5.4 Neutrality of the state towards the citizen

The English discourse is not optimally suitable for assessing the points of contention impacting the neutrality of the state towards the citizen; neither neutrality, nor the state nor the citizen are clearly defined concepts. That is not to say that neutrality of the state towards the citizen is non-existent. As previously mentioned, there certainly is an idea that the state should be neutral towards its citizens. Such neutrality is considered to take effect through the observance of the rule of law and citizens' equality before the law.

As the French discourse illustrated, the ideas on citizenship inform how the state should observe neutrality towards the citizen. The English citizenship model has been dubbed a multiculturalist model contrary to the French 'assimilation' model.[267]

---

264 *Azmi* case (2007), para. 52.
265 As can be derived from the Equal Treatment Bench Book (2010), pp. 3-18/3-4.
266 See also Bakht in Grillo and others (2009), p. 125.
267 Cf. A. Phillips, *Multiculturalism without culture* (Princeton University Press, Princeton, NJ [etc.] 2007)

Accordingly, it aims at integrating minorities in society.[268] In order to do so, England has implemented a pluralist policy. This policy does not expect individual differences regarding ethnicity, culture, religion and the like to be erased but rather specifically takes account of them. For instance, authorities explicitly consult minorities in adopting policies such as school uniform policies. The possibility of participating in such consultations by virtue of their minority status has stimulated the establishment of special interest groups, which has considerably enhanced minorities' emancipation. The wide range of associations and organisations representing subgroups with the police is illustrative.

The endeavour to actively include minority groups of all segments of society clearly emerges from the Bench Book.[269] It makes clear that the judicial system in general, and judicial proceedings in particular, should be as accessible as possible. This equally implies that it must be, and must be seen to be inclusive and representative of the whole community.[270] Accordingly, the Bench Book explicitly encourages practices which will enable as many people as possible to participate and engage with judicial processes.[271] This could mean that women with a *niqab* will be allowed to wear it in the courtroom as well, purely to enable their participation in court proceedings.[272] It was clear from the debate on religious symbols at schools that similar considerations apply to accommodating pupils concerning their religion or belief. However, this does not imply that pupils have a general right to wear religious symbols. School authorities are allowed to take measures limiting this right. But in doing so, they should ensure the proportionality of such measures in taking into account circumstantial factors such as the availability of other schools for instance.[273]

The integration model goes hand in hand with the idea that the state derives its neutrality not by representing a blank entity, dissociated with society, but by mirroring society. The affairs described previously involving the police demonstrate this. They demonstrated the importance of the police remaining connected to the community it polices. It has been recognized explicitly that such connection can be expressed by having the police reflect society. This idea was laid down in the concept of policing by consent. In the same vein, the dress policy of allowing headscarves for police officers was informed by the aspiration to attract more Muslim women.[274]

As to the point of separation of church and state, it should be noted that the established Church precludes this point from applying as such to the neutrality

---

268 Molokotos Liederman (2000), p. 113.
269 Equal Treatment Bench Book (2010), p. 3-18/2.
270 Ibid.
271 Ibid.
272 Ibid, p. 3-18/3.
273 See *Begum* case (2006) and *X* case (2007).
274 E.g. 'Great Britain, Protecting the Veil', at *Qantara News* on <www.qantara.de/webcom/show_article.php/_c-549/_nr-11/i.html>.

concept within the English context. Establishment has had a notable influence on the English system, more specifically on the conception of the public sphere and on how the public functions have been institutionalized. In tune with the non-secular nature of the public sphere, the institutions within the public sphere need not necessarily be separated from religion. As previously described, religion is indeed visibly present, for example by religious officials having seats in the House of Lords and the monarch being Head of the Church. Accordingly, the visibility of religion in itself is not considered as undermining the neutrality of the state. Other ways underscore the need of observing neutrality such as the oaths on taking judicial office; these leave no doubt that it is the law which binds a judge. The judicial oath specifically makes the oath-taker swear to do right 'after the laws and usages of this realm'. The oath for the police is equally unambiguous in holding police officers bound by the law. Thus, it should be understood that whereas the symbolic visibility of religion may be relatively uncontested, the prevalence of the law is equally straightforward. The latter entails room for debate on the concept of religion in requiring protection of certain beliefs

Even more than the other public services, public education makes clear how immensely important the influence of the Anglican Church has been, as shown for example by religious education. At any rate, education falls short of being secular.[275] Regarding religious symbols, school policies show that Christianity does not enjoy preferential treatment. A cursory glance at the uniform policies shows an overall inclusiveness of other religions. Perhaps contrary to what may be reasonably expected, the establishment of the Church turned out not to present too much of an impediment to religious minorities for being acknowledged in their claims. Instead, it was felt to create room for such claims. In general, the public sector in England has not been considered as secular and no strict separation is made between the public and private employment sector. To the extent that religion is present, in the public domain as well, it sits quite comfortably with the prevalence of the law.

7.6 CONCLUSION

The contrast of the English stereotype with the French one can be explained with reference to the different way in which England deals with neutrality and underpinning issues. The present chapter has shown that, contrary to the French version of formal neutrality, the English version is based on substantive neutrality. That said, it should be noted that state neutrality as such has not found explicit recognition in English discourse. Instead, it is implicitly assumed through the principle of the rule of law and equality before the law. Accordingly, it is not an abstract principle which imposes generic restrictions on public officials only by reason of their being public officials.

---

275 Blair and Aps (2005), p. 2.

Public officials are also not specifically seen as personifying the state, although the specificity of their function is not ignored. In the same way as Chapter 6 has examined the French context, the present chapter has looked at the English context against the background of arguments which help to refute or put into perspective the idea that state neutrality justifies and/or necessitates limitations on public officials' religious freedom. In doing so, it has used the conceptual model of Chapter 4 as a lens for looking at the English context. Four findings can be highlighted.

Firstly, 'the state' is not as strong a concept as it is in the French context. Although the English state undoubtedly exists, it has not been conceptually emphasized as a distinct entity. In the same vein, while French discourse considered public service as a monolithic sector, English discourse does not have a rigid conception of the public service. The second point, emanating from the first one, is that public officials are not seen as personifying the state to such an extent that representing the state entails setting aside individuality. Public officials are not considered to forgo the exercise of their individual rights by exercising state authority. That is not to say, however, that limitations cannot be imposed on public officials' freedom to display religious symbols. However, when such limitations are imposed, they are not justified by reference to a generally applicable principle, but on the basis of the specific circumstances. Such justification entails a proportionality test. The way in which this test is applied points in the direction of the third finding worth mentioning which relates to the way in which the English conceive religious freedom and specifically the freedom to display religious symbols. The distinction between the *forum internum* and the *forum externum* seems to be less rigidly conceptualized, in part because no absolute limitations on the *forum externum* apply. The assessment of whether limitations on the freedom to display religious symbols are justified is made in view of concrete circumstances. At this point, the fourth finding of the English context can be referred to. The display of religious symbols is not in and of itself incompatible with state neutrality. Instead of inferring a possible discriminatory effect of religious symbols worn by public officials vis-à-vis citizens, the English approach is aimed at ascertaining whether a public official in fact discriminates against citizens. The display of religious symbols is not assumed to automatically imply discriminatory treatment. This may also have to do with how the visibility of religion is looked at more generally. Partly because of the establishment of the Church, religious features have not been banned from the public sphere and they are not as such considered as jeopardizing principles such as equality.

What the English context has in common with the French one – and the Dutch one for that matter – is that debate on religious symbols has not died down. On the contrary, even the case-by-case approach in England cannot prevent disputes from emerging and resulting in legal claims. Evidently, such disputes emanate from instances where limitations have been imposed on individuals' freedom to manifest religion or belief. From lack of a general principle, domestic courts assess limitations on the basis of the specific circumstances of the case. One of the striking aspects of the judicial approach in England concerns the struggle with even a particular symbol as qualifying for protection as a religious symbol. This struggle may call to mind similar difficulties which the ECHR supervisory bodies have dealt with. In the next chapter, the conclusions address more of these parallels which can be derived from the findings of this study.

CHAPTER 8
CONCLUSION

8.1   INTRODUCTION

A proposal for a ban on Dutch municipal employees displaying religious symbols caused an enormous uproar, but the proposal had little effect in the long run. Indeed, the observation at the outset of this study that the debate on the display of religious symbols in public functions has been dragging on for some years now stands a good chance of holding true for another good few years. The MP's suggestion for the proposal did cause a fellow MP to call for a broad debate on church–state relations,[1] but this call does not seem to have led to a clear approach towards the display of religious symbols in public functions.[2] So it seems as if the issue is to remain dormant on the public agenda for now. Nonetheless, it only takes one law student to lodge a complaint after having been rejected for the judiciary training because he wears a religious symbol for the debate to reignite.

This study has confirmed that the issue of displaying religious symbols in public functions should be seen against the background of contention on broader issues having to do with the position of religion in the public domain. At the same time, the issue turned out to be particularly apt for being used as a case study to obtain clarity on these broader issues as well. It was shown that the concept of state neutrality was at the root of contention and confusion in the Dutch debate. Both proponents and opponents of imposing limitations on public officials in displaying religious symbols employed state neutrality to bolster their point. Therefore, this study has taken the point of view that clarification of the issue should begin with clarifying state neutrality and its role in the debate.

The present study has taken on this endeavour with the question as to whether state neutrality in the Netherlands justifies and/or necessitates limitations on the freedom of public officials to display religious symbols. The examination has revolved around three public functions at the forefront in the Dutch debate: the judiciary, the police and public education. While sharing responsibility for serving the public interest,

---

1   'Dibi wil hoorzitting over scheiding kerk en staat', *Trouw* (28 March 2011) on <www.trouw.nl/tr/nl/4492/Nederland/article/detail/1866029/2011/03/28/Dibi-wil-hoorzitting-over-scheiding-kerk-en-staat.dhtml>.

2   The call has caused a parliamentary committee to organize an expert meeting on the separation of church and state and fundamental rights, in Parliament, see Tweede Kamercommissie Binnenlandse Zaken, 'Rondetafelgesprek over Scheiding kerk en staat en Grondrechten', (15 september 2011, Den Haag), on <www.parlement.com/9353000/1f/j9vvhy5i95k8zxl/viq7czuiqsz6>.

255

they represent different aspects of this interest. In line with its point of view on the paramount importance of state neutrality, the study has taken a three-step approach to clarify state neutrality and its role in the debate. In the first place, it has approached the issue on the level of argument by thoroughly discussing the debate; it has disentangled separate arguments advanced to substantiate state neutrality. Secondly, it has dealt with the notion of state neutrality on a conceptual level by studying this notion and the ensuing implications for public officials' religious freedom on a theoretical level. Thirdly, it has examined state neutrality within three normative contexts: the ECHR, England and France. By doing so, the study aimed at identifying the minimum boundaries posed by human rights standards and at exploring implementations of state neutrality which are as divergent as possible, at least in the European context. The results of this examination serve as the basis for the evaluative analysis conducted in this chapter.

This evaluative analysis substantiates the twofold answer to the research question. On the one hand, it establishes that state neutrality does not necessitate limitations on public officials' freedom to display religious symbols. On the other hand, it does not rule out that state neutrality may justify such limitations, but not as a general principle. In several respects the findings of this study demonstrate that state neutrality falls short of explicitly requiring the exclusion of religious symbols in public functions. On a theoretical level, it appears that the core requirements of state neutrality do not imply such a requirement. Furthermore, by the very nature of setting a minimum yardstick, the ECHR framework does not require states to exclude religious symbols either in order to uphold state neutrality. In the Dutch context, it should be noted that the Netherlands has not endorsed a strict interpretation of state neutrality which, moreover, appeared to lack the status of an expressly enshrined constitutional principle. Traditionally, the Netherlands has been inclined to accommodate religious needs and to approach religious diversity in a pragmatic way. If state neutrality is regarded as a justification for limitations on displaying religious symbols, then it is true that the ECHR itself offers much leeway to states in imposing limitations on public officials to manifest religion or belief. However, Chapter 5 showed that the ECHR bodies do not generally identify state neutrality as a principle justifying such limitations. In sum, next to not requiring limitations on public officials' freedom to display religious symbols, state neutrality also falls short of automatically justifying such limitations. This concept can serve as a justification but only in carefully circumscribed conditions.

Accordingly, this study urges a critical eye to be cast on any limitation imposed on public officials to display religious symbols. Public officials' freedom to manifest religion or belief should be the rule and limitations the exception, not the other way around. Furthermore, when states impose limitations they bear the burden of properly justifying them. This study advocates a contextual approach. That is to say that any limitation should be justifiable in view of the public function at hand and of the specific factors at play. One might think of the capacity of the citizen with whom a public official has dealings, or of the specific setting in which a public official exercises his function. The comparative analysis of France and England conducted in this study is conducive to appreciating such factors and their weight. It is specifically by justifying that limitations are better substantiated. At this point, the search for solidly argued limitations resonates with Smits' view that legal science is meant to identify the better arguments in order to substantiate one or the other position.

Needless to say, this general answer does not allow for dealing with the nuances, which this chapter elaborates on in later sections. Before doing so, in Sections 8.2 to 8.5, this chapter recapitulates the findings of Chapters 2 to 7. Section 8.2 reiterates the findings of Chapters 2 and 3 which deal with how to clarify state neutrality in the Dutch debate by disentangling the separate underpinning arguments. Section 8.3 summarizes the conceptual findings of Chapter 4 by presenting again the conceptual model construed from these first results. This model has been used subsequently to examine the ECHR framework, as well as the French and English context. Sections 8.4 and 8.5 recapitulate the findings of this examination. In this chapter, the conceptual model helps to connect the results of the other contexts to the Dutch context. The previous explorations each deliver a part of the answer to the research question; but this chapter also develops more explicitly the implications of the answer to the research question for the Dutch context which it presents in Section 8.6. This study advocates a contextual approach to shape such implications. The following section, Section 8.2, begins the endeavour of concluding the study with a recapitulation of how the Dutch debate came about and how it was conducted.

8.2 THE MULTIPLE LAYERS OF DUTCH DEBATE

Stereotypes allow for a quick visualization of a complex reality. Naturally, they should be taken with many provisos, but they are nevertheless inspired by a grain of truth. The stereotypical image of the Netherlands has long been shaped by tolerance and multiculturalism, the two of which were often linked. The brief exploration of the Dutch context in Chapter 2 echoed this image and brought out two features of the Dutch approach to religious diversity: pluralism and pragmatism. Additionally, it showed how societal changes had created room for contestation to emerge.

8.2.1 Pluralism, pragmatism and change

Like most other countries in Western Europe, the Netherlands has been affected by the events of 11 September 2001 and their aftermath. It is arguable whether these events have actually changed the way in which countries deal with diversity, or whether they have only laid bare what was already under the surface. In dealing with the claims of various religious groups, the Netherlands has adopted a pragmatic approach in accommodating those claims. The creation of a separate space for different groups in the public realm within the so-called pillarization system exemplifies this accommodative approach. Changes in Dutch society have influenced the increasing controversy over religious diversity in general and religious symbols in public functions in particular. For the past few years, the role of religion has changed in a paradoxical manner. It has become less prominent in that increasing individualization has led people more and more to profess religion in their own private realms instead of in public communal institutions. However, the increasing drain from churches does not necessarily indicate a decline in people's religiousness. The role of religion has been transformed rather than necessarily diminished. A seemingly contrasting development is that the topic of religion has regained its position on the public agenda. There were times when it was claimed that religion would become much less relevant, in part because of secularization. Reality has refuted this expectation. More than ever, religion-related matters are capable of stirring up feelings. Another change which has loomed in the background of controversies on religion concerns the composition of the Dutch population. Years of immigration with periodic peaks has altered the Dutch population so that it now comprises a significant proportion of immigrants. A large number of them have come from Turkey and Morocco and are Muslim. The combination of these factors – the changed role of religion and the modified composition of the Dutch population – has brought to light issues long thought to be settled. The question of religious symbols in public functions is one of those issues. The lack of codification on the scope for religious symbols in public functions leaves room for varying interpretations: religious symbols may either be allowed or prohibited in public functions. Additionally, although discussion has generally been initiated by Muslim symbols, such discussion has moved onto symbols of other religions or beliefs as well.

8.2.2 Several points of contention

As with any debate, it is easy to go astray in the wilderness of arguments concerning religious symbols in public functions. Generally, a public debate does not take place along nicely defined lines. Instead, such a debate is conducted by a multitude of actors, in different contexts and across a variety of documents. Furthermore, the presentation of arguments in a debate aims at making a point and, therefore, does not necessarily have to be systematic, consistent or comprehensive. The legal discipline ultimately embraces the inconclusiveness of debate but is also capable of distinguishing between strong and weak arguments. Smits qualifies law as a science of competing positions. He considers the very role of the legal discipline to imply carefully identifying and scrutinizing the underlying arguments. Accordingly, the first challenge in obtaining an overview of the debate lies in identifying and systemizing the points of contention. In this study, disputes before the Dutch Equal Treatment Commission (Commission) served as the starting point. The reasons for having chosen this angle are twofold. Firstly, the opinions of the Commission possess authoritative value as to the interpretation of Dutch equal treatment law. Secondly, the Commission has addressed each of the three public functions examined in this study in individual cases. The examination of the cases served to supply key points of contention. Additionally, the examination has scrutinized the debate on both a political and scholarly level to see how these points of contention resounded and whether additional points had been advanced elsewhere. Subsequently, the study assembled the main underlying points of contention figuring in the debate. Accordingly, Chapter 3 proposed six main points on which the arguments centred, without assuming them to be exhaustive or strictly separated. Table 8.1 (see next page) will return to these points.

As stated in Chapter 3, this overview demonstrates three things. First, the points of contention uncover differences in various respects. To illustrate, some of the points apply to the public official individually, whereas others apply to the public service as a whole. Secondly, although the points in principle stand independently, they are also inter-connected. This might be relevant for their importance. For instance, the issue of separation of church and state can be coupled with the issue of personification in order to argue in favour of limitations on the freedom of public officials to manifest their religion or belief. Thirdly, the points of contention indicate general strands in the debate on public functions. They revolve around common aspects of different public functions. At the same time, they point to the relevance of the particular features of a public function for the effect of state neutrality. For instance, considering the paramount importance of the principle of judicial impartiality, the point of bias can be expected to have specific importance for the judiciary.

Table 8.1: Points of contention

Point of contention	Explanation
(1) Equal treatment of the public official	The state should ensure equal access to those pursuing a position in public service and moreover it should treat public officials equally. The question is how such equality is best safeguarded, by an invariable policy or by a differentiating policy?
(2) Personification of the state	Does a public official personify the state? On the one hand, a public official still has a personal capacity endowing him with individual rights. On the other hand, being a public official he possesses an official capacity and incurs an obligation of state neutrality vis-à-vis others. Therefore, the question can be asked, to what extent does his professional obligation encroach on his individual rights?
(3) Public officials' bias	The question can be asked whether public officials manifesting their religion or belief by displaying symbols convey bias. An ensuing question is whether they violate another person's right to equal treatment. This violation is mainly created by the impression which public officials give of being biased towards another person with whom they have dealings. This might justify limiting public officials' freedom to manifest their religion or belief.
(4) Risk of proselytism	This point also relates to the effect of the appearance of public officials on the rights of others. In contrast to the previous point, though, this one extends this effect further in considering the possibility of their appearance exerting an improper influence on others. This argument thus addresses the risk of imposing a religion or belief on others.
(5) Image of the state	In serving citizens of the state, public officials need to convey that the state is available for all. The question is how they can best do so, for instance by embodying some blank entity or by emphasizing their individuality and link to society?
(6) Separation of church and state	It has been suggested that the separation of church and state directly requires that public officials refrain from manifesting their religion or belief by wearing symbols. The argument presupposes public officials as personifying the state.

8.2.3 Concluding remarks

Two things are worth remarking after having briefly explored the Dutch background to the debate itself. In the first place, the history of Dutch efforts to cope with religious diversity demonstrates an approach of accommodating different religious groups. The state took on a proactive role in ensuring such accommodation which was not considered as incompatible with its neutrality. The pillar structure testified to this active role and moreover exemplified that the visibility of the presence of multiple denominations in the public sphere was not banned. Societal changes of the past few decades, related to the role of religion and immigration, revitalized the interest in religion-related issues. Religions which had not previously been prominent caused contestation which reflected on settled religions as well. These societal changes cast a different light on what state neutrality might encompass. It is in this different light that calls for strict state neutrality are made. However, the Dutch background does not appear conductive to strict state neutrality which would necessitate limitations on public officials' freedom to display religious symbols.

The second thing which the exploration showed was that the opaque concept of state neutrality encompassed multiple points of contention each of which relates to a particular element of how state neutrality plays out in the issue of public officials displaying religious symbols. These points were explanatory for how state neutrality can be employed on both sides of the debate. Depending on how the separate points of contention are assessed, one or the other position concerning state neutrality is favoured. On the one hand, these points run across all public functions. On the other hand, they demonstrate the need to differentiate according to the particularities of each public function. Accordingly, the answer to the research question might vary depending on the public function involved. In other words, the analysis on the argument level did not seem to support a catch-all version of neutrality to answer the research question.

8.3 THE TRIANGULAR MODEL

8.3.1 All roads lead to neutrality

Some notions are so elusive that they are more easily described by what they are not than by what they are. As shown in Chapter 4, state neutrality does not equate to the separation of church and state, despite having some connection to this notion. Neither is it the same as secularism. An attempt to describe state neutrality runs into three difficulties. Firstly, it is rooted in liberalism. This origin has coloured the notion of neutrality, which has been used by some to question the very neutrality implicit in the notion of state neutrality. Put simply, the concept of neutrality itself is not neutral. This metaphysical note aside, the liberal character of state neutrality further complicates the theoretical clarification of state neutrality in entwining state neutrality with big philosophical questions. These questions concern the role of the state towards citizens, the extent to which the state may interfere with citizens' lives and in doing so interfere with conceptions of the common good. The second difficulty in grappling with state neutrality is its interdisciplinary nature. State neutrality has turned out to be rooted in a politico-philosophical background; it is used in political theory, debated in legal theory and employed as a constitutional principle. The third and greatest challenge regarding state neutrality lies in its abstract nature as an ideal. As is the case with ideals, the more concrete the implementation, the more variation comes in. Hence, state neutrality does not promulgate a clear policy as regards the use of religious symbols in public functions.

Indeed, quite opposing policies can be based on state neutrality. That is, a state could claim to be neutral when adopting a policy excluding religious symbols. It could also express its neutrality by allowing public officials to display religious symbols. Theory has accepted that state neutrality can be realized through multiple pathways. In doing so, it has developed classifications to distinguish these pathways. An influential classification distinguishes two ways in which state neutrality can operate as a standard: neutrality of justification and neutrality of effect. The former standard of neutrality requires a state to advance neutral reasons for its policies, irrespective of the effects of these policies. For example, the state might decide to prohibit all public officials from wearing head coverings because a head covering is not part of the prescribed uniform. Such a policy would probably stand the test of neutrality of justification. By contrast, if it were to be assessed by the standard of neutrality of effect, the policy might turn out not to be neutral. After all, it is likely to have a greater impact effectively on particular religious groups. Indeed, the standards of neutrality of justification and effect run parallel to the conception of formal and substantive equality respectively.

The problem is compounded because the issue of religious symbols in public functions obviously also involves public officials' religious freedom. Their freedom to manifest religion or belief by displaying symbols is not absolute and can under certain conditions be limited. Such limitation is in part informed by the elusive obligation of state neutrality but possibly also by other interests, such as the rights and freedoms of others. In the case of religious symbols, the rights and freedoms of others may concern their right to equal treatment or freedom of religion or belief. Hence, so far as the issue of religious symbols in public functions is concerned, it does not even suffice to examine state neutrality in itself. The relation of state neutrality to religious freedom, on multiple levels, should also be looked at. In sum, the exploration of theory has demonstrated that although state neutrality and religious freedom seem to speak for themselves, they actually invite a wide array of understandings. When applied to the issue of public officials displaying religious symbols, both concepts imply a certain bandwidth within which this issue can be dealt with.

8.3.2 Three obligations and three actors

The previous section has underscored the complexity in defining state neutrality. One of the pitfalls in grasping state neutrality is circular reasoning: state neutrality means that public officials should be neutral. What is neutral? To whom do public officials incur an obligation of neutrality? How should they convey such neutrality? The issue of religious symbols in public functions offers a compelling occasion to deal with these questions because this issue sits right on the intersection between state neutrality and religious freedom. By looking at the interplay between these two concepts, Chapter 4 has sought to clarify the effect of both concepts on the issue of religious symbols in public functions. The convergence of both concepts on two important points, state–individual relations and the obligation of the state towards the individual, has helped to clarify the impact of state neutrality on the issue of religious symbols in public functions. The very rationale of both state neutrality and religious freedom appears to be the protection of the individual against the state. On the basis of the extensive theory on state neutrality and the interplay of state neutrality with religious freedom, this study has identified three core obligations as inherent to the general duty incumbent on the state 'to be neutral' in order to further describe this duty. These core obligations can be listed as follows:

1. the state should not evaluate, favour or disfavour religions or beliefs (in general or in its interaction with individuals and communities);
2. the state should not impose religion or belief (in general or in its interaction with individuals and communities;
3. the state should not favour or disfavour individuals or communities on the basis of religion or belief.

These core obligations still leave room for divergent interpretation when interpreting them according to neutrality of justification or neutrality of effect. For example, neutrality of justification would only require the state not to evaluate religions or beliefs explicitly, whereas neutrality of effect would also demand that such evaluation would not be the result of a policy which in itself contains no explicit evaluation. Furthermore, the study has observed that these obligations are not only effective in the relation between the state and the citizen, but also between the state and the public official and the public official and the citizen. Accordingly, Chapter 4 has proposed a triangular model of the relevant actors and their mutual relations to visualize the dynamics of state neutrality, without pretending this model to be the exclusive one to capture reality. The model can be beneficial to the understanding of religious symbols in public functions in three respects. Firstly, it clearly outlines which actors and relations are at play. Secondly, the triangle emphasizes the indivisibility of the relations between the actors and hence the effectuation of state neutrality. Thirdly, it indicates the importance which specific factors have in assessing the necessity and justifications of limitations on the freedom to display religious symbols.

8.3.3 Correspondence with points of contention

The advantage of this visualization is that it appears particularly apt to represent how the points of contention advanced (Table 8.1) play out. Indeed, some of the points of contention mainly concern the state in a more abstract sense in relation to citizens, while others turn on the relation between the individual public official and the individual citizen. Additionally, state neutrality also concerns the relation between the state and the public official. Because they concern different relations, it makes sense to consider the points of contention separately, although it should not be overlooked that they mutually reinforce each other. The points of contention can be placed within the model in the following way.

The equal treatment and personification points (1 and 2) can be linked to the dynamics between the state and the public official. Both points in fact boil down to the question of how the policy regarding religious symbols affects the treatment of public officials by the state. Secondly, the points of contention as to the public official's bias and the risk of proselytism (3 and 4) both address the question of whether public officials displaying religious symbols jeopardize the equal treatment and freedom of religion of citizens. In other words, they correspond with the relation between the public official and the citizen. Finally, the points of contention regarding the image of the state and the separation of church and state (5 and 6) concern the question of whether public officials wearing religious symbols compromise the neutral image of the state for citizens. These points centre on the relation between the state and citizens. The triangular model shows that state neutrality may play out differently across the different relations. Accordingly, it might vary in bearing on the different points of contention. That means that it allows for possibly necessary differentiation between the weight of these points of contention. The triangular model and its relation to the points of contention can be shown as follows.

Diagram 8.1

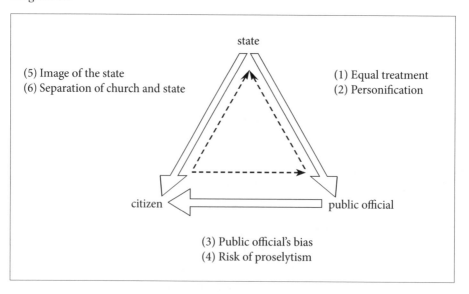

8.3.4 Concluding remarks

To prohibit or not to prohibit, that seems to be the question in the debate on religious symbols in public functions. The difficulty in answering this question with reference to state neutrality is that this concept does not provide an unambiguous solution. Indeed, state neutrality turns out to be employed by the proponents as well as by the opponents of prohibition. The theoretical exploration of the concept of state neutrality has confirmed that it leaves room for both positions. As an ideal, state neutrality cannot be taken to dictate in detail what the state is allowed to do. As shown in the conceptual analysis in Chapter 4, state neutrality should rather be imagined as a force, which variably exerts a limiting effect on the freedom of public officials to wear religious symbols. In the same vein, religious freedom can be seen as leaving room for variation depending on the limitations imposed on it. As a consequence, religious freedom and state neutrality can be reconciled to varying degrees. In other words, from a conceptual point of view, a plain answer to the research question is not available. Stated simply, state neutrality in and of itself does not justify and/or necessitate limitations on the freedom of public officials to display religious symbols. It may do so, but that depends on how it is interpreted. When employed as a standard of justification, it might do so. Additionally, the formal conception of state neutrality is likely to justify and possibly necessitate such limitations. Whether either is the case depends on the domestic implementation of neutrality.

The conceptual analysis has proposed two more ways to clarify how state neutrality may play out in the issue of religious symbols in public functions. Firstly, it has derived three core duties from the literature which can be considered as inherent to state neutrality. These duties make more explicit what state neutrality might entail. Secondly, it has proposed that state neutrality could best be imagined as taking effect within a triangle of relations between the state, the public official and the citizen. Such a visualization implies that it has posited state neutrality as a relational notion, which assumes meaning through the interactions between the actors involved. Seeing the actors involved in this way has been argued to do justice to the multifold and not necessarily consistent effect of state neutrality. Moreover, it has provided a model within which the points of contention in the Dutch debate could be placed and accordingly assessed. In sum, the conceptual analysis corroborates that the effectuation of state neutrality regarding public officials displaying religious symbols is likely to be differentiated.

8.4 Minimum ECHR standards

The research question includes a twofold test of state neutrality as a ground for imposing limitations on public officials' religious freedom: necessity and justification. The latter part refers to a human rights test. Because limitations encroach on public officials' freedom to manifest religion or belief, they must at least fulfil the requirements of the ECHR (which in this study has been taken as the main point of reference in view of the states examined). The study has used the case law to infer the minimum boundaries set by human rights law on the scope for religious symbols in public functions. Although the case law does not lend itself to propounding doctrinal truths, it does reveal indicators for such boundaries. It should be noted that the supervisory bodies have generally left a broad margin of appreciation to states in Article 9 cases. As a consequence, they have not given particular and clear guidance regarding limitations on public officials displaying religious symbols.

8.4.1 Neutrality as a pluralist and a secular principle

Chapter 5 has demonstrated that neutrality has assumed a palpable yet broad understanding within the context of the ECHR. Moreover, neutrality has played a role on a more general level and as a relatively specific principle in cases. Albeit not codified in the Convention, this concept has figured in numerous cases, to the extent that it has become one of the principles underpinning the approach towards Article 9 ECHR. Throughout the case law, neutrality has evolved from a more general obligation to a principle implying more specific duties for the state. For example, the state should not take sides in disputes between religious communities and should not assess the legitimacy of religious beliefs. Additionally, the supervisory bodies have generally coupled state neutrality with wider values such as pluralism, tolerance and the preservation of a democratic society. They have still left ample room for divergent national implementations of the principle of neutrality. Accordingly, neutrality has been found to be compatible with the Convention, irrespective of whether it is a written or unwritten principle. That said, neutrality has also played a role on a more specific level in cases. On that level, the status of neutrality within the domestic legal order is of relevance for the strictness of limitations on citizens' religious freedom. It seems that a constitutionally enshrined principle of neutrality allows for stricter limitations. Otherwise, various forms of neutrality with various rationales fall within the ambit of the ECHR definition of neutrality. For instance, there have been cases concerning political neutrality, which appeared to be informed by the integrity of the public system. Other cases referred to religious neutrality as safeguarding religious harmony in society. Such neutrality might well be implemented in a secular manner, as appeared to be the case in Turkey. In several cases against Turkey, reference has been made to combating religious extremism and safeguarding social harmony as underlying rationales of a strict version of secularism. All these forms of neutrality in themselves have been found to be compatible with the Convention. It must finally be noted that the specific context in which state neutrality is implemented matters for its application.

8.4.2 State towards the public official: rights can be limited or waived

The starting point is that a public official, as an individual, can rely on the guarantees enshrined in the Convention, including those in Article 9. Dress and symbols qualify as a religious manifestation in terms of that Article. At any rate, the *forum externum* of Article 9 is not unlimited. There are three respects in which limitations on the freedom of public officials to wear religious symbols can be justified.

First of all, the supervising bodies have reiterated on numerous occasions that freedom of religion does not protect at all times the right to manifest religion or belief in public. Secondly, not every act inspired by religion or belief is protected under the Convention. Consequently, justifying limitations on the freedom of public officials to manifest religion or belief during the exercise of their office by reference to a distinction between their private and official capacities does not in itself contravene the Convention. Thirdly and finally, public officials have been acknowledged as representatives of the state. This particular capacity may supplement justifications as to limiting public officials' religious freedom. An important strand of case law has revolved around the applicability of a 'particular regime' to justify limitations. This line of reasoning has mostly been applied in cases involving the military or education. In emphasizing an individual's voluntary compliance with the limitations of a particular regime, the ECHR bodies have accepted the legitimacy of such limitations. This is even more the case when they consider that an individual has the possibility of relinquishing that regime. In sum, in considering whether such a regime is applicable and capable of limiting individuals' rights, the ECHR bodies have looked at whether the individuals chose to become part of the regime, whether they truly had a choice, and whether they were aware beforehand of the possible limitations. It should be noted that this line of case law has not even considered Article 9 ECHR to have come into play. Stated more specifically, limitations ensuing from a particular regime have not been considered as actually interfering with Article 9 ECHR.

8.4.3 Public official towards the citizen: a religious symbol can jeopardize rights

As alluded to in the previous section, the supervising bodies have accepted that public officials are considered as representing the state. As a consequence, particular limitations may be imposed on their freedom to manifest religion or belief. Cases before the ECHR supervising bodies resonate with the Dutch debate in that states have justified limitations by reference to possible bias and the risk of proselytism. It should first be noted that, despite its pejorative connotation in the debate on religious symbols, proselytism has been included in the right to manifest religion or belief in the first significant Article 9 case, *Kokkinakis v. Greece*. The Court has ruled that improper proselytism, though, is not covered by the protection of Article 9. The

Dahlab case concerning a state school teacher can be taken as illustrating a case of improper proselytism, according to the decision of the Court. Four aspects of the case should be pointed out which were crucial to the final decision.

Firstly, denominational neutrality is an essential principle in the (Swiss) educational system. It has been codified as a strict principle. Secondly, the applicant's function as a teacher qualifies her as a 'figure of authority'. Thirdly, the 'tender age' of the pupils is considered in assuming their vulnerability to being influenced by teachers. Fourthly, the particular religious symbol, the headscarf, is deemed to be a 'powerful external symbol', the wearing of which might have a proselytizing effect. What is more, the Court argued that the wearing of the headscarf might be difficult to square with gender equality. Furthermore, the Court established that this tension between the headscarf and gender equality also makes it difficult to reconcile the headscarf with values of tolerance, respect and equality.

8.4.4 State towards citizens: a neutral and impartial organizer

In attributing to the state the role of a neutral and impartial organizer, the supervisory bodies have admitted that the state bears responsibility towards its citizens. However, just as they leave it up to states to shape their religion–state arrangements, they leave it to states to decide how to effectuate this responsibility. In accordance with this wide margin of appreciation, states have a considerable amount of freedom in terms of the ways in which they convey that they are available to citizens. Retaining public trust has been acknowledged as an important consideration in shaping the image of the state. As long as a state pursues the interests of pluralism, tolerance and democracy, however, this image itself can be exclusionary or inclusionary in nature. More specifically, it is left to the states to what extent they decide either to ban the visibility of religion in the state or even in the public sphere (exclusionary) or to include such visibility (inclusionary).

8.4.5 Concluding remarks

State neutrality has been referred to in multiple ways in ECHR case law. This concept has figured as a general principle in numerous cases, often alongside other values like pluralism, tolerance and broadmindedness. These values seem to allude to an interpretation of state neutrality which leaves room for religious manifestations. It can be concluded in any case that, in the view of the ECHR bodies, state neutrality does not necessitate limitations on religious manifestations. A scrutiny of how state neutrality has operated in concrete cases though indicates that multiple interpretations are compatible with the Convention. What is more, states relying on an exclusive interpretation of state neutrality, possibly as a constitutional principle, are allowed to invoke state neutrality as a ground to impose limitations in terms of Article 9(2)

ECHR. Stated more generally, occasional ambiguities in the case law notwithstanding, the supervisory bodies have left states with a fair amount of leeway to impose limitations on public officials' freedom to display religious symbols. Such leeway implies that state neutrality may justify limitations on the freedom of individuals to display religious symbols from the viewpoint of minimum human rights standards. Such leeway also specifically applies in the case of public officials.

As to the limitations on public officials' religious freedom, it should also be taken into account that the supervisory bodies have had regard for the associated characteristics on the special role of public officials, such as the state-representative nature of their tasks, the authority of public officials, and the loyalty which public officials owe to the state. These characteristics have been relevant for judging the proportionality of a measure interfering with Article 9 ECHR. Additionally, the extent to which the rights and freedoms of others are considered to be encroached on by an individual, possibly a public official, determine whether the interference is proportional. In the issue of religious symbols, two factors have been of particular interest: the symbol at hand and the way in which it is displayed. Thus far, the Court has notably attached significance to the headscarf as a proselytizing symbol. In so doing, the Court has not verified whether this interpretation could be corroborated by evidence. Rather, it has linked this interpretation of the headscarf to the wearer's function in assuming the possibility of such proselytism. This approach points to the relevance of the way of displaying religious symbols: when it is a public official displaying a symbol, undue influence seems to be assumed. By contrast, the Court has considered a crucifix on the wall to be an essentially passive symbol, unlikely to give rise to proselytism.

While taking into account that case law is not suitable for propounding doctrinal truths, the study has looked at whether human rights standards stop state neutrality from justifying limitations on public officials' freedom to display religious symbols. The case law analysis has demonstrated that state neutrality has the potential of serving as a justification. Then again, in line with the case-by-case approach inherent to the Convention system, it should be emphasized that the specific circumstances of a case determine whether state neutrality can indeed justify limitations. The wide margin of appreciation left to states does not allow for very clear guidelines. There seems to be a good deal of leeway for imposing limitations on the wearing of religious symbols. At the same time, the ECHR bodies indicate the minimum yardstick which states should comply with in order to observe the Convention. Furthermore, the ECHR case law should not be taken to imply that anything goes. It is striking to note that most cases regarding religious symbols centre on constitutional principles of secularism.

8.5 DIVERGENT APPROACHES IN FRANCE AND ENGLAND

In the present study, two countries have been selected to provide different contexts for examining the issue of religious symbols in public functions. As two extremes of the spectrum regarding religious diversity in the public domain, France and England were expected to provide clues for approaches which are as divergent as possible. The examination of both countries has looked at the contexts in themselves, how the conceptions within both countries fit into the conceptual model and how they thus relate to the points of contention. While not aiming at a fully-fledged comparison of the two systems, the study brings out some interesting differences between those systems which are relevant to their significance for the Dutch context.

8.5.1 Neutrality in two opposite interpretations

The wide divergence between France and England is corroborated by how they approach the issue of state neutrality. Chapters 6 and 7 demonstrated that their respective conceptions of state neutrality can be summed up in three opposites: explicit versus implied, formal versus substantive, and exclusive versus inclusive.

The French conception of neutrality cannot be seen separately from the paramount constitutional principle of *laïcité*. Neutrality is explicitly recognized and accepted, albeit in a formal version. That is to say that France disregards religion altogether as a relevant category for policy. France has a formal interpretation of state neutrality and employs state neutrality to justify its policy without looking at whether the effect of its policy is neutral. As a consequence, it does not differentiate between the various implications of neutrality, making the implementation of this principle uniform. In other words, France implements neutrality as a standard of justification. Finally, the rigid interpretation implies an absolute exclusion of religion and religious manifestations. Accordingly, French neutrality is clearly exclusionary in nature. By contrast, England has not codified or conceptualized neutrality. Instead, its existence is assumed through equality before the law. Ensuing from a substantive conception of equality, neutrality is measured by looking at the effects of a policy. Thus insofar as it is in active force, English neutrality corresponds to a standard of effect. Lacking any uniformity or rigidity, neutrality is assessed in a case-by-case manner. This concept is not *a priori* considered incompatible with religion and accordingly leaves room for religion or religious manifestations. The English approach can thus be called inclusionary in nature.

8.5.2 State towards the public official: absorption or individuality

As Diagram 8.1 showed two points, namely (1) a public official's equal treatment and (2) his personification of the state are related to the neutrality of the state towards the public official. Two characteristics of the French and English approaches can be distinguished as influencing how these arguments play out: firstly, the conception of the state and its relation to the public official; and secondly, the position of religion in the public domain. This is explained in the rest of this subsection.

First, the state and the extent to which it is considered as incorporating public officials are conceptualized differently in the French and English contexts. France exemplifies a system embracing a strong conception of 'the state'. The state as a strong entity in itself surpasses a public official's individuality. Consequently, a public official is considered as representing, or even embodying, the state. As described in the previous section, a duty of strict neutrality applies. This interpretation of neutrality entails the absolute exclusion of any personal manifestations of religion. Such exclusion makes the state religion-blind, which in French discourse does not conflict with equal treatment of public officials. This approach is not further differentiated as to the particular public function. Regardless of the function, an identical threshold applies for public officials, namely one that excludes religion. This policy is considered as enabling the state to have exclusive regard for an individual's relevant qualifications and as precluding the state from discriminating against public officials on the basis of religion or belief. In England, 'the state' has not been theorized so extensively. Public officials are thus not seen as embodying the state. This is in tune with the lack of a strict duty of neutrality imposing clear requirements on public officials regarding such embodiment. Moreover, neutrality has not been interpreted as absolutely excluding personal manifestations, including religious ones. Religion-blindness is not considered necessary for the state to be neutral towards public officials. This ties in with the second characteristic, the position of religion in the public domain.

Secondly, an obvious difference between France and England concerns the place they give to religion. Whereas the former is known as a secular state, the latter is one of the last European states with an established church. France is not only a secular state; it has also embraced a republican ideology. As a consequence, public officials embodying the state also embody this ideology, which relegates personal markers like religious ones to the private sphere and leaves room only for republican values. French ideology is based on the premise that a state can best serve its citizens by not allowing any visibility of religion to creep into public functions. It is thus assumed that visibility of religion in and of itself can be harmful to citizens. Religion is something which belongs in the private sphere. Accordingly, neutrality has assumed a strictly exclusionary character. The state is a public entity with its own values, republican values. By contrast, in England, even today the Anglican Church has significant presence for the public domain. Hence, it may not only be the lack of a strongly conceptualized state that precludes a public official from embodying the state. Another impediment for considering that public officials embody the state may be the remaining ties of the state with a religious institution like the Anglican Church.

In personifying the state, French public officials thus personify an areligious republican entity. They have been abstracted from individual markers, which are considered divisive for citizenship. In the French conception it goes without saying that public officials forgo their right to manifest religion or belief. This conception raises questions as to the extent to which a French public official can still be reasonably considered as a full subject of individual rights. The absolute limitation on public officials' rights is also related to the rigid distinction in France between what is public and what is private. As to public officials, this distinction implies far-reaching limitations on the public official's freedom in office, and more lenient limitations on his freedom outside office. By contrast, the English practice shows how religion is not necessarily considered as exclusively belonging to the private sphere. Abstract values have no comparable force in English discourse. Moreover, individual differences do not have to be completely neutralised. The imposition of limitations does not run parallel to a distinction between public and private.

8.5.3 Public official towards the citizen: appearance or conduct

Regarding the issue of religious symbols in public functions, the relation between the individual public official and the individual citizen attracts much attention. After all, it is this image which comes to mind when thinking about public officials wearing religious symbols. Two implications (the third and fourth points of contention) which emanate from the contrast between the French and English approaches bear on the points concerning this relation: (3) bias and (4) proselytism. These implications specifically concern the room for differentiation and the evidentiary basis on which to establish bias or proselytism respectively.

The first implication is inherent to the degree of abstractness of the approaches. The previous section made clear that the strong conception of the state coupled with the principles of *laïcité* and neutrality left no room for differentiation in the French approach. Accordingly, this approach disregards the particular features of a public function. It is by virtue of representing public service that a public official is precluded from wearing religious symbols. Whether he is a judge, a police officer or a state school teacher is irrelevant. The exclusion of religious symbols is assumed to protect the rights and freedoms of others. The English approach does not revolve around a theorized idea of the state and neutrality. Instead, the particular features of public functions are taken into account for assessing the possibility of wearing religious symbols. The English approach does not automatically and *a priori* assume a detrimental effect of religious symbols on other individuals. To assume or not assume the effect of religious symbols alludes to the second implication.

French history reveals the origins of an apprehensive attitude towards religion and its visibility, which is still present today. Consequently, appearance does matter in establishing whether or not someone is seen as possibly exhibiting bias or proselytizing. By contrast, appearance in itself does not have much weight under the English approach. It is rather a public official's conduct which serves as a yardstick for his objectivity. In tune with the accepted public visibility of religion, religious symbols do not have a pejorative meaning. Moreover, displaying or removing religious symbols is not considered as impacting on a person's religiousness or ability to remain neutral.

8.5.4 State towards citizens: authority or representation

Theories of state neutrality generally centre on the relation between the state and citizens. The forceful French ideology of the state pervades the way in which state neutrality vis-à-vis citizens is conceived. It has nearly made 'the state' a sacred notion, while English discourse has not embraced this notion of 'the state' to a comparable extent. A twofold divergence (related to the fifth and sixth points of contention) ensues from the different conceptions of the state. On the one hand, the discourses show how availability of the state for citizens can be expressed either by detached authority (France) or by recognizable representation (England). Thus, the discourses demonstrate how two different questions can be significant for how the state–citizen relation is shaped. Does the state invoke sufficient reverence with citizens? Or, can citizens identify with the state? This also has to do with how the public–private divide is viewed. French discourse applies a strict distinction between the state, public services and other domains. It may be said that state and society are disconnected. This is in line with the impersonal image with which the state conveys its availability. The lack of recognition of (religious) minority groups, or of any community for that matter, corroborates this point. Access to citizenship is considered as sufficiently guaranteeing an individual's rights vis-à-vis the state. By contrast, the legitimacy of the English state is in part derived from its connection with society. The idea of policing by consent whereby the police explicitly seeks to tune in with local communities exemplifies this view. More generally, the state mirroring the composition of society is seen as a tool to integrate minority groups. There is an explicit aspiration to include minority groups, without denying that these groups constitute minorities.

As to the sixth point of contention, the separation of church and state, it could be seen that there may be some correspondence between the church–state system and the way in which the state gives effect to neutrality. More generally, the way in which neutrality of the state towards citizens is shaped is naturally influenced by the position of religion in respect of the state. It is not too surprising that a state endorsing *laïcité* shapes its neutrality by excluding religion. Neither is it illogical for a state with an established church not to exclude religion. What is more, the English discourse illustrates that the Established Church has even been considered by scholars to create room for the presence and manifestations of religions other than the Anglican one.

8.5.5 Concluding remarks

In debates related to religious diversity, the French and English approaches often feature as archetypical opposites. The French are portrayed as exclusionary towards religion and the English as inclusionary. Indeed, their respective practices reflect these attitudes. While this is a finding concisely describing their practices, it does not necessarily explain them. In bringing to light the underlying reasons for this divergence, the study has shown some essential differences in the way that state neutrality is considered to relate to public officials' religious freedom. To begin with, a key difference concerns the status of state neutrality. The French view sees neutrality as part and parcel of the constitutional principle of *laïcité*. Although neutrality has not been codified, it is undoubtedly accepted as an imperative requirement incumbent on public officials. In this regard, neutrality can be considered as a purpose in itself. By contrast, the English approach does not herald neutrality as an independent notion. Rather, it is understood to emanate self-evidently from citizens' equality before the law.

This first difference – concerning the status of neutrality – impacts on the approach of each country regarding religious symbols in public functions, which constitutes the second difference. In attributing fundamental value to *laïcité* and neutrality, France has adopted an abstract approach. It has proclaimed the necessity of public officials being neutral and this principle has determined policy. Lacking an explicit principle of neutrality, England could be said to approach the question of religious symbols in public functions from a contextual point of view. Stated simply, the French approach was fixed *a priori*, whereas the English approach was adaptable. As a consequence, the difference between the two approaches can be qualified as uniform versus differentiated. Because the French point of view turns on a principle, it had a rigid conception of the state, public officials and citizens and their mutual relations. Accordingly, it does not have regard for the actors' specific features or the variables applicable to their relation. For instance, it is irrelevant how the relation between a judge and a defendant on the one hand, and a teacher and a pupil on the other hand, differ. All that matters is whether it concerns a public official and a citizen. By contrast, the English approach does not have a uniform view of the public service and leaves more room for the display of religious symbols. Moreover, specific contextual factors can be taken into account.

8.6 QUESTIONING LIMITATIONS IN THE DUTCH CONTEXT

It is time to revert to the main question: does state neutrality in the Netherlands justify and/or necessitate limitations on public officials' freedom to display religious symbols? The previous sections have examined the minimum ECHR standards and domestic approaches as divergent as the French and the English one. This examination is useful for putting flesh on the conceptual model including an appraisal of the points of contention. As the introductory chapter of this study observed, the comparative analysis with the two domestic systems cannot serve to provide a ready-to-use template for the Dutch context. Therefore, an answer in terms of 'doing like the French or like the English' is not in order. Instead, inspiration can be derived from the quest to identify the underlying reasons for one or the other approach. When dissociated from the states, the approaches of France and England can be qualified as abstract and contextual respectively.

At the outset of this chapter, it was put forward that state neutrality in the Netherlands does not necessitate limitations on public officials' freedom to display religious symbols. Still, it may justify such limitations. However, the study explicitly rejects the idea that general and uniform limitations on public officials in the Netherlands to display religious symbols are justified. This is the case in France, but it was clear that the ultimate underpinning rationale for these limitations is the constitutional principle of *laïcité*, which imbues the entire French thinking about religion in the public domain. Instead, this study argues that a contextual approach[3] is most appropriate to appraise possible limitations within the Dutch context adequately, because it can optimally employ the potential of state neutrality to be balanced with religious freedom. Such an approach is more capable of achieving proportional measures which do not unnecessarily limit public officials' religious freedom. The points of contention represent the interests to be balanced in the appraisal exercise. While a contextual approach can result in either advocating inclusive and exclusive neutrality, it does not in itself exclusively rely on either type of neutrality. Additionally, it does not qualify functions as closer or more distant from the core functions of the state, because it considers that view to be subjective and static in itself. In the Netherlands it seems to go without saying that of the three public functions, public education can least be qualified as a core state function. That this can be different is shown by the French view on the position of public education which it considers to be at the heart of the republican mission. The comparative analysis was made exactly to expand the framework of reference. In other words, the French and English practices provide inspiration for possible (other) conceptions of public functions.

The reasons for a contextual approach are explained in the following section. Subsequently, the chapter continues with assessing the interests involved in calling for a critical approach towards limitations on public officials' freedom to display religious symbols. This assessment is enriched with the knowledge derived from the evaluative analysis. While a critical attitude towards religious symbols in public functions should

---

3   In view of his research, Carens has advanced that a contextual approach 'can clarify the meaning of abstract formulations'. He has further explained that 'we do not really understand what general principles and theoretical formulations *mean* until we see them interpreted and applied in a variety of specific contexts', J.H. Carens, *Culture, Citizenship and Community. A Contextual Exploration of Justice as Evenhandedness* (Oxford University Press, Oxford 2000), pp. 2-3.

be welcomed, a critical attitude should also be taken towards limitations on these symbols. Because contrary to what current conceptions of neutrality may suggest, it is not nearly so self-evident that neutrality justifies limitations. Therefore, it is not sufficient to dismiss claims for accommodating demands to wear religious symbols in public functions by employing the elusive term 'neutrality'. As was shown throughout the study, this term may raise more questions than provide clarity. Instead, limitations on religious symbols should be carefully considered by contemplating the underlying interests. And the best way to do so is by taking a contextual approach. At least three characteristics of the Dutch context can be pointed out which provide reasons for preferring a contextual approach: (i) the status of neutrality; (ii) the visibility and accommodation of religion in the public sphere; and (iii) the conception of the state. These reasons firstly concern considerations of what is in keeping with the Dutch context and secondly they touch on more fundamental considerations.

8.6.1 An implicit concept of state neutrality

First of all, the Netherlands does not have a powerful constitutional principle advocating state neutrality. Instead, state neutrality can be derived from the constitutional provisions dealing with equality, freedom of religion and freedom of education. Situations concerning neutrality are not traced back to one and the same source. Moreover, state neutrality does not necessarily imply the same thing for all actors, but it may take different forms depending on the relation it concerns. This is corroborated by how the current practices regarding the wearing of religious symbols by the judiciary, the police and state school teachers emerged. This shows the greater correspondence of the contextual approach with the Dutch context.

As regards the substantial assessment of the approaches on state neutrality, the following can be said. The description of the French situation showed how the principle of *laïcité* coupled with neutrality informed the rigorous and absolute exclusion of religious symbols. This was confirmed once again in recent case law of the French Council of State. There is no differentiation as to the particular public function at hand; there is no difference between a police officer on the street and a secretary in the police station and it is irrelevant which religious symbol is worn. Clearly, the exclusion of religious symbols impacts on public officials' freedom to manifest religion or belief. The outright application of absolute neutrality leaves no room whatsoever for varying this policy. The result is thus identical at all times for all public functions. In this view, the proposed model of the dynamics of state neutrality would equally remain identical for all public functions. The French conception of the model is reduced to a fixed model in which state neutrality would continuously have the same implications. Such a model does not manage to acknowledge the different features of the actors and the different dynamics of their relationships. An inevitable implication is that arguments for limitations are less attuned to the specific situation.

8.6.2 Public visibility and accommodation of religion

A second reason why the Dutch context should favour a contextual approach concerns the visibility of religion and the public accommodation of religious practices. Dutch public space has not eradicated religion to the extent that French public space may be argued to have. On the contrary, the Netherlands is characterized by remnants of religious traditions scattered throughout the public space. References to God in Acts, official speeches and (occasional) prayers at some municipal council meetings are only some examples. Furthermore, religious needs have traditionally been accommodated rather than eradicated. The pillar structure serves as the textbook example corroborating such accommodation. An example specific for this study is the option for public officials to swear a religious oath when they take on their function. Another example concerns the accommodation of registrars who, for religious reasons, refuse to officiate at marriages for same-sex couples. It was in 2007 when such accommodation was provided for in the government agreement. Advocating an approach based on the absolute undesirability of religion being publicly visible thus does not correspond to the Dutch situation, notwithstanding calls to relegate religion to the private sphere. If the plea to exclude religious symbols from the public sphere because the public sphere needs to be secular were to be consistent, then first all these religious remnants would have to be removed. That said, this study reasons the other way around in taking the current situation as pleading against strict limitations, for more elementary reasons.

A rigid approach to religion qualifying the visibility of religion as unwanted at all times implies that such an approach would mean the same at all times for individuals and society. The mere fact that republicanism is an 'ism-ideology' demonstrates the doctrinal level at which the French approach is crystallized. This crystallization has set the French policy in stone in not differentiating the visibility of religion for particular situations. It may well be that the effect of religion being visible plays out differently depending on circumstances. As to the image of the state, the French and English practices exemplified an authority-based and a representation-based approach respectively. The contextual approach leaves room for varying the visibility of religion and can thus oscillate between both approaches. It may well be argued that it is desirable for the police to represent society rather than a blank body of public officials, but that the judiciary is best seen to be detached as much as possible from personal markers.

8.6.3 A differentiated conception of the state

Last but not least, the Dutch conception of the state would not be congruent with an abstract approach. French ideology exemplifies how the state can be envisaged as a dominant entity and the public service as a uniform body. While 'the English state' undoubtedly exists, it is not as strongly conceptualized. Furthermore, a uniform idea of *the* public service does not exist. This divergence has a bearing on the justification of policy regarding religious symbols. The French abstract discourse shows how the principle of neutrality is applied uniformly to the entire public service, irrespective of the different functions or specific factors. Consequently, neutrality permanently serves as the source to justify limiting public officials' freedom, and in doing so forgoes any balancing test. By contrast, the English practice illustrates how the lack of a principle of state neutrality allows cases to be assessed on their own merits considering the specific circumstances. In line with the lack of a strong principle of neutrality, an invariable conception of the public service is also lacking in the Dutch context. This can already be seen in the different policies regarding the judiciary and the police on the one hand, and state school teachers on the other hand. Moreover, the Dutch state is not considered to take over the public official to the same extent as the French state does. At present, the Dutch public official is generally recognized as holding individual rights. While limitations can be imposed on these rights, such limitations are subject to the test of proportionality. In sum, this view of the public official, his position in public service and his rights is more likely to fit the contextual approach.

On a fundamental level, the whole idea of envisaging the dynamics of state neutrality as triangular is to create room for differentiation in the meaning of state neutrality. For instance, state neutrality from the state towards citizens may have a different significance than from the state towards public officials. While the former touches on the question of the image which the state should convey to citizens, the latter is entwined with employment policies. Additionally, the triangular model makes clear that differentiation according to the type of function may be needed. A judge's neutrality towards a litigant may be important for different reasons than a teacher's neutrality towards pupils. Differentiation can make explicit what the exact implications of state neutrality on individuals' religious freedom are.

Having outlined the reasons for preferring a contextual approach in assessing the points of contention, the following section continues with doing exactly that: taking a better look at the individual points of contention raised in Dutch debate and assessing them. Such appraisal is framed within the conceptual model and is based on the previous evaluative analysis. Furthermore, the following subsections resume and further elaborate the reflection on how specific factors emanating from the conceptual model influence the assessment of the points of contention. Specifically, the evaluation takes into account the differentiation between the actors, the functions and other relevant circumstances.

8.6.4 State towards the public official: substantive neutrality

For a state to be neutral towards public officials, adopting a dress policy which imposes limitations on public officials' freedom to display religious symbols is questionable. Such a dress policy is likely to jeopardize rather than guarantee a public official's right to equal treatment (first point of contention: equal treatment of the public official). Additionally, Dutch public officials cannot be said to personify the state to such an extent that they are absolutely precluded from displaying religious symbols (second point of contention: personification of the state). Both of these points can be bolstered by taking into account relevant factors such as other available mechanisms to ensure state neutrality, the availability of alternative functions, and the setting in which a public official exercises his function.

8.6.4.1 Drawbacks of a formal dress policy for Dutch public officials

In view of the relevant factors mentioned in the previous paragraph, the application of a formal dress policy turns out to be lacking in three respects: specificity, proportionality, and effectiveness. To begin with the first respect, the specificity of the dress policies currently applicable to Dutch public officials does not go beyond a distinction between the judiciary and the police on the one hand and public education on the other hand. The former functions do not allow for visible religious symbols whereas the latter does. While the familiar is easily taken for granted, such a policy may nonetheless be called into question. When the current policy is looked at anew, does it really make so much sense? Why would it be justifiable for the state to prohibit judges and police officers from displaying religious symbols, and to allow state school teachers to do so? In being informed by a formal conception of equality and neutrality, the dress policies regarding the judiciary and the police resound with the French approach. An essential difference though is that the Dutch policies do not ensue from a solidly constitutionally enshrined principle of neutrality. Another difference is that, unlike in France, the Dutch policies are not embedded in an environment where the aim is to eradicate the visibility of religion to the greatest extent possible and where a strong conception of 'the state' is adhered to.

On a more fundamental level, it is increasingly acknowledged that a policy based on neutrality of justification is lacking in not acknowledging (intentionally) the actual effect of the policy. In the case of applying dress requirements, the effect may be that some religious groups and individuals are more adversely affected than others. As is evident from the growing body of non-discrimination case law, the justification of such an effect should meet strict requirements. More specifically, the dress requirement should proportionately pursue the aim of – in this case – judicial impartiality or neutrality of the police. Despite leaving states a wide margin of appreciation, Chapter 5 demonstrated that the ECHR institutions still require the state to guarantee that measures fulfil the requirement of proportionality. As argued in this study, the lack of a constitutional principle of secularism or neutrality makes it more difficult for the Netherlands to meet this requirement. The determination of such proportionality is inextricably linked with how the six points of contention are assessed. For example, the finding that a judge displaying a religious symbol may infringe on a litigant's individual rights (as implied by the third point of contention) might justify an employment policy imposing stricter requirements regarding religious symbols. This study has shown that as self-evident as they are sometimes claimed to be, the other points of contention concerning limitations on religious symbols within the judiciary and the police have to be critically assessed. The point of departure in the Netherlands should be that although state neutrality may justify such limitations, it does not do so automatically. As it was described in the previous sections, the Dutch version of state neutrality falls short of being equivalent to the French one which justifies limitations against the background of a comprehensive republican ideology. Dutch neutrality is not part and parcel of such an ideology. Therefore, this study proposed an even more specific application of state neutrality than is currently in place.

One of the reasons for a more specific application lies in the fact that the structure and organization of public functions in the Netherlands is diverse. For instance, the study has demonstrated in Chapter 2 that the judiciary in the Netherlands is not as monolithic as is sometimes imagined. For instance, the category of law-administering judges includes a wide variety of judges, dealing with many fields of law. Whether or not a judge manifests his religion or belief may be more or less relevant depending on the type of proceedings. Similarly, the task carried out by the judiciary is not as uniform as suggested. While judging may conjure up a typical image of a judge sitting in a courtroom, it comprehends many other tasks, many of which are deskwork. The same holds true for the police. It may certainly not be so self-evident to exclude religious symbols for such tasks 'behind the desk' as it is sometimes suggested in the pleas in favour of limitations. In that light, it may be wondered whether it makes sense to apply a dress policy to the whole of the judiciary and the police. Why not tailor dress policies to the particular function at hand? Consequently, it may be conceivable to allow for religious symbols in legal proceedings where symbols expressing personal preferences may not be detrimental to the legal questions at stake. For example, would it really be a problem for a judge who is dealing with administrative proceedings concerning building permits to wear a headscarf? On the other hand, it could well be contested that a state school teacher is currently able to wear a headscarf at all times. Could not such a general authorization be considered at odds with state neutrality? In sum, it cannot be ruled out that state neutrality may justify limitations on public officials' freedom to display religious symbols. However, such limitations should only be imposed whilst taking into account the particular factors in play. Therefore, a dress policy applied uniformly on the basis of formal neutrality fails to address the nuances of practice needed to bolster any justification.

The argument in favour of a more specific application ties in with the proportionality of dress policies tailored to formal neutrality. In the first place, apart from the factors mentioned above, other factors inherent to the selection and employment of public officials should be taken into account when considering dress policies. It might be worth looking at the educational paths leading up to selection for a public function, both in terms of specialization and selection. For instance, the recruitment trajectory for the judiciary is already specialized and strict in itself. After all, the pool from which to recruit candidates only includes academically and legally qualified individuals. In particular, candidates for the judicial training have already completed law studies. Accordingly, they can be expected to be familiar with principles of impartiality. Moreover, the selection is strict in closely screening individuals as to their competences of solid judgment, social awareness and integrity. Only a small number of persons are eligible for the judiciary. The Dutch judicial system has been professionalized entirely with no jury at any stage or in any part of the judicial system. Individuals are able to wear religious symbols for the greater part of the training leading up to being appointed as a judge. Specifically, as yet, no dress requirement applies to the stage when individuals are taking part in the specific training to be a judge. It would make sense to view the necessity for and justification of dress limitations in connection with other selection mechanisms which can ensure neutrality.

A second factor which a dress policy informed by formal neutrality fails to address is the exclusivity of the public function. An essential difference between the judiciary and the police on the one hand and public education on the other hand is that the former public functions have a monopoly whereas education can also be provided by private parties. When an individual wanted to become a teacher and could not do so in public education because he wears a religious symbol, he could still pursue this ambition in private education. By contrast, the wearing of religious symbols definitely bars an individual from becoming a judge without offering any recourse to an alternative. In other words, the impact of the exclusion of the wearing of religious symbols may vary according to the exclusivity of the function. Such an approach creates a stricter standard of justification of limitations on religious symbols.

In the third place, it can be questioned whether a dress policy based on formal neutrality is effective; this has to do with the point of personification (the second point of contention). The French and the English approaches show two very different ways of looking at this particular point. This is not surprising in view of their general approaches to religious symbols in public functions. The former approach takes it for granted that an individual public official 'becomes' the state and should refrain from any personal manifestation whatsoever. By contrast, the English approach does not have this conception and instead leaves room for individuals to retain their individuality. This study emphasizes that, irrespective of the domestic context, it cannot be overlooked that the different public officials exercise different state tasks and as a result any assumed personification does not take place in the same way. That said, such personification is not necessarily intertwined with a public official's appearance. As a consequence, measures concerning the public official's appearance may lack effectiveness for ensuring neutrality. This point is further elaborated in the next subsection.

8.6.4.2 Putting personification into perspective

An evident difference between once again the judiciary and the police on the one hand and public education on the other hand is the wearing of a uniform. In the first place, a uniform can be seen as the symbolic expression of personification. It has been suggested in the Dutch debate that, by putting on the uniform, an individual takes on his public task. Appealing as this idea may be, it is not very sophisticated. The way in which a judge wears a uniform is still different from how a police officer wears a uniform. Whereas the former in principle only dons his robes during sessions in the courtroom, the latter wears uniform permanently, at least whilst at work. It thus seems that the judicial robe is primarily ceremonial in nature. This is corroborated by the practice that not all judges don the robes. Furthermore, as alluded to above, they do not wear their robes when writing the judgment, which they may do in the confines of their offices or even of their private homes. Surely, judges cannot be assumed to be personifying the judge any less when not wearing their robes. To put it another way, it appears that the robe is not a sine qua non for individuals to personify the judge. In other words, the robe in itself might not be all that important for ensuring judicial impartiality. Accordingly, it can not only be argued that religious symbols may be compatible with the judicial robe but also that religious symbols can be worn in the first place. Inconceivable as that idea may seem, English practice shows the possibility of combining religious symbols with the judicial robe. Moreover, English practice does not seem to consider the judicial robe as essential for properly carrying out the judicial task. Quite a number of judges do not even don their robes. District judges sit in business attire and it is more than likely that they can do so while displaying personal symbols as well. Indeed, the English approach focuses on a public official's conduct instead of on his appearance to establish neutrality. As to the police in the Netherlands, the (semi) permanent wearing of a uniform is an important difference with how the judicial robe is worn. While the reasons for the (semi) permanent wearing of a police uniform are in part undoubtedly pragmatic in nature, they also seem to allude to a more essential relevance to the function itself. It could well be that the uniform itself is essential for an individual to actually personify the police officer. On the other hand, it can be seen that exactly because a police officer wears the uniform all the time during his working hours, he does not set aside his individuality in exercising his police tasks. It would be unrealistic to assume that individuals leave all personal preferences aside when personifying the police. In principle, state school teachers also perform their job in class all day. In the Netherlands, and also in France and England for that matter, they are able to do so in their own clothing. In other words, their personification with their task is thus not symbolized by a particular uniform. In the Netherlands, they are also free to display religious symbols, which is apparently not seen as barring them from personifying the pedagogic task entrusted to them.

Whether or not a public official wears a uniform, it mostly seems an illusion to think that a uniform and the exclusion of religious symbols are necessary in order for an individual to personify a public official. In that light, this study questions whether the arguments informed by the idea of personification really justify limitations on religious symbols. The hesitation about such justification is even stronger considering that compelling individuals to take off religious symbols does not guarantee that they have set aside their private ideas and beliefs too. This point can be taken even further when considering the possibility that they will almost certainly retain these beliefs but without anyone being able to see this. What is more, they may even feel more justified in letting their personal beliefs creep in once they comply with the requirement of removing religious symbols. On a different note, it may be questioned altogether whether for instance the Dutch legal system itself is as areligious as suggested in this line of argument. Take, for example, the phrase 'by God's grace' included in Acts of Parliament. This fact waters down the force of the argument that, for example, judges personify a secular institution. At any rate, considering the weighty reasons for questioning the effectiveness of measures excluding religious symbols from public functions, such measures may well not be justified by neutrality. That the plea in favour of such measures does no more than favour a neutral appearance of public officials is corroborated by the points of contention concerning the relation between the public official and the citizen.

8.6.5 Public official towards the citizen: 'keeping up appearances'

Much of the discussion on religious symbols in public functions in the end centres on the importance of a public official's appearance to the outside world. Accordingly, the third and fourth points of contention concerning the relation between the individual public official and the individual citizen, namely bias and proselytism, grasp the gist of the controversy. The present study has shown that, when contemplating these points carefully, serious questions can be raised as to the extent to which they can serve as justification for limitations on public officials' freedom to display religious symbols. In the end, causality turns out to be a dubious factor in establishing the risk which religious symbols pose to state neutrality. The reason for this is that symbols are in and of themselves ambiguous. They are attributed meaning by virtue of other people's perceptions. The meanings of some symbols will be more based on consensus than others. It is also the meanings attributed to symbols which determine the possibility of bias or proselytism. In other words, it is not the symbol itself directly causing someone to be treated unequally or experience proselytism. It is the possibility that someone assumes bias or proselytism on the basis of a symbol being worn. The actual presence of such an assumption and the extent to which it is justified is not easily established. At any rate, the question remains whether a citizen's assumptions constitute a proper criterion to decide on measures limiting the wearing of a symbol. Moreover, it can be doubted whether such measures are effective.

Before the bias point itself is addressed, it should be noted that the way in which this point is being discussed cannot be seen separately from the societal background. Somehow, being religious is set aside from being Dutch, white or female. It was pointed out at the outset of the study that in relation to state neutrality, religion in and of itself has been looked at with increasing suspicion. Against this background, people of faith seem to be increasingly questioned as to their ability to think independently, reasonably and neutrally. Be that as it may, it should be kept in mind that the discussion on religious symbols in public functions is not about whether or not to allow for religious public officials. Indeed, such a discussion would have little point, as any exclusion of individuals on the basis of their religion or belief would clearly be discriminatory and incompatible with the ECHR. Neither France, nor England have incorporated any limitations to the public functions on the (direct) basis of religion or belief. The judiciary, police and public education include people of faith in their ranks without problems, in all three states. In England, it is not uncommon for public officials also to be active members of a church community. It should be noted that England does have stricter regulations concerning political membership which can be taken as an indication that religious adherence need not be the only factor possibly influencing a public official's neutrality. Anyhow, the possibility exists that the general suspicion towards religion or belief may improperly imbue the discussion on the issue of religious symbols in public functions. In this discussion it should thus be emphasized that the only point up for discussion is really about whether or not to allow religious public officials to make their religion or belief visible to others by displaying symbols.

8.6.5.1 Presumed bias is not equal to bias

The bias point has been employed to substantiate the argument that a citizen may infer bias on the part of the public official when seeing that public official wearing a religious symbol. By virtue of his function, this argument goes, a public official should avoid, to the largest extent possible, such an impression from occurring, even when that implies he needs to refrain from manifesting his religion or belief by displaying symbols. Criticism of this argument has pointed out that it basically comes down to condoning or even endorsing prejudices. It is difficult to solve this conundrum because the very force of the argument lies in the citizen's perception, which is a subjective and variable factor, entwined with the varying attribution of meaning to symbols as pointed out above. The French and English practices represent two divergent ways of dealing with this factor of uncertainty. Either you choose to be on the seemingly safe side by prohibiting public officials from displaying religious symbols at all, thus altogether ducking the question whether a religious symbol may (rightly) cause a citizen to infer bias on the part of a public official. The actual proportionality of this limitation as regards the infringement on the public official's freedom to manifest religion or belief is left aside altogether. Or you choose not to pursue a policy of altogether excluding or including religious symbols beforehand, but to decide on a case-by-case basis on the extent to which a religious symbol creates an inadmissible appearance of bias.

Of course, as long as it is not objectively established that persons who display religious symbols are really less neutral than persons who do not, a uniform and absolute approach is in the end based on assumptions. Therefore, it should at least be questioned exactly why a bias could be rightly assumed to be more present in a religious individual displaying a religious symbol than in a religious individual not displaying a religious symbol. If that question is set aside as irrelevant, and instead all substantiation is based on the citizen's perception of bias, it should be admitted that this substantiation rests on no more than attributed prejudices. As well as endorsing such prejudices, such an approach can also be said to assume that citizens close their eyes to the human factor in all public functions. Although it might be that formality can invoke a citizen's reverence for the state, public officials and the like, it cannot alter the fact that in the end public officials are human beings. Accordingly, they have their personal beliefs, ideas and characteristics. Furthermore, it should be pointed out that the bias point also works the other way around: it can just as well be asked to what extent a seemingly non-religious person might seem biased towards a religious citizen. The two characteristics of an abstract approach, uniformity and absoluteness, bring into question the proportionality of prohibiting public officials from displaying religious symbols. Therefore, it makes more sense to tackle this point from a contextual approach. Such an approach allows for taking into account the complexity of the bias problem, the particular sub questions on which are further discussed in the next paragraphs.

As a matter of fact, the line of reasoning which employs the bias point to argue in favour of limitations on religious symbols in public functions consists of three arguments. Firstly, the mere visibility of someone's religion or belief may be problematic in itself, because citizens attribute all kinds of meanings to that visibility. Secondly, it should be relatively easy to remedy that visibility, certainly in comparison to the personal characteristics. Thirdly, the public official's act of 'intentionally' displaying a religious symbol may be problematic because that very act would impact on his neutrality. The solidity of these arguments can be questioned in the following way. To begin with the first argument, the visibility of religion or belief in comparison with the visibility of other personal characteristics such as gender and ethnicity, has been addressed in discussion. It needs to be asked whether religion has the same relation to a neutral attitude as gender and ethnicity. Although these days we may not conceive gender to impact on an individual's neutrality, there was a time when it was questioned whether or not women were too emotional to be neutral. It can be alleged that all three characteristics influence how an individual perceives and thinks about the world around him. At the same time, a typical feature of religion or belief is that it concerns a value system with particular ideas on the good life. This feature in principle distinguishes religion from ethnicity or gender neither of which propounds such value systems explicitly. However, in itself it does not justify a limitation on the wearing of religious symbols, because it was established in the previous paragraph that it is not religion or belief itself which is problematic. After all, a Christian, feminist or communist is in principle not precluded from being a public official.

The second argument relies on the relative easiness with which a religious symbol can be taken off in comparison with other personal markers. Contrary to one's gender or skin colour, it is said, a religious symbol can easily be taken off. Indeed, when thinking of a headscarf, it could be thought that it only requires untying a piece of cloth and taking it off the head. The major objection to this line of thought is that it bypasses the significance which the wearer ascribes to it. The very weight of a religious duty is a subjective experience the protection of which is guaranteed by the freedom of religion. This is not meant as a plea against limitations on religious manifestations per se. It only goes to show that the argument that taking off a religious symbol is more easily done than taking off gender or ethnicity does not hold water. Three additional doubts about whether religion is really that different from other personal characteristics can be pointed out.

Firstly, while the headscarf may seem like a clear-cut case of a religious symbol easily taken off, other religious symbols may be thought of which are not taken off so 'easily'. Take for example a beard worn for religious reasons. How feasible would it be to prohibit individuals from wearing a religious beard? Aside from the infringement on an individual's physical integrity, a prohibition raises the question how to even begin to qualify a beard as religious. Other symbols like a particular hairdo or a tattoo may be thought of to illustrate that religious symbols might not be taken off so easily as sometimes suggested. Secondly, the distinction of religious identity from say ethnic identity may not be as clear as sometimes suggested. The English practice showed them being mixed up whilst French practice showed how loaded the very concept of ethnicity is, casting a different light on these personal characteristics. Thirdly, it needs to be pointed out that not all symbols or personal markers expressing a personal lifestyle have yet been prohibited. For instance, pearl earrings which might be considered to be visibly indicating socio-economic class, are permitted, so why not religious symbols?

The third argument in favour of limitations is that displaying a religious symbol constitutes an 'intentional' act which impacts on the public official's very neutrality. This argument is employed in three ways. To begin with, displaying a religious symbol in and of itself is seen as jeopardizing a public official's neutrality. According to this view, being aware that he is wearing a religious symbol may remind an individual of his religion. Assuming that religious symbols would be capable of this effect, then all religious symbols, including the ones worn beneath the uniform, should be considered problematic. Secondly, there is the notion that those displaying religious symbols adhere to a strict observance of their religion which in itself makes them less neutral. This point reverts to the underlying religion or belief and its alleged orthodoxy. Considering the duty of the state to show interpretative restraint, this cannot serve as an argument to limit the wearing of such religious symbols. In the third place, the neutrality of a public official displaying religious symbols is contested because he should be aware of the effect the symbol might have. By choosing to display a religious symbol while knowing the possibility of such an effect, a public official basically lets his religion or belief prevail over the law. On the face of it, the argument seems very convincing. If an individual wants to become a public official, and does not want to comply with the regulations in place, because apparently he deems his religious duty to wear religious symbols more important, he lets his religion prevail over the law. He does so by not wanting to act in conformity with the dress regulations and by showing he adheres to a different value system than the law. Convincing as it may seem, the argument is limited and flawed for three reasons.

Firstly, it was argued previously that the knowledge that citizens may infer bias from a religious symbol is itself no justification for compelling a public official to take off the symbol. After all, such bias is substantiated by no more than assumptions. Secondly, the whole issue raised by the claims for accommodations brings back into question the current regulation. It necessitates looking at the current regulation beyond the level of positive law. Therefore, to argue that an individual wanting to display a religious symbol is not willing to comply with the law only holds true from a static point of view, but it begs the question of the validity of this interpretation of the regulation. Thirdly, the question really is whether an individual can display a religious symbol while applying the law neutrally. English practice shows that the two certainly are not mutually exclusive. In other words, the idea that by wearing a religious symbol an individual indicates that he attributes more weight to the value system of his religion or belief than to the value system of the law is not necessarily true. It would be different if the religion were to require him to manifest his religion or belief for instance by (actually) treating men unequally in comparison with women. But the individual religious duty of wearing a religious symbol in and of itself does not say anything about the individual's ability to apply the law.

What is true is that by wearing a religious symbol while exercising a public function, public officials expand the visibility of an allegedly active manifestation of a religion or belief to the public sphere. That makes it distinct from the manifestations which might more traditionally be thought of in the context of, for example, Christianity, like going to church, praying and reading the Bible which are mostly activities taking place in the private sphere. In the end, that is a (broader) key challenge posed by other religions: that the whole conception of religious manifestation, the sphere in which it takes place and the extent to which it is a part of religious observance, differs from those religions which have been present in the Netherlands for a longer time.

It is too simple to assume that an expanding presence of religious manifestations in the public sphere is incompatible with the Dutch secular public sphere. First of all because, as previously mentioned, the Dutch public sphere is not secular. Additionally, it would testify to a limited and inconsistent conception of how to ensure the ban on religious manifestations. As argued before, a judge does not sit in the courtroom for the entire day. Some of the time he does not wear the official robes, and is free to wear whatever he pleases including religious symbols. What is more, for all one knows, an individual judge may pray or read the Bible in his own office. So, manifesting religion or belief during the exercise of his public function in itself cannot be and probably is not eradicated. Additionally, it can be asked why a state school teacher currently is able to manifest his religion or belief at all times without any problem. In the same way that it might be argued that actively manifesting religion or belief is incompatible with applying the law, it might be said that such manifestations preclude a teacher from objectively instructing pupils. At any rate, pleas to ban religious symbols displayed during the exercise of a public function can be questioned as to their effectiveness.

In addition to the fact that for example a judge can still wear a religious symbol during other stages of the process, removing a religious symbol probably does not remove an individual's religion or belief. This ties in with the previous points made regarding bias. Such a removal can only be effective in that a particular symbol is no longer visible for citizens to assume particular ideas but, as said, citizens should nonetheless be aware that the public official is still free to adhere to such ideas. What is more, they should realize that a public official can still wear symbols which are not directly visible, like a Christian cross beneath a judicial robe.

As described above, the bias discussion runs the risk of remaining in a deadlock due to the difficulty of substantiation. Therefore, it makes sense not only to look at the issue in the abstract but also to consider within a particular context whether a possibly perceived bias could justify limitations. In the judicial context, the type of proceedings could be rather relevant in establishing the importance of avoiding such an apparent bias. How detrimental would the appearance of religious bias be in administrative proceedings on building permits? Then again, what if the building permit were to concern a mosque? Would it then matter if the judge were to wear a headscarf? An additional factor might be the impact of a citizen's reaction to a public official's functioning. In principle, how a litigant reacts to a judge does not have to affect the latter's work. By contrast, for the police, a suspect's reaction immediately impacts on a police officer's work. Therefore, the citizen's response provoked by a religious symbol might more understandably justify limitations on a police officer's freedom than on a judge's freedom. This is even more so when it is recalled that a police officer operates in an unpredictable environment and is seen by numerous persons whose reactions he cannot monitor. But then, this still does not have to result in an absolute prohibition on religious symbols within the entire police force, as the multitude of the tasks involved may not always entail such justification. On the contrary, the freedom to manifest religion or belief should remain the point of departure and the possibility of limitations the exception. When considering such exceptions the state should substantiate them with reference to the possible response by citizens or to other factors. Such other factors to consider may be mechanisms available to citizens to guarantee neutrality. For example, the judicial system incorporates mechanisms to ensure judicial impartiality. Obviously, a litigant can always rely on the judgment to see whether he has been treated neutrally. Otherwise, in case of doubt on a judge's impartiality, he can still challenge the judge. Moreover, the judge can recuse himself. These mechanisms can be seen as possibly neutralizing a judge's bias, should a litigant suspect it on the basis of a religious symbol. It is worth considering to what extent such mechanisms are available to citizens even when dealing with police officers or teachers.

8.6.5.2 Symbolic proselytism is not equal to proselytism

Next to the third point of contention (public official's bias), the point of proselytism (fourth point of contention) was made in the relation between the public official and the citizen. This point appeared to emerge mainly in the educational environment. Indeed, it can hardly be imagined how this point of contention could play out in the context of the judiciary or of the police. Generally, the moments of contact between a judge or a police officer and citizens are too brief for actual proselytism to take place, let alone for a religious symbol to have a proselytizing effect. This is different for a teacher who has a long-term relation with pupils and their parents. Moreover, as repeatedly pointed out in educational cases before the courts, both on a national and on a regional level, pupils are almost always young, which arguably makes them more vulnerable to a proselytizing influence. This influence could be exerted directly by the teacher or indirectly in endorsing a climate in which proselytism is allowed. More specifically, a young pupil may also be subjected to peer pressure; other pupils might feel confirmed in the rightness of their own practice of displaying a religious symbol when the teacher does as well. On the other hand, barring a teacher from displaying religious symbols does not necessarily remove the risk of proselytism. Of course, a teacher is still capable of actual proselytism by actively converting pupils. But with regard to his appearance, an allegedly neutral appearance, that is to say without visible religious symbols, might just as well harbour the risk of proselytism. To what extent may a secular-looking teacher be seen as proselytising religious pupils by discouraging them from manifesting their religion or belief? Another factor is that the longer time span during which a teacher is in contact with a pupil could actually be considered to neutralize the possible prejudice that a pupil may experience vis-à-vis a religious symbol. A teacher's performance of his duties is continually monitored. For instance, parents also have recurring occasions, like yearly assessments, where they can raise concerns. What is more, the structural exclusion of religious symbols may equally amount to a form of indoctrination of pupils. In the end, pupils have to learn to participate as citizens in a diverse society. This ties in with the point whether limitations ensure the neutral image of public functions.

8.6.6 State towards the citizen: recognizable state

The fifth and sixth points of contention identified regarding the relation between the state and the citizen concerned the image of the state and the separation of church and state. Although it has been suggested otherwise, the latter point turned out to refer to a primarily institutional principle which accordingly has little bearing on the question of religious symbols in public functions. The former point concerns the wider ramifications of the issue of individual display of religious symbols for the neutral image of public functions on a macro level. In general, it is not an easy task to examine the causal factors for an 'image' to come about. In a way, this refers to what was stated at the very outset of this study. While a private company can intentionally create and cultivate a particular image, the image of 'the state' or of public functions is entwined with society. Where companies can spend vast amounts on advertisements to create an image, no such means are available to the state. The triangular model of how state neutrality is effectuated amongst the three actors – state, public official, and citizen – implies interrelatedness. In other words, the conception that public officials displaying religious symbols adversely affect the neutral image of a public function is entwined with how the relation between the state and the public official on the one hand and between the public official and the citizen on the other hand is looked at. It was demonstrated in the previous section that it is far from certain that a public official displaying religious symbols acts contrary to the duty of state neutrality towards the citizen. Accordingly, the very same objections which apply to that individual relation hold true for the question whether state neutrality would justify limitations on religious symbols in public functions in safeguarding a neutral image of the state towards citizens. Additionally, with regard to the relation between the state and the public official, it turned out that a policy tailored on formal neutrality in excluding religious symbols completely, may not be justified by neutrality. Instead, in order to safeguard neutrality, it makes more sense to consider policies which have regard for the specific circumstances.

At any rate, taking into account such circumstances would also help to understand how the link between the individual display of religious symbols and harm to the neutral image of the public function would come about. It then appears that such a link is not as easily established as sometimes suggested. In other words, as detrimental as the mere thought of a judge with a headscarf, a kippah or a large visible crucifix may initially seem for the image of the judiciary, such a line of reasoning leaves aside essential nuances. A first nuance concerns the precise context in which a public official operates. The specific features of this context are relevant for the extent to which the public official's appearance impacts on the general image of the function at hand. A second nuance is the precise purpose of the task exercised by the public official.

As to the first nuance, it was made clear in the previous sections as well that the context in which a judge does his work is significantly different from the one in which a police officer works. For instance, a judge primarily works in confined spaces, be it the courtroom or his office or even his private home. That also entails that the contact he has with others takes place in a given context. Additionally, the capacity of those he comes into contact with is limited to a few roles: most probably, they are either an attorney, or a litigant. Admittedly, people can also view proceedings from the public gallery, but they are not likely to turn up in great numbers. How different this is from the police officer patrolling on the streets, having contact with numerous individuals, and being seen by even more. Just as different again is the context in which a state school teacher does his job. Similar to a judge, a teacher most of the time works within a confined space: the classroom. He comes into contact primarily with pupils, and secondarily their parents. These differences in context and in 'audience' are vital for determining whether the public officials' wearing of religious symbols affects the neutrality of the public function. If a citizen walking on the street sees a police officer wearing a headscarf, would he consider the institution of 'the police' to be more or less neutral? It should not be overlooked either that it may not be merely the public official's appearance but also that of other employees working in that context which impact on the neutral image of the institution. This diminishes the (exclusive) impact of a public official's appearance on the image of the public function. This point came to the fore in the deputy court clerk case. When, for example, the receptionist at a court building currently wears a religious symbol, this may just as well cause a citizen to question the neutrality of the court. This point can be taken two ways. Either all religious symbols within the public institution as such are prohibited, as in the French context, or they are permitted to the extent that the circumstances allow for. The current refutation is that the difference between a receptionist and a judge is the very function they exercise. But it was demonstrated in the previous section that there are also many reasons to question whether state neutrality would justify limitations on a judge's freedom to display religious symbols in light of the

291

specificities of his function. More specifically, proceedings are conceivable for which the judge's display of religious symbols may not be problematic.

What is also relevant for properly assessing the relation between an individual's display of religious symbols and the effect on the neutral image of the function, is the specific purpose of a public official's task. The difference in nature of the tasks performed in the public functions in this study may be evident. Put simply, a judge ensures justice is done, a police officer endeavours to have people abide by the law and a teacher guarantees that children receive education. In view of these different purposes, it may be more or less significant for the general image of a public function that a public official displays religious symbols. For instance, part of a teacher's task is to help children in becoming citizens able to participate in the society around them. It is conceivable that a teacher's appearance should be conducive to what a teacher is attempting to teach. In particular, when state schools aim at familiarizing pupils with societal reality, then visible diversity may be something not to exclude. By contrast, the tasks of a police officer are entwined with public order. More than any other public official, a police officer should prevent division and ensure safety. It was pointed out previously that a citizen's response to a police officer's appearance directly impacts on his functioning. More specifically, a religious symbol might cause or increase a tense situation. This could thus weigh in favour of retaining an impersonal image of the police.

At the same time, the legitimacy of the police may be experienced to increase when diversity is actually visible. English policing has been modelled on this idea. In general, apart from carefully considering the multitude of factors influencing the relation between an individual public official's display of religious symbols and the neutral image of the public function, the question remains which approach is more likely to result in a neutral image. The current situation in the Netherlands already testifies to a partly nuanced approach. It centres on a differentiation between the judiciary and the police on the one hand and public education on the other hand. By taking into account the particular factors touched on above, the Dutch approach may take its differentiation further. It might be that it is desirable to confer a blank or a representational image on some public functions or on some specific parts of these public functions.

8.6.7 Concluding remarks

The study has demonstrated that a contextual approach enables a thorough contemplation of the points of contention. It specifically favours this approach over an abstract approach because it is more apt to assess which are the better arguments. As argued at the outset of the study, such assessment is the very asset of legal science. When thus taking the debate beyond the level of state neutrality in the abstract, the study was able to question the extent to which state neutrality might actually justify limitations on public officials' freedom to display religious symbols. At any rate, individual public officials' religious freedom remains the point of departure; unlike the French approach, state neutrality in the Netherlands does not make a public official forgo this freedom beforehand. Therefore, it remains imperative that limitations on this freedom are justified. The contextual approach also exemplified how little sense it makes to refer to state neutrality as adhered to by other states without having regard for the particular circumstances. The state neutrality underlying such limitations in the Dutch context should be inclusive rather than exclusive. In other words, the visibility of religion in the public sphere should not in itself be considered as incompatible with state neutrality. Most importantly, instead of referring to state neutrality as a justification for limitations, the underlying interests should be identified to the most concrete level possible. In the same vein, it makes little sense to speak of 'public functions'. Rather, the specific public function at issue should be examined to the most specific level possible. It appeared that while state neutrality might justify limitations on public officials' freedom to display religious symbols, it did not do so lightly. Much of the discussion was based on assumptions the validity of which remains to be proved. It might well be that the legal discipline is not capable of providing such proof, in which case resort to other disciplines should be taken.

8.7 CONCLUDING OBSERVATIONS

Debate provides the oxygen for democracy.[4] Therefore, it is essential to ensure that such debate is properly conducted. This study has illustrated the vital role which legal science can play in enhancing the quality of debates. In tune with Smits' approach, this study has aimed at contributing to the debate on religious symbols in public functions by systemization and assessment of the points at issue. The main conclusion is that state neutrality in the Netherlands does not necessitate, but may justify limitations on public officials' freedom to display religious symbols. In the case of limitations, it still remains imperative to justify such limitations. The findings of this study underpinning this conclusion can be summarized on the basis of two threads.

The first thread concerns the concept of state neutrality and specifically the elusive meaning of state neutrality which accounted for confusion in the debate. Such confusion has left room for divergent interpretations and applications of the concept. This study has shown that in essence, state neutrality in and of itself is not incompatible with public officials displaying religious symbols. As long as the state does not evaluate, favour or disfavour religions or beliefs on the one hand or does not favour or disfavour individuals on the basis of religion or belief on the other hand,

---

4   This expression once coined by A.W.H. Docters van Leeuwen in 1998 has come to be an often-used adage in Dutch debating circles.

it observes state neutrality. Admittedly, these core obligations still leave quite some leeway for interpretation which is why this study has proposed really looking beyond the concept of state neutrality in the debate. In so doing, this study has demonstrated that state neutrality actually harbours six separate yet intertwined points of contention. Furthermore, it was shown that these points of contention correspond to the different actors and relations involved in the issue of religious symbols in public functions. As a consequence, different specific factors should be taken into account. Envisaging state neutrality within this indivisible triangle of actors also serves to emphasize that this concept is a relational notion. Accordingly, the meaning of state neutrality in the end takes effect between actors. Additionally, the way in which state neutrality takes effect in one relation affects the relation between other actors as well. In the end, this study has demonstrated that the different points of contention fall short of self-evidently justifying limitations on public officials' freedom to display religious symbols. The lack of self-evident justifications ties in with the second thread which revolves around the application of state neutrality as a justification.

This study has emphasized that the wide margin of appreciation which the ECHR supervisory bodies leave to states should not be taken as an argument in favour of limitations. The ECHR case law puts forward standards which states should observe but only as a minimum safeguard of human rights. Furthermore, this study has questioned the extent to which the specific context of the Netherlands would provide ground for limitations in terms of the Convention. Another finding which came to the fore in the ECHR case law and in the French context concerned the scope of Article 9. In these contexts, particular regimes or absolute *a priori* limitations were capable of leaving the right of public officials to display religious symbols outside legal protection altogether. A similar line of reasoning is applied in the judiciary and the police in the Dutch context. This study has argued against the application of this line of reasoning in the Dutch context, but instead it has advocated the importance of taking into account specific factors which can best be done by assessing the justification of limitations. Additionally, taking account of the underlying reasons for the English and the French approach, this study has identified what such specific factors could be and how they are of relevance for the points of contention.

Two more remarks need to be made. Firstly, this study has emphasized and focused on contemplating the reasons in favour of or against religious symbols in public functions. In so doing, this study has intentionally shied away from prescribing how to implement a particular policy. Such restraint is partly observed because, in the end, the formulation of dress policies is best left to the particular public institution at issue. Furthermore, as mentioned in Chapter 1, there is a wide array of policies available depending on which considerations, whether they are principled or pragmatic, prevail. And finally, the issue of religious symbols in public functions runs the risk of becoming politicized. Secondly, this study will not end the debate. On the one hand, this study has restrictions in dealing with some of the non-legal aspects which are inherent to the issue. An evident non-legal aspect is the actual effect of a religious symbol on the person seeing the symbol. Empirical research may fill that gap and thus further strengthen the discussion. On the other hand, the seemingly trivial issue of religious symbols in public functions grows on altogether contentious soil. Accordingly, while informed by 'bigger' issues, the issue and the way in which it is approached likewise has wider ramifications on these bigger issues. Such issues include but are not limited to the place of religion in the public sphere, the general scope of religious freedom for public officials, and the face of the state towards citizens. This study has advanced a case for not being too anxious about (public visibility of) religion or belief and for taking public officials' religious freedom as the point of departure. Uproar surrounding politicians' ideas to ban religious symbols from the public sphere makes for thought-provoking headlines in the newspaper. However, it is high time for a more substantial debate on the underlying points of contention which are conducive to unveiling the actual meaning of state neutrality.

SAMENVATTING

'Hennis (VVD) wil debat hoofddoek' (De Volkskrant, 15 maart 2011)

INLEIDING

Religieuze symbolen lijken een geliefde eendagsvlieg in de pers. Niettemin loont het om diepgaand onderzoek te verrichten naar dit onderwerp. Hiervoor zijn ten minste drie redenen aan te wijzen: het debat over religieuze symbolen loopt al sinds geruime tijd; dit debat raakt aan bredere vragen zoals de plaats van religie in de samenleving; bovendien overschrijdt dit debat de nationale grenzen. Deze drie redenen inspireerden de onderhavige studie, die zich richt op publieke functies waar religieuze symbolen nog meer dan in andere contexten tegenstand oproepen. De gedachte dat publieke functionarissen in belangrijke opzichten verschillen van andere individuen, vindt haar weerslag in de stelling dat publieke functionarissen de staat vertegenwoordigen en dus 'neutraal' moeten zijn. Een veelgehoorde gevolgtrekking van deze stelling is dat publieke functionarissen zich dienen te onthouden van het tonen van religieuze symbolen. Deze studie zet vraagtekens bij deze redenering door te onderzoeken of staatsneutraliteit in Nederland daadwerkelijk rechtvaardigt en/of vereist dat het tonen van religieuze symbolen door publieke functionarissen aan beperkingen onderhevig moet zijn. Daarbij limiteert de studie deze vraag tot drie beroepsgroepen die centraal staan in het Nederlandse debat: de rechterlijke macht, de politie en het openbaar onderwijs. Deze groepen zijn karakteristiek voor de publieke functies van de staat en ze kennen individuele eigenschappen die de functie in kwestie typeren. Ze zijn bovendien verschillend, waardoor de discussie bevorderd wordt.

Het doel van de studie is drieledig en hangt samen met de redenen voor de studie. In de eerste plaats is de studie gericht op een gedetailleerde ontleding van het debat over religieuze symbolen in publieke functies. Deze benadering is geïnspireerd door Jan Smits' idee dat de juridische discipline een wetenschap van conflicterende standpunten is. Dienovereenkomstig kan de discipline een bijdrage leveren door de argumenten die ten grondslag liggen aan standpunten te onderkennen en te wegen. Deze bijdrage wint aan kracht wanneer de argumenten theoretisch worden ingebed. In de tweede plaats beoogt de studie dan ook om de theorie van de twee centrale concepten, staatsneutraliteit en religieuze vrijheid, te verkennen en toe te spitsen op de hoofdkwestie. Door de onderlinge samenhang van deze concepten te beschouwen met betrekking tot religieuze symbolen in publieke functies kan de studie nagaan wat de preciezere implicaties van deze concepten zijn. In de derde plaats stelt de studie zich ten doel te komen tot een normatieve beoordeling van de verschillende argumenten in het debat over religieuze symbolen in publieke functies. Hiertoe plaatst de studie deze kwestie tegen de achtergrond van achtereenvolgens het Europees Verdrag tot Bescherming van de Rechten van de Mens (EVRM of Verdrag), Engeland en Frankrijk. De eerstgenoemde context is van belang voor het in acht nemen van mensenrechtelijke normen zoals de vrijheid van religie omdat het EVRM dwingende minimumstandaarden vereist. De Engelse en Franse context vertegenwoordigen in Europa twee uitersten ten aanzien van religieuze symbolen in publieke functies. Daarom biedt een verkenning van beide contexten een brede inspiratie voor mogelijke benaderingen in de Nederlandse context.

VEELLAGIG DEBAT

Alvorens de details van het debat ten tonele te voeren, biedt de studie in Hoofdstuk 2 eerst een globaal beeld van de Nederlandse achtergrond, onder andere door te beschrijven hoe religieuze vrijheid is geëvolueerd in Nederland. Van oudsher stond Nederland bekend om zijn tolerante en pragmatische benadering van religieuze kwesties. Een schoolvoorbeeld van dit imago is het zuilensysteem, dat ruimte bood aan verscheidene confessionele groeperingen om met gelijkgestemden hun eigen gedeelte binnen de publieke ruimte te delen. Al langer en vooral sinds 11 september 2001 is dit imago aan corrosie onderhevig. In het bijzonder twee maatschappelijke veranderingen hebben ingewerkt op de evolutie van religieuze vrijheid. De eerste verandering betreft de rol van religie die op paradoxale wijze meer en minder prominent geworden is. Enerzijds heeft religie gewonnen aan belang door weer een vaste plek in te nemen op de publieke agenda. Tegelijkertijd heeft religie een minder belangrijke positie in de maatschappij doordat ze minder geïnstitutionaliseerd is; zo zijn mensen hun religie bijvoorbeeld meer individueel gaan belijden. De tweede verandering betreft de samenstelling van de Nederlandse bevolking. Deze is de afgelopen decennia ingrijpend door immigratie veranderd, zowel in etnisch als in religieus opzicht. De combinatie van deze twee veranderingen heeft een ander licht geworpen op religieuze kwesties en dientengevolge het debat erover doen opleven. Aldus is er ook discussie ontstaan over de ruimte van publieke functionarissen om religieuze symbolen te tonen. In een notendop kan gesteld worden dat de status quo rechters en politieagenten niet toestaat om religieuze symbolen te dragen, terwijl leerkrachten in het openbaar onderwijs dat wel kunnen. De juridische regulering van deze status quo heeft echter voldoende ruimte gelaten voor discussie en doet dit tot op de dag van vandaag nog.

Geschilpunt	Uitleg
(1) Gelijke behandeling	De staat moet gelijke toegang verschaffen aan hen die een positie in de publieke dienst ambiëren en bovendien moet ze publieke functionarissen gelijk behandelen. De vraag is hoe gelijkheid het best kan worden gegarandeerd, door een onveranderlijk beleid of door beleid te differentiëren?
(2) Belichaming	Belichaamt een publieke functionaris de staat? Enerzijds heeft een publieke functionaris nog steeds een persoonlijke hoedanigheid waardoor hij zich kan beroepen op individuele rechten. Anderzijds heeft een publieke functionaris een officiële hoedanigheid waardoor hij gebonden is aan een verplichting van staatsneutraliteit ten opzichte van anderen. Daarom rijst de vraag in hoeverre zijn professionele verplichting afbreuk doet aan zijn individuele rechten.
(3) Vooringenomenheid	De vraag doet zich voor of publieke functionarissen die religieuze symbolen tonen vooringenomenheid uitstralen. Een vervolgvraag is of ze andermans recht op gelijke behandeling schenden. Deze schending ontstaat voornamelijk doordat publieke functionarissen de indruk kunnen geven dat ze vooringenomen zijn ten opzicht van een andere persoon met wie ze contact hebben. Dit kan rechtvaardigen dat hun vrijheid om religie of levensovertuiging te uiten beperkt wordt.
(4) Risico van bekering	Dit punt houdt ook verband met het effect van het voorkomen van publieke functionarissen op de rechten van anderen. In tegenstelling met het vorige punt trekt dit punt het effect verder door de mogelijkheid te beschouwen dat het voorkomen een ondeugdelijke uitwerking op anderen kan hebben. Dit argument betreft dus het risico van het opdringen van een religie of levensovertuiging aan anderen.
(5) Beeld van de staat	In het dienen van burgers moeten publieke functionarissen overbrengen dat de staat voor eenieder beschikbaar is. De vraag is hoe ze dat het beste kunnen doen, bijvoorbeeld door een blanco entiteit te belichamen of door hun individualiteit en band met de maatschappij te benadrukken?
(6) Scheiding tussen kerk en staat	Er is betoogd dat de scheiding van kerk en staat automatisch vereist dat publieke functionarissen zich onthouden van het tonen van religieuze symbolen. Dit argument veronderstelt dat publieke functionarissen de staat belichamen.

De argumentatie tegen religieuze symbolen in publieke functies is dat zulke symbolen niet verenigbaar zijn met staatsneutraliteit. Deze argumentatie lijkt meer te verhullen dan duidelijk te maken. De betekenis van staatsneutraliteit is kennelijk niet eenduidig, want waarom zou een leerkracht wel neutraal kunnen zijn met religieuze symbolen terwijl een rechter dat niet kan? Bovendien roept deze argumentatie vragen op ten aanzien van bijvoorbeeld de betekenis van de 'staat vertegenwoordigen'. In Hoofdstuk 3 geeft de studie een gedetailleerde analyse van het debat over religieuze symbolen in publieke functies om te kijken naar de achterliggende argumentatie. Als aanknopingspunt voor deze analyse dienen de uitspraken van de Commissie Gelijke Behandeling (CGB) vanwege hun belang voor het publieke debat. Bovendien hebben alle drie de functies gefigureerd in een CGB-uitspraak. Zo deed in 2001 een CGB-uitspraak over een (kandidaat-) griffier met een hoofddoek flink stof opwaaien in het nationale debat. Conform Smits' benadering richt de studie zich eerst op het identificeren en systematiseren van de centrale argumenten alvorens deze te wegen. Deze exercitie leidt tot zes punten die ten grondslag liggen aan het debat over religieuze symbolen in publieke functies. De tabel op de vorige pagina vat deze punten samen.

Deze punten tonen de gemeenschappelijke thema's die een rol spelen in het debat over religieuze symbolen in publieke functies. De vraag in welke mate een publieke functionaris de staat belichaamt doet zich voor in verband met een rechter, een politieagent en een leerkracht. Tegelijkertijd kunnen de punten verschillend uitpakken voor de drie functies. Handhaving wordt als een kernfunctie van de staat gezien, waardoor een politieagent wordt geacht de staat te belichamen. De mate waarin een leerkracht de staat belichaamt wordt in het algemeen als minder sterk beschouwd al was het maar omdat het Nederlandse onderwijssysteem ook bijzonder onderwijs kent. Ten slotte moet worden opgemerkt (zie punt (6) bijvoorbeeld) dat de punten onderling verband houden en elkaar kunnen versterken.

DRIEHOEKIG MODEL

In Hoofdstuk 4 vervolgt de studie met een theoretische verkenning van de twee concepten die centraal staan in de studie: staatsneutraliteit en religieuze vrijheid. Deze concepten hebben in het debat soms meer verhuld dan verhelderd. Als idealen laten ze ruimte voor nadere invullingen. Om zicht te krijgen op deze ruimte hebben theorieën typologieën onderscheiden. Een vaak genoemde typologie van staatsneutraliteit maakt een onderscheid tussen neutraliteit van rechtvaardiging en neutraliteit van effect. Deze twee types illustreren de mogelijke variatie van de vormgeving van staatsneutraliteit. Zo vereist neutraliteit van rechtvaardiging 'slechts' dat een staat haar beleid rechtvaardigt op basis van neutrale redenen. Een beleid dat hoofddeksels uitsluit van publieke functies om representatieve redenen kan verenigbaar zijn met neutraliteit van rechtvaardiging. Daarentegen moet een beleid dat voldoet aan neutraliteit van effect ook rekening houden met het daadwerkelijke (dus inclusief onbedoelde of onvoorziene) effect. Tegen die standaard bezien zou het voornoemde beleid wel eens niet neutraal kunnen zijn omdat het nadeliger uitpakt voor bijvoorbeeld islamitische dan christelijke vrouwen. In plaats van een eenduidige lijn biedt staatsneutraliteit eerder een bandbreedte waarbinnen verschillende soorten beleid mogelijk zijn. Dit is ook zo vanuit het oogpunt van de vrijheid van publieke functionarissen om hun religie of levensovertuiging te uiten. Deze is niet onbeperkt. De rationale van staatsneutraliteit ten aanzien van deze vrijheid is uit te drukken in de drie volgende kernverplichtingen:

300

1. de staat dient religies of levensovertuigingen niet te beoordelen, te bevoordelen of te benadelen (in het algemeen of in haar interactie met individuen en gemeenschappen);
2. de staat dient geen religie of levensovertuiging op te leggen (in het algemeen of in haar interactie met individuen en gemeenschappen);
3. de staat dient individuen of gemeenschappen niet te bevoor- of benadelen op basis van religie of levensovertuiging.

Deze kernverplichtingen drukken uit dat beide concepten samenkomen in de idee dat het individu tegen de staat beschermd moet worden. Tegelijkertijd is van belang voor ogen te houden dat in het geval van publieke functionarissen en religieuze symbolen het individu als het ware samenvalt met de staat. De studie verfijnt de gebruikelijke dichotomie staat-individu in de kwestie religieuze symbolen in publieke functies, door de publieke functionaris expliciet zichtbaar te maken Het resultaat is een driehoekig model waarbinnen de kernverplichtingen gestalte krijgen. Op deze wijze komt duidelijk naar voren (meer dan in een lineair model) welke actoren en relaties in het spel zijn. Bovendien illustreert de driehoek dat de relaties en daarmee de uitwerking van staatsneutraliteit ondeelbaar zijn. Ook kan de driehoek verduidelijken welke factoren, zoals de aard van de relatie, van belang zijn bij het beoordelen van de noodzaak en rechtvaardiging van beperkingen op het tonen van religieuze symbolen. Om een voorbeeld te geven: de relatie die een rechter heeft met een rechtzoekende is een andere dan die een leerkracht met een leerling heeft. Het model geeft ook ruimte om de geschilpunten in te delen. Zo wordt bijvoorbeeld zichtbaar dat het punt van belichaming de relatie tussen staat en publieke functionaris betreft en daarmee verschilt van het punt van vooringenomenheid dat zich voordoet tussen de individuele publieke functionaris en de individuele burger.

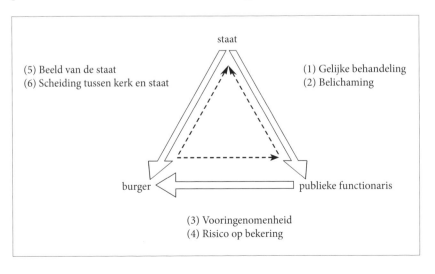

Samenvatting

Het driehoekig model met de geschilpunten dient als de lens waardoorheen de resultaten van de verkenning in de Hoofdstukken 5 t/m 7 beoordeeld worden. In hoofdstuk 5 verkent de studie de EVRM-jurisprudentie om de piketpaaltjes te vinden waarbinnen het verdrag staten toestaat om beperkingen op te leggen aan de vrijheid van publieke functionarissen om religieuze symbolen te tonen. Hoofdstukken 6 en 7 gaan na hoe staatsneutraliteit binnen respectievelijk de Franse en Engelse context geacht wordt te vereisen en/of te rechtvaardigen dat beperkingen worden opgelegd aan de vrijheid van publieke functionarissen om religieuze symbolen te tonen.

MINIMUM EVRM STANDAARDEN

Voor de mensenrechtennormen in Nederland, en overigens ook in Frankrijk en in Engeland, zijn het EVRM en zijn jurisprudentie van wezenlijk belang. Hoewel deze jurisprudentie geen bron is voor absolute waarheden, biedt ze aanknopingspunten voor de (dwingende) minimumstandaarden die lidstaten in acht moeten nemen. Voor de vraag welke ruimte Nederland heeft om beperkingen op te leggen aan de vrijheid van publieke functionarissen om religieuze symbolen te tonen biedt het EVRM en zijn jurisprudentie een waardevolle bron. In zaken over beperkingen op de vrijheid van religie laat het Hof veel ruimte aan lidstaten om beperkingen op te leggen waardoor er geen eenduidige richtlijnen van de jurisprudentie zijn af te leiden.

Staatsneutraliteit is niet opgenomen in het Verdrag en heeft geleidelijk aan vorm gekregen in de jurisprudentie tot het niveau dat deze neutraliteit nu als algemeen beginsel functioneert en gekoppeld wordt aan waarden als pluralisme, tolerantie en democratie. Daarnaast zijn er specifieke verplichtingen afgeleid van staatsneutraliteit zoals dat de staat niet mag treden in de legitimiteit van religies of levensovertuigingen; hier klinkt de echo van de hierboven onderscheiden kernverplichtingen van staatsneutraliteit. Deze beschrijving van staatsneutraliteit lijkt ruimte te laten voor religieuze symbolen. Niettemin tonen individuele zaken aan dat andere interpretaties van staatsneutraliteit, die wel beperkingen op religieuze symbolen impliceren, ook verenigbaar zijn met het Verdrag. Bovendien hebben de Straatsburgse instellingen ook de specifieke kenmerken van publieke functionarissen in acht genomen om beperkingen op hun religieuze vrijheid te beoordelen. Zo is geaccepteerd dat het vrijwillig aangaan van een bepaalde betrekking die ook weer vrijwillig neergelegd kan worden, beperkingen met zich meebrengen kan. Kort door de bocht, zou gesteld kunnen worden dat het Hof zich mild getoond heeft tegenover beperkingen op religieuze symbolen. Niettemin is het van belang om in het oog te houden dat twee factoren naar voren komen bij de beoordeling of beperkingen zijn toegestaan: het specifieke symbool en de wijze van tonen. Opvallend en controversieel is dat het Hof heeft verondersteld dat de islamitische hoofddoek een bekerende werking kan hebben. Hiervoor is wel van belang op welke wijze en overigens ook in welke context het symbool gedragen wordt. Meer specifiek, in een zaak betreffende een

302

basisschoolleerkracht nam het Hof in acht dat deze leerkracht een voorbeeldrol vervulde en dat de leerlingen door hun jonge leeftijd ontvankelijk waren voor bekering. Er kan dus niet zonder meer gesteld worden dat beperkingen op religieuze symbolen in publieke functies per definitie toelaatbaar zijn onder het EVRM. Ondanks de ruime marge die staten hebben om beperkingen op te leggen, dienen staten te verzekeren dat zulke beperkingen aan een proportionaliteitstoets voldoen. In de Hoofdstukken 6 en 7 heeft de studie twee uiteenlopende benaderingen, in Frankrijk en Engeland, onder de loep genomen om te kijken hoe staatsneutraliteit zich in die benaderingen verhoudt tot beperkingen op religieuze symbolen in publieke functies.

De uniforme Franse benadering versus de gedifferentieerde Engelse benadering

De verkenningen van de Franse respectievelijk de Engelse context richten zich eerst op algemenere vragen, zoals welke rol religie inneemt in de maatschappij en welke ruimte publieke functionarissen hebben om religieuze symbolen te tonen. Bovendien besteden ze aandacht aan de kwesties die debat hebben veroorzaakt. Want ondanks het contrast tussen beide landen ten aanzien van hun opstelling tegenover religieuze symbolen, hebben beide landen op hun eigen wijze met religieuze symbolen geworsteld. In het Nederlandse debat werd verwezen naar Frankrijk om het pleidooi tegen religieuze symbolen kracht bij te zetten. Frankrijk heeft zijn imago als 'hardliner' zeker al sinds 2004 bevestigd door religieuze symbolen op openbare scholen te verbieden. In 2011 trad een zogenaamd algemeen 'boerkaverbod' als eerste in Frankrijk in werking. Als tegenpool dient Engeland dat met getulbande rechters en gehoofddoekte politieagenten inspiratie bood voor het standpunt dat religieuze symbolen niet onverenigbaar zijn met staatsneutraliteit. Niettemin ondervinden Engelse burgers ook beperkingen bij het dragen van religieuze symbolen. In 2006 zorgde een werkneemster bij British Airways voor consternatie toen zij een kruisje zichtbaar wilde dragen op haar uniform; de kledingreglementen stonden dit niet toe. In 2012 had haar zaak haar weg gevonden naar het Europese Hof voor de Rechten van de Mens.

Na deze algemene verkenning wordt beoordeeld hoe de opvattingen binnen beide landen passen in het conceptuele model en hoe ze zich verhouden tot de zes geschilpunten. Deze beoordeling bevestigt het contrast tussen beiden landen in de omgang met religieuze symbolen in publieke functies, en bovendien komt naar voren op welke fundamentele punten de overwegingen voor deze benaderingen verschillen. Zo'n fundamenteel verschil is al gelegen in de interpretatie van staatsneutraliteit en dit verschil is samen te vatten in drie punten. Ten eerste wordt neutraliteit in de Franse context expliciet erkend terwijl neutraliteit in de Engelse context wordt verondersteld door middel van gelijkheid voor de wet. Ten tweede hanteert Frankrijk een formele versie van neutraliteit wat betekent dat religie en levensovertuiging als irrelevant criterium van beleid worden beschouwd; er wordt niet gekeken of beleid wellicht ongelijk uitpakt voor bepaalde groeperingen. Daarentegen streeft Engeland naar materiële neutraliteit waarbij oog is voor het daadwerkelijke effect van beleid. Ten derde betekent neutraliteit in de Franse context per definitie het uitsluiten van religieuze symbolen terwijl Engeland ruimte laat voor zulke symbolen.

Specifiek met betrekking tot publieke functionarissen en religieuze symbolen is het contrast tussen de Franse en de Engelse benadering uit te drukken door de kwalificaties 'uniform' versus 'gedifferentieerd' respectievelijk. Dit contrast is terug te voeren op verschillen in opvattingen over de conceptualisering van de staat, de plaats van religie in het publieke domein en het belang van schijn van de publieke functionaris. Simpel gesteld, trekt de Franse benadering een duidelijke lijn in het uitsluiten van religieuze symbolen voor publieke functionarissen. Ongeacht de specifieke functie, de situatie of het symbool is het publieke functionarissen nimmer toegestaan om religieuze symbolen te tonen. Dat betekent bijvoorbeeld dat een schoonmaker in dienst van het Ministerie van Binnenlandse Zaken zich in gelijke mate moet onthouden van het tonen van religieuze symbolen als een rechter van het Hof van Cassatie. De Engelse benadering trekt niet op voorhand een duidelijke lijn en bekijkt per geval of er noodzaak is tot beperking of mogelijkheid voor accommodatie. Toen het Londens politiekorps ondervond dat geïnteresseerde vrouwelijke kandidaten zich lieten ontmoedigen doordat het uniform niet voorzag in een hoofddoek, heeft het besloten de hoofddoek te integreren in het politie-uniform. Wanneer deze benaderingen gekoppeld worden aan het driehoekig model kan gesteld worden dat de driehoek in de Franse context onveranderlijk is voor de drie functies. Het is irrelevant om welke publieke functionaris het gaat: theoretisch heeft een rechter dezelfde neutraliteitsverplichting richting de rechtzoekende als een leerkracht richting de leerling. Daarentegen kan de driehoek in de Engelse context gedifferentieerd worden naar publieke functie waarbij de concrete omstandigheden in acht worden genomen.

EEN KRITISCHE BLIK OP BEPERKINGEN IN DE NEDERLANDSE CONTEXT

De studie sluit af door de bevindingen 'terug te koppelen' naar de Nederlandse context. Op basis van deze bevindingen concludeert de studie dat staatsneutraliteit in Nederland in ieder geval niet vereist dat er beperkingen worden opgelegd. Staatsneutraliteit zou zulke beperkingen wel kunnen rechtvaardigen, maar niet vanzelfsprekend. De studie benadrukt het belang van een deugdelijke rechtvaardiging, waarvoor een contextuele benadering geschikter is dan een abstracte benadering. Bovendien stemt een contextuele benadering meer overeen met de Nederlandse context waar staatsneutraliteit een impliciete status heeft, waar religie in het publieke domein nog zichtbaarheid en accommodatie kent en waar de publieke functionaris zich nog kan beroepen op individuele rechten.

De studie pleit ervoor om onafhankelijk van de gegeven situatie de kwestie te overdenken en schijnbaar vanzelfsprekende aannames kritisch te bevragen. Door de zes geschilpunten te doordenken tegen de achtergrond van de bevindingen over het EVRM, de Engelse en de Franse context, stelt de studie zogeheten vanzelfsprekendheden ter discussie. Bovenal benadrukt de studie om verder te kijken dan het concept van staatsneutraliteit om vast te stellen welke belangen echt in het spel zijn. Om een voorbeeld te geven, een belangrijke aanname is dat rechters moeten uitstralen neutraal te zijn en dat zo'n uitstraling minder belangrijk is voor leerkrachten. Deze aanname vindt uitdrukking in geschilpunt (3) over de vooringenomenheid van de publieke functionaris. In Hoofdstuk 8 wordt dit punt behandeld door te vragen exact waarom religieuze symbolen in de weg zouden staan aan een neutrale uitstraling. Moet de waarneming van het uiterlijk van een rechter überhaupt als criterium dienen om neutraliteit vast te stellen? Wat maakt religieuze symbolen anders dan andere persoonskenmerken? Andersom onderzoekt de studie of het wel zo logisch is dat een leerkracht op een openbare school religieuze symbolen kan dragen. Dient het openbaar onderwijs niet juist als contragewicht van het bijzonder onderwijs dat de vrijheid heeft voor een confessionele grondslag? Of past een leerkracht met religieus symbool juist uitstekend in het streven van het openbaar onderwijs neutraal te zijn in de zin van niet bevoordeeld ten opzichte van de maatschappelijke diversiteit?

Door de gedachten te laten gaan over de concrete belangen die ten grondslag liggen aan staatsneutraliteit wint het debat aan scherpte en diepgang. Bovendien biedt het meer aanknopingspunten om de sterke argumenten van de zwakke argumenten te onderscheiden. Deze benadering maakt het mogelijk om courante en snel geaccepteerde redeneringen te bevragen. Bovendien biedt een dergelijke benadering ook ruimte voor andere relevante factoren die niet vanzelfsprekend in gedachte komen bij staatsneutraliteit alleen. De identificatie van deze factoren kan bevorderen dat de proportionaliteit van een beperking beter vastgesteld kan worden. Zo is een mogelijk relevante factor, de mate van openbaarheid waarin een publieke functionaris zijn functie uitoefent. Doordat een politieagent zich op straat beweegt, wordt hij waargenomen door meer mensen dan een rechter in functie. Dit impliceert onder andere dat hij minder zicht heeft op het effect van een religieus symbool dat hij toont en dat de reactie op zo'n symbool een andere uitwerking heeft voor zijn functioneren dan bijvoorbeeld bij een rechter. Door deze punten uit te lichten beoogt de studie overwegingen zichtbaar te maken voor een deugdelijke rechtvaardiging van eventuele beperkingen.

Conclusie

De studie is erop gericht het debat over religieuze symbolen in publieke functies op een hoger plan te trekken door verheldering te brengen op argumentatief en conceptueel niveau. Bovendien wordt een beoordeling gegeven van de in het geding zijnde geschilpunten door de kwestie tegen de achtergrond van het EVRM, Frankrijk en Engeland te plaatsen. De kern van het verschil tussen deze twee archetypische tegengestelden heeft de studie verwoord in een uniforme versus een gedifferentieerde benadering. In de studie wordt betoogd dat voor de Nederlandse situatie een contextuele benadering geschikter is om te beoordelen of beperkingen op religieuze symbolen in publieke functies noodzakelijk en/of gerechtvaardigd zijn. Staatsneutraliteit in Nederland vereist in ieder geval niet dat er beperkingen worden opgelegd. Zulke beperkingen kunnen gerechtvaardigd zijn, maar vereisen nog wel deugdelijke motivering. De studie laat zien dat een dergelijke motivering niet zo vanzelfsprekend voorhanden is. Door de argumenten uiteen te rafelen en gedetailleerd te doordenken maakt de studie zichtbaar welke overwegingen die ten grondslag liggen aan staatsneutraliteit een rol spelen in het debat. De studie breekt een lans voor de vrijheid van religie door te benadrukken dat deze vrijheid ook als uitgangspunt moet dienen voor publieke functionarissen. De onderbouwing van beperkingen zou verder moeten gaan dan verwijzing naar abstracte concepten als staatsneutraliteit. Door de onderliggende overwegingen expliciet te maken wint het debat winnen aan helderheid en diepgang wat bevorderlijk is voor het ontsluieren van de werkelijke betekenis van staatsneutraliteit.

Résumé

'La contractuelle voilée en conseil de discipline. Une agente municipale de Paris risque une sanction administrative car elle refuse de retirer son voile au travail.'
(Le Parisien, 4 février 2010)

Introduction

Les symboles religieux semblent faire l'objet de unes éphémères dans la presse. Néanmoins il est nécessaire de faire des recherches approfondies sur ce thème, pour au moins trois raisons: le débat sur les symboles religieux dure déjà depuis longtemps; ce débat porte sur des questions plus larges comme la place de la religion dans la société; de plus ce débat va au-delà des frontières nationales. Ces trois raisons inspirent cette étude qui se concentre sur les fonctions publiques dans lesquelles des symboles religieux sont plus controversés que dans d'autres contextes. L'idée que des agents publics diffèrent des autres individus pour des questions plus importantes de respect s'explique par le fait que les agents publics représentent l'Etat et doivent donc être neutres. Une conclusion souvent entendue énonce que les agents publics doivent s'abstenir d'exposer des symboles religieux. Cette étude pose des questions sur ce raisonnement afin d'examiner si la neutralité de l'Etat aux Pays-Bas justifie et/ou rend nécessaire la limitation du port de symboles religieux aux agents publics. L'étude limite cette question aux trois groupes professionnels qui sont centraux dans le débat néerlandais: la magistrature, la police et l'éducation publique. Bien qu'ils soient typiques pour les fonctions publiques de l'Etat, ils ont également des propriétés individuelles qui caractérisent la fonction en question.

L'objectif de cette étude consiste en trois parties. En premier lieu, l'étude vise une analyse détaillée du débat sur les symboles religieux dans la fonction publique. Cette approche est inspirée de celle de Jan Smits, qui estime que la discipline juridique est une science où les arguments s'affrontent. En conséquence, la discipline peut contribuer à identifier et évaluer les arguments impliqués par ces points de vue. Cette contribution gagne en force si ces arguments sont ancrés dans la théorie. C'est pourquoi en deuxième lieu, l'étude vise à explorer la théorie des deux concepts centraux, neutralité de l'Etat et liberté religieuse, et à la lier au problème central. En considérant la relation mutuelle de ces concepts par rapport aux symboles religieux dans la fonction publique, l'étude examine les implications exactes de ces concepts. En troisième lieu, l'étude a pour but de faire une appréciation normative des différents arguments dans le débat sur les symboles religieux dans les fonctions publiques. Dans ce but, l'étude place le problème central dans le contexte de la Convention européenne des droits de l'homme (CEDH ou Convention), la France et l'Angleterre. Le premier contexte est important pour considérer des normes des droits de l'homme comme la liberté de religion, la CEDH exigeant un standard minimum. Les contextes français et anglais représentent en Europe deux extrêmes concernant la position quant aux symboles religieux dans la fonction publique. C'est pourquoi une exploration des deux contextes offre une inspiration la plus large possible pour des approches possibles dans le contexte néerlandais.

LES DIFFÉRENTES PHASES DU DÉBAT

Avant de présenter les détails du débat, l'étude ébauche dans le Chapitre 2 une image globale de la situation néerlandaise, comme l'évolution de la liberté religieuse aux Pays-Bas. Traditionnellement, les Pays-Bas étaient connus pour son approche tolérante et pragmatique des problématiques religieuses. Un exemple classique pour souligner cette image est le système de piliers qui offrait aux différents groupes confessionnels la possibilité de profiter de l'espace public en le partageant. Avec le temps et plus récemment à partir du 11 septembre 2001, cette image est corrodée. Deux changements sociétaux en particulier ont affecté l'évolution de la liberté religieuse. Un premier changement concerne le rôle de la religion qui, paradoxalement, est devenu à la fois plus proéminent et moins proéminent. D'un coté, la religion a connu un regain d'intérêt en étant de nouveau mise à l'ordre du jour. En même temps, la religion a perdu de l'importance parce qu'elle est moins institutionnalisée; les personnes sont tenues de professer leur religion dans une sphère plus individuelle. Un deuxième changement concerne la composition de la population néerlandaise. Celle-ci a connu des changements radicaux, tant du point de vue des ethnies que des religions. La combinaison de ces deux changements a permis une mise en lumière différente des questions religieuses et en conséquence a relancé le débat. Une discussion s'est également engagée sur les implications du port de symboles religieux par les agents publics. En un mot, il est établi que la situation actuelle ne permet pas aux juges et aux policiers d'exposer des symboles religieux tandis que les enseignants de l'éducation publique le peuvent. La réglementation juridique de cette situation a laissé l'espace suffisant pour la discussion jusqu'à aujourd'hui.

Les arguments en défaveur du port de symboles religieux dans la fonction publique sont que ces symboles ne sont pas compatibles avec la neutralité de l'Etat. Cette argumentation semble plus opaque que claire. Le sens de la neutralité de l'Etat n'est évidemment pas sans équivoque: pourquoi le fait qu'un enseignant porte des symboles religieux serait neutre alors qu'un juge agissant de même ne le serait pas? De plus, cette argumentation suppose des questions par exemple sur le sens de la 'représentation de l'Etat'. Au troisième chapitre l'étude s'engage dans une analyse détaillée du débat sur les symboles religieux dans la fonction publique afin d'envisager les questions sous-jacentes de cette argumentation.

Les opinions de la Commission pour le traitement égal (*Commissie Gelijke Behandeling*, ci-après Commission) servent comme point de départ pour cette analyse au regard de leur importance pour le débat public. De plus, les trois fonctions ont figuré dans une opinion de la Commission; par exemple, une opinion sur un (candidat-) greffier portant un voile a engendré un intense débat national en 2001. Conformément à l'approche de Smits, l'étude dans un premier temps identifie et systématise les arguments centraux avant de les évaluer. Cet exercice amène aux six points qui sont à la base du débat sur les symboles religieux dans la fonction publiques. Le tableau suivant résume ces points.

Point contesté	Explication
(1) Traitement égal	L'Etat doit donner l'égal accès à ceux qui aspirent à un emploi dans les services publics et elle doit en plus traiter les agents publics également. La question est la suivante: comment peut-on garantir la plus grande égalité possible, par une politique invariable ou par une politique différenciée?
(2) Personnification	Un agent public personnifie-t-il l'Etat? D'un coté, un agent public a toujours une capacité personnelle qui lui dote des droits individuels. D'un autre coté, un agent public a un statut officiel qui le contraint à respecter la neutralité de l'Etat envers les autres. Par conséquent, dans quelle mesure ses obligations professionnelles empiètent sur ses droits individuels ?
(3) Parti pris	La question se pose lorsque des agents publics qui exposent des symboles religieux ont un parti pris. La question se pose de savoir si ces symboles violent le droit d'autrui d'être traité également. Cette violation donne surtout l'impression que les agents publics peuvent être de parti pris envers les autres personnes avec qu'ils entretiennent des rapports. Cela peut justifier que le droit de manifester sa religion ou conviction soit limité.
(4) Risque de prosélytisme	Ce point est lié à l'effet de l'apparence des agents publics sur d'autres personnes. Contrairement au dernier point, celui-ci étend cet effet en considérant la possibilité d'une influence excessive de l'apparence sur les droits des autres. Cet argument concerne donc le risque d'imposer une religion ou conviction aux autres.
(5) Image de l'Etat	En servant les citoyens, les agents publics doivent transmettre l'idée d'une disponibilité de l'Etat à l'égard de tous les citoyens. La question est d'avoir la meilleure situation possible: par exemple en personnifiant une entité blanche ou en soulignant l'individualité des agents par rapport à la société?
(6) Séparation de l'Eglise et l'Etat	Il est suggéré que la séparation de l'Eglise et l'Etat implique automatiquement l'abstention des agents publics d'exposer les symboles religieux. Cet argument suppose que les agents publics personnifient l'état.

Ces points démontrent les thèmes communs qui jouent un rôle dans le débat sur les symboles religieux dans la fonction publique. La question de savoir dans quelle mesure un agent public personnifie l'Etat se pose également à propos d'un juge, d'un policier et d'un enseignant. En même temps, les points peuvent avoir un effet différent pour les trois fonctions. Le maintien de l'ordre public est vu comme une fonction centrale de l'Etat, et par conséquent un policier est considéré est comme une personnification de l'Etat. En général, l'enseignant est moins considéré comme une personnification de l'Etat uniquement parce que le système néerlandais d'éducation comprend également les écoles privées, qui peuvent être religieuses. Finalement, il doit être remarqué que les points sont mutuellement connectés et peuvent renforcer l'un l'autre (cf. le point (6)).

LE MODÈLE TRIANGULAIRE

L'étude continue au quatrième chapitre par une exploration théorique des deux concepts centraux: neutralité de l'Etat et liberté religieuse. Ces concepts sont parfois plus opaques que clair. En tant qu'idéaux, ils laissent une marge de manœuvre pour leur implication. Afin d'avoir plus de clarté, les théories ont distingué plusieurs typologies. Une première typologie souvent mentionnée distingue la neutralité de justification et la neutralité d'effet. Ces deux types démontrent la variation possible d'implémentation de la neutralité. Ainsi la neutralité de justification exige 'simplement' que l'Etat justifie sa politique sur la base de raisons neutres. Par contre, une politique qui correspond à la neutralité d'effet doit aussi prendre en compte l'effet réel (donc inclut les effets non prévus ou non voulus). Selon ce standard, ladite politique pourrait bien être non-neutre en ce sens qu'elle serait plus défavorable pour des femmes islamiques que pour des femmes chrétiennes. Au lieu d'offrir une approche sans équivoque, la neutralité de l'Etat laisse une marge pour différentes politiques possibles. C'est aussi le cas de la liberté des agents publics de manifester leur religion ou conviction, liberté qui n'est pas illimitée. Les raisons de la neutralité de l'Etat à propos de cette liberté se résument aux trois obligations essentielles suivantes:

1. l'Etat ne doit pas évaluer, favoriser ou défavoriser des religions ou convictions (en général ou dans son interaction avec les individus ou les communautés);
2. l'Etat ne doit pas imposer une religion ou conviction (en général ou dans son interaction avec les individus ou les communautés);
3. l'Etat ne doit pas favoriser ou défavoriser des individus ou des communautés sur la base de leur religion ou conviction.

Ces obligations essentielles impliquent que les deux concepts convergent en l'idée que l'individu doit être protégé contre l'Etat. En même temps il est important que dans le cas des agents publics et des symboles religieux, l'individu soit à égalité avec l'Etat. L'étude affine la dichotomie habituelle Etat-Individu à propos de la question des symboles religieux dans la fonction publique, en mettant en avant l'agent public explicitement. Le résultat est un modèle triangulaire dans lequel des obligations essentielles sont effectuées. De cette manière les acteurs et relations engagés sont plus évidents que dans un modèle linéaire. Le triangle démontre de plus que les relations et l'effet de la neutralité de l'Etat sont indivisibles. Aussi le triangle peut clarifier quels facteurs, comme la nature de la relation, sont pertinents en jugeant la nécessité et la justification des limitations des symboles religieux. Par exemple: la relation entre un juge et un plaideur est différente de celle entre un enseignant et un élève. Le modèle laisse de l'espace aux points contestés. Ainsi il devient visible que le point de personnification concerne la relation entre l'Etat et l'agent public, et en le faisant il est différent du parti pris qui est pertinent pour la relation entre l'agent public individuel et le citoyen individuel.

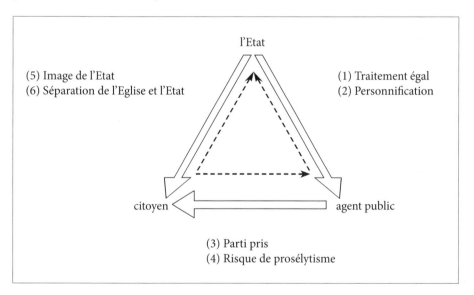

Le modèle triangulaire avec les points contestés sert comme l'angle par lequel les résultats de l'exploration aux chapitres 5 jusqu'à 7 sont considérés. Le Chapitre 5 étudie la jurisprudence de la CEDH afin de trouver les frontières dans lesquelles la Convention permet aux Etats d'imposer des limitations à la liberté des agents publics d'exposer des symboles religieux. Les chapitres 6 et 7 traitent de la neutralité de l'Etat dans les contextes français et anglais et de la façon dont elle est considérée afin de nécessiter et justifier les limitations faites aux agents publics d'exprimer leurs croyances et d'exposer des symboles religieux.

Résumé

LES STANDARDS MINIMUM DE LA **CEDH**

A propos des normes des droits de l'homme aux Pays-Bas, et d'ailleurs aussi en France et en Angleterre, on ne peut pas éviter la CEDH et sa jurisprudence. Bien que cette jurisprudence ne soit pas une source pour des vérités absolues, elle offre des indications sur les standards minimums (obligatoires) que les Etats membres doivent observer. Sur la question de la possibilité pour les Pays-Bas d'imposer des limitations à la liberté d'exposer les symboles religieux des agents publics, la CEDH offre une source valable. Dans le cadre des affaires impliquant des limitations à la liberté de religion, la Cour laisse aux Etats une grande marge afin d'imposer des limitations, de laquelle des indications claires ne peuvent pas découler.

La neutralité de l'Etat n'est pas incluse dans la Convention et vient d'être formulée dans la jurisprudence, et elle est actuellement comme un principe général et est liée aux valeurs comme le pluralisme, la tolérance et la démocratie. De plus des obligations spécifiques découlent de la neutralité de l'Etat: par exemple l'Etat n'est pas autorisé à évaluer la légitimité des religions ou des convictions; c'est ici que l'écho desdites obligations essentielles de la neutralité de l'état se fait. Cette description de la neutralité de l'Etat semble laisser de la place pour les symboles religieux. Néanmoins des affaires individuelles démontrent que des autres interprétations sont aussi compatibles avec la Convention. En outre, les institutions strasbourgeoises ont aussi rendu compte des caractéristiques spécifiques des agents publics en évaluant des limitations à la liberté religieuse de ces agents. Ainsi il est accepté qu'entrer volontairement dans une certaine relation professionnelle, et qui peut aussi être abandonnée volontairement, peut aussi impliquer des limitations. Dit simplement, la Cour s'est montrée modérée à propos des limitations aux symboles religieux. Néanmoins il est important de ne pas oublier que deux facteurs attirent l'attention quant au fait que les limitations sont acceptables: le symbole spécifique et la manière dont ce symbole est exposé. Il est frappant et controversé que la Cour ait assumé que le voile islamique peut avoir un effet prosélyte. Pour cela il est pertinent de prendre en considération la manière et aussi le contexte dans lesquels le symbole est porté. Plus spécifiquement, dans une affaire qui concerne une enseignante d'une école primaire, la Cour a pris en compte que cette enseignante avait un rôle exemplaire et que les élèves étaient si jeunes qu'ils ne pouvaient être sensibles au prosélytisme. On ne peut pas simplement dire que des limitations aux symboles religieux dans la fonction publique sont autorisées sous la CEDH. En dépit de la large marge laissée aux Etats pour imposer les limitations, ils doivent assurer que de telles limitations répondent à un test de proportionnalité. Aux chapitres suivants, 6 et 7, l'étude examinent deux approches divergentes en France et en Angleterre afin d'apprécier le rapport entre la neutralité de l'Etat et les limitations des symboles religieux dans la fonction publique.

L'APPROCHE DIFFÉRENTIÉE FRANÇAISE UNIFORME VIS-À-VIS DE L'APPROCHE ANGLAISE

L'exploration du contexte français et anglais respectivement vise des questions plus générales comme le rôle que la religion joue dans la société et quelle possibilité les agents publics ont d'exposer des symboles religieux. En outre, elle s'occupe des questions qui ont suscité débat. Malgré le contraste entre les deux pays quant aux symboles religieux, tous deux ont éprouvé des difficultés avec ces derniers. Dans le débat néerlandais, référence était faite à la France afin de soutenir l'appel contre des symboles religieux. Au moins à partir de 2004, la France a souligné son image comme 'hardliner' en interdisant les symboles religieux au sein des écoles publiques. En 2011, la première interdiction générale des voiles intégraux en Europe est entrée en vigueur en France. L'Angleterre est comme aux 'antipodes' en ayant des juges enturbannés et des policières voilées, et inspire l'idée selon laquelle des symboles religieux ne sont pas incompatibles avec la neutralité de l'Etat. Pourtant les citoyens anglais connaissent aussi des limitations aux symboles religieux. En 2006, le fait qu'une salariée à British Airways voulait porter un crucifix visible sur son uniforme a suscité une grande consternation, les règlements vestimentaires ne l'autorisaient en effet pas. En 2012 cette affaire a trouvé sa route à la Cour européenne des droits de l'homme.

Après cette exploration générale, l'étude montre que les conceptions dans les deux pays peuvent correspondre au modèle conceptuel et leur rapport avec les six points contestés. Cette évaluation confirme le contraste entre les deux pays quant à leur approche des symboles religieux et elle démontre de plus dans quels respects fondamentaux les considérations pour ces approches diffèrent. Une telle différence résulte de l'interprétation de la neutralité de l'Etat qui peut être résumée aux trois points. Premièrement, la neutralité est reconnue explicitement dans le contexte français tandis que la neutralité dans le contexte anglais est garantie implicitement par l'égalité devant la loi. Deuxièmement, la France a une version formelle de la neutralité ce qui veut dire que la religion et les convictions sont considérées comme des critères non pertinents pour la politique; ce n'est pas examiné où la politique pourrait avoir des effets inégaux pour des groupes particuliers. Cependant l'Angleterre vise la neutralité matérielle en considérant l'effet réel de la politique. Troisièmement, la neutralité dans le contexte français signifie par définition l'exclusion des symboles religieux tandis que l'Angleterre laisse la possibilité pour ces symboles. Plus particulièrement, lorsque l'on parle des agents publics et des symboles religieux, le contraste entre l'approche française et l'approche anglaise peut être qualifié 'd'uniforme' contre 'différentié'.

Ce contraste peut être dû aux différences qui existent entre diverses questions telles que la conceptualisation de l'Etat, la place de religion dans le domaine publique et l'importance de l'apparence de l'agent public. En résumé, l'approche française fixe une limite claire en excluant le port de symboles religieux par les agents publics. Sans distinction de la fonction spécifique, de la situation ou du symbole, il n'est jamais autorisé aux fonctionnaires publics d'exposer des symboles religieux. Cela signifie par exemple qu'un agent de nettoyage au service du Ministère des affaires intérieures doit s'abstenir d'exposer des symboles tout autant qu'un juge à la Cour de Cassation. L'approche anglaise ne fixe au contraire pas de limites claires et examine au cas-par-cas où il est nécessaire de restreindre ou de tempérer. Quand le corps des policiers anglais trouvait que des candidats féminins étaient découragées parce que l'uniforme ne prévoyait pas un voile, il a été décidé d'intégrer le voile à l'uniforme de police. Quand ces approches sont reliées au modèle triangulaire, on peut dire que ce triangle dans le contexte français est invariable pour les trois fonctions. Aucune considération du type d'agent public n'est prise; en théorie un juge a la même obligation de neutralité envers un plaideur qu'un enseignant envers un élève. Cependant le triangle dans le contexte anglais peut être différentiée selon la fonction publique en considérant les circonstances concrètes.

Un regard critique des limitations dans le contexte néerlandais

L'étude se finalise en se reconnectant au contexte néerlandais. Sur la base de ces résultats, l'étude conclue que la neutralité de l'Etat aux Pays-Bas en tout cas ne nécessite pas que des limitations soient imposées. La neutralité de l'Etat pourrait justifier ces limitations mais pas évidemment. L'étude met l'accent sur une justification propre pour laquelle une approche contextuelle est plus adéquate qu'une approche abstraite. En outre, l'approche contextuelle correspond plus au contexte néerlandais où la neutralité de l'Etat a un statut implicite, où la religion est toujours visible et accommodante dans le domaine public et l'agent public peut toujours recourir aux droits individuels.

L'étude expose les raisons en faveur de l'appréciation de la question indépendamment de la situation actuelle et de l'appréhension critique des prémisses apparemment évidentes. En considérant les six points contestés avec les résultats de la CEDH, du contexte anglais et français, l'étude traite de questions qui semblent évidentes. Avant tout, l'étude insiste sur l'importance de regarder au-delà du concept de neutralité de l'Etat afin d'établir les intérêts réellement en discussion. Par exemple, on peut supposer que les juges doivent transmettre la neutralité et que cette transmission a moins d'importance pour les enseignants. Cette prévision est exprimé au point contesté (3) du parti pris de l'agent public. Au Chapitre 8, l'étude analyse ce point en se demandant pourquoi une apparence neutre serait empêchée par les symboles religieux? Pour commencer, la perception de l'apparence d'un juge doit-elle servir comme un critère pour établir la neutralité? Pourquoi exactement les symboles religieux diffèrent-ils des autres caractéristiques personnelles? Inversement, l'étude examine la logique selon laquelle un enseignant dans une école publique peut exposer ou non des symboles religieux. L'éducation publique ne sert-elle pas comme un contrepoids à l'éducation privée qui donne la liberté d'avoir une base confessionnelle? Ou est-ce qu'un enseignant avec un symbole religieux ne correspond pas parfaitement dans l'ambition de l'éducation publique d'être neutre dans le sens de ne pas avoir de parti pris à propos de la diversité sociétale.

En réfléchissant aux intérêts concrets qui sont à la base de la neutralité de l'Etat, le débat peut être spécifié et approfondi. En outre, il offre davantage d'indications pour distinguer les arguments puissants des arguments mauvais. Cette approche rend possible la mise en doute des raisonnements courants et facilement acceptés. Toutefois une telle approche offre aussi la possibilité de considérer les autres facteurs pertinents qui ne sont pas au départ évidents lorsqu'il s'agit du principe de neutralité de l'Etat. L'identification de ces facteurs peut expliquer la proportionnalité d'une limitation. Ainsi l'étendue de la représentation publique d'un agent peut être un facteur pertinent. Parce qu'un policier est dans la rue, il est vu par un plus grand nombre de personnes qu'un juge en fonction. Cela implique en outre qu'il a moins d'idée de l'effet d'un symbole religieux et que cette réaction à ce symbole a un autre effet pour son fonctionnement qu'un juge aurait par exemple. En montrant ces points l'étude vise à rendre explicites les considérations pour une justification propre des limitations éventuelles.

CONCLUSION

L'étude vise à améliorer le débat sur les symboles religieux dans la fonction publique en donnant de la clarté sur le niveau argumentatif et conceptuel. En outre, l'étude a donné une évaluation des points en question en les plaçant dans le contexte de la CEDH, de la France et de l'Angleterre. La différence essentielle entre ces deux opposés archétypiques est formulée dans l'étude comme une approche uniforme versus contextuelle. L'étude soutient que pour la situation néerlandaise, une approche contextuelle est plus appropriée afin d'évaluer les situations dans lesquelles des limitations aux symboles religieux dans la fonction publique sont nécessaires et/ou justifiées. De toute façon, la neutralité de l'Etat aux Pays-Bas ne rend pas nécessaire que les limitations soient imposées. De telles limitations peuvent être justifiées mais elles ont toujours besoin d'une motivation propre. L'étude démontre qu'une telle motivation n'est pas si facilement envisageable. En démêlant et appréhendant les arguments, l'étude explique les considérations sur la base de neutralité de l'Etat. L'étude lance un appel pour la liberté de religion en soulignant que cette liberté doit rester le point de départ, également pour les agents publics. La référence aux concepts abstraits ne suffit pas pour la preuve des limitations. En rendant explicites les considérations sous-jacentes, le débat gagne de la clarté et de la profondeur, ce qui favorise le dévoilement du vrai sens de la neutralité de l'Etat.

BIBLIOGRAPHY

Books, book contributions and articles

Ahdar, R.J. and Leigh, I., *Religious freedom in the liberal state* (Oxford University Press, Oxford [etc.] 2005)

Andreescu, G. and Andreescu, L., The European Court of Human Rights' Lautsi Decision: Context, Contents, Consequences (2010) 26(9) *Journal for the Study of Religions and Ideologies*

Barmes, L. and Malleson K., 'The Legal Profession as Gatekeeper to the Judiciary: Design Faults in Measures to Enhance Diversity' (2011) 72(2) *The Modern Law Review*

Baubérot, J., 'Secularism and French Religious Liberty: A Sociological and Historical View' (2003)(2) *Brigham Young University Law Review*

– – *Histoire de la laïcité en France* (Que sais-je? 2nd edn Presses Universitaires de France, Paris 2004)

– – *Laïcité 1905-2005, entre passion et raison* (Seuil, Paris 2004)

– – 'The Place of Religion in Public Life: The Lay Approach' in Lindholm, T., Cole Durham Jr., W. and Tahzib-Lie, B.G., (eds), *Facilitating Freedom of Religion or Belief: A Deskbook* (Martinus Nijhoff Publishers, Leiden 2004)

Bauer, A., 'Les tâches de la police et les mutations de la délinquance' (2002) 3(102) *Pouvoirs*

Bedouelle, G. and Costa, J.P., *Les laïcités à la française* (Politique d'aujourd'hui, Presses Universitaires de France, Paris 1998)

de Been, W., '*Lautsi*: A Case of "Metaphysical Madness"?' (2011) Special Issue: The Lautsi Case' 6(3) *Religion and Human Rights* (2011)

Beenen, N., *Citizenship, Nationality and Access to Public Service Employment. The Impact of European Community Law* (PhD Universiteit Utrecht, Europa Law Publishing, Groningen, 2001)

Bell, J., 'Le service public: l'expérience britannique (1997) *L'Actualité Juridique – Fonctions Publiques*

Bellekom, T.L., *"Verfassungsfeinde" en openbare dienst* (PhD Rijksuniversiteit Leiden, Stichting NJCM-Boekerij, Leiden 1987)

Berger, P.L. (ed), *The Desecularization of the World. Resurgent Religion and World Politics* (Ethics and Public Policy Center/William B. Eerdmans, Washington D.C./Grand Rapids 1999)

Bermann, G.A. and Picard, E., *Introduction to French law* (Kluwer Law International, Alphen aan den Rijn 2008)

Bernts, T., de Jong, G. and Yar, H., 'Een religieuze atlas van Nederland' in W.B.H.J. van de Donk and others (eds), *Geloven in het publieke domein. Verkenningen van een dubbele transformatie. WRR Verkenningen, nr. 13* (Amsterdam University Press, Amsterdam 2006)

Berthoud, J., 'La neutralité religieuse du fonctionnaire' (2005)(12) *Semaine Juridique – Administrations et Collectivités Territoriales*

van Bijsterveld, S.C., 'Freedom of religion in the Netherlands' (1995) 29(2) *Brigham Young University Law Review*

– – *Godsdienstvrijheid in Europees perspectief* (W.E.J. Tjeenk Willink, Deventer 1998)

– – 'Scheiding van kerk en staat: een klassieke norm in een moderne tijd' in van de Donk, W.B.H.J. and others (eds), *Geloven in het publieke domein. Verkenningen van een dubbele transformatie. WRR Verkenningen, nr. 13* (Amsterdam University Press, Amsterdam 2006)

– – *Overheid en godsdienst. Herijking van een onderlinge relatie* (Wolf Legal Publishers, Nijmegen 2008)

Blair, A. and Aps, W., 'What not to wear and other stories: addressing religious diversity in schools.' (2005) 17(1-2) *Education and the Law*

Blum, N., *Die Gedanken-, Gewissens- und Religionsfreiheit nach Art. 9 der Europäischen Menschenrechtskonvention* (Duncker & Humblot, Berlin 1990)

den Boef, A.H., *Nederland seculier! Tegen religieuze privileges in wetten, regels, praktijken, gewoonten en attitudes* (Van Gennep, Amsterdam 2003)

Bowen, J.R., 'Why Did the French Rally to a Law Against Scarves in Schools?' (2008) 68 *Droit et société*

Bradney, A., 'Religion and Law in Great Britain at the End of the Second Christian Millennium' in Edge, P. and Harvey, G. (eds), *Law and Religion in Contemporary Society: Communities, individualism and the State* (Ashgate, Aldershot [etc.] 2000)

Brekelmans, F.H.J.G. and Vermeulen, B.P., 'Enkele beschouwingen over de relevantie van religie, politieke overtuiging en overheidsneutraliteit voor de rechtspositie van de leraar' in de Lange, R. and Rogier, L.J.J. (eds), *Onderwijs en onderwijsrecht in een pluriforme samenleving: opstellen aangeboden aan prof. mr. dr. D. Mentink* (Boom Juridische uitgevers, The Hague 2008)

Brenninkmeijer, A.F.M., 'Verwarring', (Mening over de stelling 'In een multiculturele samenleving is een rechter in toga met een hoofddoek een aanwinst')' (2001) 21 *Nederlands Juristenblad*

Bruinsma, F., 'Symbolische kleding (Mening over de stelling 'In een multiculturele samenleving is een rechter in toga met een hoofddoek een aanwinst') (2001) 21 *Nederlands Juristenblad*

van der Burg, W., *Het ideaal van de neutrale staat. Inclusieve, exclusieve en compenserende visies op godsdienst en cultuur* (Boom Juridische uitgevers, The Hague 2009)

– – W., Schuyt, C.J.M. and Nieuwenhuis, J.H., *Multiculturaliteit en recht* (Verslag van de op 13 juni 2008 te Dordrecht gehouden algemene vergadering van de Nederlandse Juristen-Vereniging, vol. 138, Kluwer, Deventer 2008)

Buruma, I., *Murder in Amsterdam: The Death of Theo van Gogh and the Limits of Tolerance* (Penguin Books, New York 2006)

Buwalda, M., 'De terugkeer van religie in het publieke domein' in Wetenschappelijk Onderzoeks- en Documentatiecentrum (WODC) (ed), *Religie en Grondrechten* (Justitiële Verkenningen, Wetenschappelijk Onderzoeks- en Documentatiecentrum, The Hague 2007)

Calo, Z.R., 'Pluralism, secularism and the European Court of Human Rights (2011) 26 *Journal of Law and Religion*

Carens, J.H., Culture, *Citizenship and Community. A Contextual Exploration of Justice as Evenhandedness* (Oxford University Press, Oxford 2000)

Cliteur, P., *The secular outlook: in defense of moral and political secularism* (Wiley-Blackwell, Oxford 2010)

Cortese, F., 'The*Lautsi* Case: A Comment from Italy' (2011) 6(3) *Religion and Human Rights*

Costa-Lascoux, J., 'Het individu en de godsdienstvrijheid beschermd. *Laïcité* en burgerschap in Frankrijk' in ten Hooven, M. and de Wit, T.W.A. (eds), *Ongewenste goden: de publieke rol van religie in Nederland* (Sun, Amsterdam 2006)

Cumper, P. and Lewis, T., '"Taking religion seriously"? Human rights and *hijab* in Europe – Some problems of adjudication' (2009) 24(2) *The journal of law and religion*

Curtit, F., 'Egalité vs. non-discrimination. Primauté du principe d'égalité en droit français' in Hill, M. (ed), *Religion and discrimination law in the European Union. La discrimination en matière religieuse dans l'union européenne* (Institute for European Constitutional Law, University of Trier, Trier 2012)

Dadomo, C. and Farran, S., *The French legal system* (2nd edn Sweet & Maxwell, London 1996)

van Dam, P., *Staat van verzuiling. Over een Nederlandse mythe* (Wereldbibliotheek, Amsterdam 2011)

Davie, G., 'Croire sans appartenir: le cas britannique' in Davie, G. and Hervieu-Léger, D. (eds), *Identités religieuses en Europe* (La Découverte, Paris 1996)

Davies, G., 'Banning the Jilbab: Reflections on Restricting Religious Clothing in the Light of the Court of Appeal in *SB v. Denbigh High School*. Decision of 2 March 2005.' (2005) 1 *European Constitutional Law Review*

Davis, G. and Vennard, J., 'Racism in Court: The Experience of Ethnic Minority Magistrates', (2006) 45(5) *The Howard Journal*

Dawkins, R., *The God delusion* (Houghton Mifflin Company, Boston 2006)

Deceaux, E., 'Chronique d'une jurisprudence annoncée: laïcité française et liberté religieuse devant la Cour européenne des droits de l'homme' (2010) 21(82) *Revue trimestrielle des droits de l'homme*

den Dekker-Van Bijsterveld, S.C., *De verhouding tussen kerk en staat in het licht van de grondrechten* (PhD Katholieke Universiteit Brabant, W.E.J. Tjeenk Willink, Zwolle, 1988)

Dieu, F., 'Le Conseil d'Etat et la laïcité négative' (2008) 13 *La Semaine Juridique Administrations et Collectivités territoriales*

van Dijk, P. and others (eds), *Theory and practice of the European Convention on Human Rights* (4th edn Intersentia, Antwerp [etc.] 2006)

van de Donk, W. and Plum, R., 'Begripsverkenning' in van de Donk, W.B.H.J. and others (eds), *Geloven in het publieke domein. Verkenningen van een dubbele transformatie. WRR Verkenningen, nr. 13* (Amsterdam University Press, Amsterdam 2006)

Edge, P.W., *Legal Responses to Religious Difference* (Kluwer Law International, The Hague/London/New York 2002)

Evans, C., *Freedom of religion under the European Convention on Human Rights* (Oxford ECHR Series, Oxford University Press, Oxford 2001)

–– and Thomas, C.A., 'Church-State Relations in the European Court of Human Rights' (2006) 3 *Brigham Young University Law Review*

Evans C., 'The Islamic Scarf in the European Court of Human Rights' (2006) 4 *Melbourne Journal of International Law*

Evans, M.D., *Religious liberty and international law in Europe* (Cambridge University Press, Cambridge 1997)

–– 'Historical Analysis of Freedom of Religion or Belief as a Technique for Resolving Religious Conflict' in Lindholm, T., Cole Durham Jr., W. and Tahzib-Lie, B.G. (eds), *Facilitating Freedom of Religion or Belief: A Deskbook* (Martinus Nijhoff Publishers, Leiden 2004)

–– *Manual on the Wearing of Religious Symbols in Public Areas* (Council of Europe Manuals: Human Rights in Culturally Diverse Societies, Nijhoff, Leiden 2009)

Favoreu, L., *Droit des libertés fondamentales* (3rd edn Dalloz, Paris 2005)

Ferrari, S., 'Islam and the Western European Model of Church and State Relations' in Shadid, W.A.R. and van Koningsveld, P.S. (eds), *Religious Freedom and the Neutrality of the State: the Position of Islam in the European Union* (Peeters, Leuven 2002)

Fetzer, J.S. and Soper, J.C., *Muslims and the State in Britain, France, and Germany* (Cambridge University Press, Cambridge 2005)

Fortuyn, P., *Tegen de islamisering van onze cultuur* (A.W. Bruna Uitgevers, Utrecht 1997)

Fredman, S., 'The legal context: public or private?' in Corby, S. and White, G. (eds), *Employee relations in the public services: themes and issues* (Routledge, London [etc.] 1999)

Freedland, M. and Vickers, L., 'Religious Expression in the Workplace in the United Kingdom' (2009) 30(3) *Comparative labor law & policy journal*

Gaboriau, S., 'Laïcité et Justice' in Pauliat, H., (ed), *Services publics et religions: Les nouvelles frontières de l'action publique en Europe* (Presses Universitaires de Limoges, Limoges 2006)

Galston, W.A., *Liberal purposes: goods, virtues, and diversity in the liberal state* (Cambridge University Press, Cambridge; New York etc. 1991)

Gaudu, F., 'Labor Law and Religion' (2009) 30(507) *Comparative Labor Law & Policy Journal*

Gedicks M.F., 'Religious Exemptions, Formal Neutrality, and *Laïcité* (2006) 13(2) *Indiana Journal of Global Legal Studies*

Gemie, S., 'Stasi's Republic: the school and the 'veil', December 2003-March 2004' (2004) 12(3) *Modern & Contemporary France*

Glenn, C., 'Historical Background to Conflicts over Religion in Public Schools' (2004) 33 *Pro rege*

Graham, G., *Living the Good Life: an Introduction to Moral Philosophy* (Paragon House, New York 1990)

Grillo, R. and others (eds), *Legal Practice and Cultural Diversity* (Ashgate, Farnham [etc.] 2009)

Guimezanes, N., *Introduction au droit français* (2nd edn Nomos, Baden-Baden 1999)

Gunn, T.J., 'Under God but Not the Scarf: The Founding Myths of Religious Freedom in the United States and *Laïcité* in France' (2004) 46 *Journal of Church & State*

Haarscher, G., *La laïcité* (Que sais-je? Vendôme Impressions, Vendôme 2004)

Harchaoui, S., 'Gevraagd: Analytisch vermogen (Mening over de stelling 'In een multicul-turele samenleving is een rechter in toga met een hoofddoek een aanwinst') (2001) 21 *Nederlands Juristenblad*

Henrard, K.A.M., 'De neutraliteit van openbaar onderwijs en de staatsplicht de filosofische en religieuze overtuigingen van ouders te respecteren: een zoektocht naar de gepaste grenzen in concreto' in de Lange, R., Rogier, L.J.J (eds), *Onderwijs en onderwijsrecht in een pluriforme samenleving: opstellen aangeboden aan prof. mr. dr. D. Mentink* (Boom Juridische uitgevers, The Hague 2008)

– – 'Shifting Visions about Indoctrination and the Margin of Appreciation Left to States', Special Issue: The Lautsi Case' 6(3) *Religion and Human Rights* (2011)

Heywood, A., *Politics* (3rd edn, Palgrave Macmillan, Basingstoke 2007)

Hirsch Ballin, E.M.H., 'Staat en kerk, kerk en staat' in den Dekker-Van Bijsterveld, S.C. and others (eds), *Kerk en staat. Hun onderlinge verhouding binnen de Nederlandse samen-leving* (Ambo, Baarn 1987)

Howard, E., 'School Bans on the Wearing of Religious Symbols: Examining the Implications of Recent case Law from the UK' (2009) 4(7) *Religion and Human Rights*

– – *Law and the Wearing of Religious Symbols: European bans on the wearing of religious symbols in education* (Routledge, Abingdon 2012)

Jenkins, J.E., *West Africans in Paris: an assessment of French immigration policies in the 1960s and 1970s* (VDM Verlag Dr. Müller, Saarbruecken 2008)

Joppke, C., *Multiculturalism and Immigration: a Comparison of the United States, Germany, and Britain* (European University Institute, Florence, 1995)

Kada, N., 'Service public et religion: du renouveau du principe de neutralité' (2004)(5) *L'Actualité Juridique – Fonctions Publiques*

Kastoryano, R., 'French secularism and Islam: France's headscarf affair' in Modood, T., Triandafyllidou, A. and Zapata-Barrero, R. (eds), *Multiculturalism, Muslims and Citizenship: a European Approach* (Routledge, London 2006)

Kennedy, J. and Valenta, M., 'Religious Pluralism and the Dutch State: Reflections on the Future of Article 23' in W.B.H.J. van de Donk and others (eds), *Geloven in het pub-lieke domein. Verkenningen van een dubbele transformatie. WRR Verkenningen, nr. 13* (Amsterdam University Press, Amsterdam 2006)

Kiliç, S., 'The British Veil Wars' (2008) 15(4) *Social politics: international studies in gender, state, and society*

Knights, S., 'Approaches to Diversity in the Domestic Courts: Article 9 of the European Convention on Human Rights' in Grillo, R. and others (eds), *Legal Practice and Cultural Diversity* (Ashgate, Farnham [etc.] 2009)

Knippenberg, H., 'The changing relationship between state and church/religion in the Netherlands' (2006) 67(4) *International Journal on Geography*

Kolbert, E., 'Le port du foulard islamique dans l'exercice de la fonction publique', Conclusions sur Cour administrative d'appel de Lyon, 19 November 2003 in *Revue Française de Droit Administratif* (2004)

Koolen, B., 'Intermezzo: stappen in de tijd' in van de Donk, W.B.H.J. and others (eds), *Geloven in het publieke domein. Verkenningen van een dubbele transformatie. WRR Verkenningen, nr. 13* (Amsterdam University Press, Amsterdam 2006)

Kortmann, C.A.J.M., 'Tekenen' ((Mening over de stelling 'In een multiculturele samenleving is een rechter in toga met een hoofddoek een aanwinst')' (2001) 21 *Nederlands Juristenblad*

Kuijer, M., 'Vrouwe Justitia: blinddoek of hoofddoek? (Annotatie bij Commissie Gelijke Behandeling 22 juni 2001, oordeel 2001-53)' (2001) 26(7) *NJCM-Bulletin: Nederlands tijdschrift voor de mensenrechten*

Kupperman, J.J., *Six myths about the good life: thinking about what has value (Hackett, Indianapolis* 2006)

Kymlicka, W., *Contemporary political philosophy: an introduction* (2nd edn Oxford University Press, Oxford [etc.] 2002)

Labuschagne, B.C., *Godsdienstvrijheid en niet-gevestigde religies. Een grondrechtelijk-rechtsfilosofische studie naar de betekenis en grenzen van religieuze tolerantie* (PhD Rijksuniversiteit Groningen, Wolters-Noordhoff, Groningen 1994)

Lagreé, J. and Portier, P. (eds) *La modernité contre la religion? Pour une nouvelle approche de la laïcité* (Presses Universitaires de Rennes, Rennes 2005)

Lainé, L., 'Liberté religieuse des agents territoriaux et obligation de neutralité religieuse' in J. Fialaire (ed), *Liberté de culte, laïcité et collectivités territoriales* (LexisNexis Litec, 2007)

Langan, E.S., 'Assimilation and Affirmative Action in French Education Systems.' (2008) 40(3) *European education*

Laycock, D., 'Formal, Substantive and Disaggregated Neutrality toward Religion' (1990) 39 *DePaul Law Review*

Lelièvre, C., 'The French model of the educator state.' (2000) 15(1) *Journal of education policy*

Letsas, G., 'Two Concepts of the Margin of Appreciation' (2006) 26(4) *Oxford Journal of Legal Studies*

Levey, G.B., 'Secularism and religion in a multicultural age' in Levey, G.B. and Modood, T. (eds), *Secularism, Religion and Multicultural Citizenship* (Cambridge University Press, Cambridge 2009)

Lewis, P., 'Between Lord Ahmed and Ali G: Which Future for British Muslims?' in Shadid, W.A.R. and van Koningsveld, P.S. (eds), *Religious Freedom and the Neutrality of the State: the Position of Islam in the European Union* (Peeters, Leuven 2002)

Lijphart, A., *Verzuiling, pactificatie en kentering in de Nederlandse politiek* (J.H. de Bussy, Amsterdam 1984)

Lindholm, T., 'Philosophical and Religious Justifications of Freedom of Religion or Belief' in Lindholm, T., Cole Durham Jr., W. and Tahzib-Lie, B.G. (eds), *Facilitating Freedom of Religion or Belief: A Deskbook* (Martinus Nijhoff Publishers, Leiden 2004)

Lochak, D., 'For intérieur et liberté de conscience' in Centre universitaire de recherches administratives et politiques de Picardie (ed), *Le for intérieur* (Presses Universitaires de France, Paris 1995)

Loenen, T., 'Hoofddoeken voor de klas en in de rechtbank: op weg naar een multicultureel publiek domein?' (2001) 26(7) *NJCM-Bulletin: Nederlands tijdschrift voor de mensenrechten*

– – and Terlouw, A., 'De ondraaglijke zwaarte van de hoofddoek: het EVRM bevestigt dat een hoofddoekverbod aan de Turkse universiteiten geoorloofd is (2006) 31(2) *NJCM-Bulletin: Nederlands tijdschrift voor de mensenrechten*

– – Geloof in het geding: Juridische grenzen van religieus pluralisme in het perspectief van de mensenrechten (Sdu Uitgevers, The Hague 2006)

Loof, J.P. (ed), *Juridische ruimte voor gewetensbezwaren?* (Stichting NJCM-Boekerij, Leiden 2007)

Lyon, D. and Spini, D., 'Unveiling The Headscarf Debate' (2004) 12(3) *Feminist Legal Studies*

Madeley, J.T.S., 'European Liberal Democracy and the Principle of State Religious Neutrality' in Madeley, J.T.S. and Enyedi, Z. (eds), *Special Issue on Church and State in Contemporary Europe. The Chimera of Neutrality.* (West European Politics, vol. 26, no. 1; Frank Cass & Co., London 2003)

van Manen, N.F. (ed), *De multiculturele samenleving en het recht* (Ars Aequi Libri, Nijmegen 2002)

Maris-van Sandelingenambacht, C.W., 'Hoofddoek of blinddoek?' in van Manen, N.F. (ed), (Ars Aequi Libri, Nijmegen 2002)

McCaffrey, E., 'The Return of Faith and Reason to Laïcité: Régis Debray and 'le fait religieux'' (2005) 16(3) *French cultural studies*

McClean, D., 'United Kingdom' in Hill, M., (ed), *Religion and discrimination law in the European Union. La discrimination en matière religieuse dans l'union européenne* (Institute for European Constitutional Law, University of Trier, Trier 2012)

McGoldrick, D., *Human Rights and Religion: The Islamic Headscarf Debate in Europe* (Hart Publishing, Oregon 2006)

– – 'Religion in the European Public Square and in European Public Life–Crucifixes in the Classroom?' (2011) 11(3) *Human Rights Law Review*

Messner, F., Prélot, P.H., Woehrling, J.M. (eds), *Traité de droit français des religions* (LexisNexis Litec, 2003)

Michalak, L. and Saeed, A., 'The Continental Divide: Islam and Muslim Identities in France and the United States' in *Muslim Europe or Euro-Islam: Politics, Culture, and Citizenship in the Age of Globalization* (Lexington Books ; [etc.], Lanham, MD 2002)

Modood, T., 'Establishment, multiculturalism and British citizenship' (1994) 65(1) *Political Quarterly*

– – 'The Place of Muslims in British Secular Multiculturalism' in Alsayyad, N. and Castells, M. (eds) *Muslim Europe or Euro-Islam: Politics, Culture, and Citizenship in the Age of Globalization* (Lexington Books [etc.], Lanham, MD 2002)

– – 'British Muslims and the politics of multiculturalism' in Modood, T., Triandafyllidou, A. and Zapata-Barrero, R. (eds), *Multiculturalism, Muslims and Citizenship: a European Approach* (Routledge, London 2006)

– – *Multiculturalism: a Civic Idea* (Polity, Cambridge 2007)

– – 'Muslims, religious equality and secularism' in Levey, G.B. and Modood, T. (eds), *Secularism, Religion and Multicultural Citizenship* (Cambridge University Press, Cambridge 2009)

Molokotos Liederman, L., 'Pluralism in Education: the display of Islamic affiliation in French and British schools' (2000) 11(1) *Islam and Christian-Muslim Relations*

Monsma, S.V. and Soper, J.C., *The Challenge of Pluralism: Church and State in Five Democracies* (Religious Forces in the Modern Political World, Rowman & Littlefield Publishers, Inc., Lanham (New York, Boulder, Oxford) 1997)

Monsma, S.V., 'Substantive Neutrality as a Basis for Free Exercise-No Establishment Common Ground' (2000) 42(1) *Journal of Church & State*

van Mourik, B., 'Het islamitisch hoofddoekje en het Franse *laïcité*' (2004) 29(3) *NJCM-Bulletin: Nederlands tijdschrift voor de mensenrechten*

Nehmelman, R., 'Hoe een enkel feit tot een nieuwe schoolstrijd leidt? Over het spanningsveld tussen de bijzondere school en de homoseksuele docent' in Broeksteeg, H. and Terlouw, A. (eds), *Overheid, recht en religie* (Kluwer, Deventer 2011)

– – 'Private vrijheid! Over de werking van grondrechten in het privaatrecht' (2011)(1) *Letsel & Schade*

Niessen, C.R., 'Ambtenaar en grondrechten, ofwel: leve het poldermodel.' (1999) 24(7) *NJCM-Bulletin: Nederlands tijdschrift voor de mensenrechten*

Nieuwenhuis, A.J., 'Tussen *laïcité* en AWGB: Hoofddoek en openbaar onderwijs in Frankrijk, Duitsland, Nederland en onder het EVRM' (2004)(18) *Nederlands Juristenblad*

van Noorloos, M., *Hate Speech Revisited* (PhD Universiteit Utrecht, Intersentia, Antwerp, 2011)

Oldenhuis, F.T., *Schurende relaties tussen recht en religie* (Van Gorcum, Assen 2007)

Oliva, J.G., 'Religious Symbols in the Classroom: A Controversial Issue in the United Kingdom' (2008) 20(3) *Brigham Young University Law Review*

van Ooijen, H.M.A.E., 'Boerka of bivakmuts: verbod in de openbare ruimte? Het wetsvoorstel Kamp nader onder de loep genomen' (2008) 33(2) *NJCM-Bulletin: Nederlands tijdschrift voor de mensenrechten*

– – and others (eds), *Godsdienstvrijheid: afschaffen of beschermen?* (Stichting NJCM-Boekerij, Leiden 2008)

Overbeeke, A. and van Ooijen, H.M.A.E., 'Les politiques relatives à la burqa aux Pays-Bas: une tradition pluraliste démasquée?" (provisional title)' in Koussens, D. and Roy, O. (eds), *Quand la burqa passe à l'Ouest, enjeux éthiques, politiques et juridiques* (Sciences des religions, Presses universitaires de Rennes, 2013 (forthcoming))

Parekh, B., *Rethinking multiculturalism. Cultural diversity and political theory* (MacMillan's, Palgrave 2000)

– – 'The future of multi-ethnic Britain. Reporting on a report' (2001), 362 *The Round Table* (2001)

Peiser, G., *Droit administratif général* (23rd edn Dalloz, Paris 2006)

Phillips, A., *Multiculturalism without culture* (Princeton University Press, Princeton, NJ [etc.] 2007)

Piret, J.-M., 'A Wise Return to Judicial Restraint' (2011) Special Issue: The Lautsi Case' 6(3) *Religion and Human Rights* (2011)

Post, H., *Godsdienstvrijheid aan banden* (Wolf Legal Publishers, Nijmegen, 2011)

Poulter, S., *Ethnicity, Law and Human Rights: The English Experience* (Clarendon Press, Oxford 1998)

– – 'Muslim Headscarves in Schools: Contrasting Legal Approaches in England and France' (1997) 17(43) *Oxford Journal of Legal Studies*

Prélot, H., 'Définir juridiquement la laïcité' in Gonzalez, G. (ed), *Laïcité, liberté de religion et Convention européenne des droits de l'homme* (Droit et justice edn Nemesis – Bruylant, Brussels 2005)

Rayner, J. and others, 'Public Service Ethos: Developing a Generic Measure' (2010) *Journal of Public Administration Research and Theory*

Rivers, J., *The Law of Organized Religion. Between Establishment and Secularism* (Oxford University Press, Oxford)

Robert, J., 'Religious Liberty and French Secularism' (2003) *Brigham Young University Law Review*

Robertson, R., 'Church-State Relations in Comparative Perspective' in Robbins, T. and Robertson, R. (eds), *Church-State Relations: Tensions and Transitions* (Transaction Books, New Brunswick, New Jersey, [etc.] 1987)

Rorive, I., 'Religious symbols in the public space: in search of a European answer.' (2008-2009) 30(6) *Cardozo Law Review*

Rouban, L., *La fonction publique* (La Découverte, Paris 1996)

Rousseau, J.-J., *Du contrat social* (Flammarion, Paris 1992)

Roy, O., *Secularism confronts Islam* (Holoch, G. (tr) Columbia University Press, New York, N.Y. 2007)

Sadurski, W., 'Neutrality of law towards religion' (1990) 12 *Sydney Law Review*

Saharso, S. and Verhaar, O., 'Headscarves in the Policeforce and the Court: Does Context Matter?' (2006) 41(1) *Acta politica: tijdschrift voor politicologie*

Saint-James, V., 'La liberté religieuse du fonctionnaire' (2005)(12) *La semaine juridique – Edition administrations et collectivités territoriales*

Salon, S. and Savignac, J.C. (eds), *La fonction publique; documents réunis et commentés*, (La Documentation Française, Paris 1999)

Sandberg, R., 'A Uniform Approach to Religious Discrimination? The Position of Teachers and Other School Staff in the UK' in M. Hunter-Henin (ed), *Law, Religious Freedoms and Education in Europe* (Cultural Diversity and Law, Ashgate, Farnham [etc] 2011)

– – *Law and Religion* (Cambridge University Press, Cambridge 2011)

Saxena, M., 'The French Headscarf Law and the Right to Manifest Religious Belief' (2007) in 84 (5) *University of Detroit Mercy Law Review*

Sayyid, S., 'Contemporary politics of secularism' in Levey, G.B. and Modood, T. (eds), *Secularism, Religion and Multicultural Citizenship* (Cambridge University Press, Cambridge 2009)

Scheffer, P., 'Het multiculturele drama' in *NRC Handelsblad* (29 January 2000)

– – *Het land van aankomst* (De Bezige Bij, Amsterdam 2007)

Schuyt, C.J.M., 'Publiekrecht in een multiculturele samenleving' in van der Burg. W., Schuyt, C.J.M. and Nieuwenhuis, J.H. (eds), *Multiculturaliteit en recht. Verslag van de op 13 juni 2008 te Dordrecht gehouden algemene vergadering van de Nederlandse Juristen-Vereniging* (vol. 138; Kluwer, Deventer 2008)

Schwartz, R., *Un siècle de laïcité* (Le point sur, Berger-Levrault, Paris 2007)

Sengers, E., 'Kwantitatief onderzoek naar religie in Nederland' in ter Borg, M. and Borg-man, E. (eds), *Handboek religie in Nederland: perspectief, overzicht, debat* (Meinema, Zoetermeer 2008)

Shadid, W.A.R. and van Koningsveld, P.S. (eds), *Religious Freedom and the Neutrality of the State: the Position of Islam in the European Union* (Peeters, Leuven (Paris-Sterling) 2002)

Sher, G., *Beyond Neutrality. Perfectionism and Politics* (Cambridge University Press, Cambridge 1997)

Sloot, B., 'Moeten rechters lijken op de Nederlandse bevolking? Over de wenselijkheid van descriptieve representatie door de rechterlijke macht' (2004)(2) *Trema*

Smits, J.M., *Omstreden rechtswetenschap. Over aard, methode en organisatie van de juridische discipline* (Boom Juridische Uitgevers, The Hague, 2009)

– – 'Redefining Normative Legal Science: Towards an Argumentative Discipline' in Coomans, A.P.M. and Grünfeld, F. (eds), *Methods of human rights research* (Intersentia, Antwerp, 2009)

Snik, G. and de Jong, J., 'Moet een liberale overheid bijzondere scholen bekostigen?' (2001) 21(3) *Pedagogiek, wetenschappelijk forum voor opvoeding, onderwijs en vorming*

Tahzib, B.G., *Freedom of religion or belief. Ensuring Effective International Legal Protection* (PhD Universiteit Utrecht, Martinus Nijhoff Publishers, Leiden 1995)

Taylor, C., 'Foreword: What is secularism?' in Levey, G.B. and Modood, T. (eds), *Secularism, Religion and Multicultural Citizenship* (Cambridge University Press, Cambridge 2009)

Taylor, P.M., *Freedom of Religion. UN and European Human Rights Law and Practice* (Cambridge University Press, New York 2005)

Temperman, J., 'State Neutrality in Public School Education: An Analysis of the Interplay Between the Neutrality Principle, the Right to Adequate Education, Children's Right to Freedom of Religion or Belief, Parental Liberties, and the Position of Teachers' (2010) 32(4) *Human Rights Quarterly*

– – *State-Religion Relationships and Human Rights Law: Towards a Right to Religiously Neutral Governance* (Martinus Nijhoff Publishers, Leiden/Boston 2010)

Terrier, J., 'The idea of a Republican tradition: Reflections on the debate concerning the intellectual foundations of the French Third Republic.' (2006) 11(3) *Journal of political ideologies*

Thomas, E.R., 'Competing Visions of Citizenship and Integration in France's Headscarves Affair' (2000) 8(2) *Journal of European Area Studies*

– – *Immigration, Islam and the Politics of Belonging in France. A Comparative Framework* (University of Pennsylvania Press, Philadelphia 2012)

Tigchelaar, J., 'Het kledingprobleem van Vrouwe Justitia: kan een hoofddoek op een toga?' (2001) 17(4) *Nemesis: tijdschrift over vrouwen en recht*

Trigg, R., *Religion in public life: must faith be privatized?* (Oxford University Press, Oxford 2007)

Troper, M., 'Sovereignty and laïcité' (2009) 30(6) 30 *Cardozo Law Review*

Uitz, R., *Freedom of religion: in European constitutional and international case law* (Council of Europe Publishing, Strasbourg 2007)

Uzman, J., 'Procola-spook of broedende kip? Noot bij oordeel 2008-123 in Gerards, J.H. and Zoontjens, P.J.J. (eds), *Gelijke behandeling: oordelen en commentaar 2008* (Wolf Legal Publishers, Nijmegen 2008)

Ventre, A.M., 'Les polices en France' (2002) 102 *Pouvoirs. Revue française d'études constitutionnelles et politiques*

Verhaar, O. and Saharso, S., 'The Weight of Context: Headscarves in Holland' (2004) 7(2) *Ethical Theory and Moral Practice*

Verhulp, E., *Vrijheid van meningsuiting van werknemers en ambtenaren* (PhD Universiteit van Amsterdam, Sdu, The Hague 1996)

Vermeulen, B.P., 'Religieus pluralisme als uitdaging aan de 'neutrale' rechter' Themanummer 'Ieder z'n recht, magistraat in een pluriforme samenleving' (2005) *Trema*

– – 'On Freedom, Equality and Citizenship: Changing Fundamentals of Dutch Minority Policy and Law (Immigration, Integration, Education and Religion)' in Foblets, M. and others (eds), *Cultural diversity and the law. State responses from around the world* (Bruylant [etc.], Brussels 2010)

Vertovec, S. and Rogers, A., *Muslim European Youth: Reproducing Ethnicity, Religion, Culture* (Ashgate, Aldershot [etc] 1998)

Vickers, L., *Religious freedom, religious discrimination and the workplace* (Hart, Oxford [etc.] 2008)

– – 'Religion and Belief Discrimination and the Employment of Teachers in Faith Schools' (2009)(4) *Religion and Human Rights*

Viljanen, J., *The European Court of Human Rights as a developer of the general doctrines of human rights law: a study of the limitation clauses of the European Convention on Human Rights* (Tampere University Press, Tampere 2003)

Vroom, H.M., ''Church'-state relations in the public square: French laicism and Canadian multiculturalism' in van de Donk, W.B.H.J. and others (ed), *Geloven in het publieke domein. Verkenningen van een dubbele transformatie. WRR Verkenningen, nr. 13* (Amsterdam University Press, Amsterdam 2006)

Walker, R.J. and others, *Walker & Walker's English legal system* (9th edn Oxford University Press, Oxford 2005)

Wall, S., 'Neutrality and Responsibility' (2001) 98(8) *Journal of Philosophy*

Weil, P., *Qu'est-ce qu'un français? Histoire de la nationalité française depuis la Révolution* (revised edn, Gallimard, "Folio Histoire", Paris, 2005); translated in English: C. Porter (tr), *How to be French. Nationality in the Making since 1789* (De University Press, Durham 2008).

– – 'Why the French *laïcité* is liberal' (2009) 30(6) *Cardozo Law Review*

Weller, P., 'Equity, Inclusivity and Participation in a Plural Society: Challenging the Establishment of the Church of England' in Edge, P. and Harvey, G. (eds), *Law and Religion in Contemporary Society: Communities, individualism and the State* (Ashgate, Aldershot [etc.] 2000)

Werdmölder, H., 'Headscarves at Public Schools. The Issue of Open Neutrality Reconsidered.' in Loenen, M.L.P. and Goldschmidt, J.E. (eds), *Religious Pluralism and Human Rights in Europe: Where to Draw the Line?* (Intersentia, Antwerp-Oxford 2007)

Willaime, J.P., 'European Integration, *Laïcité* and Religion' in Leustean, L.N. and Madeley, J.T.S. (eds), *Religion, Politics and Law in the European Union* (Routledge, Abingdon, 2010)

Woehrling, J.M., 'Réflexions sur le principe de la neutralité de l'état en matière religieuse et sa mise en oevre en droit français' (1998) 101 *Archive de sciences sociales des religions*

Wolff, T., *Multiculturalisme & Neutraliteit* (Vossiuspers, Universiteit van Amsterdam, Amsterdam 2005)

Yourow, H.C., *The margin of appreciation doctrine in the dynamics of European human rights jurisprudence* (PhD University of Michigan Law School, Kluwer, The Hague 1996)

Zauberman, R. and Lévy, R., 'Police, minorities, and the French Republican ideal' (2003) 41(4) *Criminology*

Zoontjens, P.J.J., 'Bijzonder en openbaar onderwijs' in T. Bertens (ed), *Recht en religie* (Ars Aequi, Nijmegen, 2003)

Reports and advices

Association of Chief Police Officers (ACPO), Home Office (HO) and the Association of Police Authorities (APA), 'The Employment Monitoring Duty. Guidance for the police service in England, Wales and Northern Ireland'

Barnett, L., 'Freedom of Religion and Religious Symbols in the Public Sphere' (Parliament of Canada, Ottawa 2011) Background paper no. 2011-60-E

Commissie Gelijke Behandeling, 'Advies Commissie Gelijke Behandeling inzake uiterlijke verschijningsvormen politie. Pluriform uniform?' (November 2007) 2007/8

Commission de réflexion sur l'application du principe de laïcité dans la République, 'Rapport au President de la République' (Paris 2003)

Commission nationale consultative des droits de l'homme (CNCDH), 'La laïcité aujourd'hui' (2003)Conseil d'Etat, 'Rapport Public 2004: Jurisprudence et avis de 2003. Un siècle de laïcité' Conseil d'Etat (Paris)

Commission on the Future of Multi-Ethnic Britain (Chair: Bikhu Parekh) 'The Future of Multi-Ethnic Britain' (London, 2000)

Conseil d'Etat, 'Réflexions sur la laïcité. Considérations générales. Un siècle de la laïcité.' (2004),

Chérifi, H., 'Application de la loi du 15 mars 2004 sur le port des signes religieux ostensibles dans les établissments d'enseignement publics' Ministère de l'éducation nationale de l'enseignement supérieur et de la recherche (Paris)

Kosmopolis, 'Geloof en Staat, Helderheid in een verwarrende relatie' (Rotterdam, 15 april 2007)

Gerin, A. and Raoult, E., 'Rapport d'information fait en application de l'article 145 du Règlement au nom de la mission d'information sur la pratique du port du voile intégral sur le territoire national' (Assemblée nationale, Paris 2010).

Haut Conseil à l'Intégration (HCI), 'Projet de charte de la laicite dans les services publics. Avis à Monsieur le Premier ministre', (Paris 2007)

Report of the Home Affairs Committee 'Freemasonry in the Police and the Judiciary' (House of Commons, 1997)

Krishnaswami, A., 'Study of Discrimination in the Matter of Religious Rights and Practices' United Nations (New York 14 October 1959) UN Doc. E/CN.4/Sub.2/200/Rev.1 79

Lord Chancellor and Secretary of State for Justice, The Governance of Britain: Judicial Appointments, 2007, no. Cm 7210

The Netherlands, 'Fourth Periodic Report submitted to the Human Rights Committee' (30 July) 9 May 2007 CCPR/C/NET/4

SOPEMI (Système d'observation permanente des migrations), 'Immigration et presence etrangère en France en 2010' Secretariat Général à l'Iimmigration et à l'Intégration

Ministère de l'Intérieur, de l'Outre-Mer, des Collectivités Territoriales et de l'Immigration (Paris)

Ministerie van Binnenlandse Zaken, Nota 'Grondrechten in een pluriforme samenleving', *Kamerstukken II* 2003/04, 29 614, no. 2

Nederlandse Juristen-Vereniging, Handelingen NJV, 'Multiculturaliteit en Recht' (Dordrecht, 13 June 2008, vol. 138(2))

R. Plant (Lord Plant of Highfield), 'A Public Service Ethic and Political Accountability' (2003) 56 (4) *Parliamentary Affairs*, p. 564

Raad van State, 'Advies over het initiatiefvoorstel Wet normalisering rechtspositie ambtenaren', *Kamerstukken II* 2010/11, 32 550, no. 4

– – 'Advies ten aanzien van het Voorstel van wet houdende de instelling van een algemeen verbod op het dragen van gelaatsbedekkende kleding, met memorie van toelichting', *Kamerstukken II*, 2011/12, 33 165, no. 4

Rapport du groupe de travail (présidé par A. Rossinot) 'La laïcité dans les services publics' (2006)

Royal Commission on the Reform of the House of Lords (Chairman: the Rt Hon Lord Wakeham DL) 'A House for the Future' (January 2000)

Vereniging van Nederlandse Gemeenten (VNG) en het Ministerie van Binnenlandse Zaken en Koninkrijksrelaties, 'Tweeluik religie en publiek domein' (2009)

TABLE OF CASES

United Nations Human Rights Committee

Hudoyberganova v. Uzbekistan, (82nd session) Views Communication 931/2000, 5 November 2004

Ranjit Singh v. France (102nd session) Views Communication no. 1876/2000, 27 September 2011

European Commission of Human Rights/European Court of Human Rights

Ahmed and others v. United Kingdom, Appl. nos. 65/1997/849/1056 2 September 1998 (ECtHR)

Ahmet Arslan and Others v. Turkey, Appl. no. 41135/98, 23 February 2010 (ECtHR)

Altin v. Turkey, Appl. no. 39822/98, 6 April 2000 (ECtHR)

Arrowsmith v. United Kingdom, Appl. no. 7050/75, 16 May 1977 (ECnHR)

Buscarini v. San Marino, Appl. no. 24645/94, 18 February 1999 (ECtHR)

Campbell and Cosans v. United Kingdom, Appl. no. 7511/76, 7743/76, 25 February 1982 (ECnHR)

Chaplin v. United Kingdom, Appl. no. 59842/10 (ECtHR)

Dahlab v. Switzerland, Appl. no. 42393/98, 15 February 2001 (ECtHR)

Dimitras and Others v. Greece (no. 2), Appl. nos. 34207/08 and 6365/09, 3 November 2011 (ECtHR)

Dogru v. France, Appl. no. 27058/05, 4 December 2008 (ECtHR)

Efstratiou v. Greece, Appl. nos. 77/1996/696/888, 18 December 1996 (ECtHR)

Engel v. the Netherlands, Appl. nos. 5100/71, 5101/71, 5102/71, 5354/72, 5370/72, 8 June 1976 (ECtHR)

Eweida v. United Kingdom, Appl. no. 48420/10 (ECtHR)

Folgerø and others v. Norway, Appl. no. 15472/02, 29 June 2007 (ECtHR)

Francesco Sessa v. Italy, Appl. no. 28790/08, 3 April 2012 (ECtHR)

Grzelak v. Poland, Appl. no. 7710/02, 15 June 2010 (ECtHR)

Hauschildt v. Denmark, Appl. no. 10486/83, 24 May 1989 (ECtHR)

Ivanova v. Bulgaria, Appl. no. 52435/99, 12 April 2007 (ECtHR)

Jakóbski v. Poland, Appl. no. 18429/06, 7 December 2010 (ECtHR)

Kalaç v. Turkey, Appl. nos. 61/1996/680/870, 23 June 1997 (ECtHR)

Kjeldsen, Busk Madsen and Pedersen v. Denmark, Appl. nos. 5095/71, 5920/72, 5926/72, 7 December 1976 (ECtHR)

Knudsen v. Norway, Appl. no. 11045/84, 8 March 1985 (ECnHR)

Kokkinakis v. Greece, Appl. no. 14307/88, 25 May 1993 (ECtHR)

Konttinen v. Finland, Appl. no. 24949/94, 3 December 1996 (ECnHR)

France (including opinions of the HALDE)

en vertu d'un contrat d'accueil et d'intégration (CAI) (no 2008-193, 15 September 2008) (HALDE)
Dlle Weiss, 28 April 1938 (CE)
Mlle Marteaux, Avis no. 217017, 3 May 2000 (CE)
Madame M., décision no. 286798, 27 June 2008 (CE)
M.S., décision no. 285394, 5 December 2007 (CE)

England

Azmi v. Kirklees Metropolitan Borough Council, 30 March 2007 (EAT)
Chaplin v. Royal Devon & Exeter NHS Foundation Trust, 6 April 2010 (ET)
Ms. N. Eweida v. British Airways PLC, 20 November 2008 (EAT)
Eweida v. British Airways, 12 February 2010 (EWCA)
Lillian Ladele v. The London Borough of Islington, 15 December 2009 (EWCA)
Mandla and another v Dowell Lee and another, 24 March 1983 (UKHL)
McFarlane v. Relate Avon Ltd, 29 April 2010 (EWCA)
Pay v. Lancashire, 29 October 2003 (EAT)
R. (on the application of Begum (by her litigation friend, Rahman)) v. Headteacher and Governors of Denbigh High School, 22 March 2006 (UKHL)
R. (on the application of Playfoot) v. Governing Body of Millais School, 16 July 2007 (EWHC)
R. (on the application of Sarika Angel Watkins-Singh (A child acting by Sanita Kumari Singh, her Mother and Litigation Friend)) v. The Governing Body of Aberdare Girls' High School, 29 July 2008 (EWHC)
R. (on the application of X (by her father and litigation friend)) v. The Headteachers of Y School, The Governors of Y School, 16 July 2007 (EWHC)

The Netherlands (including opinions of the Equal Treatment Commission)

Appellant t. de Korpsbeheerder van de politieregio Rotterdam-Rijnmond, LJN: BK8782, 24 December 2009 (Centrale Raad van Beroep)
Beslissing in de zaak onder nummer van 5499, 11 December 2009 (Hof van Discipline)
Oordeel 1999-18, 9 February 1999 (CGB)
Oordeel 2001-53, 22 June 2001 (CGB)
Oordeel 2005-19, 11 February 2005 (CGB)
Oordeel 2006-30, 2 March 2006 (CGB)
Oordeel 2008-123, 23 October 2008 (CGB)
Trambestuurder t. GVB, LJN: BK6378, 09-1165 14 December 2009 (Rb Amsterdam)

CURRICULUM VITAE

Hana van Ooijen attended the *gymnasium* of the Corderius Lyceum in Amersfoort. After studying psychology for a year, she changed to studying law. She then pursued her legal education at Utrecht University and Université Toulouse I. In 2006, she received her LL.M. in international and European law. Her end project for international law was to participate in the Philip C. Jessup Moot Court Competition where she and her team reached the international rounds in Washington D.C. For European law, she wrote her master's thesis at the T.M.C. Asser Institute in the framework of the European Arrest Warrant Project. From 2007 onwards, she has worked at the Netherlands Institute of Human Rights as a Ph.D. researcher and a co-lecturer in Comparative Human Rights. For the comparative parts of her research she stayed at Oxford Brookes University, the PRISME centre of the Université de Strasbourg and the CREDOF centre of the Université Paris Ouest Nanterre. During the first few years of her research, she was a member of the Ph.D. Council of the UU Faculty of Law, Economics and Governance. Since 2010, she has been the book review editor of Religion & Human Rights. Alongside her dissertation, she has published on related topics.

SCHOOL OF HUMAN RIGHTS RESEARCH SERIES

The School of Human Rights Research is a joint effort by human rights researchers in the Netherlands. Its central research theme is the nature and meaning of international standards in the field of human rights, their application and promotion in the national legal order, their interplay with national standards and the international supervision of such application. The School of Human Rights Research Series only includes English titles that contribute to a better understanding of the different aspects of human rights.

For previous volumes in the series, please visit http://shr.intersentia.com.

Published titles within the Series

47 Otto Spijkers, *The United Nations, the Evolution of Global Values and International Law*
    ISBN 978-1-78068-036-1

48 Karin Veegens, *A Disrupted Balance? Prevention of terrorism and compliance with fundamental legal rights and principles of law – The Dutch anti-terrorism legislation*
    ISBN 978-1-78068-042-2

49 Antenor Hallo de Wolf, *Reconciling Privatization with Human Rights*
    ISBN 978-1-78068-049-1

50 Marie-José van der Heijden, *Transnational Corporations and Human Rights Liabilities: Linking Standards of International Public Law to National Civil Litigation Procedures*
    ISBN 978-94-000-0195-4

51 Marthe Lot Vermeulen, *Enforced Disappearance. Determining State Responsibility under the International Convention for the Protection of All Persons from Enforced Disappearance*
    ISBN 978-1-78068-065-1

52 Vera Vriezen, *Amnesty justified? The need for a case by case approach in the interests of human rights*
    ISBN 978-1-78068-075-0

53 Maite San Giorgi, *The Human Right to Equal Access to Health Care*
    ISBN 978-1-78068-081-1

54 Jeroen Blomsma, *Mens rea and defences in European criminal law*
    ISBN 978-1-78068-104-7

55 Masha Fedorova, *The Principle of Equality of Arms in International Criminal Proceedings*
    ISBN 978-1-78068-111-5

56 Martine Boersma, *Corruption: A Violation of Human Rights and a Crime Under International Law?*
    ISBN 978-1-78068-105-4

57 Hein Lubbe, *Successive and Additional Measures to the TRC Amnesty Scheme in South Africa*
    ISBN 978-1-78068-116-0